ROUTLEDGE INTERNATIONAL HANDBOOK OF MULTIDISCIPLINARY PERSPECTIVES ON DESCENDANTS OF HOLOCAUST SURVIVORS

The *Routledge International Handbook of Multidisciplinary Perspectives on Descendants of Holocaust Survivors* offers a comprehensive collection of cutting-edge studies from a wide range of fields dealing with new research about descendants of Holocaust survivors. Examining the aftermath of the Holocaust on the Second Generation and Third Generation, children and grandchildren of Holocaust survivors, it is the first volume to bring together research perspectives from history, psychology, sociology, communications, literature, film, theater, art, music, biology, and medicine.

With contributions from international experts, key topics covered include survivor characteristics and experiences; the phenomenological experience of transmitted trauma legacies; the creation of Second Generation groups; the epigenetics of inherited trauma; the development of Second Generation writing; representation of Holocaust survivors in film; music and the transmission of memory; art, music, and the Holocaust; ancestral trauma and its effect on the ageing process of subsequent generations; 2G and 3G health issues and outcomes. Divided into two sections, the first deals with the humanities: history and testimony, literature, film and theater, art, and music. The second section, focusing on the social sciences and health-related sciences, contains chapters dealing with studies in the fields of psychology, sociology, anthropology, communication, gerontology, nursing, and medicine.

This insightful handbook is a contemporary anthology for advanced students and scholars in the humanities, along with those in behavioral, social, and health-related sciences concerned with research about second- and third-generation Holocaust survivors.

Judith Tydor Baumel-Schwartz is Director of the Arnold and Leona Finkler Institute of Holocaust Research, Abraham and Edita Spiegel Family Professor in Holocaust Research, Rabbi Pynchas Brener Professor in Research on the Holocaust of European Jewry, and Professor of Modern Jewish History in the Israel and Golda Koschitzky Department of Jewish History and Contemporary Jewry at Bar-Ilan University, Ramat Gan, Israel.

Amit Shrira is the chair of the Department of Social & Health Sciences at Bar-Ilan University, Israel. He supervises the social sciences track at the interdisciplinary graduate program in gerontology at Bar-Ilan University, Israel. His research program focuses on late-life effects of massive trauma and its intergenerational transmission.

ROUTLEDGE INTERNATIONAL HANDBOOKS

ROUTLEDGE INTERNATIONAL HANDBOOK OF MULTIDISCIPLINARY PERSPECTIVES ON DESCENDANTS OF HOLOCAUST SURVIVORS
Edited by Judith Tydor Baumel-Schwartz and Amit Shrira

ROUTLEDGE INTERNATIONAL HANDBOOK OF VISUAL-MOTOR SKILLS, HANDWRITING, AND SPELLING
Edited by Yanyan Ye, Tomohiro Inoue, Urs Maurer, and Catherine McBride

ROUTLEDGE HANDBOOK OF ENVIRONMENTAL POLICY
Edited by Helge Jörgens, Christoph Knill and Yves Steinebach

THE ROUTLEDGE HANDBOOK OF SOFT POWER (2ND EDITION)
Edited by Naren Chitty, Lilian Ji, Gary D Rawnsley

THE ROUTLEDGE HANDBOOK OF URBAN LOGISTICS
Edited by Jason Monios, Lucy Budd and Stephen Ison

For more information about this series, please visit: www.routledge.com/Routledge-International-Handbooks/book-series/RIHAND

ROUTLEDGE INTERNATIONAL HANDBOOK OF MULTIDISCIPLINARY PERSPECTIVES ON DESCENDANTS OF HOLOCAUST SURVIVORS

Edited by Judith Tydor Baumel-Schwartz and Amit Shrira

Routledge
Taylor & Francis Group
LONDON AND NEW YORK

Cover image: Getty Images/Andriy Onufriyenko

First published 2024
by Routledge
4 Park Square, Milton Park, Abingdon, Oxon OX14 4RN

and by Routledge
605 Third Avenue, New York, NY 10158

Routledge is an imprint of the Taylor & Francis Group, an informa business

British Library Cataloguing-in-Publication Data
A catalogue record for this book is available from the British Library

Library of Congress Cataloging-in-Publication Data
Names: Baumel-Schwartz, Judith Tydor, 1959- editor. | Shrira, Amit, editor. (To be estab)
Title: Routledge international handbook of multidisciplinary perspectives on descendants of Holocaust survivors / edited by Judith Tydor Baumel-Schwartz and Amit Shrira.
Description: Abingdon, Oxon ; New York, NY : Routledge, 2023. | Series: Routledge international handbooks | Includes bibliographical references and index.
Identifiers: LCCN 2023003852 (print) | LCCN 2023003853 (ebook) | ISBN 9781032254333 (hbk) | ISBN 9781003283157 (ebk)
Subjects: LCSH: Children of Holocaust survivors. | Grandchildren of Holocaust survivors. | Holocaust, Jewish (1939-1945)—Influence.
Classification: LCC D804.3 .R77 2023 (print) | LCC D804.3 (ebook) | DDC 940.53/18—dc23/eng/20230216
LC record available at https://lccn.loc.gov/2023003852
LC ebook record available at https://lccn.loc.gov/2023003853

ISBN: 978-1-032-25433-3 (hbk)
ISBN: 978-1-032-25432-6 (pbk)
ISBN: 978-1-003-28315-7 (ebk)

DOI: 10.4324/b23365

Typeset in Bembo
by Apex CoVantage, LLC

Dedicated to the Survivors, Without Whom There Would Not Have Been Future Generations

CONTENTS

CONTRIBUTORS

Batya Brutin is an art historian researcher of art during and after the Holocaust and Holocaust monuments in Israel and worldwide. She published academic books and articles and educational materials on these subjects. As a curator, she curated Holocaust art exhibitions in Israel and abroad. From 2000 to September 2018, she was the director of the Holocaust Teaching in Israeli Society Program at Beit Berl Academic College in Israel. Dr. Brutin received the Yad Vashem award of lifetime achievement in the field of Holocaust education in 2018.

Melvin Jules Bukiet is the author of eight books of fiction including *After, Signs and Wonders* and *Strange Fire* and the editor of several anthologies including *Nothing Makes You Free.* He teaches at Sarah Lawrence College and lives in Manhattan.

Dr. Irit Felsen, PhD is a clinical psychologist, born in Israel. She studied psychology at the Hebrew University in Jerusalem and got her PhD from the University of Hamburg, Germany, and then trained at Yale University. She is in private practice in New Jersey, and she teaches at Columbia University in New York.

Atarah Fisher is a music therapist with experience with autism and Down syndrome. She is a lecturer at Efrata College of Education, Bet Rivka College, and Levinsky College on special education, music therapy, and Holocaust art. Her PhD dissertation from the Department of Music Therapy at Bar-Ilan University is on the subject "The Role of Music in Terms of the Relationship between Holocaust Survivors and their Children, from the Perspective of the Second Generation". Dr. Fisher lectures at conferences in Israel and at international conferences on music therapy with an emphasis on Holocaust trauma. She has published articles in international journals.

Roy Horovitz was born in Israel, 1970. He is a graduate of Nisan Nativ Acting Studio, BA and MA (with distinction) from Tel-Aviv University. His PhD is from the Department of Comparative Literature in Bar-Ilan, where he is currently a senior faculty member. Horovitz has performed many roles for various theaters and has been awarded Best Actor at the International Haifa Festival, 1997. He also won the Best Director award for directing *Pollard's Trial* (The Cameri Theatre, Tel-Aviv). His film work includes *The Body* with Antonio Banderas. He directed a succession of critically acclaimed productions (including *Not About Nightingales* by Tennessee Williams and *Rabbit Hole* by David Lindsay-Abaire). He was artistic director of the Mara theater in Kiryat Shmona, dramaturge of Beer-Sheba Theatre, and a visiting professor at the University of Texas in Austin and the American University in Washington DC. His book, *World of Innocents – The Dramatic Afterlife of the Bible in Yaakov Shabtai's Plays*, was published in 2021.

Samuel Juni is Professor Emeritus at New York University. He founded the Graduate Program in Cross-Cultural Psychology at NYU Tel Aviv, which he has headed since 2009. An international lecturer, author, and renowned expert in character disorders, psychiatric/psychological diagnostics, and psychoanalytic theory, he has conducted numerous research studies investigating cutting edge issues at the intersection of psychopathology and personality adjustment. Holding a doctorate in clinical psychology and a post-doctorate in psychiatric diagnostics, Dr. Juni also maintains a clinical differential diagnosis practice in Jerusalem. He was raised in a community of survivors and their families, a number of whom became his patients. Years ago, he began to notice distinct pathology syndrome patterns among the Second Generation of Holocaust survivors. Research with colleagues and discussions with peers from his Yeshiva days led him to formulate a personality profile of the cohort, which he published in a series of professional scientific research papers.

Natan P.F. Kellermann was born in Sweden, studied psychology at the University of Stockholm, and moved to Israel in 1980. For many years, he worked in Amcha – an Israeli treatment center for Holocaust survivors and their families – and lectured on Holocaust trauma at the International School for Holocaust Studies in Yad Vashem.

Carol A. Kidron is Associate Professor in the Department of Anthropology at the University of Haifa, Israel. Kidron has undertaken comparative ethnographic work on familial and collective memory of Holocaust descendants in Israel and children of Cambodian genocide survivors in Cambodia and Canada. Kidron has examined the localization of Euro-Western discourses on memorialization, justice and reconciliation, victimhood, and trauma in Cambodia, exploring sites of friction in local-global encounters. Kidron's publications include: "Toward an Ethnography of Silence: The Lived Presence of the Past in the Everyday Life of Holocaust Trauma Survivors and Their Descendants in Israel" (*Current Anthropology* 2009), "Alterity and the Particular Limits of Universalism: Comparing Jewish-Israeli Holocaust and Cambodian Genocide Legacies" (*Current Anthropology*, 2012), "Trauma as Badge of Honor: Phenomenological Experiences of Holocaust Descendant Resilient Vulnerability" (*Social Science & Medicine* 2019) and "The 'Perfect Failure' of Communal Genocide Commemoration in Cambodia: Productive Friction or 'Bone Business'? (*Current Anthropology*, 2020).

Lital Keinan-Boker has been on the faculty in the School of Public Health, the University of Haifa since 2005. Additionally, she has been nominated Director of the Israel Center for Disease Control in the Israel Ministry of Health in 2019, after having served as Vice-Director since 2003. Prof. Keinan-Boker received a PhD (2002) from the Julius Center for Epidemiology and Public Health of the Utrecht University, Utrecht, the Netherlands. Her MPH degree (1997, with distinction) was obtained from the Hebrew University in Jerusalem, Israel, during her residency in public health. She has received her MD degree from the same institute (1988). Prof. Keinan-Boker's research focuses on cancer epidemiology, including etiology and prevention, early detection, late outcomes, and rehabilitation. Additionally, she has a keen interest in long-term effects of exposure to extreme circumstances (famine, PTSD) and has studied Holocaust survivors in this respect. To date Prof. Keinan-Boker has published over 200 scientific papers in peer-reviewed journals.

Laurence J. Kirmayer, MD, FRCPC, FCAHS, FRSC is James McGill Professor and Director, Division of Social and Transcultural Psychiatry, Department of Psychiatry, McGill University. He is Editor-in-Chief of the journal *Transcultural Psychiatry* and directs the Culture & Mental Health Research Unit at the Institute of Community and Family Psychiatry, Jewish General Hospital, in Montreal, where he conducts research on culturally responsive mental health services, psychiatric anthropology, and the philosophy of psychiatry. His publications include the co-edited volumes: *Cultural Consultation: Encountering the Other in Mental Health Care* (Springer, 2013); *Re-Visioning Psychiatry: Cultural Phenomenology, Critical Neuroscience, and Global Mental Health* (Cambridge, 2015); *Culture, Mind and Brain: Emerging Concepts, Methods, and Applications* (Cambridge, 2020); and *Healing and the Invention of Metaphor: Toward a Poetics of Illness Experience*. He is a fellow of the Canadian Academy of Health Sciences and the Royal Society of Canada.

Rachel Kollender is a graduate of Bar-Ilan University, a musicologist and ethnomusicologist with particular interest in Jewish music, Karaite sacred music, women and music in Jewish societies, and Jewish music during the Nazi era. Her scholarly essays have been published in academic periodicals and books. She is presently a lecturer at Bar-Ilan University and retired head of music department at the Jerusalem Girls' Teaching College.

Dan M. Kotliar is a lecturer (assistant professor) at the Department of Sociology, The University of Haifa. Kotliar's research spans the sociology of knowledge, sociology of the internet, science and technology studies, and the sociology of emotions. His more recent works explore the ways big-data algorithms change our understanding of key sociological concepts such as identity, choice, power, emotion, and morality. Kotliar has published in leading journals such as *New Media & Society*, *Theory & Society*, *Science, Technology & Human Values*, *Social Science & Medicine*, and more.

Phyllis Lassner is Professor Emerita at Northwestern University. Her publications include studies of Holocaust literature, film and art, and women writers of the 1930s, World War II, and after. In addition to many articles, her books include *British Women Writers of World War II, Colonial Strangers: Women Writing the End of the British Empire* and *Anglo-Jewish Women Writing the Holocaust*. Her most recent book is *Espionage and Exile: Fascism and Anti-Fascism in British Spy Fiction and Film*. She co-edited the volumes *Antisemitism and Philosemitism in the Twentieth and Twenty-first Centuries* and *The Palgrave Handbook of Holocaust Literature and Culture.* She also co-edited the new edition of Gisella Perl's memoir, *I Was a Doctor in Auschwitz*. She was awarded the International Diamond Jubilee Fellowship at Southampton University, UK and serves on the Education and Exhibition Committees of the Illinois Holocaust Museum and Education Center.

Motti Neiger is Associate Professor at the School of Communication at Bar-Ilan University. His scholarly interests include mediated collective memory and Holocaust commemoration; journalism studies in the digital age (news temporalities media ethics and journalistic work during conflicts), and culture mediators (e.g., the book publishing industry in Israel). He is also Founder of OtheReality, a startup that leverages Virtual Reality technology to boost empathy in the healthcare sector.

Miriam Neiger-Fleischmann holds a PhD from the Hebrew Literature Department at the Hebrew University. She is an independent scholar, a poet, and a visual artist. Following her dissertation, she recently completed a comprehensive scholarly monograph on the poetry of Avigdor Hameiri.

Katalin Pécsi-Pollner PhD is a literary scholar living in Budapest, Hungary: an essayist, educator, and a lecturer on the field of the contemporary Jewish literature and film and numerous issues related to the Holocaust and women. She was the curator of the international traveling exhibition: *"... sticking together ..." – Personal Stories of Hungarian Survivor Women.* She has been the director of the project *"Hungarian Jewish Women who rescued fellow Jews during the Holocaust"* – in cooperation with the Memorial of the German Resistance (GDW) and the International Auschwitz Committee (IAK), Berlin. She is the founder and president of Esthers' House Association for the Jewish Culture and the Feminist Values. She is also a member of the organization International Council of Jewish Women (ICJW).

Liat Steir-Livny is Associate Professor in the Department of Culture at Sapir Academic College. She also teaches in the Cultural Studies MA program and in the Department of Literature, Language, and the Arts at the Open University of Israel. Her research focuses on Holocaust commemoration in Israel from the 1940s until the present. It combines Holocaust studies, memory studies, cultural studies, trauma studies, and film studies. She is the author of many articles and five books: *Two Faces in the Mirror: the Image of Holocaust Survivors in Israeli Cinema* (Eshkolot-Magness, 2009, Hebrew); *Let the memorial hill Remember: Holocaust Representation in Israeli Popular Culture* (Resling, 2014, Hebrew); *Is It O.K to Laugh about it? Holocaust Humour, Satire and Parody in Israel Culture* (Vallentine Mitchell, 2017); *Three Years, Two Perspectives, One Trauma* (The Herzl Institute for the Study of Zionism, University of Haifa, 2019, Hebrew); and *Remaking Holocaust Memory: Documentary Cinema by Third-Generation Survivors in Israel* (Syracuse University Press, 2019).

Andrea Zielke-Nadkarni, R.N., is a nurse teacher with a Dr. Phil. in education (1992) who practices habilitation in nursing science. She is Professor for nursing science at the Muenster School of Health, Applied University of Muenster. Her special research areas include: care needs of sociocultural minorities and of vulnerable populations and women's health.

INTRODUCTION

Amit Shrira and Judith Tydor Baumel-Schwartz

"Where can I find an archive of Second Generation Interviews?" The question, coming from a friend who is both a psychiatrist and a daughter of two Holocaust survivors, caught me by surprise. "Holocaust survivor interviews conducted by the Second Generation?" I asked. "No, interviews done with people like us, members of the Second Generation. In a few years there won't be any more survivors, and we will be left to tell the tale", she responded. "Besides, we also have a story to tell. We also went through something. Remember – we survived the survivors".[1]

While her last statement was made half tongue-in-cheek, it contained more than a handful of truth. Since the beginning of the 21st century there has been a new wave of interest in the special character of the Second Generation, far beyond the understanding of the topic that has already existed since the mid-1970s when the term was coined by the American Psychoanalytic Association to replace "children of Holocaust survivors" that had been used until then. Focusing on the nature and character of members of this generation as independent entities and not just defining them as appendages of their parents had been the first step. Then came the first Second Generation awareness groups, later the local and national original organizations, and, eventually, internet-based international Second Generation discussion groups.

Initial studies of the Second Generation, often known by the initials 2g (or G2), were part of a second wave of Holocaust-related studies. During the first decades after the war's end scholars writing about the Holocaust focused upon what they saw as "major topics". These included Nazi anti-Jewish policy including ghettos and camps, Jewish leadership and resistance, and attempts to rescue Jews. By the 1970s, academic Holocaust-related historical scholarship had expanded to include social and cultural topics, while the fields of psychology and, to a degree, sociology were already exploring the Holocaust's aftermath, including that pertaining to offspring of Holocaust survivors, the Second Generation. As time passed, studies of 2gs began to surface in other disciplines including history, communications, law, literature, education, and film. More recently, we have seen studies in biological and health-related sciences including the epigenetics of inherited trauma and health issues of the Second Generation.

Studies have appeared in all these fields; however, there have been few attempts to put together a more comprehensive volume encompassing more than one field and, to the best of our knowledge, no attempts until now to put together a multi-disciplinary perspective of new and hitherto unpublished studies dealing with research about offspring of Holocaust survivors. This volume will

DOI: 10.4324/b23365-1

attempt to fill this lacuna. Divided into two sections, the humanities and the social and health-related sciences, it charts and analyzes past and current studies having to do with the Second Generation in thirteen fields.

Judith Tydor Baumel-Schwartz recounts and analyzes the history of Second Generation organizations in Israel and the United States over four generations. Second Generation writer Melvin Jules Bukiet explores the metamorphosis of Second Generation literature over a 30 year period, using his own work as a case study. Katalin Pécsi-Pollner discusses literature dealing with the Second and Third Generations in Hungary, where some members of the Third and even Fourth Generations have slowly begun to investigate the repressed memory of their families.

Moving from Literature to Film, Phyllis Lassner examines the 2016 film *Past Life* directed by Avi Nesher as dramatizing the search for the Holocaust diary of survivor Baruch Milch by his two daughters, showing it to be an inquiry into the nature of Holocaust memory. Liat Steir-Livny focuses on the perception of time in five Second Generation Holocaust survivor documentaries since the 1980s, showing how these films reflect a perception that time has stood still for the survivors and their children although outwardly they live their Israeli lives.

Specializing in the medium of theater, Roy Horovitz explores Jewish-Australian playwright Ron Elisha's prolific body of work as a "Holocaust playwright", following the sources of his inspiration, analyzing the main themes of his play, documenting the work process on the Israeli production, and examining the way it was received.

Art scholar Batya Brutin examines how Second Generation Israeli artists use the motif of *Arbeit Macht Frei* to show reality and meaning in their attempt to deal with the memory of the Holocaust. Rachel Kollender explores how music shapes and transmits Holocaust memory to the Second and Third Generations, using her experiences in teaching Holocaust-related music as a springboard for the discussion. In her study of music as a therapeutic tool, Atarah Fisher interviews Second Generation musicians, asking them to prepare three musical extracts representing their mother, their father, and themselves. Analyzing these compositions, she probes the mechanism of how some Second Generation musicians use music in dealing with their complex connection with their parents.

Transitioning from the humanities into the social sciences, Samuel Juni analyzes an ongoing survey he is conducting regarding the effects of the Holocaust on the Second Generation. Among the topics he discusses are the personality, religiosity, and interpersonal relationships of the Second Generation. Irit Felsen focuses on intergenerational transmission of the experiences of aging members of the Second Generation during the COVID pandemic in the United States. In it, she reports how adult children of Holocaust survivors have navigated the largest-scale pandemic of the last hundred years, as well as the convergence of socio-cultural, political, and economic crises that came in its wake. Discussing past, present, and future perspectives of Holocaust trauma transmission, Natan Kellerman presents a critical overview of past psychological research, discusses the current shift from a psychosocial to a neurobiological focus, and suggests avenues for future studies.

Carol A. Kidron and her colleagues provide a social anthropological account of Second Generation Israelis and suggest a shift from binary representations of resilience and vulnerability (e.g., wellness and distress) to more intricate descriptions of 2gs in which strength intermingles with distress so that emotional wounds are simultaneously perceived as "scratches" and as a "badge of honor".

In the field of communications and social media, Motti and Miriam Neiger explore a fascinating digital space: the closed Facebook group titled "Yes, I'm a Second Generation Holocaust survivor", which numbers 9,750 members. Based on interviews, a survey, and a qualitative analysis of posts and discussion, they present six functions of social media for the Second Generation.

Moving into health-related sciences, Amit Shrira focuses on gerontological issues and questions whether ancestral trauma can affect the aging process of subsequent generations. By creating a model for the Second Generation, he shows how the consequences of parental trauma on aging offspring become most pronounced under adverse conditions.

Andrea Zielke-Nadkarni focuses on the life and care of members of the Second Generation in Germany, presenting the results of a qualitative explorative study on the biographies of Second and Third generation members living there today with special focus on that group's trauma inheritance and their dependence on professional care providers when in need of nursing care.

Finally, Lital Keinan-Boker analyses the long-term physical health outcome in child survivors and offspring of Holocaust survivors. One long-term physical outcome that she mentions regarding the Second Generation is their being potentially susceptible to certain chronic conditions, especially metabolic disease, and she suggests focusing attention on primary prevention and early detection in this population.

The lives of the Second Generation are an ongoing story. Studies into those lives show an ever-changing dynamic in all fields, with common denominators for large groups of 2gs alongside distinct and separate tendencies and inclinations for various subgroups. We hope that this multi-disciplinary collection of studies will cast light on some of those dynamics, tendencies, and inclinations in order to provide insight into the lives of a group whose very existence is testimony to the survivors' motto of "We are here!"

Note

1 Telephone conversation between Dr. Jacqueline Heller Kahane and Judith Tydor Baumel-Schwartz, July 13, 2022.

PART I

Humanities

1

CREATING SECOND GENERATION GROUPS IN THE USA AND ISRAEL

A Four-decade Perspective

Judith Tydor Baumel-Schwartz

Introduction

There is a story told in Jewish administrative circles that encapsulates the modern Jewish response to meaningful events. "It happened. It ended. We celebrated/mourned. We ate/fasted. Now let's form an organization about it, fight over it, and remember it forever". Whether apocryphal or authentic, it epitomizes a postwar Jewish response to the Holocaust: the creation of numerous Holocaust-related organizations – or modification of existing associations and alliances – to reflect a Holocaust-related essence. Some were survivor organizations characterized by places of origin, wartime locations, or sites of liberation. Others were groups of former refugee adults or children, *Landsmanschaft*-style associations, and those composed of partisans. Because of the sociological and geographical dynamics of the Jewish wartime experience, it was not uncommon to be a member of several such organizations at once. And, of course, there were competing organizations as per the dictum, "two Jews, three *shuls* (synagogues). Yours, mine, and the one neither of us would ever step foot into".

As time passed and the next generation came of age, new Holocaust organizations were established that focused on them: children of refugees, children of Jews from area X; children of deportees, children of Jews liberated from this camp or that ghetto, and, finally, local, national, and international organizations created by and for descendants of Holocaust survivors according to that term's broadest definition. Some lasted; others disappeared. Some morphed into new organizations; others split, reunited, and split again, proving that the Jewish tradition of factionalism had lost none of its fervor when bequeathed to children of Holocaust survivors, known in colloquial parlance as the "Second Generation" (2g).

This article focuses on the dynamics behind the creation and operation of "Second Generation" Holocaust organizations established in the USA and Israel, two countries in the free world with large numbers of 2gs, over a period of four decades, from the early 1980s up to 2022.[1] What was the impetus for their genesis and who were their creators? What activities did they focus on, and how did this focus change over time? Why were some successful while others were not? Why did certain organizations continue to exist for years while others disappeared after a short period of activity? Did 2g organizations whose members had a common denominator in addition to being a descendant of Holocaust survivors have a greater chance of succeeding? What conclusions have research-focused 2g organizations reached in their studies regarding issues of identification and

DOI: 10.4324/b23365-3

belonging among the Second and Third Generations? These are some of the questions that I will probe in the following pages.

Research Framework

If most nations commemorate their triumphs and successes, Jews tend to immortalize their defeats and catastrophes, undoubtedly from having had to deal with so many of them throughout the ages. Organizations formed by Holocaust survivors were an almost traditional response to the cataclysm, but 2g groups were an innovation that only became possible in a world that had experienced the social changes and cultural revolution of the "turbulent 60s", focusing on personal identity, psychological wellbeing, healing, and a positive sense of "self".

What worked for descendants of Holocaust survivors turned out to be equally supportive for offspring of populations experiencing trauma. Adopting the "Second Generation" nomenclature, they, too, spoke of coming to terms with a traumatic heritage (also known as "transgenerational trauma"), forming groups and utilizing other tools to deal with that troubling legacy. Consequently, like the Holocaust affiliations preceding them, 2g Holocaust groups became an organizational paradigm, epitomizing genocide's generational aftermath.

Second Generation Holocaust groups did not function in a vacuum. All "Second Generation" organizations are part of an expanding research category that combines collective memory, postmemorial activity, and response to transgenerational trauma. Collective memory, as posited by Halbwachs, is a social group's shared pool of memories, knowledge, and information that is significantly associated with its identity.[2] *Postmemory* is one's relationship to the memory of others that one has taken upon oneself. Originally a term coined by Marianne Hirsch in 1992 to describe the relationship between children of survivors and their parents' memories,[3] it quickly expanded to mean the relationship that later generations bear to traumas they didn't experience but that were transmitted to them by those who experienced them (transgenerational trauma). When dealing with a traumatic event such as – but not limited to – the Holocaust, postmemory can become a toxic, negative element in one's life. To alleviate the negative aspects of those memories, one solution is to turn to "postmemorial activity", the metamorphosis of negative trauma into positive action.

Are 2g organizations a form of postmemorial activity? A brief survey of postmemorial activities that deal with transgenerational trauma illuminates four recurring templates. The first is the creation of frameworks for Second Generation psychological counseling.[4] As psychologist Samuel Juni explains, these offer strength-based interventions to work through trauma and achieve recovery. The second evokes the use of literature and the arts in working through transgenerational traumas.[5] In her exploration of the Tamil diaspora community in Canada, Ann Satkuman illustrates how Second Generation women whose parents survived the civil war in Sri Lanka negotiate trauma and identity through art.[6] The third involves creating communal institutions in which the Second Generation plays an important role. As trauma specialist Rachael Goodman shows us, these institutions provide an ecological framework that fosters resilience in healing from transgenerational trauma.[7] The fourth and final response is the development of Second Generation organizations whose members explore issues of identity and self while recalibrating negative or complex encounters that they experienced with their parents.[8] In their studies of Second Generation Cambodian-Americans and the Kiowa Tribe of Oklahoma, two groups experiencing transgenerational trauma, Jordan[9] and Chhun,[10] analyze how Second Generation organizations help descendants of those groups recognize, define, and evaluate their own roles by inverting victimhood and developing agency.

Of all the template's alternatives, Second Generation Holocaust organizations appear to be the most comprehensive response, often including components from each of them. Some were self-help therapy groups, initially led by 2g therapists/facilitators who boosted group psychological dynamics to promote healing. Others encourage members to work out transgenerational traumas through art and bibliotherapy, while acting as an initial audience for the results. Certain Second Generation groups are devoted to social action, working hand-in-hand with new or existing communal institutions. And, of course, there can be any combination of these possibilities. Consequently, Second Generation organizations have the potential to become the most versatile and comprehensive form of postmemorial activity of all the aforementioned alternatives.

How did these the dynamics develop within Second Generation organizations of descendants of Holocaust survivors? How did the geographical and sociological differences between the organizations in various countries express themselves? To answer these questions, we must go back in time to before such organizations existed, when the term "Holocaust" was used solely for Jews and the memory of that cataclysm was of an event that had taken place during most people's lifetimes.

How It All Began

The first documented 2g groups were short-term awareness groups, run by psychologists Bella Savran and Dr. Eva Fogelman at Boston University (1976) and then by Fogelman at the Hebrew University of Jerusalem (1978).[11] Their inspiration came from reading what they felt was an eye-opening dialogue between children of survivors that had been published in *Response: A Contemporary Jewish Review* in 1975. Meeting for eight to twelve sessions, these were the first 2g groups that discussed issues pertaining to the lives of children of survivors.

By that time, the term "Second Generation", not just "Children of Survivors", was being used by the American Psychoanalytic Association, and the group was being viewed as an independent entity with its own identity and not as an appendage to the survivors. Welcoming Fogelman to the annual meetings of their newly established "Group for the Psychoanalytic Study of the Effect of the Holocaust on the Second Generation", they learned from her about the results of the short-term awareness groups, while emphasizing the significance behind the use of a new nomenclature.[12] *Second* implies continuity, a continuation of survivor trauma, albeit in a different form. It also implies a connective chain and degree of dependance, as there is no "second" without "first". At the same time, it also gives expression to that generation's emerging adult identity and cohesion, no longer individual "children" but an entire generation with common denominators, stemming from its members' Holocaust heritage. Terminology is an important shaper of identity, and I will revisit these terms later in a different context.[13]

Interest in the Holocaust reached unparalleled heights following the broadcast of NBC's 1978 docudrama by that name and the publication of Helen Epstein's path-breaking 2g introspection, *Children of the Holocaust*.[14] Bringing the topic of Holocaust survivors' descendants to the forefront, the first 2g Holocaust organizations began to crystallize in the United States and Israel. In November 1979 the First Conference of the Second Generation, held at Hebrew Union College, laid the groundwork for a 2g organization that would be established a year and a half later, following the World Gathering of Jewish Holocaust Survivors held in Jerusalem in June 1981.[15] Although it was called "The International Network of Children of Jewish Holocaust Survivors" (INCJHS), it soon became a primarily American organization, headed by 2g activist and lawyer Menachem Rosensaft, son of post-war activists Josef and Dr. Hadassah Bimko-Rosensaft, a founding member of the United States Holocaust Memorial Council.

The first Israeli initiative to establish a 2g organization predated the American one. In March 1980, having heard about the American 2g conference, historian Judy Tydor Baumel (later Baumel-Schwartz) and psychodrama specialist Ya'akov Naor founded the *Irgun Yaldei Nitzolei Shoah*

Beyisrael – The Israeli Organization for Children of Holocaust Survivors, a long-named, short-lived body that lasted for less than six months due to discord over its organizational focus. Should its 40 or so members devote their energies to hashing out personal fallout from their 2g background, or should they use that time to volunteer among elderly or indigent survivors? Were they meant to be a "rap (discussion) group" or to devote themselves to social action? Could they do both?

Unable to reach a consensus, even between the organizers, the group disbanded a year before its American counterpart was established. Nevertheless, it heralded the creation of a larger Israeli 2g organization, *Irgun Dor Hemshech Limoreshet Hashoah VeHagevurah* (Second Generation Organization for the Legacy of Holocaust and Heroism), which, like the INCJHS, was also – unsurprisingly – formed in the wake of the 1981 World Gathering in Jerusalem. "The Second Generation will never know what the First Generation does in its bones, but what the Second Generation knows better than anyone else is the First Generation", writes 2g author and literary critic Melvin Jules Bukiet.[16] When survivors gather, their children are rarely far behind.

It was not by chance that both the American and the Israeli 2g national organizations were catalyzed by a Holocaust survivor conference and supported or partially initiated by survivor organizations of activists (including during the Holocaust) with organizational clout and financial resources. In Israel, leaders of the Partisans, Underground, and Ghetto Resistance Fighters Organizations, such as Bela-Elster-Rotenberg ("Wanda"), Ya'akov Greenstein, Stefan Grayek, and Moshe Kalcheim, initiated the creation of *Irgun Dor Hemshech*, while Ya'akov Zilberstein, head of the Organization of Former Nazi Prisoners, financially assisted the organization at various junctures. In the United States, Benjamin Meed, President of the American Gathering of Jewish Holocaust Survivors and a founder of WAGRO, the Warsaw Ghetto Resistance Organization (1963), helped spearhead the American initiative.

Are "initiated" and "active" synonyms for "controlling"? It depends on who one asks. Finances "make or break" many organizations, and 2g bodies suffered from chronic deficits. The backing of survivor organizations was often critical to their continued existence. Inevitably, the interconnection between survivors and 2g groups led to tacit power struggles between survivors wishing to see their legacy continue and 2gs determined to set their own path. Debates over policy and practice did not always end with hugs and smiles. Like families where children are considered adults only at middle age, it sometimes took a generational transition for 2gs to come into their own.

"Second Generation" members worldwide may embody similar characteristics, but the same is not true of 2g organizations. It is not by chance that the major American and Israel 2g organizations had different names stemming from the different Holocaust narratives and disparate natures of the survivor and 2g communities in those countries. While neither organization used the term "Second Generation", the American organization emphasized "Jewish" Holocaust Survivors, which in Israel was unnecessary. And although both groups had strong connections with Holocaust partisan organizations, only in Israel did the 2g organization's name refer to "Holocaust and Heroism" instead of "Holocaust", reflecting the prevalent Israeli Statist terminology and narrative.

Another difference was geographical. At an early stage, the American and Israeli 2g endeavors took on different trajectories, influenced by geography and organizational culture. The sheer geographical vastness of the United States and a tradition of decentralization encouraged the development of local 2g groups throughout the country. These were organized by activists such as Jeanette Friedman (New Jersey), Charlie Silow (Michigan), and others and flourished in cities such as Atlanta, Cleveland, Detroit, Los Angeles, Miami, New York, Philadelphia, San Francisco, St. Louis, Teaneck, and Washington DC from the mid-1980s onward. Certain local groups, like that founded by Friedman in Teaneck, echoed the debate that had effectively shut down the first Israeli 2g organization between those advocating for it to become a social action body as opposed to those wishing for it to remain a "rap group".[17] Some groups were connected to the INCJHS, while others began as independent discussion groups. There were also 2g groups that began as a section within an existing Holocaust-related organization such as WAGRO, whose members were acutely aware of the aging process and wished to create reserves for the future.[18]

Second Generation organizations in Israel developed somewhat differently as circumscribed geographical parameters precluded the need to develop local 2g groups. During the early 1980s the national *Dor Hemshech* organization, whose members met in the greater Tel-Aviv area, included several dozen 2g activists from all over the country, some of whom would eventually become major academic figures (Rafi Cohen-Almagor, Gad Barzilai, Gideon Greif, Shmuel Refael), or national 2g activists (Tzippi Kichler, Billie Laniado). A number had been approached about joining the initiative by Israeli Knesset Minister and Holocaust survivor Dov Shilansky, others by Moshe Kalcheim and Ya'akov Greenstein of the Partisan Organization.

Numbering close to 1,400 members, the organization continued to function under this name until 1986–87 when several active members left the country to study abroad, while others finished their studies and had little time for 2g activities. There were also financial difficulties regarding publications and mailings, making it necessary to constantly beg funds from survivor organizations. Consequently, the organization diminished in size, was reinvented with a different name, and continued to function for more than a decade before undergoing a more radical organizational change. Like its American counterpart, the Israeli organization held national conferences and promoted Holocaust-related educational activity. It did not sponsor psychological discussion groups like those of the local American 2g organizations, possibly because of its being a national organization (neither did the American national organization) or because of the different cultural attitude in Israel of the 1980s towards self-awareness groups. Most of its efforts were devoted to public conferences, and towards the end of the decade, it became active in promoting educational missions to Poland and supporting the March of the Living, initiated in 1988.[19]

An additional Israeli organization functioning during that period to promote Holocaust education and commemoration was *Lapid* – The Movement to Teach the Lessons of the Holocaust. Although not specifically a 2g group, it was founded by a 2g, lawyer and educator Aryeh Barnea, and it had a large 2g following. Functioning between 1986 and 1994, *Lapid* promoted several educational goals including those pertaining to the Holocaust's Zionist lessons, rescue during the Holocaust, the fate of North African and Middle Eastern Jews, and the responsibility to help victims of contemporary genocides.[20]

As survivors everywhere recognized that their biological clock was ticking, 2g sections were also being formed in Israeli-based survivor organizations and *Landsmanschaften* such as the Organization of Jews from Salonika, The Association of Jews from Bochnia, and the *She'erit Hapletah* – Bergen Belsen Organization in Israel. Like in America, the relationship between the survivors and 2gs in these frameworks was often fraught with undercurrents, recalling those between survivors and their children everywhere.[21]

New Stages in 2g and 3g Organizational Identity

From the mid-1990s onward, a new stage began in 2g organizational development propelled by generational transitions and technological developments.

In Israel, a small national 2g organization continued to exist, working in cooperation with groups such as *Amcha,* the Israeli association for mutual aid, memory processing, and grief resolution for survivors. But it took another decade (2005) until the *Amutat Dorot Hahemshech – Nosei Moreshet Hashoah VeHagevura* (the Next Generations to Holocaust and Heroism Association) was established, which, like its predecessors, focused on commemoration and educational endeavors.[22] One explanation for the organization's renaissance and expansion was the gradual disappearance of the older survivors, combined with the Second Generation's aging, leading to a heightened awareness that they would soon have to continue their parents' legacy alone. Another explanation was the internet's proliferation that brought the organizations' existence to the attention of 2gs throughout the country, while eliminating the mailing costs that had financially paralyzed previous Israeli 2g organizations.

The generational transition was also felt among the *Landsmanschaft* organizations, such as that of Jews from Bochnia, where a 2g assumed leadership of the entire organization while campaigning to bring in large numbers of previously unaffiliated 2gs whose parents had been longtime members.[23] Although not declared 2g organizations, in practice, as the survivor generation dwindled, their membership was composed primarily of survivors' children. Such organizations were not devoted to 2g issues but rather to maintaining the communal legacy and commemorating its Holocaust martyrs.

The same generational transition and technological innovations existed in the United States but took a somewhat different form. One was the creation of online 2g communities, the first of which was known as the 2nd Gen List. Begun in 1995, the "List" was the brainchild of Paul Foldes, a 2g electrical engineer and consumer attorney turned businessman, who hadn't been able to find a face-to-face 2g group in the Washington DC area where he lived. Knowing that online communities were an opportunity to reach beyond local meetings, he founded the List even before the web existed.[24]

As an internet-based group, the List bypassed certain problems that face-to-face 2g groups had grappled with. It was the first to break local and national barriers to become a truly international, English speaking, 2g framework. Unlike 2g face-to-face organizations, it required no funding. Freed from having to pander to various groups for financial support, its active members could devote their energies to their favorite 2g activities: discussing their past and arguing about their present and future. Ultimately succumbing to internet ills such as flaming, trolling, and cyberbullying, the List went through several metamorphoses. Meanwhile, suffering from moderator burnout, its founder and some active members eventually left not only their moderating positions but the group. The List was also affected by platform instability, forced to migrate from one free platform to another until becoming a Google group where it functions today.

As the List celebrated a decade of existence, Facebook was born, offering another platform for 2g encounters. Since then, a plethora of 2g Facebook groups have been created to disseminate information about Holocaust-related and 2g events, share experiences, and focus on specific issues such as 2gs obtaining European citizenship.[25] While perusing the numerous English-language Facebook groups created for descendants of Holocaust survivors, one is struck by their vast geographical, political, and social diversity. American political ideologies, attitudes towards European governments – particularly those in Eastern Europe – and debates over the policies of the State of Israel are a few of the more common topics that surface continuously in some groups to become acrimonious discussions.

Certain groups are public; others are closed. Some allow free expression; others ask members to refrain from making political statements of any kind. Some boast thousands of members, while others have only a handful. Some become platforms for what is facetiously known as the "Suffering Olympics", comparing who among their members endured more as a 2g, while others only discuss educational matters.[26] Many of these groups became a lifeline for 2gs during the COVID-19 pandemic when face-to-face meetings often came to an abrupt halt. At the same time, the well-documented, darker side of relying on Facebook for social interaction also became evident in some of the 2g discussions.[27]

The move to online 2g organizations in America preceded such a move in Israel by almost half a decade. Several years after English-language 2g Facebook groups were established, the first of three 2g Hebrew Facebook groups was launched – *Dor Sheni Lenitzolei Shoah* (Second Generation to Holocaust Survivors) established as a public group in 2010.[28] It was followed by two private groups created in 2013 (*Dor Sheni Lashoah* – Holocaust Second Generation) and 2014 (*Ken, Ani Dor Sheni (Shoah)* – Yes I am Second Generation (Holocaust)).[29] While there are specific 2g geographical Facebook groups in the United States that are outgrowths of previous face-to-face groups,[30] Israel's circumscribed geography and centralized 2g organizational tradition has prevented the creation of similar online local groups.

The internet's international nature and characteristic of becoming a great equalizer has enabled English-speaking (or reading) Israelis to actively participate in international 2g online groups. A quarter of the active members of the List live in Israel. A considerable number of Israeli 2gs participate in both public and private 2g international Facebook groups.

And what of the 3gs? Despite officially belonging to another generation, it is not uncommon to find 2gs and 3gs of the same age. The oldest 3gs are even older than the youngest 2gs. At the beginning of the 21st century, face-to-face 3g groups were organized in America and on Facebook.[31] In Israel, the national organization for descendants of Holocaust survivors was already called *Amutat Dorot Hahemshech* – the Next Generations, an inclusive name that would cover all generations of Holocaust survivor descendants.

As the masses of 3gs are primarily under 50, and many are in their 30s and younger, their involvement in these groups is still minimal. It will be interesting to note whether they follow their parents' pattern and become more involved in Holocaust issues as they grow older or whether the extra generation's distance from the Holocaust and the fact that they were not raised by survivors will act as a distancing mechanism from such organizations.

Researchers Remember

Until 2018 almost all 2g groups in the USA or Israel, whether online or face-to-face, were discussion groups, therapy groups, social action groups, groups created for purposes of Holocaust education or a combination of these. Almost none were created for research purposes. This changed when I became Director of the Finkler Institute of Holocaust Research at Bar-Ilan University in Israel and formed a 2g Forum focusing on descendants of survivors worldwide who chose a profession with a strong research component. The hypothesis was that many 2gs grew up with Holocaust-related questions they were afraid to ask their families or in a household unconducive to such discussions. If so, we asked, was there any connection between their Holocaust heritage and their choice of a research profession (academic, medical, legal, etc. and not necessarily Holocaust related) that forced them to continuously ask questions, probe, and reflect? By doing so, did research become an arena of memory and commemoration for of them? The forum, initially focusing on 2g researchers, grew to include 3gs as well.

Ultimately, the "Researchers Remember" forum included 250 researchers worldwide and is still growing. Three focus groups with a total of 30 participants from 7 countries met monthly to discuss these questions, eventually becoming the basis for the *Researchers Remember* book.[32] Forum participants were asked to fill out a detailed questionnaire probing the connection between their personal and professional choices and their 2g/3g background, ranking their degree of identification with Holocaust-related statements in several frameworks. The first was their parental home with statements such as: "When I was young, I asked my parents a lot of questions about their Holocaust experiences";"When I was young, it often scared me when my parents would begin talking about the Holocaust".

From there they progressed to educational and personal choices. Those statements included: "I wanted to succeed in my studies to compensate my parents for what they experienced during the Holocaust";"When I was younger, I felt that my parents' Holocaust experiences greatly influenced my daily life". They were then asked to rate personal experience statements such as "I occasionally still feel like a 'memorial candle' for my relatives who were killed during the Holocaust" and "I have visited the camps, ghettos or hiding places where my parents were during the Holocaust".

Finally, they noted their identification with statements about their professional choices: "I think there is a connection between my choice to be a researcher and look for solutions and insights and my 'Second Generation' background", "I think that 'Second Generation' researchers have unique common denominators that they don't share with their research colleagues who are not part of the 'Second Generation'", etc.

When analyzing the completed questionnaires, some responses were expected while others were a surprise. Three quarters of the 2g researchers living outside Israel still felt themselves to be "memorial candles", as opposed to less than half of those living in Israel. Close to 80% of the 2g researchers living outside of Israel felt a strong connection between their Holocaust heritage and their choice of a research profession as opposed to less than 40% of the Israeli 2gs. Unlike the diaspora where the Holocaust (and Israel) plays a major role in Jewish identity – and not just for 2gs – living in Israel appears to provide 2gs with a national and social framework that may lessen the need to use the Holocaust as a marker of collective identity.

Similar dichotomies existed in terms of age groups. Twice as many older 2g researchers (born before 1950), than younger ones (born after 1970) stated that the Holocaust was very present in their homes and that they spoke about it often with their families. Over half of the older 2g researchers stated that the connection between their Holocaust heritage and choice of a research profession grew stronger with time, as opposed to only a third of the youngest 2g group. Thus, the length of time that passed between the end of the Second World War and the birth of 2gs appears to play an important role in the centrality of the Holocaust in their lives.

Then there were the 3g researchers of whom fewer than half admitted to being "obsessed by the Holocaust" in their youth, as opposed to more than two thirds of the 2g researchers their age, all born after 1970. Fewer than a third connected their strong research drive to their Holocaust heritage, as opposed to over half of the 2g researchers their age. Finally, almost no 3g researchers stated that they would find it difficult to participate in joint research projects with non-Jewish German researchers, while over a third of the 2g researchers in their age bracket admitted to finding such professional cooperation against their liking.

One important conclusion of this study is that generational separation from the Holocaust, as opposed to chronological age, appears to be a decisive factor regarding the impact of a Holocaust legacy and relationship to the first generation. Even if they were the same age, from the same social milieu and the same country, 2gs and 3gs responded differently to Holocaust-related issues. Being raised by survivors appears to be very different than being raised by their children. Another conclusion is that geography and culture play important roles in the lives of 2gs and 3gs, as is seen by the difference in response between 2gs/3gs raised in Israel and those raised elsewhere.

New Insights

Let us return to our starting point – a comparison between 2g organizations in the United States and in Israel created over a period of four decades. Three interrelated issues characterize the differences between them – terminology, mission, and geographical trajectory – and all organizations function within the prevalent Holocaust narrative in their country at a particular time.

Terminology is related to self-image and social acceptance. In America, the term "Holocaust Survivor" came into common use during the mid- to late 1970s. Prior to that they were called "liberated Jews" or "displaced persons" and then "refugees" or "immigrants". Sometime during the 1970s they were reclassified as "survivors", a more positive term showing strength, persistence, heroism, and even agency.[33] In Israel, survivors were commonly called *nitzolim* (those saved by others), a passive term in view of the heroic Israeli hierarchy of ghetto fighters, resistants, and partisans. Only during the second decade of the 21st century did the term *sordim* (survivors) come into use, as a more positive and active term expressing a degree of agency.

Terminological differences left their mark on 2g organizations. While the first 2g organization in Israel used the term *Yaldei Nitzolei Shoah* (children of those who were saved) in its title, all later Israeli 2g organizations eschewed the term. Instead, they chose a title representing future and continuity ("Next Generation"), while adopting the Israeli statist narrative of Holocaust and Heroism, created to focus on the Holocaust's aspect that did not clash with the Zionist ethos of physical heroism. This is not surprising as the initiative to create a national Israeli 2g organization came from the Organization of Partisans, Underground, and Ghetto Resistance Fighters, and the official name of Israel's Holocaust Memorial Day, declared by the Knesset in 1959, is *Yom HaShoah VeHagevurah* (Holocaust and Heroism Day). Eventually, the Israeli concept of heroism was broadened to include cultural, educational, and religious resistance, but by then the 2g organization's nomenclature and implied narrative had been set, despite some of the 2g leadership being children of partisans or ghetto fighters and the changes already being evident in the Israeli Holocaust ethos by the early 1980s.

In the United States, the national 2g organization calling itself "Children of Holocaust Survivors" gave survivors equal billing in its self-definition/image, but most local groups called themselves the "Second Generation". While there is no "Second Generation" without a first, these groups focused on themselves without overtly including other populations or ideologies in their title.

Nomenclature is intrinsically connected with mission and, here, with geographical trajectory. While the major national 2g organization in the USA promoted Holocaust education, commemoration, and social action, the country's vast geography encouraged the development of local groups, each choosing its own mission. In America of the early 1980s, where psychological wellbeing was a premium and therapy was considered a normal step towards that wellbeing, many 2g groups devoted their meetings to self-exploration, discussing the unique and often painful experiences of being a 2g.

Intergenerational transmission of trauma is dependent upon parents' agency and communication styles. As Diane Wolf shows us, a positive, open, age-appropriate communication style can mitigate the intergenerational transmission of trauma. As that was not the style used by many Holocaust survivors to share their experiences with their children, 2g discussion groups helped downsize the central role of trauma among their members.[34]

In Israel of the 1980s, the national 2g organization was devoted to education, commemoration, and social action. Being a small country, the geographical trajectory did not actively encourage the development of local 2g groups that might have adopted other missions. Although certain members of the first, short-lived Israeli 2g organization had wanted it to become a discussion group, that was not the direction taken by any of the national 2g groups established afterwards. Furthermore, as self-exploration and therapy were not yet mainstream public activities in Israel of those years, even if local 2g groups had been established, it is questionable whether they would have developed then in that direction.

Amcha, the Israeli organization for mental health and social services for survivors, with 14 branches throughout the country, eventually added "and the Second Generation" to its title and has offered individual and group therapy to 2gs for years. These are not discussion groups but therapy groups run by professionals in the framework of what was originally a survivor-focused organization. Even the "Researchers Remember" forum of the Finkler Institute, initiated in 2018, was not created initially to be a 2g discussion group but a research forum. Ultimately, the focus group dynamics turned them into something approximating American local and regional 2g discussion groups of the 1980s.

Second Generation organizations often echo their country's Holocaust narrative while mirroring their politics of Holocaust identity. During the 1980s, the Holocaust was a central link connecting American Jews to their past and its commemoration offered the United States a framework in which to make amends for not having saved European Jews. As introspection and self-analysis were commonplace; 2g action and discussion groups could flourish there while including an educational and commemorative component.

In contrast, in an Israel that still emphasized victimization and marginalization, the first 2g groups were propelled towards extroversive (educational, commemorative, and social action) activity rather than introspection. It would take another two decades before the need for self-analysis and understanding among Israeli 2gs would express itself overtly, but eventually it happened, with 2gs creating online Hebrew discussion groups, compensating for the lack of local face-to-face 2g groups of that kind.

Conclusion

In the end, as Melvin Jules Bukiet reminds us, all 2gs boil down to the same thing and all 2g groups are based on the same premise: the need to remember, render, and attribute meaning to being a descendant of Holocaust survivors.[35] The ways in which 2gs express that need are manifold and have changed as they transition through various stages of life. They are shaped by the existing dynamics in the societies and countries in which they live, while simultaneously shaping Holocaust consciousness in those societies and countries. As 2gs age in the years to come and the mantle of creating memory and meaning will be transferred to the next generation, the 3gs, it will be interesting to see how a new generation of Holocaust descendants will choose to express their legacy.

Holocaust Organizations:

Amcha – the Israeli center for social and emotional support of survivors and the Second Generation, www.amcha.org/node/72 retrieved on November 6, 2021.

Second and Third Generation Online Groups:

2g Second Generation Children of Holocaust Survivors 4.9 k members in 2021 (created in 2013, name change in 2019) www.facebook.com/groups/2GSecongGeneration. retrieved on October 31, 2021.

Allgenerations Inc. (survivors and 2, 3, 4, g), 151 members in 2021 (created in 2015) www.facebook.com/groups/374780785962698/about retrieved on October 31, 2021.

Austrian Citizenship Holocaust Descendants, 1.1k members in 2021 (created in 2019) www.facebook.com/groups/ACHDs retrieved on November 7, 2021.

Children of Holocaust Survivors, with 11.9 K members in 2021 (created in 2007) (www.facebook.com/groups/childrenOHS/about) retrieved on October 31, 2021.

Children of Holocaust Survivors 2g, 757 members in 2021 (created in 2015) www.facebook.com/groups/COHS2ndGeneration retrieved on October 31, 2021.

Descendants of Holocaust Survivors (2G Greater New York) 1.3K members in 2021 (created in 2021) www.facebook.com/groups/557145015152591 retrieved on October 31, 2021.

Generations of the Shoah International (GSI), 6.1K members in 2021 (created in 2009) www.facebook.com/groups/genshoah/about. retrieved on October 31, 2021.

Generational Holocaust Survivors and Descendants, 97 members in 2021 (created in 2021) www.facebook.com/groups/1391150541260503 retrieved on October 31, 2021.

Holocaust Second Generation, 3.1K members in 2021 (created in 2013) www.facebook.com/groups/dorsheni retrieved on October 31, 2021.

Holocaust – the Third Generation, 247 members in 2021 (created in 2013) www.facebook.com/groups/426696890758459/about retrieved on Nov. 3, 2021.

Second Generation Holocaust Survivors, with 1.3K members in 2021 (created in 2015) www.facebook.com/groups/601578856610348 retrieved on October 31, 2021.

Second Generation Holocaust Survivors without Censorship, 5 members in 2021 (created in 2019) www.facebook.com/groups/2454321674606549 retrieved on October 31, 2021.

Second Generation to Holocaust survivors, with 48 members in 2021 (created in 2008) www.facebook.com/groups/28135391466/about retrieved on October 31, 2021.

Second Generation to Holocaust Survivors, with 12K members in 2021 (created in 2010) www.facebook.com/groups/dorsheny retrieved on October 31, 2021.

Yes, I am Second Generation (Holocaust) with 9.7K members in 2021 (created in 2014) www.facebook.com/groups/813800091992522 retrieved on October 31, 2021.

Author's correspondence and online interviews:

Author's correspondence with Aryeh Barnea, July 13, 2021; Nov. 14, 2021.

Author's telephone interview with Prof. Gadi Barzilai, August 9, 2021.

Author's Zoom interview with Prof. Rafi Cohen-Almagor, July 19, 2021.

Author's correspondence with Helen Epstein, July 16, 2021.

Author's correspondence with Dr. Eva Fogelman, July 18, 2021.

Author's correspondence with Paul Foldes, July 1, 2021.

Author's correspondence with Jeanette Friedman Sieradski, Aug. 17, 2021.

Author's correspondence with Prof. Gideon Greif, July 29, 2021.

Author's correspondence with Dr. Rachel Kolender, July 25, 2021.

Author's correspondence with Billie Laniado, July 13, 2021.

Author's telephone interview with Prof. Shmuel Refael, July 13, 2021.

Notes

1 There are no precise statistics as to the number of 2gs with estimates of the American 2gs ranging from 250,000 to much less than that number and Israeli 2gs being estimated at around 750,000 to a million. See: Stein, 2014: 9 and Brown, 2015; author's correspondence with Billie Laniado, former President of the *Dorot Hahemshech* organization for descendants of Holocaust survivors in Israel, October 29, 2021. Also see Second Generation estimates of *Amcha* – the Israeli center for social and emotional support of survivors and the Second Generation, https://www.amcha.org/node/72 retrieved on November 6, 2021.

2 Halbwachs, 1992.

3 Hirsch, 1992: 3–29.

4 Juni, 2016: 97–111.

5 Bukiet, 2002.

6 Satkunam, 2016.

7 Goodman, 2013: 386–405; Jacobs, 2017.

8 Baumel-Schwartz, 2022.
9 Jordan, 2011.
10 Chhun, 2016.
11 Author's correspondence with Dr. Eva Fogelman, July 18, 2021; author's correspondence with Helen Epstein, July 16, 2021.
12 Fogelman, 2022.
13 Wolf, 2017.
14 *Holocaust*, 1978; Epstein, 1979.
15 Friedman Sieradski, 2013.
16 Bukiet, 2002: 14.
17 Friedman Sieradski, 2022.
18 Author's correspondence with Dr. Eva Fogelman, July 18, 2021; author's correspondence with Jeanette Friedman Sieradski, Aug. 17, 2021.
19 Author's correspondence with Prof. Gideon Greif, July 29, 2021.
20 Author's correspondence with Aryeh Barnea, July 13, 2021, Nov. 14, 2021.
21 Author's correspondence with Billie Laniado, July 13, 2021; author's telephone interview with Prof. Shmuel Refael, July 13, 2021; author's Zoom interview with Prof. Rafi Cohen-Almagor, July 19, 2021; author's correspondence with Dr. Rachel Kolender, July 25, 2021; author's correspondence with Prof. Gideon Greif, July 29, 2021; author's telephone interview with Prof. Gadi Barzilai, August 9, 2021.
22 In 2020 the organization had over 7,000 members on its mailing lists. Author's correspondence with Billie Laniado, July 13, 2021.
23 Author's correspondence with Rachel Kolender, 2g and chair of the organization of Jews from Bochnia, July 25, 2021.
24 Author's correspondence with Paul Foldes, July 1, 2021.
25 See, for example: Austrian Citizenship Holocaust Descendants https://www.facebook.com/groups/ACHDs retrieved on November 7, 2021.
26 "Children of Holocaust Survivors (2007); Second Generation to Holocaust survivors (2008); Generations of the Shoah International (GSI) (2009); 2g Second Generation Children of Holocaust Survivors (2013); Second Generation Holocaust Survivors (2015); Children of Holocaust Survivors 2g, (2015); Allgenerations Inc. (2015); Second Generation Holocaust Survivors without Censorship (2019); The new Second Generation Holocaust survivors (2020); Generational Holocaust Survivors and Descendants (2021).
27 Hu et al., 2017.
28 Second Generation to Holocaust Survivors (2010).
29 Holocaust Second Generation (2013); Yes, I am Second Generation (Holocaust)(2014).
30 Descendants of Holocaust Survivors (2G Greater New York) (2021).
31 Holocaust – the Third Generation (2013).
32 Baumel-Schwartz and Refael, 2021.
33 Wolf, 2017.
34 Wolf, 2019.
35 Bukiet, 2002: 17.

Bibliography

Baumel-Schwartz, Judith Tydor (ed.), 2022. *The List: The Making of an Online Transnational Second Generation Community*, Bern: Peter Lang.

Baumel-Schwartz, Judith Tydor, and Refael, Shmuel (eds.), 2021. *Researchers Remember: Research as an Arena of Memory for Descendants of Holocaust Survivors, A Collection of Academic Autobiographies*, Bern: Peter Lang.

Brown, Ian, 2015. "The Holocaust's Long Reach: Trauma is Passed on to Survivors' Children", *The Globe and Mail*, https://beta.theglobeandmail.com/life/the-holocausts-long-reach-trauma-is-passed-on-tosurvivors-children/article23793425/?ref=www.theglobeandmail.com& retrieved on October 29, 2021.

Bukiet, Melvin J., 2002. *Nothing Makes You Free: Writings by Descendants of Jewish Holocaust Survivors*, New York and London: WW Norton and Company.

Chhun, Korlany, 2016. *Transgenerational Trauma Among Second Generation Cambodian-Americans*, PhD Dissertation, Alliant International University, Sacramento, CA.

Epstein, Helen, 1979. *Children of the Holocaust*, New York: Putnam.

Fogelman, Eva, 2022. "Generations of the Holocaust: Invisible to Visible Identity and Community", in: Judith Tydor Baumel-Schwartz (ed.), *The List: The Making of an Online Transnational Second Generation Community*, Bern: Peter Lang.

Friedman Sieradski, Jeanette, 2013. "Rabbi 'Yitz' Greenberg at 80: A Paradigm Changer", *Jewishlink*, June 27, https://jewishlink.news/features/1000-rabbi-yitz-greenberg-at-80-a-paradigm-changer retrieved on August 11, 2021

Friedman Sieradski, Jeanette, 2022. "Ta'aseh Lach Chavurah – Create Your Own 'Hood'", in: Judith Tydor Baumel-Schwartz (ed.), *The List: The Making of an Online Transnational Second Generation Community*, Bern: Peter Lang.

Goodman, Rachael D., 2013. "The Transgenerational Trauma and Resilience Genogram", *Counseling Psychology Quarterly* 26 (3–4): 386–405.

Halbwachs, Maurice, 1992. *On Collective Memory*, Chicago: University of Chicago Press.

Hirsch, Marianne, 1992. "Family Pictures: *Maus*, Mourning, and Post-Memory", *Discourse* 15 (2): 3–29.

Holocaust, written by Gerald Green, directed by Marvin J. Chomsky, April 16–19, 1978, www.imdb.com/title/tt0077025/ retrieved on August 11, 2021.

Hu, Xiaomeng, Kim, Andrew, Siwek, Nicholas, and Wilder, David, 2017. "The Facebook Paradox: Effects of Facebooking on Individuals' Social Relationships and Psychological Well-Being", *Frontiers in Psychology* 31 (January), https://doi.org/10.3389/fpsyg.2017.00087 retrieved on October 31, 2021.

Jacobs, Janet, 2017. *The Holocaust Across Generations: Trauma and its Inheritance Among Descendants of Survivors*, New York: NYU Press.

Jordan, Michael P., 2011. *Reclaiming the Past: Descendants Organizations, Historical Consciousness and Intellectual Property in Kiowa Society*, PhD Dissertation, University of Oklahoma, Norman, Oklahoma.

Juni, Sam, 2016. "Second-generation Holocaust Survivors: Psychological, Theological and Moral Challenges", *Journal of Trauma Dissociation* 17 (1): 97–111.

Satkunam, Ann, 2016. *Nor Your Mother's Culture – Second Generation Tamil Women Negotiating Trauma and Identity Through Art*, MA Thesis, Reyerson University, Toronto.

Stein, Arlene, 2014. *Reluctant Witnesses: Survivors, Their Children, and the Rise of Holocaust Consciousness*, New York: Oxford University Press.

Warsaw Ghetto Resistance Organization Formed in USA, 1963, www.jta.org/1963/02/19/archive/warsaw-ghetto-resistance-organization-formed-in-u-s-by-ex-members retrieved on August 16, 2021.

Wolf, Diane L., 2017. "What's in a Name? The Genealogy of Holocaust Identities", *Genealogy* 1: 19. https://doi.org/10.3390/genealogy1040019 retrieved on October 31, 2021.

Wolf, Diane L., 2019. "Postmemories of Joy? Children of Holocaust Survivors and Alternative Family Memories", *Memory Studies* 12 (1): 74–87.

2

THE METAMORPHOSIS OF SECOND GENERATION WRITING

Just When I Thought I Was Out – A Case Study

Melvin Jules Bukiet

Introduction

In an interview that I gave years ago I stated the following: "As a novelist, I'd prefer it if people apprehended the Holocaust through the lens of history. Of course, they won't".[1] In fact, more people know about history because of novels they've read (or movies they've seen) than because of nonfiction. Just as liturgy is poetry made theological, so history is a story that serves collective memory. Historical research on the Holocaust remains vital, but the sheer power of stories is more likely to determine our perception of history over time, whether historians like it or not.

Second Generation literature – that written by children of survivors such as me – is a clearly defined and uniquely characteristic sub-category of Holocaust fiction. This brings up several questions. As the Second Generation ages, how does its storytelling change? What type of metamorphosis has Second Generation literature undergone during the past two decades?

In the following chapter I will discuss the changes in my own writing over that period as a case study of the continuous development of Second Generation literature. At the same time, I address the question of Second Generation writers' attitudes towards dealing with the Holocaust in general. What happens to us as we grow up? Grow older? Reach the age our survivor parents were in their prime? After their prime? Let's begin.

Does Genocide Have a Future?

Whither the Holocaust? Will it wither away as many antisemites and, frankly, many Jews except for a few museum directors and commemoration managers might prefer? Twenty years ago, I would have laughed at the idea. Back then, there seemed to be an inexhaustible craving for striped pajama imagery and gas chamber nightmares. Concentration camps were grand opportunities to wring the handkerchief of woe and fly the happy flag of resilience and quasi-Christian resurrection. It was a party everybody could join.

Distrusting many writers' easy acquaintance with atrocity, I would have begun a discussion of the subject with a verbal smack in the face. Something like, "Hello Auschwitz fans and lovers". Too often, genocide was used to lend gravitas to anything from one's romantic life to outrage at man's inhumanity to chickens. True that; I once received a vegan screed called *Eternal Treblinka*. It's available

DOI: 10.4324/b23365-4

on Amazon, next to an album of the same title by a band called Death Cult. I find the latter more appealing.

And yet there may not be much of a category difference between dubious and "authentic" renderings of genocide, and I'm as guilty as anyone, maybe guiltier because I did more than work those mines. I edited an anthology that aimed to canonize the best ore-producers, and then, having retired from writing about the Holocaust, recently fell off the wagon and returned to Shoah business. As some of the greatest Jew-killers of all time used to say, "Mea culpa".

People – including my editors here – consider me a novelist of the Holocaust, but I've always felt uncomfortable with the rendering of atrocity in fiction. Instead, I'd prefer that it remain in the realm of facts, figures, train schedules, the chemical formula for Zyklon B, and the single clamorous, ubiquitous number, six million.

Unfortunately, I'm a writer, consequently amoral when material is available. Just compare the riches of genocide to the meager rewards of parlor dramas or personal angst. Lionel Trilling said people had come to believe that "evil was the very essence of reality". Never mind that he said that skeptically, in defense of domestic realism; it's true that some people believe that, and I believe they are right. Moreover, it's not like the portrayal of evil is easy. There are innumerable ways to muck up a Holocaust novel, but at least you've got a subject of undeniable value.

If you were born to survivors, you'd be an ingrate to ignore the pivotal life (and, predominantly, death) experiences of your family. My father didn't go to Auschwitz so that I could write about the Upper West Side. Of course, he didn't go to Auschwitz so that I could write about that either. Nor did Tadeusz Borowski go to Auschwitz so that he could write about it. But let's leave all that be, and agree that since the Holocaust has taken a central, *bima*-like place in modern Judaism, it would be quasi-apostatic to eschew it. And those with the greatest knowledge bear the greatest responsibility. Like our Third Generation children in the sandbox, we had to learn to share. Still, I couldn't get over the giant anti-fictional, barbed wire fence I'd erected around the subject.

So I granted myself a chronological dispensation.

Not daring to trespass on the Unholy of Unholies, I wrote one book set in a shtetl before the war (*Stories of an Imaginary Childhood*), another that commenced with the liberation of the camps (*After*), and yet another in which a Holocaustal consciousness afflicted contemporary Germany on the verge of the millennium (*Signs and Wonders*), as well as multiple short stories and essays pertaining to the *Churban*. But I never set a scene between September 1939 and May 1945.

Of course, this temporal gerrymandering was logically defective. Could I, for example, have drawn a geographical line instead of a chronological one, thereby allowing myself to write about New York in 1943? Of course. What about Paris instead of New York? Sure. Or Warsaw instead of Paris? What about a Jewish shtetl instead of a secular city? Could I write about the shtetl, but not the ghetto? The ghetto but not the camp? The camp but not the chamber? Andre Schwarz-Bart goes into the chamber in *The Last of the Just*, and he does so out of sober necessity. So perhaps, all I can say in order to be consistent is not that *one* must not write about the war but that *I* cannot write about it.

But that, too, is sophistry, because all my books that live an inch beyond the boundaries were shaped by the extremities within the boundaries.

A Word from the First Generation

OK, that's a good start. Let's take a short break here for my favorite Holocaust story, the term itself comprehensible only by the Shoah community.

The mother of my friend Larry was one of the last prisoners at Auschwitz. Why she wasn't marched out along with my father in the winter of 1944, I have no idea. But there she was in the spring of 1945 when the Russians arrived. One Soviet soldier discovered a German hiding. Rather than place the man in prison, he got an idea. He handed his gun to the emaciated former prisoner and offered to let her kill her former master. "It's easy", he said. "No one will ever know. Just pull the trigger". But it wasn't easy. She trembled and threw the gun down. Now, most people would say that the moral of this story is that we are nothing like the people who tried to kill us. But Larry's mother drew a different lesson. As she later told her son about her refusal to become a murderer, "I've regretted that every single day for the rest of my life".

A Return to Our Subject

Back to Second Generation literature. My own transit moved from the making of dubiously justified Holocaustal narratives to editing *Nothing Makes You Free*, an anthology of prose by descendants of survivors. So why was the project mine to execute? First, it was my idea. Also, I knew the territory. Finally, it seemed appropriate (as well as vain) to put my name on the cover. In editing this volume, I had the distinction of rejecting not one but two (so far) subsequent Nobelists. Yet I found Elfriede Jelinek to be grossly sensationalist, and Patrick Modiano to be so subtle as to evaporate from the page. On the other hand, I now wish that I had not included an excerpt from Carl Friedman's *Nightfather,* because it turned out that some of her identity was self-created.

But did anything else link the pieces besides my taste at that moment? Only in retrospect have I noticed connections to which I was editorially oblivious. National differences were most evident. The Americans like Alan Kaufman and Sonia Pilcer were more explicit and unafraid to show – or show off – their anger, perhaps a result of New World comfort – or, as we say nowadays, privilege. Several Europeans for whom antisemitism was not solely a phenomenon of the past were more elusive. Consider "The Gospel According to My Father" in which David Albahari presents a father and a son on a bridge in Belgrade. The father gazes over the balustrade and says, "Where is the water? Where did the water go?" As far as I was concerned, that was a Holocaust story. Then there were Israelis like Lea Aini who tended to pathologize the survivors in their fictions. At the risk of a making an overly broad generalization, I believe this comes from the nation's precariousness in the years when the writers were coming of age. Israel needed soldiers, not victims. Lastly, there were a few transnational experimentalists who played with form (Art Spiegelman) and a smaller number of outright hysterics (sigh, me).

Yet no matter the geographical divide among American, European, and Israeli Second Generation writers, the essential unity of those writers has become more obvious in the two decades since my book was published (2002). Rather than assimilated citizens of the global village, we remain isolated representatives of our upbringing. And some critics claim that the same can be said about Third Generation authors.[2] But they are not my focus, so let us return to the Second Generation.

What Have You Done for Me Lately?

Where are we now? I'm afraid that I can't summon a *minyan* of likely suspects to ask if and how their work has changed over the last 20 years. I can only look at myself as pretty much the end point on the fury scale. Go ahead, ask me about "righteous gentiles". Better yet, don't. But let's consider one of the most common slogans attached to the Holocaust, "You may forgive, but you must never forget". It's catchy, but it's wrong. I don't know anyone of my or my father's generation who wouldn't be delighted to wake up one morning without that abiding sense that everything we know and love can be crushed in an instant. Forgetting would be heaven. But forgiveness – no way.

Maybe that's why I – an otherwise standard issue New York liberal – am in favor of the death penalty. Yes, there have been terrible miscarriages of justice. So, raise the bar for proof until it is as undeniable as the sun's rising in the east. Then chop the culprit's head off. Sure, studies prove that the death penalty has no deterrent value, but deterrence is not the reason why I'm in favor of legal slaughter. It's sheer vengeance.

These days, however, rage doesn't come as naturally as it once did. I've got to summon it and wait a few minutes until my vital fluids heat up. Indeed, much of the animating frenzy that gave my books their character has dissipated.

The event that most immediately tempered my volcanic rage was 9/11. Yes, the Germans murdered two of my grandparents and approximately 5,999,998 other Jews a decade before I was born, but it was a new sensation for me when a handful of Arabs tried to kill my two daughters who were in high school three blocks from the World Trade Center. Though comparing atrocities is always stupid, I suddenly felt the difference between the historical apotheosis of Jew-hate and a clear and present danger (that incidentally carried the fragrant whiff of antisemitism). And yet, I couldn't bring myself to hate everyone with an olive complexion. Why not? Maybe it was simply impractical because there were too many of them. Or maybe the nature of their Moslem faith was too varied. That one a dark and stormy Wahabist. This one a sunny Sufi. Or maybe 9/11 happened too suddenly to absorb. After all, I'd been steeped in the world of the Holocaust for decades before I began to write about it.

How much of that steeping had to do with my father? It's not as if I wrote for him. In fact, I was never sure whether he read my books, although he took great pride in their existence. Nor did he ever play a guilt card (his game was gin), though he was pleased when I attended American Society for Yad Vashem board meetings with him. Back then, we convened in a back room in the garment district, available only via the freight elevator. When he died, I took his seat.

My best guess is that once my father couldn't be hurt anymore, I relaxed. Indeed, many members of the Second Generation were unusually protective of their parents. Of course, this was absurd, because they had a – slightly – more difficult coming of age than we did. Still, it seemed grotesque for them to suffer any more than they already had. In the market for misery, they'd paid in full.

The last factor in moderating my outlook was time. Even the sharpest rocks erode. I no longer see *everything* through my Shoah-colored glasses. Then again, I don't need to, because the world provides constant reminders of the past. Israel (no perfect place, as any sane Israeli will tell you) is blamed for human rights abuses by politicians on the left and the right who ignore worse behavior in China every day. Charlottesville, Virginia brought us the "Jews will not replace us" parade. And just a few weeks before writing this, I heard one of the speakers on behalf of Derek Chauvin, the murderer of George Floyd, say (sorry, this is a paraphrase) "He was such a good policeman. If his captain had asked him to dig a ditch, he would have picked up a shovel and started digging without asking a question". We've heard this defense before.

Although it is impossible to extrapolate from my own example, I believe that other writers have also wearied. After Spiegelman's *Maus II*, which followed the son rather than the father, there was no *Maus III* about the son becoming a father. Instead, he wrote *In the Shadow of No Towers* about 9/11. Eva Hoffman, whose *Lost in Translation* is one of the great chronicles of cultural estrangement of our time, wrote the strangely amelioratory *After Such Knowledge*. I wouldn't say that we as a cohort exemplified a "Been there. Done that" mentality. More like "Been there, and it ate my guts out, so leave me alone". As the survivors themselves aimed to make new lives after the war, the Second Generation writers may have aimed to find other subjects beside the war.

One More Short Break

I am reminded of another story, because this chapter puts me in a tale-telling mood. During the 1930s many German towns enacted laws against their Jewish citizens. One such small town confiscated the local synagogue and rented it out to a regional egg market. But then came Kristallnacht when synagogues were burnt from one end of Germany to the other. Unfortunately, this town no longer had a synagogue. The town fathers therefore took it back from the egg merchants and returned it to the Jewish community and insisted that they furnish the interior better than ever, with finer materials and tapestries and mosaics and gorgeous wood carvings. Then they burnt it.

A Different Kind of Break

Was I the only Second Generation writer to take a Holocaust time-out? Certainly not. More than a few of my peers seemed to have been exhausted by immersion in the topic. The reasons vary among individuals, but if I had to sum them up, I would include contemporary traumas (such as 9/11), generational transitions (such as losing our parents and having to take their place in the world, although we *know* that we can never fully do so), and the passage of time.

Or maybe we just needed to breathe.

Escaping to Other Topics, Temporarily

I wrote about the Vatican library. I wrote a parable of authoritarian control over society. I produced a dabble of this, a dollop of that. A well-known (Iraqi!) filmmaker has asked me to write a script about a Jewish teenager's trip to Poland. Maybe the DNA of these various projects contained trace elements of the *Churban*, but they were mongrel admixtures, and I was OK with that.

Or so I thought until I was once more confronted with the thing itself. Never mind the precipitating cause; that's a minor matter of personal biography. The point is that I was as susceptible to the lure of the Holocaust as a former addict who thinks he can handle just one last fix.

Literature of recurrence can't be the same as it was the first time we took a seat on the merry-go-round. To start, we've already written the books that define us to a reading public. More importantly, as we had to figure out how to write about the Shoah as 30- or 40-year-olds with aging parents, we now have to figure out how to write about the subject as 60-year-olds with dead parents.

In my case, there's a major emotional difference between *After* – the book that still seems to define me – and the novel I am currently working on. *After* was widely deemed a "black comedy" though I didn't intend it that way. Well yeah, I suppose that one character's plan to sell DPID's (Dead Person's Identification Papers) to vacuum up Yankee dollars in post-War Germany owes more to Gogol than Tolstoy. So let's call it black exaggeration rather than comedy. Indeed, the word I used to define my style when I was attached to a torture device like a university panel was "extremity". I thought that was the only prose proper for its extreme subject.

Yet just as I feel more subdued these days, my work has shifted in the direction of tranquil recollection or – a word never applied to me – realism. Here, I understand a little something about my motivation for the change; it's failure.

No one who's written a perfect book writes another book. Fortunately for Amazon, nobody's ever written a perfect book. And if failure is a natural presumption of literary endeavor, it is more so when the subject is genocide and exponentially more so when the author's connection to the material is genetic. That's why many of our current books engage in between-the-lines dialogue with our previous volumes. To contort Harold Bloom, the influencers we are anxious about are our younger selves. "Here's where you went wrong", our new work declares, "now watch me get it right". Uh huh.

Years ago, I wanted my books to be like the title film of David Wallace's *Infinite Jest*, so dangerous that to grasp them would be fatal. Alas, no one died after reading *After*. And so, I decided to do an upside-down about-face and try realism. On the other hand, there's a good chance that some writers of realistic tendencies have moved to the pandemoniac dark side as a counter-intuitive remedy for their own failures. Each of us is as doomed to our own artistic ruin as any dead grandparent who thought that they were going to be relocated in the east.

My first time around the block, I'd learned exactly what I'd known since childhood, perhaps in utero: the only lesson the Holocaust teaches us is that there are no lessons. The only thing that suffering teaches us is that we are capable of suffering. The only thing that knowledge of the past teaches us is that the future will be the same.

Back to Our Regularly Scheduled Programming

Repeating this from a literary perspective: all that stories can tell us is that we can write stories.

To put it another way: all we can do is write stories.

And we all know what stories are ours to tell.

So no matter how the Second Generation may try to escape the Holocaust, they are inevitably drawn to it.

Question: do moths know what flame will do to them? Do they jump into the fire anyway?

That's what I set out to do. Again. Once, I'd written a book set before the war and another book set immediately after the war and then a crazed parable set in the further future. Recently, it had become apparent to me that a mysterious mid-range that adhered to my chronological restrictions and happened to coincide with my childhood was free for the claiming.

In my mind, I saw two brothers on a boat steaming into New York harbor in 1948. They had no home, no family, no prospects, and they couldn't speak the language. On the other hand, no one wanted to kill them. *Dayenu.*

Soon enough, the brothers went about earning a living and creating a family. They moved swiftly from manual labor to owning a small supermarket – a bodega by any other name would smell as cheap – to real estate. Their business expanded from slum dwellings to skyscrapers. That is an extraordinary journey for any immigrant but minor compared to the journey out from behind the *Arbeit Macht Frei* sign. I suppose that's the point. All the novel aspires to say is that nearly everyone died while these two guys both moved on and paradoxically remained behind.

I guess that's accurate, but there is one more thing. It's small. Hardly worth mentioning. Not once in this book do I mention the H world. Nor do I mention any J words. I don't hide my brothers' origins – the book is sprinkled with Yiddishisms – and this glaring absence may even serve to highlight their identity through the use of a Keatsian negative capability. I don't know. I'm no good at reading my own motives. Nonetheless, I feel that it's the right thing to do.

Writing today is rife with references to the suffering undergone by protagonists who – no surprise – bear a racial, religious, national, or sexual resemblance to their authors. Of course, race, place, religion, sex, etc. have powerful effects on us, but the contemporary novel often feels more about context than the individual within a context. That's not fiction; it's sociology.

There's one more little thing I should confess. No, it's not another gap. It's an addition, only six words. Except those words will appear on the cover because they're the title. *Protocols of the Remnants of Zion* may be willfully provocative, but it's also accurate. The novel tries to be a sober record of two survivors and their community after *After.*

But that's sophistry, too, because mere accuracy should never be the goal of artistic endeavor. Connotation is more vital than denotation, and that title could be translated into Yiddish as "*Baren ir*". Now who is that fat, fictional middle finger addressed to? Could be almost anyone. The Germans, all Germans, including those who weren't even born at the time of the crime, have been perennial victims of my perpetratorship. Then there are the American Jews who worshipped the Great Roosevelt and did nothing. Or my dear readers who never quite get me, which is a shame because I'd really like them to explain me to me sometime.

Looking at things in a broader perspective, the processes that I went through appear to be more common than I thought among Second Generation writers. But were the reasons for these changes the same everywhere? Were others more successful than I in trying to leave the Holocaust arena for greener (as opposed to bloodier) pastures? Or did they end up being drawn back to the topic, as I was?

To find answers one would have to ask each Second Generation author these questions, after which it might be possible to analyze the phenomenon at large. Meanwhile, I can only speculate, offer hypotheses, posit deductions, and postulate conjectures. In other words, guess. As writers, sometimes, that's just what we do. After all, as I began this essay, we aren't historians bound hand and foot to documental evidence, leading to deep or broad considerations. But people will remember us – or at least the stories we write – especially those about our legacy, the Holocaust. Or so we hope. Or fear.

Conclusion

Wavering between avoidance and immersion, I sometimes feel like Michael Corleone in *The Godfather*. Chosen son of a Mafia dynasty in which family and death are the two abiding verities, Michael loves and respects – and benefits from – the secret knowledge that only those on the inside share, though he also understands how it has warped him. For this reason, he dreams of going straight. Yet something always happens to thwart his plans. The business needs him. The family can't do without him. As he so memorably puts it, "Just when I thought I was out, they pull me back in". More likely there's something inside him – a faith, a flaw – that can't resist the lure, and gives him an excuse to return to the horrible place where he truly feels at home.

Notes

1 Quoted in https://www.yadvashem.org/articles/interviews/melvin-jules-bukiet.html, accessed on Oct. 15, 2021.

2 Victoria Aarons and Alan L. Berger (eds.), *Third-Generation Holocaust Representation: Trauma, History and Memory* (Evanston, IL: Northwestern University Press, 2017).

3

LITERARY WORKS ON THE SECOND AND THIRD GENERATIONS OF HOLOCAUST SURVIVORS IN HUNGARY – PRESENCE OR ABSENCE?

Katalin Pécsi-Pollner

My first reaction, after I began to look for literary works on the Second and Third Generations of Holocaust survivors in Hungary, was that we did not actually have any literature of that kind. There are no literary works at all about Jews here. In Hungary, no one likes to belong to a religious or ethnic minority – even less to write about their identity and troubled history. Let me bring two personal examples to illustrate my statement that seem to be extreme and exemplary at first glance.

Labels

A few years ago, I organized a roundtable discussion on "Jewish Women Writers". It was the closing act of an all-day conference. Six renowned writers and poets sat on the stage, in a semicircle around the table – four older Holocaust survivors in the middle – and two younger women on the two edges, both Second Generation. The poet, sitting on the left, started, raising her voice thoroughly, stating that she was not a "woman" poet. When it was her turn, the other younger writer on the right side shouted into the microphone in a passionate voice, "Just because my grandmother and 16 other relatives were murdered in Auschwitz, I am still not yet a 'Jewish writer'!" At that point the audience started shouting, too, and there was such a tumult that I, as a moderator, had to turn off the microphones for a few minutes, until the room calmed down.

An example from a much earlier period concerns the special reception of a Hungarian writer of Jewish descent. In the mid-1970s, I was working at a publishing house as a young editor, just graduated from university, and the editor-in-chief commissioned me to "erase" the "Yiddish intonation" from the manuscript of a book of short stories being prepared, that of Miklós Vámos, a young novelist, who was already a well-known and even popular writer, whose stories focused mostly on young people's feeling of life. It was not a secret that he lived in a downtown neighborhood, Újlipótváros, that has been particularly popular for Jewish intellectuals, since being built in the late 1930s.[1] His stories usually took place there, as well. My editor-in-chief, relying on the biographical records, thought the author was Jewish, although not a single word about Jewish people or Judaism was uttered in the text. Furthermore, the writer's name was Hungarian, the characters were Hungarian,

 DOI: 10.4324/b23365-5

and he wrote the book in Hungarian – what can the term "Yiddish tone"[2] mean in Budapest? In addition to that – in a written text? At first, I only felt instinctively that I heard antisemitic remarks in the Hungarian state publishing house; then I became enlightened: the editor-in-chief, representing the "majority Hungarians" just got scared – perhaps he was just worrying about his own job when he wanted to protect the Hungarian reader from discovering a Jew, hiding under the guise of a Hungarian writer.

Perhaps the explanation for my second example is simpler: in communist times, it was not good to stand out with any kinds of differences – but open antisemitism was not rewarded by the political system. The situation evoked in my first example is more complicated: why this reluctance, on the part of some Hungarian women poets and writers of Jewish origin to be considered a woman or Jewish writers – in other words, for their works to be considered a part of women's or Jewish literature?

Jewish vs. Hungarian

The famous Hungarian Jewish poet Miklós Radnóti[3] wrote the definitive pronouncement on the subject, in a literary letter, in the early forties. He refused to contribute poems to a Jewish anthology, during a difficult period, when it was impossible for him to publish his writings in non-Jewish Hungarian publications. Miklós Radnóti died in 1944 as a victim of the Holocaust, but till the end of his life, he considered himself a Hungarian poet and he refused to enter a denominational ghetto.

> I never denied my Jewishness, but I do not feel Jewish. I was never taught to be religious; I do not feel a need for it, I don't practice it. . . . My Jewishness has become the problem of my life, but it is circumstances, laws, the world that made it so. The problem was forced on me. Otherwise, I am a Hungarian poet.

For the majority of Hungarian literary artists of Jewish descent, Radnóti's credo is still a model for themselves – especially for those who survived the Holocaust, even as babies or small children. Ivan Sanders,[4] a literary critic thinks that their motive is not a sense of shame or inferiority, not even a desire to forget their cultural heritage or some misplaced, exaggerated nationalist feeling. I think, in agreement with him, that Jewish writers and poets are reluctant to consider themselves anything but Hungarian, because they view any other, additional labels as inappropriate, retrograde, or even degrading. They insist on being only Hungarian because they have a vivid historical memory or because they find the path or the Hungarian literature broader, more universal then the narrow-minded or "particular" works of the Jewish culture and literature.

So then, who is the Jewish writer? The language question can be ruled out: everyone in Hungary writes in Hungarian. Religion is not a literary category in itself – unless it becomes a topic of a literary work. Whose biography contains any information about their origin? Or who is the member of the Jewish Community or some organizations? Or who is considered Jew by Gentiles – mostly antisemites?[5]

In my opinion, only those literary works can be classified as "Jewish" – regardless of the origin of their author – that thematize Judaism or that focus on Jewish identity in some way. If we examine some literary works representing the Second Generation, we need to do that in this context. Our first question is whether only Jews or non-Jews also can write about Jewish themes.

Auto- and Hetero-representation

In Hungary, the philosopher Ágnes Heller[6] was the first who raised the question of representation, which today is even more acute – thanks to the Black Lives Matter[7] movement. The question is whether the life of a particular ethnic, religious, or other minority group can be authentically depicted from the outside – that is, if it can be represented by a writer or artist who to that group is an outsider. If women are represented by male writers or Jews are represented by non-Jews. However, Jews and non-Jews live together, Heller says, so it would be unreasonable to totally separate the two groups.

Nevertheless, it is worth looking at how contemporary Hungarian writers portray Jews today. To say it simply: the out-group perspective is rare; non-Jewish writers almost never pick this topic. They do not know that group well enough: their Jewish peers, being the children of grandchildren of Holocaust survivors, were born at the end or just after the war. Even the slightest misunderstanding can be embarrassing for both Jews and non-Jews, because nobody risks facing the slightest accusation of antisemitism. Recently a popular Hungarian writer, János Háy,[8] published fiction with a protagonist who happens to be an uneducated Roma woman. The novel is her monologue. The writer has been strongly criticized by Roma activists as well as by some literary critics, accusing him with prejudices and racism, since the ethnicity of his text is evident and the representation of her Roma character is based on media stereotypes.

From the perspective of an "out-group", stereotypes can be implicit, explicit, conceptual, or sub-textual.

Out-groups – Representation of Jews by Two Non-Jewish Hungarian Writers

I find it important to speak about their novels because both of the stories are based on stereotypes – either in a negative or a positive way. Stereotyping of Jews and Jewishness can significantly facilitate understanding on the part of the readers – but it can spread uneasy feelings in the members of the in-group.

One of my examples is the first novel of a woman writer, Rita Halász.[9] Her protagonist, a middle-class woman in her late thirties, comes from a Christian Hungarian family – her thematized background means she is declared non-Jewish. Christian-Hungarians belong to the mainstream, while Jewish Hungarians belong to a weird subculture – this is the implicit message of the story. The Jewish character of the novel is the woman's first love, who 20 years later, as a married man, becomes her casual lover.

In the story, the Jewishness of the young man is mentioned both implicitly and explicitly – though never related to his beliefs. The "Other One" is construction here, as the opposition of other kinds of attributions or values. From all the irrelevant and insignificant features, the opposite image of the Christian protagonist and her family can be formed. The Jewish-Christian difference is based on old stereotypes; in addition to these details of the story, the ex-husband and the father are hard drinkers and quite violent men – while the Jewish lover is a gentle person who does not drink at all and so on.

To put it bluntly, the word "Jewish" is uttered only twice in an explicit way, by the protagonist's father (if we don't count the notices about "Jewish women with big buttocks"). This incident happened when the protagonist was still in elementary school. Unexpectedly, he inquired her daughter about a classmate of hers: "How is that handsome, 'Jewish boy' going?" Then the father added it unexpectedly: "I just don't want you to marry a Jewish boy". The girl was amazed: she wasn't even aware that there were Jewish children in her class.

This episode is just an incident without any more explanation in the story, and it is not actually thematized; in other words, it shows what it feels like for the protagonist to go to a "mixed class" with Jewish and Gentile students who even socialize together. As for the father, it was just an unconscious, slightly antisemitic outburst on his part.

Them and Us. Although the "Jewish motive" has no role at all in this story, it must be the secret of the author, why she included it in her storyline.

"Are You a Jew?"

The book by Gábor Németh[10] with its provocative title on the cover *Are you a Jew*? is another example that is on the opposite side of the scale. In this novel, the Jewishness is conceptual and not sub-textual. This is the theme of the book: what does it mean to be a Jew – or an imaginary Jew? The narrator-protagonist who speaks in the first person has been considering himself a Jew since he was a schoolboy. He feels different than the other kids, but he is not aware of the reason. When he is forced to see a documentary film about the liberation of a concentration camp, together with the other children of his summer camp, he realizes why he is an outsider among his classmates: he's a secret Jew. He has something to do with the concentration camps, but for some reason, his parents just don't want to tell him the truth. He even doesn't understand the word "Jew", yet he deciphers it from the film: "guilty" – that's what it means. "Jewish shame was so deep that no questions could penetrate" – he thinks as a 12-year-old or so boy. He researches what happened behind the "tattooed number" or "lampshade". His parents are open-minded, tolerant people, but they are unaware of the problem, and they just don't understand what their child is suffering from. After a while, the boy seeks the company or association of other Jewish children, but he has no idea how to recognize them or what a "sign" is. Then he starts to learn the "signs" slowly, but he fears that even if he used them (like his sense of humor or a *Mogen Dovid* in silver on his neck) the real Jews would expose him as a "fake" Jew. He also learns, both at school and on the street, that the word "Jewish" can be also a slur – similar to "Gypsy" or "gay" – that is, being "Jewish" also means he will be beaten every now and then. Later, when he is already a teenager or a young adult, people consider him a Sephardic Jew, because of his dark complexion, brown eyes, and dark, curled hair – it's true, he says; his cousins living in Holland and being observing Christians, look the same. . . . He starts to be identified with this role more and more. "You're ashamed and disproportionate to look elsewhere". At the end of the novel, as a young adult, he is sailing on Lake Balaton and thinks: "Now I'm leaving from here. It is good to be everywhere, but it is the best elsewhere". This is exactly the opposite of the Hungarian saying: "It is good to be everywhere, but it is the best is at home".

In this novel of Németh, too, a "Jew" is also an "Other" but in a positive sense: Jewishness for the author mostly means sensibility and identification with the Jewish fate. The protagonist himself turns his own otherness and rootlessness into a positive value. Accepting his Jewish identity, at last, is boundless liberty for him.

Second Generation Writers Break the Silence

While my previous examples were published in the last 20 years, well after the regime change, the truly new, paradigm-shifting works were written much earlier. For me, Mihály Kornis's[11] book *(Napkönyv)* was the very first among my lectures, which presented the trauma of the Holocaust and the following years, from the perspective of the children of Holocaust survivors. I read György Dalos's's[12] novel *The Circumcision* very soon after *Daybook* by Kornis, both in the early 90s. *The Circumcision* opens the perspective even wider, as he not only uses allusions, but the themes like Jewishness and Judaism are at the center in his story. Certain sensitive, painful, even taboo subjects are treated more freely, at last. Probably, Dalos wrote his book much earlier, using his own memories from his childhood, but he had a ban of publication for political reasons. By the early 90s, just after the political changes in Hungary, it was possible for him to write openly about topics like Holocaust trauma, Jewish identity and Jewish religious life during the early communist years.

To Be a "Hidden Jew" – Mihály Kornis

Mihály Kornis, himself a child of Holocaust survivors, was among the first ones in the Hungarian contemporary literature to write about the shared experience of the Second Generation: to be a "hidden Jew". The short story – which is a chapter of a book – is expressing the common experience of the Second Generation: the silence of the survivors. The short story has the title *nicht fordem kind.* In his narrative, the character, speaking in first person, tells the reader how it felt to live as a "non-Jewish" Jewish child, in the shadow of the trauma of his own family. The perspective and the voice are of a young boy. The child has heard and seen a lot of strange fragments from his family members, but he is not able to put them together: the small pieces in the kaleidoscope just don't want to come together into a single picture. In the unforgettable story by Kornis this little child visits the Jewish cemetery with his parents at a point in the 50s. His parents take him to visit the newly erected "Wall of Martyrs", searching for the names of their own lost loved ones. But the child cannot understand the situation, and he does not dare to ask his parents why they are there. . . . The text is the child's monologue: it's about attraction and repulsion – interpretation and misunderstanding.

"We are such unfortunate Jews", thinks that narrator (the little boy) in the Jewish cemetery. The reader doesn't know exactly whether he means the dead or the live persons:

> By now the 'proletarian state' allows us Jews to be ordinary working people like anyone else, and if we don't act superior, we can stay alive and even we can have our own special cemetery, true it is a bit far away, in the middle of nowhere. . . . The most important thing is that we shouldn't over- emphasize it or even brag about it or just show off.

Much of the family was destroyed in the Holocaust; others may have chosen to emigrate, so parents and the surviving grandfather could rightly believe that no one would reveal the past to their child – and the entire generation of the child.

"You guys are Jews too, aren't you? It doesn't mean a thing – your children will grow out of it. What is it you want – you're the lucky ones!"

Only the children didn't grow out of it. In fact, the second and the Third Generation just "grew into it, turning into a very different generation than that of their parents".[13]

György Dalos: A Glimpse into the Hungarian Jewish World of the 1950s

The protagonist of György Dalos's novel *The Circumcision* is also a child, and the story also takes place in the 1950s. The main character is a 12-year-old boy, Robi, who lives in a Jewish children's home and returns home just for the Shabbat and weekends. The family is communist; however, they observe Jewish traditions as well. The little boy is even getting ready for his bar mitzvah. The grandmother is the head of the family who treats her grandson as an equal adult and talks openly about everything – politics and family affairs – with him. "If anyone asks you about your origins or your religion", the boy's grandmother advises, "you'd better tell them frankly that you are a Hungarian Jewish communist".

In this novel, the second generation story is much more elaborate than in any other novel. Robi supports his mother, who is not yet old but has been devastated by the Holocaust. She is obese, neglected, suffering from a few illnesses, and still needs the be helped and assisted by both her mother and son. Robi accompanies his mother down the street, and as if the parent-child role is turned over, he seems to be the adult, while his mother is the "child".

The depiction of the Jewish foster home is also interesting. (Without this novel, I wouldn't have known much about its existence at all, because by the 90s they were already fading from our cultural memory.) In these Jewish institutions, children and educators are connected by a close, loving relationship – as in a good family. All this is contrary to the traditional public school still typical in Hungary nowadays, which is based on Prussian discipline and authoritarianism. The protagonist can discuss issues of Judaism with his teacher in the same way he discusses his family problems. The style of the novel is ironic, as is that of Kornis's narrative – it is the great value of both novels that the style is distant and childishly grotesque at the same time.

De-Judaization in Hungarian Jewish Literature

György Spiró[14] and Péter Lengyel[15] belong to the same generation, both were published at a young age in the 1970s, and both quickly became popular among young intellectual readers as they brought a new sound and vision to Hungarian literature. In their novels, however, they omit Jewish themes, even though they themselves belong to the Second Generation of survivors. In several of his interviews, Spiró Görgy even stated that he is not a Jewish writer – for reasons more or less like poet Miklós Radnóti's, decades earlier. At the same time, his interest in Holocaust literature is striking in his studies: in addition to Borowski and Primo Levi, he also praised the novel *Fatelessness* by Imre Kertész at Hungarian literary reviews – years before Kertész's Nobel Prize. In his prose, however, he avoids thematizing Jewish topics or motives – at most we can try to decipher some motives and allusions. (He still has one, very successful, Jewish-themed novel, but the story takes place in ancient Rome and Jerusalem).

Péter Lengyel masks, universalizes, and submerges his Jewish themes, too; Jewishness in his works becomes a subtext that must be decoded, deconstructed, in a way. "A novel", Ivan Sanders[16] reminds us, "can be about Jews even if it doesn't explicitly say it is about them". In the early 2000s, the philosopher Ágnes Heller noticed this tendency and analyzed the phenomenon in a conference lecture. It was about three Hungarian Jewish writers, whose novels are de-judicated. In a much-quoted essay, based on her lecture, entitled significantly "De-Jewification in Hungarian Jewish Literature", she discusses the phenomenon regarding three writers, one of them a contemporary author, Péter Lengyel.[17] She concludes that his characters are Jewish characters, but the writer elides their Jewishness and purposely de-Judaizes them. This procedure might stem from a degree of self-denial or even self-hate. A de-Judicated literary work, at the same time, can be suggestive or, of course, can also be impoverished, since it might be largely universalized.

In Péter Lengyel's novel titled *Cseréptörés* (*Tile Breakage*), some elements of the events are undefined, so ordinary Hungarian readers might not realize the exact story. It is about a young man who lost his father during the Second World War, when he, the son, was a three year old. His memory of his father is blurred, and the lack of his memories from his early age prevent him living a "normal" life. So at a point, as a young man, he tries to put together the pieces of a puzzle; he researches archives, collecting old photos, interviewing elderly people who used to know his father. While the protagonist learns more and more details, the narrator does not tell us that his father did not actually serve in the regular Hungarian army, but instead he was a Hungarian Jew sent to Forced Labor Service, then imprisoned in a POW camp in Russia. That was one of the typical fates of Jewish men in Hungary unless they were directed to the ghetto or deported to concentration camps. While the main character is searching for the true story of the life and death of his father, the readers need to find their way in the labyrinths of allusions and ambiguous hints for putting together the puzzles and understanding the important events. On one hand, this procedure of erasing the specific features of a story can add some excitement to reading, because the reader is turned into a detective, a fellow conspirator; on the other hand, we have the feeling that something is missing from the coherent story.

Let me illustrate these statements with one more example from the novel. The main character, János was a half orphan kid, raised by her working mother, so he was sent by her mother to several orphanages, both during and after the War. (The protagonist as well as the author was born during the Holocaust, and was a small child at the Liberation, in 1945 – so we can call both as someone from the one and a half generation).[18] The first of his orphanages, during the war, was run by the Red Cross, and we know well, that these institutions were opened especially for the Jewish orphans during the Holocaust. After the liberation, János was again sent by his mother to some children's homes, but these were already communist institutions – one of them named "Stalin". Anyway, the friendly and cozy atmosphere there was contrasted by the impersonal and unfriendly public schools, where he and his roommates went while staying in their children's home. I assume they must have been Jewish children's homes, like the one where György Dalos and his protagonist used to live as a young boy.

Stories of Missing Tradition

The missing Jewish tradition is the main motive in Gábor Szántó's old short stories and recent novels, as well. Since the Hungarian Jewry had tragically lost their roots because of the Holocaust, they have the choice of a variety of traditions to reach back to. The Second and Third Generations after the Holocaust often had to discover Judaism for themselves. For lack of a family recipe, they were not always sure where to look for a point of orientation. Traditions were almost completely lost in the Holocaust and the subsequent 40 years of Communist dictatorship.

While the prose written by the mainstream of Hungarian Jewish writers can be considered only "Jewish-related literature",[19] Gábor Szántó T. is reaching back to the old generations for whom Jewishness obviously meant religion.

According to Gábor Fináli,[20] a young rabbi from the Second Generation, Hungarian Jewish identity is not self-evident:

> It is built on the legacy of the Holocaust. In other words, it does not relate directly to our home and to the present. . . As for the Holocaust: unfortunately, even among the third and fourth generations, it was more of a force in the Holocaust: in community-building than the morals, richness, or beauty of the Torah. Auschwitz has a greater impact on us than Mount Sinai.

Gábor Szántó T. is the only one in our contemporary prose who tries to find his identity inside of the traditional frames.

Is There a Jewish Identity at All?

Péter Nádas[21] is not only the greatest Hungarian writer and a Nobel Prize nominee for many years, but his novels have the full spectrum depicting – or even omitting – the Jewish theme. He was also born during the Holocaust like Péter Lengyel or György Dalos, and he also became known as a writer in the 70s. For many years, Jewish topics or characters did not appear in his works at all – we could only guess from indirect signs, such as home interiors, whether a given character may be of Jewish origin. However, an autobiographical episode unexpectedly appeared in a story of his in 1989: The main character, a school child, recalls an antisemitic remark heard from schoolmates before his father, who leads him in front of the mirror and tells him, "Then look at this guy well – said quietly, there is a Jew to be hated, in front of you".

In his most recent book, a memoir with the title *Lightning Details*, he speaks about his large family, so he must also speak out about his own Jewishness. His personal story begins after the siege of Budapest (at that time he was two years old), which is used by the writer as a euphemism for the words *war*, *persecution*, or even *Holocaust*, a term that did not even exist at the time.

This great book is about the assimilation history of an extensive Jewish family – and more specifically about its integration into Hungarian society. The complexity of the history of Hungarian Jewry can be seen in Nádas' own family: there are conservative and liberal among his ancestors, some atheist revolutionaries, and even a superstitious Galician grandmother, who does not even accept her own modern daughter – Nádas's mother. His personality has been shaped by every spiritual heritage, both what he accepts and what he rejects from what is offered. Though as an adult Péter Nádas is proud of his ancestors and his parents, as a young boy it was hard for him to bear his orthodox Jewish maternal grandmother, speaking half-Yiddish, with her own ritualistic, tribal thinking. He felt not only her as a burden but his enthusiastic, antifascist, then-communist parents, as well. His father and mother both were extremely involved in the communist movement in the 50s. Speaking about his grumpy and intolerant grandmother with her small talks and poor Hungarian or about his stubbornly enthusiastic mother, he represents all of them in an ironic way, but the pain is also mixed into his humor. The characters – his family members – are not one-sided: his mother, for example, a blindly devoted communist in the 50s, earlier, in the 40s, during the Holocaust, was a brave resistant and rescuer of fellow Jews, making fake IDs and other documents for them, along with her husband and sister-in-law.

Jewish Themes in Contemporary Hungarian Novels – Transgenerational Holocaust Trauma Transfer

In recent years, with the Third Generation already in its fifth decade, the Jewish theme or motives have finally appeared in several novels and short stories. Interestingly, all three "pioneers" are female writers. In fact, in the narratives of Anna Gáspár-Singer,[22] the Jewishness of her protagonist, speaking in the first person, is present only in shortcomings or "lacks".

In one of the short stories in her book, the protagonist is a 26-year-old university student who goes for *Taglit* (birthright), a "roots tour" in which Jewish youth can visit Israel for free. She knows absolutely nothing about Judaism or about her own roots, and she is not even interested in Israel, either. She feels herself not only a stranger but an alien there, even much more than most non-Jewish tourists who are at least curious and open to sightseeing or to the local gastronomy. The representation of her experiences is distant and oscillates emotionally between the indifferent and the negative.

The story that follows is about the Jewish high school that the protagonist-narrator used to attend. We can understand her behavior and attitude better, why she was so uninterested and unmotivated in Israel, in the previous story. She is Jewish only on her paternal side; furthermore her secular family never "brought up the Jewish theme earlier". They have not even spoken about the grandparents' experiences of the Holocaust, and after several years at this Jewish school, she feels herself an outsider who is unsuccessful as a Jew.

Her situation is not unique at all. The Jewish tradition passed down from generation to generation was discontinued radically with the Holocaust. Even Holocaust survivors wanted to spare their children from the stigma of Jewishness: it was the "strategy of silence".[23] However, nostalgia arises in the grandfather, so he sends his grandchild to the Jewish foundation school as soon as it opens. As for himself, he starts going to the synagogue again – thanks to the school. This was a typical process in the early 1990s. In a paradoxical way, in Eastern and Middle Europe, young children taught their parents about Judaism, some Hebrew words, or how to celebrate Jewish holidays at home. Thanks to Jewish schools, summer camps and youth organizations, a generation and a half after the Holocaust, the Jewish life in Hungary was reborn somehow – but of course, this too-rapid process also produced its own "dissidents" with critical voices. ("I never wanted to see a long skirt again".)

Already after I finished writing my chapter, a new story was published by Anna Gáspár-Singer, which would be a pity not to mention, as it is about today's overt antisemitism and racism – a topic that is still missing in Hungarian literature. The protagonist is a middle-aged mother called to school: she must talk to her child's teacher, headmistress, and a parent about whether another child is regularly bullying and beating her son for racist reasons. The narrative is still calm and detached, and this style highlights the protagonist's helplessness, who feels like a stranger in the company of the uncomprehending teachers and the other parent, unable to get her son's truth.

I would also like to mention two other writers from the Third Generation: Ágnes Gurubi[24] and Eszter Rubin.[25] Both of their novels are contemporary stories; still, at a point, the Holocaust trauma of the grandparents and great grandparents comes up unexpectedly and affects the life of the protagonists. Both the writers are women in their forties, and their protagonists, too, are well-educated, middle-class, single mothers with good jobs but who have serious identity problems.

In Ágnes Gurubi's novel, her teenage daughter has developed an auto-immune disease. This severe health problem drives her mother – who herself suffers from allergic syndromes – to wrap up her family past. Her family members were reluctant to speak openly about their Holocaust experiences, but at a point in the story, the protagonist, the mother of a teenage girl, flies to New York, then to Buenos Aires, just to meet her grandmother's two emigrant sisters, for the first time, to find out what happened to her ancestors in 1944–45. She faces the repressed stories of her great-grandmothers and grandmothers, then realizes that the transferred trauma *might cause her daughter's auto-immune disease*.

In Eszter Rubin's book, it is not the child but the mother – the author's alter ego – who is severely ill with auto-immune disease. Doctors are helpless, but the reader realizes after a while that her mysterious disease must have to do something with her inherited anxiety, which went from generation to generation in her family. A turning point comes in Hanga's condition when she accidentally sees a French Holocaust film about children on the TV. Although being shocked by the topic, she watches more and more traumatic films purposely, day by day. After a state of stupor and sobbing endlessly, she just realizes that the untold stories of her own family might make her sick: their repressed memories have taken her vitality.

Eszter Rubin's novel is interesting from another point of view, too: her story continues to our days, and she starts to get better during the pandemic lockdown. In a paradoxical way, the monotonously repetitive rites of staying at home and disinfecting her household scrupulously help her get back her spiritual balance.

Instead of a Conclusion

"You have to fight for your identity as a Jew", says Diana Groó, a young filmmaker from the Third Generation, speaking about herself in an interview[26] in the early 90s. For many of the children and grandchildren of the survivors, the meaning of their Jewishness is contested. Ferenc Erős,[27] a social psychologist, explains it: the "strategy of silence" means a conscious effort on the part of the parents to conceal the fact of their belonging to the once-persecuted group. "Children growing up in these families experienced an inconceivable family secret and were socialized in an environment where tradition had been eliminated, and the generational continuity of the family history broken".

However, from the literary works discussed here, we can see that the most authentic works were written by members of the Second Generation, as they happened to be close with their parents and grandparents who knew Jewish life before the war and suffered the Holocaust. Seen from another point of view, some of our most prominent writers have dared to confront their own Jewish heritage – while younger generations tend to feel only the absence and use their imagination to fill in the gaps in family memory.

It is not clear how Jewish or Jewish-related literature will develop in the future. Probably, as the Fourth and Fifth Generations will not be able to have personal contact with Holocaust survivors, the future of the so-called Holocaust literature is uncertain or, at least, quite limited. At the same time, the tendency of secularization and assimilation has been accelerated – so getting back to the traditions does not seem to be a real literary topic.

Contemporary Hungarian Jewish novels and short stories that represent the current situations and challenges of Jewish life today have not been created yet. So, the next generations will have no idea what Jewish life in the early 21st century was in Hungary. Antisemitism, the ambivalent relationship of the Diaspora with Israel, aliya and returning stories, Jewish schools, Jewish-Gentile mixed marriages, raising children in a "Jewish way", and so on could be missing themes and topics.

Notes

1 The "International Ghetto" was in Újlipótváros during the Holocaust. With the help of Swiss and Swedish diplomats Karl Lutz and Raoul Wallenberg, thousands of Jews moved into the quarter's so-called Swiss or Swedish "protected houses", using fake passports.

2 Hungarian Jews never spoke Yiddish, but refugees from Galicia whose native language was Yiddish had arrived before the Holocaust. Their "singing" way of intonation might have influenced the intonation Jewish people living in Budapest or probably also the German language, as the urban Jewish citizens spoke mostly German at home. To this day, in contrast to the Hungarian intonation rule, this kind of Jewish speaking is typical: the melody of the sentence goes up instead of down, so Antisemitic ears can hear this as Yiddish.

3 Radnóti, 1989: 210.

4 Sanders, 2004.

5 On what basis do antisemites consider someone "Jewish"? Antisemites compile lists of Jewish writers, artists, etc. But these lists include, in addition to those who are truly of Jewish descent, some intellectuals and artists who are Christians or even of aristocratic descendants – simply because they are liberal.

6 Heller, 1997.

7 Flaring international debates: for example, should the poem of an Afro-American poet and civil rights fighter be translated by a non-minority translator, who is not even a woman? In Hungary, after an unlimited professional debate, the right to translate it was given to some Roma female students, instead of a professional translator.

8 Háy, 2021.

9 Halász, 2020.

10 Németh, 2004.

11 Kornis, 1994.

12 Dalos, 1990.

13 Krasztev, 1999.

14 Spiró György, an acknowledged writer of plays, novels, poems, and essays.

15 Lengyel, 1978.

16 Sanders, 2013.

17 Heller, 1997.

18 Susan Rubin Suleiman used the term "*1.5th generation*" to describe people like herself, whose early childhood was in Europe during the war years and who, after the war, were raised by mothers who were adult survivors of the Holocaust. Rubin Suleiman, 2011.

19 Sanders, 2004.

20 Fináli, 2017.

21 Nádas, 2017.
22 Gáspár-Singer, 2019.
23 Erős, 1993.
24 Gurubi, 2020.
25 Rubin, 2021.
26 Portuges, 2007.
27 Erős, 1993.

Bibliography

Dalos, György, 1990. *A körülmetélés* (The Circumcision), Budapest: Magvető.

Erős, Ferenc, 1993, "The Construction of Jewish Identity in Hungary in the 1980s", *Civilisations* 42–2: 141–150.

Fináli, Gábor, 2017. "Is There a Hungarian Jewish Identity and Does It Have a Future?", *Hungarian Free Press*, November 5.

Gáspár-Singer, Anna, 2019. *Valami kék* (Something Blue), Budapest: Kalligram; 2022.

Gurubi, Ágnes, 2020. *Szív utca* (Heart Street), Budapest: Kalligram.

Halász, Rita, 2020. *Mély levegő* (Deep Breath), Budapest: Jelenkor.

Háy, János, 2021. *Mamika* (Mummy), Budapest: Európa Kiadó.

Heller, Ágnes, 1997. "Zsidótlanítás a magyar irodalomban" (De-Judaization in Hungarian Jewish Literature), in: Török Petra (ed.), *A határ és a határolt -Töprengések a magyar-zsidó irodalom létformáiról* (The Limit and the Limited – Contemplations about the Existing Forms of Hungarian-Jewish Literature), Budapest: Rabbiképző – Yahalom.

Kornis, Mihály, 1994. *Napkönyv* (Day Book), Budapest: Pesti Szalon.

Krasztev, Peter, 1999. "Confronting Jewishness, Part II", *Generating a Generation. Central Europe Review* 1: 9.

Lengyel, Péter, 1978. *Cseréptörés* (Title Breakage), Budapest: Szépirodalmi.

Nádas, Peter, 1989. *Évkönyv (Year Book), Budapest, Szépirodalmi Könyvkiadó 2017, Világló részletek* (Lightening Details), Budapest: Jelenkor Kiadó.

Németh, Gábor, 2004. *Zsidó vagy?* (Are You Jewish?), Budapest: Kalligram.

Portuges, Catherine, 2007. "Third Generation: Hungarian Jews on Screen 1", *Hungarian Cultural Studies*, https://ahea.pitt.edu/ojs/index.php/ahea/article/view/21.

Radnóti, Miklós, 1989. *Napló* (Diary), Budapest: Magvető Könyvkiadó.

Rubin, Eszter, 2021. *Minek szenved, aki nem bírja (Why Do You Suffer, If You Don't Stand It)*, Budapest: Kalligram.

Rubin Suleiman, Suzanne, 2011. *Budapest Diary, in Search of the Motherbook*, Lexington: Plunkett Lake Press.

Sanders, Ivan, 2004. "Jewish Themes and Issues in Post-1989 Hungarian Literature", *Hungarian Studies* 18 (2): 2013.

Sanders, Ivan, 2013. "Two Ways of Being a Jewish Writer: Ferenc Molnár and Arthur Schnitzler", *European Cultural Review* 26, www.c3.hu/~eufuzetek/en/eng/bookshelf/index.php?mit=12-sanders-twoways

Szántó, T. Gábor, 1995. "A temetés" (Burial), in: *A tizedik ember* (The Tenth Man), Budapest: Belvárosi Kiadó; 2012. Édeshármas (Threesome), L'Harmattan.

4
PAST LIFE
A Cantata for Holocaust Voices Past and Present

Phyllis Lassner

In her reflections on the legacies of the Holocaust in *After Such Knowledge*, Eva Hoffman questions the viability of the term *Holocaust memory* as well as how it is transmitted, understood, and interpreted. From her perspective as a child of Holocaust survivors, the meanings attributed to Holocaust memory are never self-evident or transparent. "To make a sequential narrative of what happened would have been to make indecently rational what had been obscenely irrational. It would have been to normalize through familiar form an utterly aberrant content".[1] As so many survivors attest, because their memories of torturous and disorienting experiences and responses remain incomplete, sometimes self-censoring, and often lacking documentation, their accounts question the possibility of translating them into coherent and persuasive narratives.[2] What they are able to offer, in Lawrence Langer's succinct analysis, is "a lexicon of disruption, absence, and irreversible loss" that reflects their being "hostages to a humiliating and painful past that their happier future does little to curtail".[3] Extending the challenges of translating and transmitting Holocaust experience, Noam Tirosh maintains that Holocaust memory "is not just a neutral representation of the past. Rather, it is a unique exploration of one's identity and self-consciousness, and it carries ethical implications".[4]

The transmission of Holocaust memory from survivors to their children has been represented in recent feature films as the urgent search for knowledge and recognition of the losses that have shaped the lives of both generations so irrevocably. What had been, in the words of Eva Hoffman, "an internalized past" is dramatized as it "reverberates through the minds and lives of subsequent generations".[5] Despite the historical and psychological importance of this transmission, as Liat Steir-Livny proffers, its representation as cultural artifacts raises critical questions: "should the cultural debate on the Holocaust be limited to realistic representations, or can it be represented fictionally, metaphorically?"[6] Deploying conventions of psychological suspense narratives, recent films such as *The Testament* (2017) and *The Secret* (2007) plot the intergenerational transfer of Holocaust knowledge as searches for the truth underlying the damage of Holocaust secrets on survivors and their families. In contrast, while Avi Nesher's 2016 film *Past Life* also uncovers a Holocaust family secret, it questions the viability of acquiring Holocaust knowledge as equivalent to truth and self-reflexively addresses the questions Steir-Livny poses. Nesher's cinematic language and forms question what other films take for granted by calling critical attention to the ethical and aesthetic challenges of representing Holocaust memory, its lacunae, transmission, and aftereffects. Presented in both realist and figurative terms, the film is an inquiry, a pursuit by the children of survivors to validate their father's story of surviving in hiding.[7]

DOI: 10.4324/b23365-6

Nesher, the son of survivors, explains, "I didn't feel myself capable of telling a Holocaust story. I wasn't there, and it's an unimaginable horror – I can only talk about my generation as survivors and our experience, I can't really talk about our parents' experience".[8] Both the film's characterizations and events are fictional constructions, fulfilling Nesher's narrative imperative to explore the emotional, aesthetic, and ethical effects of withholding and revealing Holocaust knowledge.

The film's narrative crux is the urgent search for the Holocaust diary of survivor Baruch Milch by his two daughters, Sephi (Ella Milch-Sheriff) – a composer and choral singer – and Nana Milch, portrayed in the film as a leftist investigative journalist.[9] After Baruch's death, Sephi found and published his diary with the title *Can Heaven Be Void?* Before the search, he had never spoken about his Holocaust past to anyone and no other knowledge of it had surfaced. As Baruch's actual daughter Ella Milch-Sheriff declares,

> My father's diary, which had revealed to me the true story of his life as well as a personality I had never really known, did not let me rest. I knew I had to write to connect to this painful and terrible text.[10]

Past Life plots a mythic search for Baruch's lost diary as though it will restore his humanity and heal the family's frayed bond. As material evidence of his innocence in a tragic accident, the diary is crucial to repairing his bitter, self-incriminating guilt. Finding the diary also promises to revitalize the sisters' self-determination, which, in the film's narrative logic, has been stymied by the loss of the Milch family's origin story concealed in their father's silence and transcribed in his diary. However, even with the possibility of a definitive outcome, the diary may not resolve a different tragedy: the story of Agnieszka and Yuli Zielinski, sisters who become tragically entangled with Baruch in the war's aftermath. Typical of quest narratives, the real and imagined challenges and insights garnered along the way become as significant as any catharsis or resolution.

Past Life dramatizes the quest for Baruch's diary as an imagined investigation of Holocaust memory and its transmission. Eva Hoffman reflects on the challenges of defining Holocaust memory and finding the medium and forms to represent the process through which it is transmitted and becomes a shaping force:

> The Holocaust, in my first, childish reception, was a deeply internalized but strangely unknown past. It has become routine to speak of the "memory" of the Holocaust. . . . We who came after do not have memories of the Holocaust. Even from my most intimate proximity I could not form "memories" of the Shoah or take my parents' memories as my own. Rather, I took in that first information as a sort of fairy tale deriving not so much from another world as from the center of the cosmos: an enigmatic but real fable.[11]

Akin to Hoffman's unfixed taxonomy, "a sort of fairy tale" and an "enigmatic but real fable", *Past Life* dramatizes the search for Baruch's diary as a multi-genre narrative. Constant cross-cutting between primary and parallel events and using both realist and enigmatic images and atmospherics as the film's language of transmission creates the effect of jostling among different narrative genres, including melodrama, the Gothic, and the quest adventure.[12] Viewed holistically, Nesher creates a metanarrative quest for a cinematic equivalent of representing, transmitting, and interpreting the opposing memories of two Holocaust survivors for their children and as a public commemoration. To achieve all of this, the film intercuts between the aftereffects of Baruch Milch's lost but obliquely expressed Holocaust memory on his family and the chase across Israel and Eastern Europe, all the while yielding false and real clues and raising and dashing hopes for resolution.[13] Binding the film's alternating incidents and locations as well as informing them is Nesher's design of mournful yet ominous coloration and soundtrack, composition, and performance.

Hovering over the Milch family's tensions are, in Dominick LaCapra's formulation, "the hauntingly possessive ghosts – of traumatic events" and of the lost and their untold stories.[14] Despite their indeterminate appearances and unknowability, these ghostly losses persist as a shaping force of the characters' development and the film's trajectory. For Eva Hoffman, the uncanny embodies the Holocaust past:

> In our small apartment, it was a chaos of emotion that emerged from their words rather than any coherent narration. Or rather, the emotion, direct and tormented, was enacted through the words, the form of their utterances. The memories – no, not memories but emanations – of wartime experiences kept erupting in flashes of imaginary; in abrupt, fragmented phrases; in repetitious, broken refrains. They kept manifesting themselves with a frightening immediacy in that most private and potent of family languages – the language of the body.[15]

As though entangled in inexpressible, unending, and irreparable grief, Baruch Milch is portrayed as a frozen and silent body, performing but neither feeling nor relating to life in the present. Like other survivors who feel unable to articulate and therefore share their Holocaust experiences, Baruch's silence has not been a healing experience for him or a comforting one for his family.[16] Instead, the pain resulting from the unresolved moral quandary at the center of his story has enveloped him and his family, almost crushing them. An uncanny force, Baruch's unrecounted story has been expressed in his abusive and controlling behavior towards his daughters.[17] The unfolding goal of the sisters' quest is to reanimate their father's Holocaust past so that the present materializes as a forgiving time and place.

The Imagined Story of Baruch Milch

Baruch Milch was working as a medical doctor in Tluste, Ukraine when the Germans invaded the Soviet Union in June 1941 and began their mass killings of the Jews. Although his medical practice saved him and his family for two years, in May 1943, 2,000 local and nearby Jews were murdered.[18] In both reality and in the film, Milch's wife Peppa, baby son, mother-in-law, and sister-in-law were among the victims and Baruch, his brother-in-law, and his child faced further tragedy. Nesher, however, changes the subsequent events as follows. Faced with omnipresent danger, the film imagines Baruch and his brother-in-law Romek signing a contract with a Polish farmer named Zielinski to hide Baruch's wife Peppa and baby son Lunek along with Romek's son also named Lunek in exchange for money and a promise of land. They were hidden in a crawl space under Zielinski's house and in the attic. In Nesher's account, the farmer planned to move Peppa and Lunek from their apartment the next day, but they had already been captured and shot. Despite the paralyzing impact of this tragedy, Baruch and Romek remain determined to survive, keeping Romek's baby with them and allowing themselves to be reassured by the news that the Russians were approaching, "that the nightmare was about to end". The worst, however, "was still to come", as Baruch attests. That same night, the SS discover the farm, conduct a relentless search, and interrogate the farmer. Although Zielinski did not betray the hidden Jews, an accident impels Baruch's silence as well as the film's investigation of its effects on his daughters. To avoid capture by the SS, Romek covers his child's face with his hand to keep him quiet, inadvertently suffocating him and producing a double tragedy. Their two sons, both named Lunek, were now dead.

> I looked at Romek. He accused me of forcing him to do it, but that wasn't true! I'm a doctor. I don't kill. He let go of the child, covered him in a blanket, sat in the corner and muttered: I

> am damned for all eternity. And I thought, so am I. So am I. You realize that everything you were taught in school, morality and justice are nothing but man's pathetic attempt to pretend that he's more than an animal.

Despite Baruch's detailed disclosure and moral commentary, his story reflects the anxiety accompanying the attempt to recount an elusive but determining memory. Like Hoffman, the second generation characters in Nesher's film experience their parents' memories as a "deeply internalized but strangely unknown past".[19] Enacted as turbulent family relationships and accompanied by ominous overtones, the past in this film is fraught with secrets that prevent parents and children from knowing or understanding each other. Nesher has commented on the emotional challenges of being a child of Holocaust survivors: "I strongly identified with the two of them having to struggle with parents who they loved but couldn't really relate to".[20] The thematic motivation for *Past Life* concerns intergenerational breaches within the Milch and Zielinski families who are bound in opposing versions of the past. In search of the truth and reconciliation across the two generations, Baruch's daughter Sephi joins forces with Agnieszka's son Thomas to search for the lost diary.

A Holocaust Mystery Story

The film is set in 1977 and begins at a choral concert in West Berlin in which Thomas Zielinski conducts and Sephi Milch performs. Casting an ominous tone over Sephi's success, with ambient sounds of thunderous rain, the Holocaust past bursts into the celebration reception. Suddenly, after seeing the name "Milch" on the program, Agnieszka Zielinski approaches Sephi. As the camera moves to a close-up, it registers the older woman's face as contorted by a menacing frown and obdurate sense of purpose: she grabs the young woman's wrist, and, spitting out her words, pronounces Sephi guilty of being the daughter of a murderer. With an uncanny sense of self-justification, captioning her assault, Agnieszka Zielinski exclaims, "You look just like him" – a hyperbolic pronouncement unsupported by the camera's close-up of Sephi's face. Nonetheless, the imputation aligns Sephi with her father's contested Holocaust past as though she has inherited his guilt epigenetically.

Despite the antipathy her accusation establishes, Agnieszka and Baruch are constructed as two mutually contested versions of the same story, both imprisoned by memories of an all-consuming past. With no other material evidence and no witness testimony, the startling allegation and its determining aftereffects are both empowered and unsettled by a pervading sense of the uncanny.[21] More of an atmosphere than a spectral presence, dark reds bleeding into black shadows, storms juxtaposed with characters' outbursts, and discordant music throughout the film call attention to the epistemological gaps in the search for a verifiable Holocaust past. Thomas's attempt to provide a rational explanation for his mother's behavior only highlights its insubstantiality: "My mother went through hell in the war. She wanted to see the daughter of a murderer". In step with the uncanny, coincidence, a familiar device of melodrama, performs the illusion of causality by entwining the Baruch daughters and the Zielinskis as well as endowing the uncertainties of the survivors' stories with an aura of mythic fatedness. As Nana tells Sephi: "In Berlin you unintentionally opened Pandora's box". With interwoven narrative contours, the film's opening scene establishes Holocaust memory and its determining power as a historical mystery that must be investigated to save the Second Generation from being victimized by unsettled questions about the nature of Holocaust guilt and innocence. The question lingers, however, if resolution is possible since each survivor remembers the Holocaust in hostility to the other.

The film's approach to the challenges of defining and substantiating Holocaust memory, its iteration and transmission is set in motion with the multivalent quandaries contained in the opening scene. Characterizing Agnieszka as traumatized accuser and Baruch as the traumatized accused raises questions about the emotional and moral challenges and costs of attempting to survive the Nazi occupation of Europe and the aftermath. For both the Milch sisters and Thomas, the search for Baruch's diary is predicated on the urgent need for a reparative narrative. From the beginning, however, despite the fatefulness of coincidence, the film's portentous atmospherics, emotional outbursts, and mordant silences predict an uncertain outcome about the meanings of Holocaust victimization and memory.

Dramatized with disorienting visual metaphors, the film pivots between vast, perilous spaces and dark, claustrophobic interiors, Gothic tropes that suggest that the search for Baruch's diary is both propelled and troubled by an ineffable but determining terror. While the Gothic emerged in the 18th century, Sara Wasson observes its application to representing 20th-century horror: "In the modern Gothic, the world, be it supernatural or natural, is witnessed through a lens of terror, anguish, paranoia or a perverse emotional deadness. Madness, dread or despair color Gothic narrative".[22] Accompanied by mournfully discordant music that expresses anguish and escalating anxiety, the suggestively Gothic settings of *Past Life* illuminate and yet obscure the Holocaust past, conveying the sense that home, art, and nature have been invaded by traces of Holocaust memories that cannot otherwise be expressed or transmitted. The atmosphere is so often toxic, the characters seem to be choking on it, as Sephi's silences and Nana's outcries reveal.

The film's representation of uncanny, indeterminate but determining forces suggests that neither the definition of Holocaust memory nor its transmission can be stabilized. Instead, Holocaust memory and its effects are fixed only as they remain in flux, across space and time, tethering past and present, survivors and the Second Generation. Holocaust memory therefore dislodges any sense of continuity in the generational time and relationships through which it moves. The effect of this haunting instability on the Second Generation is experienced as a "fearful weight of densely packed feeling", as Eva Hoffman intones: "The fragmentary phrases lodged themselves in my mind like shards, like the deadly needles I remember from certain fairy tales, which pricked your flesh and could never be extracted again".[23] Whatever documented facts are discovered, as Ella Milch-Sheriff attests, they cannot be absorbed as objective:

> The work was unbearably difficult for me. The thought that it was my own father who was talking about all the horrors he went through left me full of tears, unable to continue. In order to go on with the composition of the music, I had to detach myself emotionally and to imagine that I was writing about a stranger and not someone so close to me.[24]

In its persistent cross-cutting between scenes in Israel, Germany, and Poland, *Past Life* shows us that the narration of Holocaust memory is resistant to containment and linear progression. As though condensing the factors that have wreaked havoc on the Milch and Zielinski families' relationships, the film shifts between several intersecting yet discontinuous narrative planes: the investigation by Sephi, Nana, and Thomas into Baruch's Holocaust past, Sephi's frustrated musical career path, the discovery of Nana's cancer, and Baruch's reading of his reconstructed diary.

Reading the Reconstructed Past: "I Remember Every Word I Wrote"

Questions about Holocaust memory, its transmission, and aftereffects permeate the scenes of Baruch reading his reconstructed diary to his daughters. The design of these scenes, in which Baruch and his daughters sit back-to-back in near darkness and which are intercut with other incidents, undermines any expectation that the reconstructed diary is material evidence of an actual Holocaust past.

Instead, as Eva Hoffman's formulation suggests, the disjointed reading conjures "not memories but emanations – of wartime experiences", expressed in the visual equivalent of "abrupt, fragmented phrases; in repetitious, broken refrains". In ironic contrast to the comforting bedtime stories Baruch recalls having invented "on the spot", he now divulges a harrowing if self-consciously constructed account of his efforts to save himself, his first wife and son, and her brother's family from certain death. As though the medium is the message, he reports, "I wrote a diary with tiny pieces of pencil. I want to write it again so that you'll get the most accurate picture, as if you were there yourselves in Hell". Compounding his claim for coherence, however, Baruch's account consists of labyrinthine detours, double identities, interruptions, and protracted tension, structurally analogous to the "information" Hoffman recalls "taking in" as "an enigmatic but real fable".

The film represents Baruch's response to the tragedy at the Zelienski farm as a fable about the enigmatic presence of loss in an everlasting surfeit of guilt. He implores his daughters: "Please put yourself in my place. The first of September, 1939 was the beginning of the end of my life. I never imagined the war would last so long and that people were capable of such atrocities". Despite this historically verified indictment of actual perpetrators, Baruch identifies himself as culpable, as though the prolonged duration of the war's horrors eroded the possibility of maintaining a state of innocence, as he tells his daughters: "I didn't know that in two years they'd both be dead because of me. . . . Not a night goes by that I don't think of them standing there so scared and I'm not with them". Baruch's guilt has materialized as the ghost of himself, shadowing the devastating loss that has anchored him in the past as a driving force ever since. He remains haunted by images he can only imagine but that he experiences as reflecting an unforgiving memory caught in the interstices between his helplessness and failed responsibility. The film's exclusion of any flashback images of Baruch's first wife and child renders them lost twice over, but their absent presence has governed not only Baruch's life but also his daughters. As Joanne Pettit posits, "Such haunting is, in other words, the effect of unresolved trauma".[25]

As Baruch recounts his terrifying experience in hiding, he asks his daughters to join him in his anxious grief and therefore merge with his memory: "Imagine me helpless in the cellar, listening to the yelling and footsteps on the ceiling . . . staring at the ceiling the whole time". While he speaks, the camera shifts to Sephi's reaction, apprehensively staring up at their living room ceiling where an image of slightly open slats reveals the boots of the SS who are scouring the farmer's house for the hidden Jews. Depicted realistically in high resolution and sharply contrasting coloration, the image is overdetermined, synecdochally representing the Final Solution while validating both Baruch's memory and Sephi's identification with his terror.[26] Expressing Baruch's revivified fear, the film's visual composition, its camera work and set design, align him and his daughters as inhabiting the same imprisoning space, the same immutable, horrific memory.[27]

That traditional notions of morality and justice are destabilized by the Holocaust's exigencies become visible in the film's unrelieved counter narratives between the quest for Baruch's documentary validation, the suffering of his daughters, and the excruciating memory of Agnieszka Zielinski. Although Baruch's original diary and receipt are finally discovered in the storage room where he left them with the Jewish committee in Katowice, the search has taken on a moral life of its own. Its frantically paced representation suggests that what is at stake in the present as well as the future is driven by desperation about the past. Baruch's account of his survival in hiding also enacts the filmmaker's goal: "I would like people to think of their own past and how it shapes, for better or for worse, their own present".[28]

A practicing gynecologist and evidently very competent and compassionate, with his daughters, Baruch is embittered, both emotionally withholding and explosive. He is especially brutal to Nana, which is evinced in a fleeting flashback image of beating her when she was young. In Hoffman's words, "that most private and potent of family languages – the language of the body", punishes the child who reminds her father of his helplessness in failing to save his first wife and their son. Baruch convicts himself despite the fact that the conditions of hiding precluded any type of resistance. That his character and behavior as a father have been formed by his victimization is revealed further when Nana criticizes Israel's treatment of the Palestinians and Baruch retorts scornfully by refocusing the issue of oppression on the Jews' fate in the Holocaust. The real-life Baruch Milch revealed his own disaffections in his memoir, in which he wrote his personal Ten Commandments, such as

> "Thou shalt have no other God before yourself," "Do not have faith – the sky is empty," "Toughen your heart and do not heed it" and "Do not get close to people, and do not bring them close to you." Everything I did was to build a good life for the family. You and your sister live in a world where everything is normal and you can't understand the world back there.[29]

Whereas for all too many years Baruch is unable to differentiate his daughters' selfhood from the bitter lessons he gleaned from his Holocaust past, reading his reconstructed diary becomes a form of mediation that enacts a process of self-affirming separation for both generations while negotiating their stultifying interdependence. Although he is shown reading his reinscribed account, implying that despite his silence, his memory can be accessed and therefore readily transcribed, Nesher's design troubles this possibility. Instead, his film emphasizes the disjunctive workings of Holocaust memory, its iteration, and its transmission. The film disrupts any resemblance to a holistic, cohesive account by constantly interrupting Baruch's faltering, muted reading with screen shots of defining contemporaneous moments, including a TV image of President Sadat's speech to the Israeli parliament in November 1977 and Thomas Zielinski's appearance in Sephi's class while she sings. The cross-referencing to catalyzing personal and political flashpoints reveals that crisis and "the chaos of emotion" are both emanations of Baruch's Holocaust memory and serve as exegetical commentaries. Each insertion expresses the family's tortuous relations, as we see in several incidents to which the film intercuts. Examples include the nosebleeds of his wife Luisa that coincide with Baruch's or Nana's emotional eruptions and the onset of her cancer. The juxtaposition of bodily pain and the past that Luisa Milch would prefer to keep hidden undercuts Baruch's attempts to reassure her that he will take care of things as he always has. In effect, the film creates a collage of multiple, dissonant voices, building towards a contrapuntal, critical relationship between the Holocaust past and present and between survivor parents and their second generation children.

Coincidence and Counterpoint

Although the friendship between Thomas Zielinski and Sephi Milch appears to develop out of their shared musical interests, the film establishes it as predetermined. The opening scene situates their relationship as part of a narrative pattern in which fateful coincidences collapse the temporal distance between the Holocaust past and the present and lock the two generations into each other's narrative orbit. At birth, Thomas, Sephi, and Nana are already entangled in each other's lives as heirs to their parents' opposed but interdependent stories of the Holocaust past. Suffering the uncertainties of cancer treatment, Nana interprets Einstein as support for her fateful sense that "Everything is predetermined by forces over which we have no control. We all dance to a mysterious tune intoned in the distance by a mysterious piper". With no other explanation for her feeling of entrapment, she turns to coincidence: "So dad has the blood of a boy on his hands".

If Nana and the film's many coincidences offer little allowance for the contingencies of experiential reality or narrative realism, Nesher also grants her and other characters the power of insight as resistance. For example, in response to his mother's inability to confront an open-ended future, Thomas is "amazed at the powerful grip the past has on her". Yet in the same breath, he realizes that this grip "doesn't allow for much present". Speaking on behalf of the film's alignment of its polysemous narrative forms and the vicissitudes of transmitting memories of the Holocaust past, Nana reflects:

> In tragedy you can't escape fate. This is a comedy. Purists will point out too many coincidences in our story and will insist that in fact it's a farce. And if there is a god then the critics will tear him apart for his mixture of genres.

Nana's irony accords with Sara Horowitz's critical observation about "the inadequacy of conventional generic boundaries regarding Holocaust testimony".[30] As though in response, Nesher positions *Past Life* on a "borderland between fiction and nonfiction" that aligns with Hoffman's liminal designation of "half awful reality, half wondrous fairy tale".[31]

Equivalent to an omniscient narrator, coincidence also transforms from a conventional plot device to assuming an explanatory and developmental dimension. We learn, for example, that one reason why the receipt for Baruch's diary is so difficult to locate is that his name wasn't Milch at the time but Zielinski. The farmer Zielinski gave Baruch the identity papers of his son Jan Zielinski, who died in the war. The seminal power of the repeated name intensifies when Thomas tells Sephi that he took his mother's name because his father was a German officer. Interrelating First and Second Generations, in both cases the name Zielinski is adopted as an escape from Nazi terror – symbolic in Thomas's case and real in Baruch's. In its compressed, coincidental use, the name Zielinski forges the two families' inextricably interdependent histories. Whether it is possible for the two families to reconcile their differences and for the Second Generation to extricate itself from the painful legacy of their parents' memories is embedded in the quest for Baruch's diary. Once again, coincidence is a mechanism of inquiry as depicted in Thomas's unexpected appearance in Sephi's choral music class. Barely a minute after he enters the room, Thomas interrupts her instructor who, echoing her father, is censuring her ambitions to become a composer. In counterpoint, Thomas expresses his support for Sephi, asserting the power of self-determination as resistance to the oppressive dominance of the past. The work of these coincidences and their unraveling becomes entwined with the search for the truth of Baruch's and Agnieszka's contested memories.

"Please Put Yourself in My Place"

According to Nesher's construction of Baruch's story, in the immediate postwar, he and Yuli Zelienski became lovers and she became pregnant with their child, but the possibility of building a life together ended when a priest told him that the Jews died because they had crucified Jesus: "He even wanted to baptize me. I was so helpless after the cellar they could've done anything with me". Jolted out of passivity by this post-Holocaust replay of virulent antisemitism, Baruch decides to reactivate his Jewish identity, but what seems like an act of reparation raises questions about its ethical implications. When Yuli became desperately ill while pregnant, despite Baruch's claim that he was sympathetic, his primary concern was to have

> a family like I had. So I suggested that Yuli abort the baby. I'm a gynecologist so I could do it. I didn't realize how my offer affected her. She didn't blame me with all I had gone through but she didn't want an abortion because it's a sin against God

and committed suicide. The next morning her sister found her. He finishes his story by pointing to a scar: "I got this from her sister Agnieszka, with a kitchen knife. She tried to kill me". In the film's penultimate scene, Thomas pleads with his mother to attend Sephi's concert, meet Baruch, and attempt some kind of reconciliation, but she tells him that she cannot because she believes that Baruch killed Yuli and made it look like suicide: "If I see him, I'll want to kill him. That man is just like the Nazis! I want him to suffer like my sister, like me".

Although Baruch expresses no responsibility for Yuli's suicide, its narrative position, proximate to his overwhelming guilt about losing his first family and to Agnieszka's denunciation, relates questions about ethical choices to the unrelieved pain of loss transmitted to the Second Generation. Eva Hoffman reflects that for the children of survivors, "The presence of suffering was powerful enough so that it had to be absorbed" along with the "mythology [that] the good was closely equated with suffering".[32] Baruch's plea for understanding and Agnieszka's grievous accusation should be understood in the context of discussions about ethical relationships between Holocaust testimony and the aesthetics of representation. As Jeremy Hawthorn posits, the "accounts by and about single individuals to depict aspects of the Holocaust is very far from uncontentious. . . . But to convey the humanity of victims and the full extent of the guilt of perpetrators and bystanders, accounts by and about individuals are irreplaceable".[33] Sara Horowitz analyzes how the intelligibility of Holocaust accounts depends on a discomforting aesthetics of representation: "artistry resides in the meshing of disparate fragments into a cognitive, psychological, and ethical whole that unsettles the viewer. In other words, the artistry is not merely an overlay on already known facts, but itself constitutes and interprets".[34] *Past Life* complicates viewers' responses by mediating Baruch's diary, its quest and its interpretations, through a self-reflexive narration that commingles translation, transmission, and intervention. With a similar approach, Hofmann and Reuter discuss the translation of Holocaust memories as combining "the psychological mechanisms and cultural processes involved when members of successive generations grapple with the experiences, testimonies, and material remains of their predecessors".[35] *Past Life* represents itself as translating, and transmitting Baruch Milch's Holocaust memory and account as a fraught, intergenerational odyssey, coalescing into a fictionalized film that is both a work of art and its interpretation.

"The Time Will Come"[36]

Past Life narrates the transmission of a Holocaust story and its legacy for the Second Generation and its reverberations in collective memory through musical expression. The film ends with the concert of Sephi's cantata, "The Time Will Come", for choir and conducted by Thomas Zielinski. With Baruch, Lusia, and Nana Milch in the audience, the scene is structured metaphorically as a cinematic cantata, giving voice to the possibility of reaching out across history and memory in an attempt to exorcise the pain transferred from survivors to their children. In Eva Hoffman's words, "Just as for some survivors only full remembering could bring about some catharsis, so for the second generation, only a full imaginative confrontation with the past – however uncanny, however unknown – can bring haunting to an end".[37] Leaving this possibility as indeterminate, while Sephi's family responds to her song with tears of recognition, Agnieszka Zielinski remains at home, staring at a photo of herself with her sister Yuli and Baruch. In the only gesture she can manage to reach towards the present and the future, she turns on her TV to watch the concert and cries.

Sephi's music that completes the film was composed by Ella Milch-Sheriff who explains that it "is taken from a long poem in Polish that my father, Baruch Milch, has written during hiding and after the war with some additions of mine".[38] The lyrics, reprinted here, express Milch-Sheriff's hope and plea to reconcile the past with the present and future through a poetic monologue addressed to her father. The poem acknowledges both the debt her life owes to her father's stalwart efforts to survive and that "the thread" of her life, begun before her birth and that of her sister, will always be interlaced with her father's. Nonetheless, with a simultaneous crescendo, the poem and the film proclaim her self-determination. The poem's reference to the biblical story of Noah and the flood echoes the catastrophe of the Holocaust but then makes a promise to "fight" for a survival in a time and meaning she will call her own.

> "The Time Will Come"
> But when the time comes and cease the stormy waves,
> And the time of storms and human beasts on two will come too.
> And yet, I hope to save the thread of my life,
> I will try to fight for my soul, not to kneel
> Until my defeat, if occurred, will still have value.
> With bare hands, you fought, Father,
> You have given me life.
> Now it's my turn.
> This is my time.

Notes

1 Hoffman, 2004: 15.
2 Reading Eva Hoffman, Van Alphen offers a critical perspective on what he views as the continuity implied by the theory of Postmemory: "the dynamics between children and survivor parents is rather defined by . . . disconnection not in an emotional, personal sense but in terms of intelligibility . . . to posit that connection as the basis of what happens is, it seems to me, close to a form of literally, wishful thinking" (Van Alphen, 2006: 493).
3 Langer, 1991: xi.
4 Tirosh, 2020: 221.
5 Hoffman, 2004: 103.
6 Steir-Livny, 2019: 1.
7 Baron notes that "Plumbing the recesses of memory to comprehend how parents' wartime traumas impact their children became a more prominent theme in both German and Jewish movies in the 1980s" (2005: 221).
8 The son of Holocaust survivors, Nesher believes that his film's core issues relate directly to Israel, where he lives: "I feel that I live in a country which is trapped in its past and, most particularly, in its traumas" but that this can "be solved culturally, and cinema is a great catalyst for initiating such a process" (Zacharias interview).
9 Milch-Sheriff, 2020. In actuality, Ella's sister was Dr. Shosh Avigal, "an important theatre critic, director of various cultural institutions, adviser, researcher, and lecturer on theatre at many universities".
10 Milch-Sheriff, 2020.
11 Hoffman, 2004: 6.
12 Insdorf discusses the evolution of Holocaust film genres, from those "focused on Jewish victims and Nazi villains" to "dark comedy" and documentaries, all evincing "creative confrontation" with the Holocaust (Insdorf, 2003: 247–248). Maron argues that melodrama serves a "mollifying function that can potentially reconcile the tension between historical objectivity and subjectivity, as well as between intellectual engagement and emotional integration" (2009: 73). In his *LA Time* review of *Past Life,* Turan notes that "if the plot has too many potboiler elements, the characters are considerably more convincing in their disturbed emotions" (2017).
13 In her discussion of the haunting impact of traumatic experience on the second generation, Schwab asks "How does one write from . . . within a loss that is less remembered as a story or an image or a thought than as a mood, an existential void, or a sense of annihilation?" (2010: 60).
14 LaCapra, 2001: xi.

15 Hoffman, 2004: 9.
16 The issue of silence also assumes historiographic importance in Cesarani's discussion of the "myth" of silence based on the mistaken assumption that survivors "wanted to forget their experiences and build new lives" that was refuted by the discovery of memoirs written during the war and shortly after (2012: 2–3).
17 In LaCapra's terms this would be a form of"acting out," a symptomatic after effect . . . in which the past returns and the future is blocked or fatalistically caught up in a melancholic feedback loop" (2001: xi, 21). While LaCapra is concerned with trauma and its aftereffects on the second generation, Van Alphen argues that "Children of survivors can be traumatized, but their trauma does not consist of the Holocaust experience, not even in indirect or mitigated form. Their trauma is caused by being raised by a traumatized Holocaust survivor" (486).
18 According to the "*Sefer Tluste*", held by the New York Public Library, "Tluste was the last city in Eastern Galicia to undergo the process of total extermination, so it contained those Jews who had survived earlier '*Aktions*' in the neighbouring towns. Out of the three thousand Jewish residents ofTluste and the thousands of refugees from the neighbouring towns, less than five hundred survived at the end of the Second World War" (http:www.tovste.info.Personalities/BaruchMilch.php).
19 Samuel Juni, psychologist and son of Holocaust survivors, explains that "Second-generation survivors often see themselves as living replacements (or even incarnations) of those annihilated. . . . One's very existence is thus compensatory in its every essence (2016: 204).
20 Zacharias, 2017.
21 Grimwood, 2007, notes that "the absence of firsthand experience of the Holocaust "is often an uncanny presence in their writing" (3).
22 Wasson, 2010: 2.
23 Hoffman, 2004: 11.
24 Milch-Sheriff, 2020.
25 Pettit, 2018. "Such haunting is, in other words, the effect of unresolved trauma".
26 Elsaesser discusses how photographic and film images "have altogether dissolved the boundaries once separating *memory,* as the sense of the past experienced by a living consciousness, from *history,* as the professionally legitimated and collectively negotiated version of that past" (47–48). Von Alphen explains how children of survivors might acquire Holocaust knowledge as "a process of conveying, of combining historical knowledge and the memories of others. And importantly for constructing, it is the result of a strong identifications with (the past of) the parents, of projecting historical, familial knowledge of a past one is disconnected from onto one's life history" (Van Alphen, 2006: 491).
27 Hirsch posits that "camera images mediate the private and the public memory of the Holocaust, [and] generate a memorial aesthetic for the second and even for subsequent generations" (1999: 5).
28 Quoted in Mann.
29 Quoted in Mann.
30 Horowitz, 1997: 7.
31 Art Spiegelman quoted in Horowitz, 1998: 282; Hoffman, 2004: 11.
32 Hoffman, 2004: 13.
33 Hawthorn, 2012: 144.
34 Horowitz, 1997: 6–7.
35 Hofmann and Reuter, 2020: 8.
36 Milch and Milch-Sheriff, 2016.
37 Hoffman, 2004: 73.
38 Milch-Sheriff email to author, 8 December, 2021. Poem reprinted with permission of Ella Milch-Sheriff.

Bibliography

Baron, Lawrence, 2005. *Projecting the Holocaust into the Present: The Changing Focus of Contemporary Holocaust Cinema*, Lanham, MD: Rowman and Littlefield.

Bayer, Gerd, 2010. "After Postmemory: The Holocaust and the Third Generation", *Shofar* 28 (4): 116–132.

Cesarani, David, and Sundquist, Eric J., 2012. *After the Holocaust: Challenging the Myth of Silence*, New York: Routledge.

Elsaesser, Thomas, 2014. "Migration and Motif: The (Parapractic) Memories of an Image", in: Griselda Pollock and Max Silverman (eds.), *Concentrationary Memories: Totalitarian Terror and Cultural Resistance*, London: I. B. Tauris: 47–58.

Grimwood, Marita, 2007. *Holocaust Literature of the Second Generation*, Basingstoke: Palgrave.

Hawthorn, Jeremy, 2012. "The Face-to-Face Encounter in Holocaust Narrative", in: Jakov Lothe, Susan Rubin Suleiman, and James Phelan (eds.), *"After" Testimony: The Ethics and Aesthetics of Holocaust Narrative for the Future*, Columbus: Ohio State University Press: 143–161.

Hirsch, Marianne, 1999. "Projected Memory: Holocaust Photographs in Personal and Public Fantasy", in: Mieke Bal, Jonathan Crewe, and Leo Spitzer (eds.), *Acts of Memory: Cultural Recall in the Present*, Hanover: University Press of New England: 3–23.

Hoffman, Eva, 2004. *After Such Knowledge: Memory, History, and the Legacy of the Holocaust*, New York: Public Affairs.

Hofmann, Bettina, and Reuter, Ursula (eds.), 2020. *Translated Memories: Transgenerational Perspectives on the Holocaust*, Lanham, MD: Lexington Books.

Horowitz, Sara, 1997. *Voicing the Void: Muteness and Memory in Holocaust Fiction*, Albany: State University of New York Press.

Horowitz, Sara, 1998. "Auto/Biography and Fiction after Auschwitz: Probing the Boundaries of Second-Generation Aesthetics", in: Ephraim Sicher (ed.), *Breaking Crystal: Writing and Memory After Auschwitz*, Urbana: University of Illinois Press: 276–296.

Insdorf, Annette, 2003. *Indelible Shadows: Film and the Holocaust*, Cambridge: Cambridge University Press.

Juni, Samuel, 2016. "Identity Disorders in Second Generation Holocaust Survivors", *Journal of Loss and Trauma* 21 (3): 203–212.

LaCapra, Dominick, 2001. *Writing History, Writing Trauma*, Baltimore: Johns Hopkins University Press.

Langer, Lawrence, 1991. *Holocaust Testimony: The Ruins of Memory*, New Haven: Yale University Press.

Lothe, Jakob, Suleiman, Susan Rubin, and Phelan, James (eds.), 2012. *"After" Testimony: The Ethics and Aesthetics of Holocaust Narrative for the Future*, Columbus: Ohio State University Press.

Mann, Iris, 2017. "Holocaust is Passed Down and Always Present in *Past Life*", *Jewish Journal*, May 30, https://jewishjournal.com/culture/arts/hollywood/219715/holocaust-passed-always-present-past-life/ retrieved on November 19, 2021.

Maron, Jeremy, 2009. "Affective Historiography: *Schindler's List*, Melodrama, and Historical Representation", *Shofar* 27 (4): 66–94.

Milch, Baruch, 2003. *Can Heaven Be Void?*, New York: Ktav Publishing.

Milch, Baruch, and Milch-Sheriff, Ella, 2016. "The Time Will Come", *Composed for Avi Nesher's Movie Past Life*. Author's Email with Milch-Sheriff.

Milch-Sheriff, Ella, 2020, *Can Heaven Be Void*? www.ellamilchsheriff.com/can-heaven-be-void retrieved on December 2021.

Past Life, 2016. Avi Nesher, Dir. Israel.

Pettit, Joanne, 2018. "Holocaust Narratives: Second-Generation 'Perpetrators' and the Problem of Liminality", *Toward New Paradigms* 23 (3): 286–300, http://doi.org/10.1080/10848770.2017.1419668 retrieved on November 10, 2021.

Pollock, Griselda, and Silverman, Max (eds.), 2014. *Concentrationary Memories: Totalitarian Terror and Cultural Resistance*, London: I. B. Tauris.

Schwab, Gabriele, 2010. *Haunting Legacies: Violent Histories of Transgenerational Trauma*, New York: Columbia University Press.

The Secret, 2007. Claude Miller, dir. France.

Sicher, Ephraim (ed.), 1998. *Breaking Crystal: Writing and Memory After Auschwitz*, Urbana: University of Illinois Press.

Steir-Livny, Liat, 2019. *Remaking Holocaust Memory: Documentary Cinema by Third Generation Survivors in Israel*, Syracuse, NY: Syracuse University Press.

The Testament, 2017. Amichai Greenberg, dir. Israel and Austria.

Tirosh, Noam, 2020. "Understanding @eva.stories: Holocaust Memory in the Instagram Era", *Jewish Film & New Media* 8 (2), Fall: 217–225.

Turan, Kenneth, 2017. *In Avi Nesher's 'Past Life,' the Bitter History of a Holocaust Survivor is Passed to His Children*, www.latimes.com/entertainment/movies/la-et-mn-past-life-review-20170601-story.html retrieved on November 20, 2021.

Van Alphen, Ernst, 2006. "Second Generation Testimony, Transmission of Trauma, and Postmemory", *Poetics Today* 27 (2), summer: 473–494.

Wasson, Sara, 2010. *Urban Gothic of the Second World War*, Basingstoke: Palgrave.

Zacharias, Ramona, 2017. "Telling my Story Through Someone Else's Story: Avi Nesher on *Past Life*", *Creative Screenwriting*, May 31. www.creativescreenwriting.com/past-life/ retrieved on October 10, 2021.

5

TIME STANDS STILL

Acting Out the Trauma in Second Generation Israeli Documentaries

Liat Steir-Livny

Introduction

Eretz-Israeli documentaries began dealing with the topic of Holocaust survivors in the immediate aftermath of World War II. Cinema from the late 1940s up to the 1960s was primarily a form of Zionist propaganda. The films focused on the Zionist struggle, the establishment of a Jewish state in Eretz Israel, and financial support for the State after its founding. Thus, many films were produced in English and then translated into numerous other languages for worldwide distribution.

Filmmakers during these years created a linear narrative that moved from an abstract national disaster to a national renaissance. The documentaries did not include interviews with survivors, neither were they given a voice in any other way. The narrator provided commentary on the visuals, describing a collective transformation from ashes to revival. This narrative clearly reflected and corroborated the Zionist account, which regarded the Land of Israel as the only place where survivors could heal and begin a new life (*The Road to Liberty)* [Norman Lurie, 1946], and *Our Way of Life* [Baruch Dinar, 1958]).[1]

The few documentaries that were produced after the 1961 trial of Adolf Eichmann until the 1980s differed from earlier documentaries in terms of their greater identification with the Jewish diaspora in Europe before, during, and after the Holocaust. For example, in the trilogy *The 81st Blow* (1974), *The Last Sea* (1979), and *Flames in the Ashes* (1985) by Jacques Ehrlich, Haim Gouri, and David Bergman,[2] the survivors' voices are heard in the soundtrack as they personalize the trauma, but the survivors were not filmed.

Multiple factors led to the growth of Israeli Holocaust awareness in the 1980s. The first high school delegations to visit former concentration camps in Poland travelled in 1988. During this time, many Holocaust survivors retired and began to publish their memoirs in increasing numbers. Members of the Second Generation, mostly born after 1945, were now adults who began to discuss the ways in which the trauma had affected their lives and to depict their relationships with their parents.[3]

The international acclaim for Claude Lanzmann's monumental documentary *Shoah* (1985), together with the acknowledgment that Holocaust survivors are an aging population and the greater use of video which cuts production costs, prompted a burst of Israeli Holocaust documentaries from the late 1980s onward. These Israeli documentaries centered on stories of survival filtered through the perspectives of the Second Generation.[4]

DOI: 10.4324/b23365-7

Marianne Hirsch suggested that the Holocaust, as represented in the works of second generation survivors, creates an indirect affinity structured on inherited imagination and memory.[5] This is what she termed *postmemory*, which characterizes the experience of those controlled by events that happened before they were born, who apply their imagination to places they cannot remember. Yosefa Loshitzky called the second generation documentaries produced in Israel since the 1980s "postmemory cinema", since they represent an imagined collectivity of ghosts and shadows.[6] These films turned second-generation directors into listeners – "witnesses through imagination" or "surrogate witnesses" – whose gaze and voice defined a new form of empathy towards survivors.[7]

Most documentarists did not look for stories of heroism but rather chose to focus on the "ordinary" individuals. These documentaries rejected the utopian notion of a linear time frame that begins with the Holocaust and ends in a fully integrative process. Rather, they depicted a range of Holocaust survivor identities, living between the past and the present, between the trauma they suffered and the new lives they have built. The present in Israel is constantly interrupted by memories of the past so that the survivors and their children live their lives in two trajectories: a linear Israeli time and a circular time of the traumatic past. The next two subsections analyze the depictions of time standing still for the survivors and their children in a number of key films.

The Survivors – The Past Within the Present

The way in which traumatized individuals perceive time has been examined in psychological research since the days of Sigmund Freud. Freud considered melancholy and mourning to be two contradictory forms of coping with trauma. He theorized that an individual in a melancholic state identifies with the lost object, in a way that suspends time. Freud believed that one of the central concepts in melancholy was "repetition compulsion": the need to return to the trauma while blurring the boundaries between past and present, thus re-experiencing it. This repetition causes suffering and undermines the sufferer. In contrast, the mourner undergoes a healthy process of internalization which enables him or her to deal with the past by creating distance from it. Mourning brings with it the possibility of starting a new life, and any interruption to this process can be detrimental.[8]

Post-traumatic stress disorder (PTSD) was first included in the American Psychiatric Association*'s Diagnostic and Statistical Manual of Mental Disorders* in 1982. This disorder causes individuals who have experienced traumatic events to continue to relive the trauma in the form of intrusive, recurrent recollections of the past in the present.[9] Dominick LaCapra distinguished between two forms of dealing with the trauma of the Holocaust. The first, "acting out", construes the past as events that are reborn and experienced as though integral to present-day life, rather than as remote events that are long resolved or as distant memories. The second, "'working-through", maintains clear boundaries between past and present, and there is awareness of the differences between "then" and "now". While there is also a return to the past in "working-through", it is accompanied by conscious control of the past. A critical distance is maintained, and it is viewed from a detached perspective.[10] Israeli documentaries since the 1980s have examined various forms of working through and acting out as discussed later. The directors represent in various ways what they perceive as the PTSD of the survivors and its effect on their children.

Because of That War tells the story of two parent/child, first/second generation Holocaust survivor relationships: Halina Birenbaum and her son Ya'acov Gilad and Jacko Poliker and his son Yehuda Poliker. The film represents a series of moving conversations, during which Jacko describes his deportation from Thessaloniki to Auschwitz in cattle cars, as well as his futile attempts to save his family. Halina discusses the deportation of the Jews of Warsaw to Treblinka, Majdanek, and Auschwitz. Both survivors discuss their relationships with their children – who are musicians – and how they grew up in the shadow of their parents' trauma. Together, the two musicians produced the album *Ash and Dust* (*Efer ve Avak*) in 1988, which deals with their parents' trauma and its influence on them as second generation survivors.

The ways in which the survivors' transition from acting out to working through their trauma is revealed as Halina describes how she has dedicated her life to commemorating the past. She translates texts from Polish, to make sure they will not be lost, thus inserting the Jewish-Polish culture she grew up with into the Israeli culture of today. She writes about the Holocaust and frequently addresses high school students. When she faces them in the auditorium, she performs her life story. She creates a mental barrier between herself and her past trauma, so she can relate her story from a distance (sometimes reenacting herself as a small child, sometimes as the perpetrators) and corrals her emotions.[11] But when she returns home Halina tells director Ben-Dor that the present disappears and the ghetto "swallows me up. . . . It is not a past; it will never be a past for me". Halina confesses that the fear that her son will grow up to be "like them" (the Nazis) has shaped her mothering, noting "they had mothers as well". After returning from a trip to Poland and the Majdanek former concentration camp, she remarks to Ya'acov that she feels empty. Ya'acov is insulted – more than 30 years have passed since the Holocaust, she has built a family in Israel, a life, so why does she feel empty? Why does she feel she belongs there? Halina insists that what she experienced there was larger than herself, and at a certain moment, she would have preferred to stay there and die. She "belongs" in Majdanek, where she was imprisoned at the age of 13, where she lost her mother, and where her mother and relatives remained in "the mountain of ashes". "This is the place I most strongly belong to . . . this is eternity . . . and Ya'acov cannot understand it".

Jacko Poliker's story presents the tragic fate of the Greek Jews, especially the Thessaloniki community that perished in the Holocaust. After World War II, he started a new family in Israel, worked, and raised his children, but alongside his new life he continued to act out the trauma. For example, Jacko says that each day after work, he would go out to look for his children. They were used to him suddenly appearing at basketball practice. His son, Yehuda, tells the camera that Jacko obsessively played melancholic Greek music in their home. Yehuda begged him to stop, but he would not, claiming that his children needed to know that once there had been a great and happy family and that happiness ended tragically. Jacko describes his son Mordechai's bar mitzvah. He was so flooded with the memory of his murdered family members and began to yell and throw dishes. "The whole event was ruined", he comments.

Daddy Come to the Fair traces the Vilozny family's journey back to father Mordechai's childhood hometown in Poland and, later, to the Auschwitz-Birkenau Museum, following in the footsteps of his family members who were murdered in the Holocaust. Mordechai is a quiet, gentle man. When he returns to his birthplace, he speaks Polish. He appears weak and submissive next to his proud and domineering son Shmuel, who is an Israeli stand-up comedian and actor. The film indicates that Mordechai did not discuss the trauma for many years after the Holocaust. During the journey, Mordechai becomes emotional every few minutes, weeping, opening up to his children, and sharing anecdotes. When they meet a Polish soldier in a cemetery, Mordechai admits that, even though decades have passed since the Holocaust, seeing a Polish soldier paralyzes him with fear.

The journey back to Mordechai's roots revives the trauma. When the family reaches his hometown, he tries to explain to his children what the place looked in the 1940s. He matter-of-factly describes where his house stood, where the synagogue stood, where the wagons passed. But when he comes to the site where the *Aktzia* took place and where he saw his father for the last time, he stops. "I can see it right in front of my eyes . . . you cannot imagine what I'm seeing right now", he states. The stories of the past give way to a personal appeal to his dead father. He turns to his dead father and addresses him in the first person as an eight year old, as though standing next to him.

Pizza in Auschwitz follows Holocaust survivor Danny Chanoch and his two children, Shraga (Sagi) and Miri, during a six-day journey to Lithuania and Poland. The film shows how Danny uses black humor to cope with the horror of the past and work through it. He states that he stopped crying as a child in Birkenau, makes jokes about his "BA degree"("Bachelor of Auschwitz"), his "personal doctor" (Mengele), and the "high season" (according to him – the days surrounding Holocaust Martyrs' and Heroes' Remembrance Day).

Although Danny is obviously trying to work through the trauma, he is still completely immersed in the past. The survival tactics he used as a child to escape the *Kinder Aktion* in Kovno and survive Auschwitz have influenced the way he brought up his children. Miri says that he taught them to trust no one, to keep running, to do the opposite of what they are told. Miri explicitly criticizes the fact that this mindset was taught to them at an early age, but Danny does not accept the criticism, since he feels he has successfully brought up strong children.

Unlike the persecuted child he was in the Holocaust, Danny has developed his identity as a confident man, who walks proudly in the European cities even though they meet local Jews who remove their kippot when they step out of the synagogue and warn Danny about local antisemitism. He interrupts the conversations of locals, forcing them to listen to stories of how the Jewish dead were plundered. When they encounter a group of German teens at the Auschwitz-Birkenau Museum, he makes them listen to his stories, eventually declaring that all Germans are the same, "something deep inside them is rotten".

Along the way, he seems to have become rejuvenated by the encounter with his childhood. This reaches its surreal pinnacle when Danny expresses his desire in Auschwitz to spend the night on the bunk in the same barracks where he slept as a prisoner. His children finally convince him to leave. Film scholars Hagai Dagan and Gidi Dishon maintain that *Pizza in Auschwitz* features a unique form of "nostalgia" since trauma and nostalgia are generally considered contradictory. *Pizza in Auschwitz* reveals that nostalgia can also be applied to a traumatic past. This form of nostalgia is not sweet and wistful, but rather ironic and combative, yet it still allows for reminiscence of the past, which helps Danny cope with his suffering.[12]

In *Six Million and One,* the four children of Holocaust survivors Yosef and Mali Fisher travel to Austria where he was imprisoned. They follow his whereabouts during the Holocaust using his secret diary, which was discovered after his death. While alive, Yosef had told very short, fragmented stories about the past including half-sentences such as "we were deported from the village in trains . . . hunger, thirst, suffering, agony . . . Auschwitz, Mengele . . . left-right . . . me and my sister were the only ones who survived".[13] The diary reveals that Yosef was briefly in Auschwitz. He spent most of his time in the Austrian Gusen and Gunskirchen camps. After he passed away, none of his children wanted to read his account of these painful memories except David, the film director. Sections of the diary, narrated throughout the film, reveal that in Israel Yosef led a double life: on the outside he seemed to have started a new life, working hard and raising a large family, but inside, he was haunted by the past. Excerpts from his diary, which manifest it, are read in the soundtrack:

> People often tell me that I'm sad and melancholic. I know that it is hard for people to accept this hybrid which is me. My dear children, even in the happy times in my life [the present with the family] I'm there [in the camps]. I often regret that I survived and I say 'why me.' I'm convinced that all those who belong to my category are like me; they are all actors.

The scenes of his children's journey are interspersed with scenes of an actress standing in front of the camera reciting the various ways people died in the camps (hanging, hunger, heart attack, shooting, etc.). These scenes "haunt" the viewers, just as the sites of these multiple deaths haunted his life.

In *Choice and Destiny*, director Reibenbach documents the everyday life of her parents, Fruma and Yizhak Goldberg, now in their seventies. Throughout the film, Reibenbach conducts an ongoing discussion with Yizhak about his whereabouts during the Holocaust, and he speaks fluently, if distantly, about daily life in the camps. Fruma is unable to discuss the past. Her demeanor and body language tell a story of turmoil, fear, and anxiety. At first glance, the film appears to show a discrepancy in her parents' post-traumatic responses, i.e., "working through" versus "acting out". But the cinematic editing and the film's leitmotif of the grandfather clock suggest that Reibenbach believes that in their home, alongside the building of new lives in Israel and raising a family, time has stood still.

Throughout *Choice and Destiny* Yizhak cites his faith during the Holocaust and about daily survival in the camps. He describes taking the belongings of people who had been sent to the crematoria, buying tobacco and selling it for bread, throwing the dead off their beds to make room for the living, etc. Most of the time Yizhak tells his stories in such a detached manner that he seems to be talking about someone else. He describes being ordered to move the fence in Płaszów where he was imprisoned. When the workers finished, they discovered that they were outside the perimeter. They began debating whether to run away but then decided that there was nowhere to go. When they asked the guards to let them in, the guards refused. After all, they had not registered when they "left" the camp. Reibenbach listens in astonishment and asks, "Why didn't you run away?" "We had nowhere to go", Yizhak answers. "You could have escaped into the woods and hid with the partisans", Reibenbach says. "Nonsense" Yizhak interrupts her. "Polish partisans also killed Jews".

Fruma, who does not talk about the past, frowns when she hears Yizhak's stories. In some scenes she gets up and leaves the room, unable to hear any more. At other times, the only way she can ease her soul after hearing his stories is by obsessively cleaning. Reibenbach documents Fruma polishing the already spotless kitchen, preparing food, and carefully securing the multiple locks on the front door when Yizhak goes out shopping. Towards the end of *Choice and Destiny,* Fruma relents and relates small parts of her life story. She describes the wife of an SS officer who abused her. Her stories provide viewers with insights into other ways of acting out. Fruma says that when she lies in bed, traumatic images from the Holocaust stop her from falling asleep. When she is home alone, she calls out the names of the dead, those who perished without leaving a trace, "without a tomb to put a stone on".

Fruma's silence can be interpreted as an inability to translate the trauma haunting her into words, but this may also be a rational decision. Yohai Ataria claims that survivors may make the conscious choice to maintain silence based on the belief that words normalize the trauma by turning it into a narrative. Silence is an expression of rebellion in a world where words are everything – it is a choice to avoid participating in the game.[14]

As most documentaries contrast Israeli linear time with the circular time of the past, *Choice and Destiny* moves in two timelines: the past, as depicted in Yizhak's stories of the war years from beginning to end and the present, in the form of Yizhak and Fruma's life in Israel. The narrative of the past is linear, in that Yizhak's stories are arranged chronologically from 1939 to 1945. In contrast, the timeline that deals with the present is circular: Yizhak and Fruma are documented as they wake up, shop for groceries, cook, and clean. Yizhak sets the big grandfather clock; they watch some TV and go to sleep. The film's pace is slow and, in that sense, reflects the couple's life in their old age. The precise routine, which gives the couple reassuring comfort, contrasts sharply with their chaotic past, as recollected in Yizhak's stories.[15] But actually, Yizhak and Fruma's routine in Israel is submerged in the past. They speak Yiddish to each other, use very old cutlery (including a spoon that Yizhak took from one of the camps), and when Yizhak leaves the house to go shopping, Fruma tells him to be careful. Even when they watch TV, the program is Polish Prime Minister Lech Walesa apologizing for the Poles' deeds during the Holocaust.

The merging of past and present is also highlighted by the cinematic editing of Yizhak's stories. When he is documented playing with his grandchildren in a park in Israel, Reibenbach embeds his voice-over describing his family in Poland; when Yizhak is filmed in the shower at home washing his face, the soundtrack is made up of his stories about the showers in Auschwitz; when Reibenbach documents a conversation between them over dinner, she asks him specific questions about food in the camps. At the end of each major sequence, Reibenbach returns to the same scene in which Yizhak climbs a ladder and winds the large grandfather clock. For both of them, the Holocaust has not – and never will be – relegated to the past. This repeated scene and the ticking of the clock, a central part of the film's soundtrack, turn the clock into a symbol of the fusing of past and present. It suggests that, for Fruma and Yizhak, time stands still. For both of them, the Holocaust has not – and never will be – relegated to the past.

Second Generation: Transgenerational Transfer and Secondary Traumatic Stress

The term *Second Generation* was coined by Canadian psychoanalysts as a clinical concept, and today it is commonly used to denote the children of Holocaust survivors. In the 1960s, when the issue was first studied, it became clear that second generation survivors shared certain unique mental health characteristics. Since then, more than 400 articles have been written on the question of intergenerational transmission of Holocaust trauma. In the last few decades, the perception that they make up a separate group has been questioned; in particular, whether second generation individuals are a distinct population that has unique and/or more substantial psychological disorders than others. The interpretations can be divided into several main schools of thought: the first suggests that the Second Generation have clear characteristics that are unique and that distinguish them from other groups. These include suspicion, fear, over-protectiveness, interpersonal problems, anger, social detachment, and a constant and haunting preoccupation with the Holocaust.[16] In contrast, the second school of thought considers the Second Generation to have no significant psychological disorders and sees no long-term consequences of the Holocaust. They dismiss the conclusions drawn by proponents of the first school of thought as stereotypical, false generalizations.[17] A third school of thought acknowledges a form of interaction between parents and children that is unique to the relationship between Holocaust survivors and their offspring but considers that it is expressed in many different ways and varies from family to family.[18] Researchers have compared various groups of survivors (differentiated, for example, by the way they survived) to assess the Holocaust's influence on their children.[19]

Holocaust documentaries in Israel since the 1980s have only partially reflected these differences and have mainly portrayed the Second Generation as a separate group who have been affected by their parents' trauma. The common thread is that they were subjected to "transgenerational transfer of the trauma"[20] or "secondary traumatic stress": the indirect exposure to trauma that affects those who were not involved in the actual events. Secondary traumatic stress can be found in the friends and relatives of the traumatized persons, as well as in wider circles. Research has shown that indirect exposure to trauma through an intense cultural and media debate (television, radio, journalism, internet, etc.) can affect people who were not involved. PTSD symptoms, such as stress and anxiety, can appear in people who suffer from secondary traumatic stress, albeit less intensely.[21]

Because of that War begins with the song entitled "Because of that War" from Gila'ad and Poliker's album *Ashes and Dust*. The phrase "because of that war" suggests that World War II and the

Holocaust traumatized not only the survivors but also their children. Gila'ad says he does not have good memories from his childhood, and he does not miss it. "I always remember that I saw myself as different [from the other children] wanting to be like everyone else but cannot". He tells Ben-Dor, the director, that the Holocaust was connected to every facet of his childhood as his mother Halina had turned the past into an integral part of his present: she sang songs from the ghetto, made him a rag doll like the one she had, and when he got bad grades she yelled at him, "Is this why I survived Auschwitz? To see you come home with those grades?" Gila'ad says that in their home the dead were no less alive than the living. All children have a moment of shock where they discover the meaning of death and mortality, but he never experienced this breaking point because he has always lived with the dead.

When asked to discuss his childhood, Yehuda Poliker refers to it as a sequence of Holocaust-related traumas. He says that Jacko, his father, always ate bread greedily, in big bites because that was what he was used to in the camps, "a habit from the Holocaust". One day, when Yehuda was five or six, his father suddenly began choking, and since then Yehuda has stuttered. His parents' extreme worries and anxieties prompted him to live with his parents until he was 30 years old. "I couldn't get out of there" even though he wanted to "I wanted to break free . . . live my life . . . but I cannot leave them . . . they went through so much and suffered so much. When I left, I know it was a trauma for them".

In *Daddy Come to the Fair*, second generation Shmuel uses humor as a defense mechanism against the transgenerational transfer of trauma. The journey to Poland is interspersed with scenes taken from his stand-up routine in a Tel-Aviv club in which he uses black humor to comment on his life as a member of the Second Generation. Shmuel maintains a humorous façade that contradicts the serious purpose of the journey. In the grim atmosphere of his father's search for the dead, Shmuel deliberately wears red, flashy trousers and a red clown nose. Using vulgar humor, he voices his aversion to the Polish surroundings, which remind him of the traumatic past. He criticizes the "ugly, shabby houses" as the family travels through the countryside on the way to his father's hometown. "This is disgusting", he tells his father as they sit and eat in a local restaurant. "I'm going to settle something with you now, you piece of crap. Every Friday you forced me to eat that soup with those 'lokshen' you need to fish out with a snorkel". He says, "perhaps you can still be saved" to a baby at a restaurant. Shmuel is extroverted and loud. He is rude to the Poles, exclaiming, "where were you when they took my grandfather away? Probably as drunk as you are today". He tries to convince himself and the viewers that this journey has nothing to do with him, that it is his father's mission. As far as he is concerned, as he explicitly tells his father, the point of this trip is to put the past behind them, to leave the memories in Europe. His sister, Yael, plays a very important part in the journey. While her role in the film is relatively minor and her voice is rarely heard, the few scenes where she talks to Shmuel about their experiences indicate that she has a positive, warm relationship with their father, filled with empathy and compassion. These scenes are crucial because they upend the image of second generation Holocaust survivors as a homogenous group. Even children brought up in the same family can have different relationships with their parents, alternate perceptions, and different mechanisms to cope with the trauma.

Eventually, the past that Shmuel has tried to detach himself from strikes him in the face during their visit to Auschwitz-Birkenau Museum, where his grandfather perished. Mordechai is shaken by the place, but Shmuel is the one who breaks down, and his defense mechanism disintegrates, causing him to sink into the horrors of the past. He lies down on the ground, crying and saying he wants to die. The same person who had previously wished that his father would disconnect from the past now takes rocks and grass from Auschwitz so he can "plant them" in Tel Aviv.

Shmuel's postmemory is very vividly represented in the Auschwitz scenes. Talking to the camera, Shmuel recounts that, as a child, he would imagine hearing the sound of boots crunching on the gravel and would aimlessly wander along railroad tracks for hours. He calls himself a "coward", saying that had he been a prisoner at Auschwitz, he would probably have tried to escape. Mordechai's experience in Auschwitz allows him to feel as though he has symbolically paid his final respects to his own father. Following this catharsis, Shmuel and Mordechai become closer. Shmuel admits that while he has always wished to become the opposite of his father, he is, in fact, much like him and has even imitated him in many ways. Mordechai realizes that his silence has created difficulties in his relationship with his son. The two agree that the Holocaust was – and still is – a central aspect of their lives as a family, but having openly dealt with it makes it possible for them to become closer.

The film ends with mutual understanding. Shmuel states that the journey has changed his outlook on life. He says that what is left to do now is to walk "into the sunset" of Poland like a clichéd Hollywood ending, and the two laugh together. Yet, like many Holocaust documentaries from that era, the film does not end with full closure. In the final scene, Shmuel attempts to sing the children's song, "Daddy Come to the Fair" [*Abbaleh, bo l'luna park*], which he dedicates to his father, but he finds himself choking with sobs. The film's message is that the secondary traumatic stress cannot be erased from the soul of the Second Generation.

In *Six Million and One,* during the journey to their deceased father's past, the brothers and sister discuss the various ways the silenced trauma shaped their childhood. As they all sit in one of the tunnels the prisoners were forced to dig underground, David's sister, Esti, describes herself growing up with the Holocaust as "an open wound". She exclaims that she does not need this trip to know what her parents went through or the precise experiences her father described in his diary to appreciate him more. "I have lived with it my entire life. . . . Do I look normal to you? Do I look like a person who grew up in a normal family? Every day I bleed. I'm Holocaust from head to toe". During her outpouring of emotion, she also exposes her postmemory, claiming that she does not need to travel to the Mauthausen camps complex to "feel the Holocaust": "I knew exactly how it looks. I wasn't there but I know exactly what it looks like".

> it pisses me off that someone or something prevented me from having parents who love me like parents are supposed to love their daughter. Why?? Why?? . . . My childhood with these parents was not normal, and was fucked up and screwed up, like growing up inside a freezer. . . . I was screwed up.

She describes how she grew up as a child without love, without touch ("mother didn't touch me. She couldn't touch me"). Her brother, Ron'el, like Shmuel in *Daddy Come to the Fair,* deals with his secondary trauma by using black humor. He sardonically suggests that they should start therapy groups in tunnels. He remarks that he, as well, felt the echoes of the trauma, growing up without physical displays of affection from his cold and detached father, a man without feelings, a man of numbers and lists. Gideon disagrees with both of them. He defends their father, reminding his siblings that "our emotional scars are nothing compared to what he went through". He sees their parents as heroes and his memories are of a childhood that was warm and filled with love. He does see himself as suffering from the transgenerational transfer of trauma. His words reflect the discrepancies that exist within families regarding childhood and parental figures. "I didn't have a 'freezer' at home. I had an 'oven.' I had a father who took us on weekends. He devoted his free time to us. He never let us feel that he was a broken, miserable person, who dwells in sadness".

In *Pizza in Auschwitz,* Miri narrates the film with her voice-over, which reveals that, like her father, black humor helps her deal with her inherited trauma. She remarks: "I'm trapped in a week-long reality show about the Holocaust". Her description of their trip indicates that the past is mixed with the present: "We are leaving the hotel and moving onwards, like father and his family left for the ghetto". When the visitors leave a wreath at the place where the family was deported to the camps by rail, a train comes along and cuts through the frame. While eating bread, they comment sardonically that they have now finished their "two-day allowance". The traffic jam at the border is referred to by Miri as a "station along the transfer on the way to the *Lager*".

The film suggests that Miri's intense use of black humor is her way of avoiding drowning in the trauma that she has inherited. She describes how the experiences of her father, who has been telling her brother and her stories about the Holocaust since infancy, affected their childhood negatively. His stories about walking barefoot in the snow were a realistic substitute for Hansel and Gretel. Miri explicitly criticizes telling stories like these to such young children and is opposed to burdening them with details of the Holocaust. She says that having that knowledge made her fear every knock on the door, as she thought it might be the SS. This confession helps explain why, as an adult, she tries to create a mental barrier between her psyche and the trauma through the use of black humor. Miri is also fearful of her surroundings, unlike Danny, her father, who sees no problem in his Orthodox son walking in Vilnius from the synagogue to the hotel on foot on the Sabbath.

As in *Daddy Come to the Fair*, their arrival in Auschwitz-Birkenau reveals just how fragile this defense mechanism is. While visiting the barracks in which Danny was imprisoned and after having heard difficult stories about his life there, Miri breaks into a harsh, piercing monologue, in which she demands, hysterically, that they leave the place because she can no longer handle that amount of horror. At the end of both the journey and the film, Miri concludes:

> When I got off the airplane in Israel, I felt like somebody was following me. It was the Holocaust. It looked tired and a bit worn out. Maybe Zimmerman [the director] was right, when he said that there was no such thing as Holocaust survivors.

Similar to other second generation documentaries, *Pizza in Auschwitz* highlights the trauma and the secondary trauma from which neither generation can break free.

In conclusion, second generation documentaries produced in Israel in the last 30 years tend to focus on individual Holocaust survivors and their stories and devote a great deal of screen time to their memories. These films deal with their experiences under the Nazis and the ways in which their lives after the war were shaped by what they had experienced, while marginalizing the story of national redemption. Many films depict family journeys to Europe to trace family roots and the familial history before and during the Holocaust (primarily in Eastern Europe). They also often focus on the second generation survivors' secondary traumatic stress. They do not reflect the disparities in research on the Second Generation, and represent the offspring as a separate population that has inherited their parents' trauma. The survivors and their descendants deal with it in a variety of ways: but, for both, the trauma blends with the present and time stands still.

Notes

1 Liat Steir-Livny, *Shtei panim bamar'a: yezug nitzolei hashoah bakolnoa haisraeli* (Hebrew) (Jerusalem: Eshkolot-Magnes, 2009), pp. 7–68; Nurith Gertz, *Makhela aheret: nitzolei shoah zarim v'aherim* (Hebrew) (Tel Aviv: Am Oved/The Open University, 2004), pp. 16–37; Moshe Zimmerman, *Al tigu li bashoah* (Hebrew) (Haifa: Haifa University Press, 2002), pp 125–215.

2 Steir-Livny, *Shtei panim bamar'a*, pp. 69–95; Gertz, *Makhela aheret*, pp. 37–41; Zimmerman, *Al tigu li bashoah*, pp. 216–249.

3 Dina Porat, *Café haboker b'reach ha'ashan* (Hebrew) (Jerusalem: Yad Vashem: Am Oved, 2011), pp. 379–396; Dalia Ofer, "The Past That Does Not Pass: Israelis and Holocaust Memory," *Israel Studies* 14, no. 1 Spring (2009), pp. 1–35; Gulie Ne'eman Arad, "Israel and the Shoah: A Tale of Multifarious Taboos," *New German Critique* 90 (Autumn 2003), pp. 5–26.

4 Michal Friedman, "The Double Legacy of Arbeit Macht Frei," *Prooftexts* 22, no. 1+2, Winter/Spring (2002), pp. 200–220; Michal Friedman, "Witnessing for the Witness: Choice and Destiny by Tsipi Reibenbach," *Shofar* 24, no. 1, Fall (2005), pp. 81–93; Steir-Livny, *Shtei panim bamar'a*, pp. 96–127, 150–165.

5 Marianne Hirsch, "Past Lives, First Memories in Exile," *Poetics Today* 17, no. 4 (1996), pp. 659–67.

6 Yoseffa Loshitzky, "Post-Memory Cinema: Second-Generation Israelis Screen the Holocaust," in: Yoseffa Loshitzky (ed.), *Identity Politics on the Israeli Screen* (Texas: University of Texas Press, 2002), pp. 32–71.

7 See for example Loshitzky, "Post-Memory Cinema," pp. 32–71; Gertz, *Makhela aheret*, pp. 42–77; Zimmerman, *Al tigu li bashoah*, pp. 250–334.

8 Sigmund Freud, *Hatipul ha-psichoanaliti* (Hebrew) (Tel Aviv: Am oved), pp. 138–171.

9 See Judith L. Herman, *Trauma v'hachlama* (Hebrew) (Tel Aviv: Am Oved, 1994); "PTSD," in: American Psychiatric Association (ed.), *Diagnostic and Statistical Manual of Mental Disorders*, 5th ed. (Arlington, VA: American Psychiatric Publishing, 2013), pp. 271–280.

10 Dominick LaCapra, *Writing History, Writing Trauma* (Baltimore: Johns Hopkins University Press, 2000), pp. 37–74.

11 Gertz, *Makhela aheret*, p. 93; Zimmermann, *Al tigu li bashoah*, pp. 259–260.

12 Hagai Dagan and Gidi Dishon, "Nostalgyat shoah: iyun mehudash betrauma ubenostalgia leor hamikre shel 'pizza beauschwitz'," (Hebrew) *Teoria v'Bikoret*, Winter (2011), pp. 185–209

13 Nirit Anderman, "The Journey the Lad to the Film 'Six Million and One'," *Ha'aretz*, March 19, 2012 (Hebrew), https://www.haaretz.co.il/1.1666762

14 Yohai Ataria, "Truyma: ne'emanut lashtika," (Hebrew) *History and Theory* 29 (n.d.), http://bezalel.secured.co.il/zope/home/he/1376936935/1388333556.

15 Gertz, *Makhela aheret*, pp. 90–93; Friedman, "Witnessing for the Witness," pp. 87–88.

16 For example, Dina Wardi, *Nosei haHotam* (Hebrew) (Jerusalem: Keter, 1990); Carol A. Kidron, "Hahavnaya haHevratit shel Dor Sheni laShoah," in: Zehava Solomon and Julia Chaitin (eds.), *Yaldut bezel hashoah* (Hebrew) (Tel Aviv: Hakibbutz Hameuchad, 2007), pp. 261–285; Julia Chaitin, "Yeladim venechadim shel nizolim mitmodedim im haSshoah," in: Zehava Solomon and Julia Chaitin (eds.), *Yaldut bezel hashoah* (Hebrew) (Tel Aviv: Hakibbutz Hameuchad, 2007), pp. 304–336.

17 For example, Yoram Hazan, "Dor Sheni laShoah," *Sihot: Israel Journal of Psychotherapy* 1 (1987), pp. 104–108 (Hebrew); Avraham Sagi-Schwartz, et al., "Does Intergenerational Transference of Trauma Skip a Generation? No Meta-Analytic Evidence for Tertiary Traumatization with Third Generation Holocaust Survivors," *Attachment and Human Development* 10, no. 2, June (2008), pp. 105–121.

18 For example, Eva Hoffman, *After Such Knowledge: A Mediation of the Aftermath of the Holocaust* (London: Vintage, 2005). See p. 28; Dan Bar-On, *Bein pahad letikva* (Hebrew) (Tel Aviv: Beit Lochamei Haghetaot and Kibbutz Hameuchad Press, 1994); Iris Milner, *Kirei avar* (Hebrew) (Tel Aviv: Am Oved, 2004), pp. 19–35.

19 Yael Vilchik Aviad and Diana Cohenca-Shibi, "Hakesher shebein nesibot hahisardut shel nitzolei hashoah levein simptomim shel dicaon veharada bekerev bnei hador hasheni lashoah," *Sugiot hevratiyot beisrael* (Hebrew) 16, Summer (2013), pp 113–131. See especially pp. 117–118.

20 Amos Goldberg, "Interviewer," *'Acting Out' and 'Working Through' Trauma*, Excerpt from interview with professor Dominick LaCapra (Cornell University, June 9, 1998).

21 Charles R. Figley, "Compassion Fatigue as Secondary Traumatic Stress Disorder: An Overview," in: Charles R. Figley (ed.), *Compassion Fatigue: Coping with Secondary Ttraumatic Stress Disorder in Those Who Treat the Traumatized* (New York: Brunner-Routledge, 1995), pp. 1–20.

Bibliography

Anderman, Nirit, 2012. "The Journey the Lad to the Film 'Six Million and One'", *Ha'aretz*, March 19, 2012 (Hebrew), www.haaretz.co.il/1.1666762

Ataria, Yohai, no date. "Truyma: ne'emanut lashtika" (Hebrew), *History and Theory* 29 (n.d.), http://bezalel.secured.co.il/zope/home/he/1376936935/1388333556.

Bar-On, Dan, 1994. *Bein pahad letikva*, Tel Aviv: Beit Lochamei Haghetaot and Kibbutz Hameuchad Press (Hebrew).

Chaitin, Julia, 2007. "Yeladim venechadim shel nizolim mitmodedim im haSshoah", in: Zehava Solomon and Julia Chaitin (eds.), *Yaldut bezel hashoah*, Tel Aviv: Hakibbutz Hameuchad: 304–336 (Hebrew).

Dagan, Hagai, and Dishon, Gidi, 2011. "Nostalgyat shoah: iyun mehudash betrauma ubenostalgia leor hamikre shel 'pizza beauschwitz'", *Teoria v'Bikoret*, Winter: 185–209 (Hebrew).

Figley, Charles R., 1995. "Compassion Fatigue as Secondary Traumatic Stress Disorder: An Overview", in: Charles R. Figley (ed.), *Compassion Fatigue: Coping with Secondary Ttraumatic Stress Disorder in Those Who Treat the Traumatized*, New York: Brunner-Routledge: 1–20.

Freud, Sigmund, 1977. *Hatipul ha-psichoanaliti*, Tel Aviv: Am Oved (Hebrew).

Friedman, Michal, 2002. "The Double Legacy of Arbeit Macht Frei", *Prooftexts* 22 (1+2), Winter/Spring: 200–220.

Friedman, Michal, 2005. "Witnessing for the Witness: Choice and Destiny by Tsipi Reibenbach", *Shofar* 24 (1), Fall: 81–93.

Gertz, Nurith, 2004. *Makhela aheret: nitzolei shoah zarim v'aherim*, Tel Aviv: Am Oved/The Open University (Hebrew).

Goldberg, Amos, Interviewer, 1998. *'Acting Out' and 'Working Through' Trauma, Excerpt from Interview with Professor Dominick LaCapra*, Cornell University, June 9, 1998.

Hazan, Yoram, 1987. "Dor Sheni laShoah", *Sihot: Israel Journal of Psychotherapy* 1: 104–108 (Hebrew).

Herman, Judith L., 1994. *Trauma v'hachlama*, Tel Aviv: Am Oved (Hebrew).

Hirsch, Marianne, 1996. "Past Lives, First Memories in Exile", *Poetics Today* 17 (4): 659–667.

Hoffman, Eva, 2005. *After Such Knowledge: A Mediation of the Aftermath of the Holocaust*, London: Vintage.

Kidron, Carol, 2007. "Hahavnaya haHevratit shel Dor Sheni laShoah", in: Zehava Solomon and Julia Chaitin (eds.), *Yaldut bezel hashoah*, Tel Aviv: Hakibbutz Hameuchad: 261–285 (Hebrew).

LaCapra, Dominick, 2000. *Writing History, Writing Trauma*, Baltimore: Johns Hopkins University Press (Hebrew).

Loshitzky, Yoseffa, 2002. *Identity Politics on the Israeli Screen*, Austin, TX: University of Texas Press.

Milner, Iris, 2004. *Kirei Avar*, Tel Aviv: Am Oved (Hebrew).

Ne'eman Arad, Gulie, 2003. "Israel and the Shoah: A Tale of Multifarious Taboos", *New German Critique* 90: 5–26.

Ofer, Dalia, 2009. "The Past That Does Not Pass: Israelis and Holocaust Memory", *Israel Studies* 14 (1), Spring: 1–35.

Porat, Dina, 2011. *Café haboker b'reach ha'ashan*, Jerusalem: Yad Vashem: Am Oved (Hebrew).

"PTSD", in: American Psychiatric Association (ed.), *Diagnostic and Statistical Manual of Mental Disorders*, 5th ed., Arlington, VA: American Psychiatric Publishing, 2013: 271–280.

Sagi-Schwartz, Avraham et al., 2008. "Does Intergenerational Transference of Trauma Skip a Generation? No Meta-Analytic Evidence for Tertiary Traumatization with Third Generation Holocaust Survivors", *Attachment and Human Development* 10 (2), June: 105–121.

Steir-Livny, Liat, 2009. *Shtei panim bamar'a: yezug nitzolei hashoah bakolnoa haisraeli*, Jerusalem: Eshkolot-Magnes (Hebrew).

Vilchik Aviad, Yael, and Cohenca-Shibi, Diana, 2013. "Hakesher shebein nesibot hahisardut shel nitzolei hashoah levein simptomim shel dicaon veharada bekerev bnei hador hasheni lashoah", *Sugiot hevratiyot beisrael* 16, Summer: 113–131 (Hebrew).

Wardi, Dina, 1990. *Nosei haHotam*, Jerusalem: Keter (Hebrew).

Zimmerman, Moshe, 2002. *Al tigu li bashoah*, Haifa: Haifa University Press (Hebrew).

6

THE REPRESENTATION OF SECOND GENERATION HOLOCAUST SURVIVORS AND MURDERERS IN *CERTIFICATE OF LIFE*

On and Off the Stage

Roy Horovitz

Introduction

The Holocaust takes center stage in Israeli theater. Over a hundred original Israeli plays can be classified as "Holocaust plays" (with varying degrees of distinctiveness), thereby making the Holocaust the most "popular" theme in local dramaturgy, far ahead of other central themes (the Israeli-Palestinian conflict, religious–secular, Ashkenazi and Mizrahi. . . .).[1] At any given moment one can find productions of Holocaust plays on the Israeli stage, whether based on original Israeli plays or translated ones.

From the 1980s onwards, Holocaust discourse began to revolve more and more around the life of the Second Generation survivors and intergenerational transference. Thus, these issues also found their way to local drama. Plays like *Shop* and *A Tourist's Guide to Warsaw* (Hillel Mittelpunkt), *Biboff* (Yossi Hadar), *Rochelle Is Getting Married* and *I Am Speaking to You Chinese* (Savyon Liebrecht), *Why Didn't You Come Before the War* (Lizzie Doron), *Elka's Gold* (Yosef Bar-Yosef), *Memories of Second Generation in the bosom of the old city* (David Maayan), *Whereabouts Unknown* (Nava Semel), *Whistle* (Hadar Galron and Jacob Buchan), and others focus on the Second Generation and give them a voice.[2] This stream of original Israeli productions naturally focuses on the stories of the children of the victims.[3] Yet, through the use of foreign translated plays, sons of the victimizers also made their way onto the Israeli stage. Thus, for instance, *Born Guilty* (George Tabori's adaptation of Peter Sichrovsky's book, which is based on interviews the author conducted with children of Nazi families) was staged at the Kahn theater in 1988, at Yoram Levinstein Actors Studio in 1992, and again in 2008 at Tzavta theater.[4]

Ron Elisha's *Certificate of Life* directed by the author of this chapter at The Cameri Theater in 2017 takes the work of representing both the "sons of Abel" and the "sons of Cain" a radical step forward. For the first time, the two traumas from the two opposite sides are given the same space and arranged in an almost symmetrical fashion. The play can be categorized as a "dark comedy" that ends in a kind of "happy end", in which the two sides find peace. Moreover, the play's production in Israel was its world premiere and enjoyed a unique casting, while the biographies of the three

DOI: 10.4324/b23365-8

actresses uncannily resembled those of their characters. Thus, the line between "fiction" and "reality" was exceptionally blurred.

In the spirit of Balme's argument that every theatrical performance moves beyond the stage and takes hold in the space and discourse of its time and locality,[5] this chapter seeks to examine the play and its production through the prism of the representation of second generation Holocaust survivors and murderers. It will then examine the literary and theatrical merits of the work, the biographical links of the cast members and the affinity of the material to the field of the history of the collective memory of the Holocaust in Israel.

Certificate of Life – Plot Summary and Characters

The play unfolds the story of three women who meet once a year at the German council offices: Clara Reich, a Holocaust survivor; her devoted daughter Hilda; and Heidi Rommel – the German clerk who is assigned to their case. The plot stretches over a decade, as each year Clara is required to provide evidence that she is still alive in order to continue receiving her stipend from the German government. This bureaucratic process engenders a series of painful yet humorous encounters: Clara, who is cynical and harsh takes advantage of her yearly summons to make the young German clerk (whose surname is Rommel) miserable. She uses Heidi to settle her historical score ("Frau Rommel's welfare is not my primary concern",[6] she continues to justify her behavior). Clara's daughter Hilda, who accompanies her mother to the offices with due diligence and devotion, finds herself, time and time again, embarrassed by her mother's conduct. She finds excuses for her mother (and in return receives herself a stream of insults from Clara), while Heidi tries to do her work to the best of her ability and avoid unnecessary conflicts. As the years progress, despite the mother's adamant objection, the two young women, the Jew and the German, form a close bond. They learn to recognize the similarities between their life stories and establish both a dialogue and a friendship. Towards the end of the play, Clara begins to suffer from dementia (which also manifests in her forgetting the most crucial event in her life, the Holocaust) and the play ends with her death and burial. Heidi and Hilda emerge from the cemetery holding hands and walking towards a new future. The playwright, then, endows the Second Generation, whose members have gone through the process of working through their history, with the rare gift of living a fuller emotional life and receiving a "certificate of life".

In terms of style, the play excels in its acerbic dark humor, which marks a new stage in the artistic representation of the Holocaust and typifies many of the works written over the past few years.[7] An example of the use of this style can be found in Clara's monologue, in the second scene, in which she makes fun of the absurd situation:

> The German people expended every fibre of their being in annihilating us. They tried everything in their power, from bullets to piano wire to starvation to torture to gas. And then, the war ended and the dust settled and, to their utter disbelief, there we were. The Jews. Still alive. How could this be? ... And so, every year since the fall of the Reich, the very same Germans who were consumed with orchestrating our deaths insist that we prove to them that we are still alive.... So I ask you: Is that or is that not an irony of the most delicious order?
>
> (p. 18)

Certificate of Life was written by Ron Elisha, the "first Australian-Jewish playwright". Elisha was born in Jerusalem in 1951 and immigrated with his family to Melbourne Australia in May 1953. He graduated from medical school in 1975 and for many years worked as a family physician while also writing plays, stories, sketches, and scripts. In 1978, Melbourne Theater Company produced his play

In Duty Bound. Much like *Certificate of Life*, *In Duty Bound* also focuses on second generation Holocaust survivors, and its staging generated a heated debate on xenophobia and racism amongst the Jewish community in Melbourne. His second play, *Einstein*, won both the Australian Writers Guild (AWGIE) for Best Stage Play and Best Script in 1982 and was later produced in the United States and New Zealand. In the following years, his plays were also produced in the United Kingdom, Canada, Poland, France, Belgium, and, of course, Israel. Elisha has won many awards for his writing, including four Australian Writers' Guild Awards, the Mitch Matthews Award (2006), as well as the Houston International Film Festival Award for Best Screenplay.

Elisha's family has not gone through the horrors of the Holocaust. But, in Elisha's 30 years of experience as a physician, he has taken care of hundreds of Holocaust survivors and their families. His patients and their families gave him a rare close glimpse of their world and inspired his intensive writing on this topic. Seven of his "Holocaust plays" have so far been produced,[8] and there are many more waiting in the drawer.[9] For instance, he based the character of Frau Reich, the protagonist of *Certificate of Life*, on one of his patients, Clara Deutsch, a Holocaust survivor from Hungary, who, once a year on the day she had to renew her "certificate of life" would dress up and put on her make up.[10] In an interview he gave a few years ago, Elisha described his dramaturgical work as follows:

> The purpose of my writing is to restore the value of human life to its rightful place. This value is self-referential. Life is its own meaning. There is only one field of human endeavor which drives home this message with any real power: drama. And there is only one tool which is sharp enough to enable drama to rise to the occasion: irony. Taking as its foundation the twin pillars of the precepts 'Live and let live' and 'Do unto others . . .' the forgoing underpins all that I have written.[11]

As stated earlier, the play explored here revolves around the tense encounter between Germans and Jews. Thus, it provides a clear and valuable glimpse not only of the family dynamic that is so typical of the First and Second Generations of the Holocaust (victims and victimizers alike) but also of mother-daughter relationships as is. "What are you – my psychiatrist?" (23) Clara asks Heidi and continues to mock her, "what are you – Oprah?" (36). And still, it is difficult not to comment on a few of the play's psychological aspects: the characters (and their relationships) exist within in a constant dialectic between life and death, a dialectic that is a cornerstone of human life. Clara, who has survived the horrors of the Holocaust, choses life but also holds on to the dead with no ability to let go. Her emotional world is locked in a capsule of rage, bitterness, hatred, and vengeance. She is stuck in a psychic place with no movement, a zone of emotional death. She is an educated and complex woman who has lost her ability to trust people. Even though she denies it, she is overwhelmed with overbearing guilt over her very survival ("guilt? I have nothing for which to apologize", [21]). This is a known phenomenon, which professional literature calls "survivalist guilt". Over the years, Clara has developed a tough exterior to protect herself from her own frightening vulnerability (humor, as we know, functions as a healthy defense mechanism that makes it possible to cope with difficult emotional overloads). A typical dialogue between mother and daughter sounds like the following:

Clara: You're too easily offended.
Hilda: Strangely enough, only when I'm with *you*.
Clara: It's as if you're *looking* for reasons to get upset.
Hilda: I don't have to look very hard.
Clara: It's the one area where we failed you, your father and I. Letting you grow up with a thin skin.
Hilda: It's called sensitivity, mum. And it happens to be one of my *better* qualities.

Clara: Where does it get you, this sensitivity?
Hilda: Not everything in life has to "get" you somewhere, mum.
Clara: Try boarding the train to Auschwitz with a suitcase full of sensitivity.
Hilda: Why do you measure everything against the Holocaust?
Clara: The Holocaust is absolute zero. There's nothing colder. Nothing gets past it. Nothing even gets close. It's always there. Over your shoulder. No matter what. The perfect litmus.
Hilda: You do it on purpose. Because it reduces everything else to insignificance. Including me. And whatever I say, and whatever I do, and whatever I think.
Clara: There's that sensitivity again.

p. 19–20

After the ongoing trauma she experienced in the war, Clara goes into a survivalist mode of doing things – she immigrates, cleans houses for money, marries, has a child, builds her own business, and never stops fighting for her existence. She believes that everything she does is for the benefit of her daughter. Yet, her daughter feels that her mother does not see her. Ever since infancy, Hilda has yearned for a place in Clara's heart; she wishes for nothing but closeness and intimacy, essential nourishments for her psychic existence. However, Hilda keeps failing to reach her mother, since her mother remains attached to the life of her infant daughter who was brutally murdered by the Nazis, thus making it difficult to make room for her living daughter. Paradoxically, the dead daughter lives in the mother's mind much more than her living, breathing daughter.

In *Memorial Candles: Children of the Holocaust*, Dina Wardi describes how second generation children take on the role of "memorial candles". They are born to heal the trauma of their parents who have survived the Holocaust and create a path for the future. Hilda functions as a "memorial candle" for her older sister and is even given her name. She was meant to fill the void in her mother's broken soul. Yet, not only did Hilda not choose this role, she is also guaranteed to fail, since she can never really erase her mother's memory of the trauma. In the fourth scene of the play, Hilda tries to convince her mother to accompany her to the "March of the Living" in Poland. She believes that this trip can help them grow closer and help them heal the wounds of their past. Clara responds to the offer with horror and dismissal:

Clara: I swore in May 1945 that I would never set foot in Europe again. Ever. I see no reason to break that oath now.
Hilda: Do it for me. For my sake.
Clara: I can't. I can't go back there. . . .
Hilda: We're doing a march, mum. Not a death march. A march of the living. You and me together. Saying to Hitler: See? I'm back. Here. Where you tried to kill me. I'm alive. And so's my daughter. Alive. In spite of everything. . . .
Clara: I don't want you to be there. In the gas chambers. Where it happened. I don't want you to breathe that air. . . . It's not an amusement park! . . . It's a place where people died! Innocent people! Agonizing deaths! We don't belong there! You don't belong there!
Hilda: I don't belong *any*where. That's the problem.
Clara: What are you talking about?
Hilda: I don't trust anyone. . . . I'm always afraid that one day they'll turn around and point me out: "There's the Jew!" And that'll be the end of it. . . . I don't want to live that way. I hate living that way! I want to make peace. I want to go back there, where it all happened, and make peace.
Clara: With whom? The neo-Nazis?
Hilda: With myself.

p. 34–38

It is no surprise, then, that these messages drive Hilda to attempt suicide, realizing this death wish would make it possible for her to receive the same status as her dead sister:

> Do you have any idea how many times I've heard that story?. . . . I'm not just hearing the story. I *was* the girl on the bayonet. Hilda. That was her name. Same as mine. And she died. And her father died. And my mother married a man who wasn't good enough to tie her bootlaces. That's *my* father. And she spent thirty years in a brutal, abusive marriage, until I moved out. Then she left him. And spent every waking hour since that day cursing his name. Why she married him, and stayed with him, and had a child with him, God only knows! Why she had a child at *all* utterly defeats me! There was no way any child on the face of this earth was *ever* going to be able to compete with the girl on the bayonet!
>
> p. 28–29

But like many other of her endeavors, this attempt also ends in failure. Hilda's need for an emotional bond threatens Clara. Her bitter experience has taught her that emotional bonding is a dangerous thing that could lead to further unbearable loss. A mother-daughter bond is, by its very nature, strong and complex. In a healthy development, it starts with symbiosis in infancy and should reach a state of independent "separation" and individuality when the child matures. This is not the case for the two women in this play: Clara is in a state of chronic mourning that is turned into melancholy, she identifies with her dead husband and daughter and so is unable to invest her life energy in forming relations with others (as the daughter tells her mother: "you've cut yourself off from the whole world" [49]). Clara and Hilda's relationship encapsulates strong feelings of mutual commitment, concern, vulnerability, rejection, and guilt. They are so symbiotically "intertwined" that it is difficult for them to develop into two separate and independent individuals, who live their life to the fullest (even though they continue to exclaim: "Hilda: I have to listen to you belly-aching every day/Clara: Who asks you to listen? You don't want to listen? Go. I don't need an audience" [22]).

Heidi enters this ambivalent dyadic relationship as a third element. She undermines the delicate status quo that exists between Clara and Hilda and helps tip the balance in favor of the latter. Heidi herself is also trapped in a family story filled with death, lies, and guilt: her father died as a prisoner in a Nazi concentration camp. Heidi was raised believing that father was a political prisoner (red triangle), yet she later discovers the truth that was hidden from her throughout the years – her father was sent to the camps because of his homosexuality (pink triangle).

The relationship between the three women starts on the formal-bureaucratic level but quickly becomes emotionally charged and falls into a pattern of victim-victimizer. Clara sees Heidi as a representative of the German people, the representative of evil; and the encounter between them makes it possible for her internal drama to receive a cynical and aggressive manifestation in reality. Clara was never able to process the trauma she experienced, and her verbal attacks bring her past to life ("you can't blame Hitler for everything . . . He's been dead for sixty years. . . . You can't keep using him as an excuse" [79]), as her daughter tries to remind her to no avail. It is an endless cycle of "repetition in action" or, as Clara herself astutely testifies:

Clara: I have a form saying I'm alive. It's valid for a year. And if that form says I'm alive, then I'm alive. And my pension's alive. Which means they have to keep paying it. Every last Deutschmark. From every last pocket in Germany. So they'll never forget. Until the day I die.

Hilda: So you're going to live forever.

Clara: If that's what it takes.

(p. 33–34)

Unlike her daughter, Clara rejects any thought of death and or suicide. As she states, she needs to stay alive at all costs: "If I die. . . . If I die! . . . Hitler wins. Finally (33). It is of little surprise then, that Clara sees Hilda's budding relationship with Heidi as bitter betrayal:

> Seven billion friends to choose from, and you had to come up with a German. . . . It's too soon! Sixty years is too soon! . . . You want to kill me, don't you. . . . You found a way to kill me.
>
> p. 55–56

Despite Clara's furious objection, the two girls, both Second Generations of the war, find a common language. Both grew up in the shadow of a domineering mother who has lost her husband in the war. Moreover, they have similar experiences (depression, loneliness, and an ongoing inability to maintain romantic relationships with men) and can truly understand one another. The emotional connection between the two women helps create a bit of space in the all-too-close relationship between Clara and her daughter and makes it possible for them to step out their stagnation. Within the newly formed triangle, Hilda tries to shield Heidi from the secret Clara is keeping about Heidi's father, while Heidi tries to mediate Hilda's suffering to Clara: "My own feeling is that Hilda suffers terribly from the legacy of the Holocaust" (44). Heidi slowly transforms from a stereotypical German character to a three-dimensional human being with her own painful story, which slowly unfolds and dismantles the exclusivity of the Jewish suffering. Clara, on her part, remains entrenched in this exclusivity and refutes any attempt to include any of the other victims:

Clara: Communism is not my favorite ideology.
Hilda: But this is a human being in a Nazi concentration camp! Like you! How can you condone that!?
Clara: Because the difference is, he *chose* to become a communist.
Hilda: So!?
Clara: So he knew the score.
Hilda: So he should be murdered for it.
Clara: The communists did their fair share of murdering.
Hilda: Doesn't make it right!
Clara: No, just inevitable

p. 25

In this regard, Clara is not alone and, as mentioned earlier, she reflects the way the Holocaust was commemorated for many years in Israeli society.[12]

Lies and secrets seem to organize the plot of the play as its main motif. As the play progresses, we witness an unfolding of a complex tapestry of lies, half-truths, white lies, and pretenses. These games of truths, lies, and deceit not only play out on the technical and formal procedures (confirming the identity of the Holocaust survivor who will enjoy the stipend) but also and mainly in the play's interpersonal and intimate relationships: the mother, Clara, lied about her age and runs a business for selling wigs (which cover thinning hair and bald spots . . . how symbolic!). Her daughter, Hilda, hides her new friendship with the German clerk, while Heidi also grows up under a "smoke screen" of secrets and half-truths.

Numerous statements throughout the play reveal the central role of lies in it and the characters own awareness of it:

> I've cheated death before. And won. Against odds you wouldn't believe
>
> p. 34

> A person *needs* a little dishonesty. The honest ones died first
>
> p. 39
>
> God only knows the depths of deceit to which the corrupt Hun might sink
>
> p. 17
>
> It's self-interest that got me through Auschwitz. Not honesty.
>
> p. 26

And the most poignant motto, which appears already in the opening lines of the play: "Sometimes, in our twisted little world, corruption *is* the only form of decency" (8).

The characters of the play, though, constantly try to uncover the lies layer by layer and stand before the naked truth, despite the price tag that is attached to it. Unlike their mothers, the second generation daughters recognize their similarities, form an intimate relationship, and most importantly are willing to finally confront their mothers and their past. No wonder, then, that the play ends when Clara is buried with a Jewish ceremony, even though she objected to the idea while she was alive. In the new world, created after the death of the "desert generation", there is no more room for pretense and cover ups: Clara was born Jewish, she lived Jewish, and she will be buried a Jewish woman. The play's final accord sends a clear message: the protagonist failed to reach her goal. She did not reach the immortality she hoped for and cannot continue in her quest for vengeance. Ironically, the daughters of the Second Generation, who longed for death, eventually receive the gift of life and end up with the upper hand in their struggle against their parents. Their clear victory is not merely a result of a numerical advantage (two against one) but also and mainly the result of their ability to grow from hardship. Their story points towards the possibility to move to a new phase and open a new chapter, enjoying a "certificate" for a full life, based on an empowering dialogue and belief in kindness.

Producing the Play at the Cameri Theater – It's All About Casting

Marvin Carlson's book *The Haunted Stage: The Theater as Memory Machine*, which was published in 2003, established the holistic conception of theater as a "memory machine". This metaphor points to the fact that each member of the theatrical event (the written play, the creators, the actors, and even the theater building itself) carry with them a meaningful cultural past. Thus, one of the salient traits of any theatrical performance is its "ghosting": each participant in the creative process is haunted by his own personal and professional "ghosts", which are incorporated into the theatrical work:

> Everything in the theater, the bodies, the materials utilized, the language, the space itself, is now and has always been haunted, and that haunting has been an essential part of the theater's meaning to and reception by its audiences in all times and all places.[13]

However, "ghosts" do not belong solely to the addressers in the theatrical interactions. The addressees, that is, the audience, also come to the theater haunted by their own biographies, artistries, and prepositions, which shape their viewing experience and the reception of the theatrical work.

The encounter between actors and spectators, the pillar of every theatrical event, does not, then, take place in an empty mental space. The actor brings with him the baggage of his own (physical and mental) selfhood and the accumulation of his past roles that accompany him as a shadow, while members of the audience bring their own memories of past experiences and use them to interpret the show.

The audience's body of knowledge also includes a place for what they know about the biography of the actor performing before them. When the actor is famous, a "celebrity", the "memory machine" works overtime and the "ghosts" play an even more distinctive role: the viewer has at his disposable a relative abundance of information about the performers, and the fame of these actors becomes an inseparable part of their theatrical persona and their work. Michael Quinn, who has explored the acting semiotics of famous actors, argues that their performance often brings with it a real collision between the "personal" and the "performative" and fashions a kind of "double identity".[14]

A famous actors' double identity can of course be used in a conscious and artistic manner. Recycling biographical and professional materials is one of the trademarks of postmodernism, and casting famous actors for certain roles can be viewed as part of this general phenomenon and as a dramaturgical strategy of the highest order. This strategy shapes the way the fictional world will be received. When it is done, the actor's personality and his life are turned into an independent text which exists as entity in itself within the artistic productions. This strategy becomes even more significant in historical plays, in which, as Freddie Rokem notes in his book *Performing History*, the actors are not only "performers" but also "witnesses" and "hyper historians".[15]

The casting of the world premiere of *Certificate of Life* at the Cameri theater made, as stated earlier, conscious and maximal use of these tools and included three famous actresses. Miriam Zohar, laureate of the Israel Prize for her body of work, played Clara. Like her character, Zohar is also a Holocaust survivor and receives a stipend from Germany. Odeya Koren (Hilda) is a classic "Second Generation" Holocaust survivor and has also taken care of her deeply traumatized mother for many years. And finally, Sara Von Schwarze (Heidi) comes from a German family of nobility; her grandfather served in the Wehrmacht, while her parents converted to Judaism and even made *aliyah* to Israel ("my parents made me as Germans but had me already as Jews", as she likes to joke). The actresses' affinity for the material of the play, their familiarity with many of its aspects ("I have to do this part", Koren told me after first reading the play, "it has so many things that I wanted to tell my own mother, but didn't dare"), introduced a dimension of authenticity and integrity to the production, for better and for worse. During rehearsals, which often spilled into long personal conversions, I found myself, many times, having to stop and remind the actresses that the play is not "about them". It may be written as a realistic play that strives to represent "truth" and "reality" on stage, yet it is still a "play". It is still a work of art and its executers are still required to keep a measure of aesthetic distance from it that can make it possible for them to "lie" and act as fictional characters within a fictional framework.

The production was set at Hall III, Cameri's most intimate hall, and it took a minimalistic approach. The small stage was divided into three clear acting zones: to the left – Clara's house (marked only with a round table and two seats), to the right – the German clerk's office (a desk, an office chair, and two basic wooden seats for the "visitors"). A green and yellow chest was placed along the entire back wall of the stage. A hospital bed (for the scene that followed Hilda's suicide attempt) and a park bench (on which Hilda and Heidi sit when they meet) emerged out of the green and yellow chest towards center stage. The lighting helped to isolate each scene and hide the other areas of the stage. The play was one hour and twenty minutes long, with no intermission, and the audience was divided into three blocks that "closed" the stage from its three sides. Thus, the claustrophobic sense of suffocation and cramped space in which the characters find themselves was manifested in the physical space. The physical proximity between the audience's chairs and the stage also conflated the distinction between stage and audience and helped the actresses settle for a more "nuanced" performance. In many ways, their acting was cinematic and did not require them to raise their voices or make grand gestures. The minimalistic approach of both the direction and design stems from the desire to turn the spotlight to the performance of the three actresses as the key element in the creation of the theatrical experience.

Zohar was born in Romania in 1931. At the age of nine she was sent to the labor camps in Transnistria, and there she also fell ill with typhus. Her father did not survive the war and she came to Israel with her mother and her brother in 1949, after spending a year in the refugee camps in Cyprus (where she also first took to the stage). It was not long until she became part of the National Theater Habima, where she had a thriving career with dozens of roles. Zohar wished to leave her past behind her and for many years refused to perform in "Holocaust Plays":

> I raised a wall between myself and what I went through there. I barely remember things from there. Only my father getting beat up not far from me at the camp we were taken to at Tul'chyn, and my mother's cries of despair when I was sick with typhus and almost died in her arms. I don't remember and I don't want to remember. I never even filled a "witness page" for my father at Yad Vashem.[16]

Zohar and I have worked together in the past and, after long and adamant attempts, I finally managed to convince her to take the part of Clara. Despite a certain obvious biographical similarity between the actress and the character she plays and Zohar's personal acquaintance with the bureaucratic process of issuing a "certificate of life", they are two very different types of individuals. While Zohar is a real "lady", polite and delicate, Reich is the embodiment of sarcasm and bitterness. Zohar worked very hard to convey Clara's harsh and bitter tone and in the end proved her virtuosic abilities and won the praises of audience and critics alike. The Israeli audience especially enjoyed watching the debates that Zohar as Clara Reich had with her German clerk and viewed Clara's sharp answers as a "fitting Zionistic answer" to their murderers and their decendents. Zohar's complex performance, which oscillated between moments of strength and weakness, helped the audience see the "wounded person" hiding behind the cynical armor and develop sympathy towards Clara's prickly character. Of course, the Israeli audience's long-standing acquaintance with Zohar's personal life story and the deep respect they have for her also helped the audience warm up to Clara's character.

Koren, too, went through an emotionally tumultuous journey when she worked on her role as Hilda. In the text she wrote for the playbill, she shares with the audience her own personal "ghosts":

> I thought it would be easy for me to play Hilda. After all, I know her so well. My mother is a Holocaust survivor, and I am Second Generation. . . . We were also seemingly only mother and daughter, like Clara and Hilda. But it was only seemingly. It was actually very crowded, because the six million also lived with us. They ate dinner with us, sat with us for Passover Seder, walked around our house at night and screamed and cried and woke up my mother. They were with us in our toughest moments to remind me that my life is a piece of cake, and that I don't know the meaning of hunger/freezing/loss/suffering. They were with us in our celebrations to keep us from letting the joy go up to our heads. They were the masters of my mother's guilt for surviving and the kings of my own guilt that I am not a deserving substitute for those who are gone.
>
> I thought it would be easy to play Hilda. . . . In one of the rehearsals, I even brought Miriam Zohar my mother's purse. I thought it would cement my link to the character. It was awful. I was paralyzed, I couldn't speak, I couldn't act I could not even remember the lines. It was too close. . . . I took back my mother's purse.

Hilda's process of freeing herself from her mother's clutches and from taking care of her in the play ("I really don't care. I feel like I've spent my whole life talking about my mum. And I'm sick of it", [73]) is in many ways isomorphic to the process Koren has gone through with her own mother.

Every night, she finished the show and the Kaddish that Hilda says for her mother, in the last scene of the play, with tears washing down her face.

Von Schwarze's performance as Heidi constituted yet another poignant momentum in the play. The monologue she performed at the end of the first scene constitutes an exceptional example of the manner in which an "actor" turns himself into a "text" and the constant tension that exists in his work between "being" and "becoming". Having a German actress speak in Hebrew on an Israeli stage automatically raises the question of who exactly is the speaker: is it the fictional character Heidi? Heidi-Von Schwarze? Von Schwarze herself? Or are all the answers actually correct?

> Frau Reich, I'm going to say this once and once only. The loss of members of your family is truly tragic. But I did not kill them. Nor did my parents. Nor did my uncles nor my aunts.... On behalf of the German nation, I extend to you a profound and heartfelt apology for what happened to you, your family and every other family caught up in the Nazi Holocaust.... I cannot bring back the members of your family. I cannot ease your pain or lessen the injustice done to you. I can only disburse monetary compensation of a pre-determined nature. In order to do so, I must process your paperwork, honestly and impartially. You are not the only Holocaust survivor with whom I must deal, and I am not prepared to fight you tooth and nail every step of the way. Whatever requests I make shall be made in accordance with statutory requirements, and I expect you to comply with such requests, readily and without argument. Have I made myself absolutely clear?
>
> p. 10

The play's authentic casting was also not missed by the critics:

> In many moments throughout the moving performance of *Certificate of Life* ... I felt as if Ron Elisha, who was born in 1951 at exactly the same year that Zohar was accepted to Habima, wrote this play especially for her. Miriam Zohar together with Odeya Koren and Sara Von Schwarze endow their roles and the plot the unique gravitas of their personalities.[17]

Yet, the actresses were not the only members of the production to have an affinity for the fictional material. Many of the creators shared in this history: the late Nava Semel, who translated the play into Hebrew, was also a second Generation descendent, and in her extensive oeuvre as a writer, screenwriter and playwright, she continuously returned to the horrors of the Holocaust and its transgenerational ripples. The writer of these very lines, who also directed the play, comes from German-Jewish descent. My father was born in Berlin in 1927, and my grandfather was smart enough to escape with his family right after the Nazis rose to power. And finally, the play's composer, Shmulik Neufeld, grew up with Holocaust survivors. Of course, the very existence of such an affinity does not guarantee the quality of the final product, and yet the enthusiasm with which the production was received by both critics and audience testifies that, at least in this case, the attempt was successful.

The fact that these materials were so deeply ingrained into our being and the way in which the different roles in the play became a metaphor for the lives of the actresses contributed immensely to the successes of this production, which ran at the Cameri theater for four years in a row.

Summary

Certificate of Life is, in a very deep sense, a humane play. It sketches complex and emotionally fraught relationships and continuously reminds its audience of the simple fact that we are all human. Thus, we all need to occasionally stop and examine the way our history dictates the choices we make. We all have to find the courage within us to redirect our path as individuals.

As the play shows, work does not "liberate", oblivion also does not "liberate"; a humane, honest, and open dialogue is the precisely what can help us free ourselves. Staging the play in Israel bore a special significance, one that exceeded the confines of the theater. After all, the production denied the exclusivity of the Jewish victim and shed light on the suffering of the Second Generation descendants of the murderess. Undoubtably, the use of humor contributed to the smooth delivery of such humanistic messages and their warm acceptance by the Israeli audience. For the first time in its history, the Israeli stage represented Second Generation Holocaust survivors side by side with the Second Generation victimizers of the Holocaust. The international première of the play at the Cameri theater was especially unique, since the similarity between the actresses and their characters was underscored. The Third Generation of survivors may not be represented here on stage, but many of its members were present in the theater when the play was staged. Where will they take things? What kind of "Certificate of Life" will they issue for themselves? What historical memory will they fashion and what will they chose to cede?

Notes

1 Feingold's research mentions around 80 Holocaust plays that were written up until 2010. In the time that has passed, many more plays have been added. Feingold, 2012: 43.

2 The essay focuses on the theatrical representation of Second Generation Holocaust survivors. Later, Third Generation survivors will also receive similar treatment, for instance in Yael Ronen's play *Third Generation*, which debuted in 2009 as a co-production of the Schaubühne, Berlin, and Habima National Theater.

3 Israeli Holocaust plays reflect the zeitgeist in Israeli society while also being part the inspiration of this very same geist. As such, they deal exclusively with the horrible destiny of the Jewish victims.

4 Filling gaps in the local art scene by translating and adapting foreign works is a common and well-known pattern. For instance, Ben Ari has shown how translated literature can be used as a central tool to undermine the Puritan norms that original Israeli literature had adapted in relation to erotica and sex. "Translation", she argues, "is not merely a representation of culture or any other literature, but an intentional action of choice, assembly and reproduction accompanied by direction, manipulation, distortion and concealment of information and planting hidden messages" (Ben-Ari, 2006: 16, Hebrew, my translation). Local readers usually treat translated works more forgivingly, since they believe these works represent norms of a different culture. Thus, translated works can become trailblazers and "break different kinds of taboos from an aspiration to refresh the system or fill the gap with new genres" (Ben-Ari: 128). Of course, we may also extend this logic from literature to theater (which, unlike other cultural channels, is funded mainly by public institutions and is dependent on the agreement of the audience to buy tickets and attend), and it is easy to use translated plays to promote ideological alternative and subversive messages. The assumption is that these messages will be encountered "first through translation and then in the original" (Ben-Ari: 334).

5 Balme, 2010.

6 Quotes from the play are taken from the version that was given to the Cameri Theater and never published (p. 52). All subsequent references to the play are from this unpublished edition of the text, referencing page numbers in brackets.

7 Roberto Benigni's film *Life is Beautiful* (1997), which won the Oscar for best foreign film and sparked controversy, constitutes a good example for this style.

8 These plays include: *In Duty Bound*, *Two*, *The Levin Comedy*, *The Goldberg Variations*, *Death Duties* (*teleplay*), *Certificate of Life* and *Anne Being Frank*.

9 From a conversation I had with the playwright on November 27, 2021.

10 From a conversation I had with the playwright on November 27, 2021.

11 Wayback Machine (archive.org)

12 For more on this, see for instance Yablonka and Cohen, 2022.

13 Carlson, 2003: 15.

14 Quinn, 1990: 155.

15 Rokem, 2000.
16 From a conversation I had with Miriam Zohar on July 3, 2020.
17 Goren, 2017 (my translation)

Bibliography

Balme, Christopher, 2010. "Playbills and the Theatrical Public Sphere", in: Charlotte M. Canning and Thomas Postlewait (eds.), *Representing the Past: Essays in Performance Historiography*, Iowa City, IA: University of Iowa Press: 37–62.

Ben-Ari, Nitsa, 2006. *Suppression of the Erotic: Censorship and Self-Censorship in Hebrew Literature 1930–1980*, Ottawa: University of Ottawa Press.

Carlson, Marvin, 2003. *The Haunted Stage: The Theater as Memory Machine*, Ann Arbor: University of Michigan Press.

Elisha, Ron, 2017. *Certificate of Life.*

Feingold, Ben-Ami, 2012. *The Theme of the Holocaust in Hebrew Drama (2010–1946)* (Hebrew), Tel Aviv: Hakibbutz Hameuhad.

Goren, Zvi, 2017. "'Certificate of Life' – the Price of Survival" (Hebrew), *Habama*, www.habama.co.il/Pages/Description.aspx?Subj=1&Area=0&ArticleID=28399 retrieved on July 21, 2022.

Quinn, Michael, 1990. "Celebrity and the Semiotics of Acting", *New Theater Quarterly* 4: 154–161.

Rokem, Freddie, 2000. *Performing History – Theatrical Representations of the Past in Contemporary Theater*, Iowa City: University of Iowa Press.

Wardi, Dina, 1992. *Memorial Candles: Children of the Holocaust*, London: Routledge.

Yablonka, Hanna, and Cohen, Yigal, 2022. "Jews, You Were Not the Only Victims of the Nazis" (Hebrew), *Haaretz*, February 16, 2022.

7

ARBEIT MACHT FREI

Reality and Meaning in Second Generation Israeli Artists' Artworks

Batya Brutin

Introduction

Concentration camps were a central element in the oppressive structure of the Nazi regime that was imposed on government opponents, minorities, and Jews. The camps were characterized by severe corporal punishment of the prisoners, terrible work conditions, inhuman treatment by the camp staff, and death. On most concentration camps' gates, the phrase *Arbeit Macht Frei* ("Work sets you free") was inscribed in various visual forms.

Arbeit Macht Frei was a common German saying in various forms among German and German-Swiss peasants as part of the Protestant labor ethic. The origin of the phrase is in the name of a novel from 1873 written by the German philologist and novelist Lorenz Diefenbach (1806–1883).[1] In its original meaning, the phrase in the novel was used to describe the way gamblers and crooks go through a process of "repentance" and adopt moral norms of honesty, through productive work that creates value and benefit for them and their environment.

In 1928 the government of the Weimar Republic adopted the phrase as an encouraging message to its proactive work policy, intending to reduce the level of unemployment in post-World War I Germany. In fact, following their rise to power in 1933, the Nazis continued to use the term in its original meaning as part of their efforts to reduce the enormous level of unemployment that still existed in Germany. The Nazi Party in Germany adopted this slogan as an instrument to encourage massive construction policy and initiative of public works that they, too, instituted, as part of the efforts to fight unemployment. When the Nazis established concentration camps for dissidents in Germany, it was only natural for them to place the phrase *Arbeit Macht Frei* on the camps' gates. But this time they used it as a deception, with contempt and irony to instill false hopes in the prisoners' minds and prevent resistance and insurrection. They continued this trend after the invasion of Czechoslovakia when they established the ghetto/camp Theresienstadt and after the occupation of Poland and the establishment of the Auschwitz I camp. Israel Gutman (1923–2013), a Polish-born Israeli historian and a Holocaust survivor, explained:

> Whoever passed through the gate that bears the inscription charged with falsehood, cynicism, and ridicule – *Arbeit Macht Frei* – and the prisoner, is completely deprived of his human

DOI: 10.4324/b23365-9

> existence. Within minutes the prisoner at once lost his name, his identity, his family, his home, his clothes, his body hair, the precious souvenirs in the form of a photograph or letter that connected him with his past, and the freedom to move, to decide where he would go, to be a master of his destiny and future.[2]

The phrase, *Arbeit Macht Frei*, especially the one in Auschwitz I, became a symbolic image of the Holocaust in general and the camps in particular. It was used by artists to depict the harsh reality of incarceration in the camps and to engage with the denial of human freedom, due to the prisoners' opposition to the violent and oppressive regime.

In this article, I will discuss artworks created by second generation Israeli artists who used the *Arbeit Macht Frei* slogan to explain what it meant them and present their interpretation of it.

Life in the Shadow of the Caption

Several studies from the mid-1980s onward have demonstrated the impact of the Holocaust on visual art – in particular for artists who themselves experienced the agony of the Holocaust – but also among their contemporaries.[3] Now, more than 70 years after the Holocaust, it is apparent that its impact has carried over into the works of second generation artists as well.

The term *Second Generation* in this context refers to children born after World War II to parents who lived in Europe under the Nazi regime and suffered its horrors, whether in the ghettos, the camps, in hiding, fleeing from place to place, or as fighters and partisans. It is an international, socially heterogeneous group whose members come from different religious, economic, political, and educational backgrounds. The circumstances of their parents' survival varied from case to case; likewise, some survivors spoke of their brutal experiences while others suppressed their traumatic past beneath a blanket of silence. In both cases, however, the Holocaust has been a presence in the lives of the Second Generation and an inescapable influence.[4]

Second Generation artists, children of Holocaust survivors who were in Auschwitz, have used the Auschwitz gate sign *Arbeit Macht Frei* as a motif in their art from a personal point of view. Haim Maor (b. 1951) is one example of those second generation artists, children of Auschwitz survivors in Israel, who could not stop thinking about their parents' Auschwitz experience, and he dealt with the Auschwitz gate sign *Arbeit Macht Frei* directly. He was born as Haim Binyamin Moshkovitz, named after his grandfather who was murdered in Auschwitz. His father David Moshkovitz (1927–2005) reached Auschwitz with his family in 1942. Of all his extended family of about fifty members, only four survived. In *ARBEIT MACHT FREI* (see Figure 7.1), Maor arranged three wooden panels, two on both sides with rounded shape at the top and closed with a black metal arc colored in blue and a vertical rectangle panel in the neutral color of the wood in the center. The side panels are reminiscent of the Tablets of the Covenant, representing the Jewish people and their law. The central panel divides them in two. On the top of this panel, Maor placed a copper portrait in profile relief within a black ellipse frame of Suzanna, his German friend.[5] She represents the Germans who brought the Holocaust disaster upon the Jewish people. Maor disassembled the phrase *Arbeit Macht Frei* into three separate words, ARBEIT – MACHT – FREI and posted them each one on a different panel. By doing so, every word expresses a new meaning: work – the Nazis used the Jews for forced labor; making – the Nazis executed the murder of the Jews; freedom – the Nazis stole liberty from the Jews.

Figure 7.1 Haim Maor, *ARBEIT MACHT FREI,* 1990, triptych, wood, copper, metal, high-gloss paint, and diverse dimensions. Collection of the artist, Meitar, Israel.

In contrast to Maor, Pnina Liebermann (b. 1954) addressed the *Arbeit Macht Frei* phrase in an emotional, expressive, and direct approach. Her father Haim Baruch (1920–1994) was deported to Auschwitz in 1942. His entire family perished in the Holocaust. In *The Gate to Hell* (Figure 7.2), Liebermann created a theater scene in which the spectators are seen from the rear, observing a horrible "theater performance" of what happened at the Auschwitz gate. She depicted a blurred convoy of people, men, women, and children of different ages passing through the Auschwitz I gate with the inscription *Arbeit Macht Frei*. The people are trapped between the barbed wire fences from all sides. It looks like they are in flames to emphasize the way they were murdered. The artist wishes to deliver information about what happened to the Jewish people during the Holocaust to the next generation, so it will be remembered.[6] The title and style are influenced by *The Gates of Hell*, the monumental bronze sculpture by Auguste Rodin depicting a scene from Dante Alighieri's *Divine Comedy* (1308–1320).

Figure 7.2 Pnina Liebermann, *The Gate to Hell*, 2021, oil on canvas, 35 x 35 cm. Collection of the artist, Ramat Gan, Israel.

Paraphrase of the Phrase

Several artists have changed the words of the original phrase *Arbeit Macht Frei* and presented it not in its original language but in Hebrew, to convey a different message that interested them and paraphrase the original phrase. The first artist to do so was Maor when in 1986 he presented the inscription *Haavoda Meshchreret (Labor Sets You Free)* in his Installation *A Message from Auschwitz – Birkenau to the Han – Jerusalem* (Figure 7.3). Under the sign with the phrase *Haavoda Meshchreret* in black scripture letters on a white background, Maor placed two panels of starched cloth on a hidden wood frame, on which he depicted naked figures, a man on the right and a woman on the left and a black velvet cloth between them to represent the "black hole" of the Holocaust.

On the left end of the right panel, Maor depicted his naked figure in a shameful position with a black shadow behind him. This description is influenced by the documentary photographs showing

Figure 7.3 Haim Maor, *Haavoda Meshchreret (Labor Sets You Free),* 1986, installation, fabric, high-gloss paint, and diverse dimensions. Detail from the installation *A Message from Auschwitz – Birkenau to the Han – Jerusalem.* Collection of the artist, Meitar, Israel.

the Jewish victims being stripped naked and shot into the death pits during the Holocaust. On the left end of the left panel, he depicted a naked woman covering her private parts with her hands and a black shadow on her side.

The woman's pose is reminiscent of the Jewish women victims being stripped naked and shot into the death pits during the Holocaust. At the same time, the artist was influenced by descriptions of the classic figure ofVenus Pudica ("ModestVenus"). By placing the two figures on the left side of the panels Maor created an illusion of imbalance and instability to emphasize the uncertainty and unstable fate of the victims. Maor wanted to show the vulnerability and the humiliation of these figures who represent the Jewish victims and, at the same time, the Nazis' use of a false declaration that "work" will save them from death.[7]

Dvora Morag (b. 1949), the eldest daughter of Auschwitz survivor parents, altered the original phrase into *Haomanut Meshachreret* (Art Unleashes) as part of her *Don't Eat with Open Mouth* installation (Figure 7.4). This artwork is the artist's expression as a daughter of Holocaust survivors, of her struggle with motherhood, caring for her parents, and her own personal fulfillment in life. She placed two unstable chairs holding a long, narrow table with a slit in the center to present the problematic domestic situation she was dealing with. On the table, she attached general and personal photographs from World War II to convey the legacy of the Holocaust to future generations as a commitment to her parents. The artist placed a pair of red shoes under the chairs in shape and size that cannot be worn, to emphasize her situation that prevents her from proceeding on another path of life to make her happy. By altering the negative Auschwitz phrase that Morag, as a daughter of Auschwitz survivors, lived with to a positive expression, she helped free herself from the "chains" and the burden "lying" on her shoulders.[8]

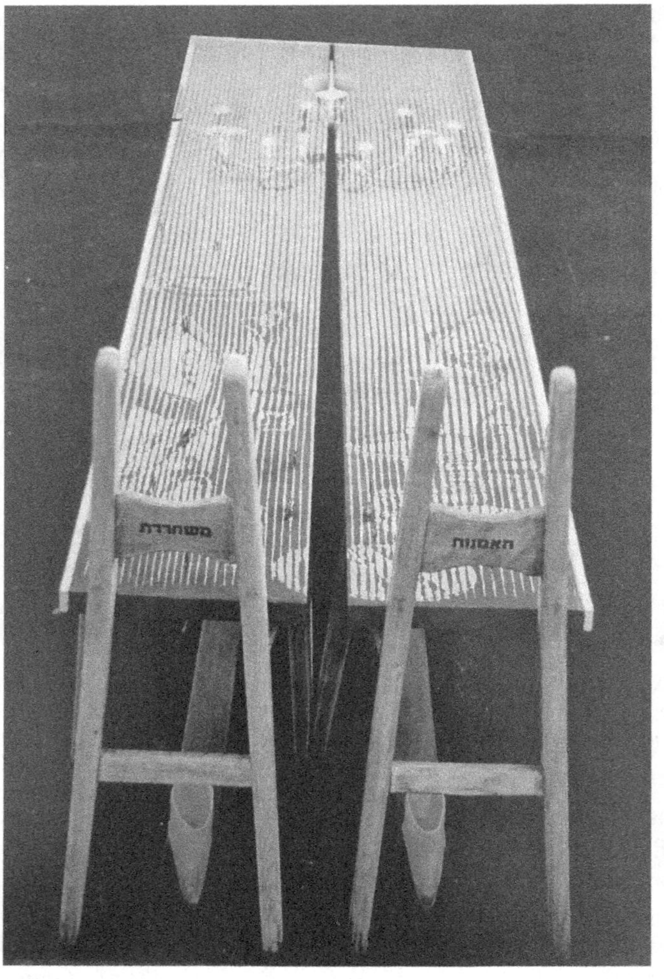

Figure 7.4 Dvora Morag, *Haomut Meshchreret* (*Art Unleashes*), 1996, installation, acrylic paint on wood, fragments of chairs, iron, polyester, photographs, and diverse dimensions. Detail from the installation *Don't Eat with Open Mouth*. Collection of the artist, Tel Aviv, Israel.

Arnon Avni (b. 1953) and Nechama Golan (b. 1947) used the iconic shape of the original phrase *Arbeit Macht Frei* on Auschwitz I's gate, but each one of them installed a different text in Hebrew on it to present their own message. Avni, a cartoonist and illustrator and a son of a Holocaust survivor mother from Bulgaria, responded to demonstrations against the disengagement and displacement of Jewish Israeli settlements from Gush Katif, a bloc of 17 settlements in the southern Gaza strip in 2004, in his cartoon *Hachutzpa Meshchreret* (The audacity unleashes) (Figure 7.5).

The intensified wave of protests was symbolized by the orange color and was one of the strongest protests in the history of Israeli democracy. Although opponents of the disengagement and displacement included both secular and ultra-Orthodox, the overwhelming majority of the protesters belonged to the national-religious stream. The artist, on the other hand, belonged to a small group that came to support members of Kibbutz Kissufim, located adjacent to the Gaza Strip on the Israeli side,

Figure 7.5 Arnon Avni, *Hachutzpa Meshchreret* (*The Audacity Unleashes*), 2004, cartoon, digital drawing (vector image), and diverse dimensions. Collection of the artist, kibbutz Nirim, Israel.

who agreed to establish the disengagement administration offices in their area. Gush Katif settlers were angry about this and threatened to turn the lives of the kibbutz residents into hell.[9]

In *Hachutzpa Meshchreret* Avni responded to the sight of several families, belonging to the protesters, who wore an orange badge on their chests in the shape of a Star of David, a badge that is reminiscent of the yellow badge that the Nazis forced the Jews to wear during the Holocaust. Avni depicted a national-religious family emerging from an undefined background, wearing an orange badge in the shape of a Star of David on their chests, standing under a shaped gate sign reading *Hachutzpa Meshachreret.* The artist protests against their audacity to treat the Holocaust and its memory disrespectfully. He claims that they think that their audacity releases them from basic human manners.

Nechama Golan, daughter of a Holocaust survivor father, also imitated the original iconic shape of Auschwitz I's gate and placed the phrase *Haemuna Meshachreret* (*The Faith Unleashes*) in Hebrew on it (Figure 7.6). The gate is depicted against a gray background of clay and earth to symbolize the ashes of the Jewish victims who were murdered in the death camps. From the difficult atmosphere of death she portrayed, Golan raises the question of faith in God during the Holocaust. The sad and bitter answer lies in the phrase saying that faith liberates from physical to spiritual life. Many Jews continued to believe in God until the last moments of their lives and went to their deaths while praying the *Shema Yisrael* prayer. The question "where was God during the Holocaust" is a philosophical one, which the artist is trying to answer with visual images. Faith in God's purity is transmitted through the white letters of the phrase, while the answer to the difficult question is portrayed as the ashes of the dead.[10]

Figure 7.6 *Nechama Golan, Haemuna Meshchreret* (*The Faith Unleashes*), 2021, installation, clay, soil, 80 x 60 cm. Collection of the artist, Ramat Gan, Israel

Moral Messages

Golan created several artworks depicting the Auschwitz I's gate through which she conveyed moral messages. In both artworks titled *Untitled*, she used the full original photograph of Auschwitz I's gate. In the first artwork (Figure 7.7), Golan substituted the original inscription with a quote in Hebrew from the book of Leviticus 19:18, "*veahavta lere'acha kamocha*" ("love thy neighbor as thyself"). The letters are written in yellow in the biblical style of Torah scrip. This verse is one of the positive commandments and a fundamental Torah concept.

Through the "new" caption on the gate, the artist emphasizes two messages. First, the fact that the Nazis did not behave according to these moral standards. Golan implied the Nazis' crimes through the use of the camp gate and the yellow color, reminiscent of the yellow Star of David they compelled the Jews to wear, to oppress, to humiliate, and to murder them, asking us not to forget. At the same time, the second message reminds the visitors who pass through this open gate, welcoming them to enter, of the value of human love, to prevent the recurrence of cases such as the Holocaust that happened to the Jews.[11]

In the second artwork, Golan clearly and directly intensified the moral message by using a famous saying by Hillel HaZaken (Hillel the Elder)[12] from Babylonian Talmud, Shabbat, 31a, "*Ma shesanu aleicha al taase le'chavercha*" (What is hateful to thee, do not do unto thy fellow man). The Hebrew letters are written in black print. The artist chose to show the camp's gate closed to stress the inscribed sentence and to compel the visitors to "read" and internalize it before they visit the camp site.

Figure 7.7 *Nechama Golan, Untitled*, 2008, digitally manipulated photograph, 60 x 50 cm. Collection of the artist, Ramat Gan, Israel.

Figure 7.8 *Nechama Golan, Untitled*, 2008, digitally manipulated photograph, 60 x 50 cm. Collection of the artist, Ramat Gan, Israel.

Political Message

Some artists have used the *Arbeit Macht Frei* image to convey political statements and messages. For example, Avni, whose artwork we have already seen, responded also to the actual disengagement of Jewish settlements from southern Gaza Strip in his *Noo, Ma Ata Matchil Shuv Im Hamitnachalim Ha'ele . . .* (so, what are you starting with these settlers again . . .) of 2005 (Figure 7.9).

Avni portrayed a couple watching television. The man changes stations with the television remote control and stops at a station describing the events of the Holocaust showing the Auschwitz I's gate and a camp prisoner wearing a striped uniform with a yellow badge with the letter "J" on his chest to emphasize that he is Jewish. The woman is confused between current events of the disengagement from Gaza and the events of the past in the Holocaust, so she says *Noo, Ma Ata Matchil Shuv Im Hamitnachalim Ha'ele . . .* The reason for the confusion is the yellow badge on the chest of the Holocaust victim and the pictures frequently shown on television, of the orange badge worn by the settlers and their supporters against the evacuation. Here the artist protests against the political use of Holocaust symbols and sees this as a deterioration of Holocaust memory to the point of degrading the Holocaust. He added,

Figure 7.9 Arnon Avni, *Noo, Ma Ata Matchil Shuv Im Hamitnachalim Ha'ele . . .* (so, what are you starting with these settlers again . . .), 2005, digital drawing (vector image), diverse dimensions. Collection of the artist, kibbutz Nirim, Israel.

> The citizens of Israel no longer distinguish between the events. Every time we talk about current events and link them to the Holocaust, it is a disregard for what happened in the Holocaust. I showed with caricaturist exaggeration that every time people see the Auschwitz I's gate and a camp prisoner, they think they are settlers.[13]

Remembering the Holocaust

Several artists dealt with the memory of the Holocaust by selecting the phrase *Arbeit Macht Frei*. For example, Michel Kichka (b. 1954), a cartoonist and illustrator whose father was an Auschwitz survivor, referred to the way his father passes on the memory of the Holocaust to future generations in *Memory*, in a personal approach (Figure 7.10). At the age of 70, his father began to accompany groups of high school students from Belgium to the extermination camps as a witness to the Holocaust. It

Figure 7.10 Michel Kichka, *Memory*, 2004, ink and watercolors on paper, 30 x 30 cm. Collection of the artist, Jerusalem, Israel.

became the most important thing in his life. Kichka portrayed his father in front of a group of students at the entrance of Auschwitz I's gate with the inscription *Arbeit Macht Frei*. He holds the flag of Belgian Holocaust survivors, which he takes to every ceremony and trip with students. He is wearing a prisoner's striped hat and a jacket with badges of honor on the chest area. He says (inside the round bubble): "Since my release from the death camps, I have become a lifelong prisoner of my memories".[14]

In contrast, Maor dealt with the memory of the Holocaust with a general approach through a single Holocaust victim in *Alma Rosé: Violin in Auschwitz-Birkenau* (Figure 7.11). This artwork is part of the exhibition *Haim Maor: My Dear Heroes* which deals with the collective and personal memory of the Holocaust.[15] In this painting on wood, Maor refers to the initiative and belief in the power of creativity that made it possible to survive the inferno and the inhuman physical and emotional conditions that prevailed in Auschwitz-Birkenau.

Figure 7.11 Haim Maor, *Alma Rosé: Violin in Auschwitz-Birkenau,* 2021, Acrylic and varnish on wood, 140 x 60 cm. Collection of the artist, Meitar, Israel.

Maor depicted Rosé's portrait, on the upper part, based on a photograph of her from 1927, and below it he wrote her signature and full name. At the lower part, Maor painted three paintings depicting Rosé based on three of her photographs from her pre-World War II performances.

Between the top two paintings, Maor portrayed the inscription *Arbeit Macht Frei* as a veil that connects Rosé's two portraits to emphasize her imprisonment in Auschwitz, to remind people of the harsh reality of incarceration in camps and to deal with the Nazi's denial of human freedom throughout their violent and oppressive regime. In addition, he wished to portray the meaning of the Nazi false phrase *Arbeit Macht Frei* as deception. In Rosé's case, even though she actually "worked" in the camp, she did not survive.[16]

Universal Message

Unlike the uses of the phrase *Arbeit Macht Frei* that we saw until now, Ayana Friedman (b. 1950), daughter of a Holocaust survivor mother, presents a universal message through her perception of the dialog between mankind's actions – in this case, the Nazis' deeds – and the eternal nature, the sea, using the inscription from Auschwitz I's gate in *My Gaze at the Horizon* (Figure 7.12). On the upper part, against the backdrop of a photograph of striped prisoners' camp uniform, Friedman printed the *Arbeit Macht Frei* image three times in an ongoing wave. To highlight the text, she turned it white and framed it with a black contour line.

On the lower part, Friedman placed a photograph of white waves sliding to the seashore. The artist emphasizes the stiffness of the vertical uniforms' stripes and the frozen wave of the inscription versus the soft, horizontal stripes of the waves. In the meeting line between the two parts on the left, there is a shadow of a breakwater with a fence and people walking on it. This shadow conveys an immediate connotation of a Nazi concentration camp and a feeling as if the prisoners' clothes are emerging from the waves.

Friedman's message here is that nature has cycles and viability and so does human history. In her gaze to the horizon, she longs to find vitality and continuity in nature as well as in human deeds to be moral, respectful, with compassion and humaneness.[17]

Figure 7.12 Ayana Friedman, *My Gaze at the Horizon*, 2021, Digital printing on canvas, 140 x 800 cm. Collection of the artist, Ramat Gan, Israel.

Epilogue

On several concentration camps' gates, the inscription *Arbeit Macht Frei* ('Work sets you free') appeared. This inscription on the Auschwitz I's gate became an icon of the Holocaust, and many artists used it as their artistic expression about the Holocaust. Some artists used the phrase *Arbeit Macht Frei* to convey moral, political, and universal messages, while others dealt with the memory of the Holocaust by portraying the phrase *Arbeit Macht Frei.* The Auschwitz I's gate image with the phrase *Arbeit Macht Frei* is a vivid icon of the Holocaust in art today, 77 years after the war's end. Will it continue to be such an icon for future generations, or will it fade away? Only time will tell.

Notes

1 Diefenbach, 1873.
2 Gutman and Berenbaum, 2003: 7–8.
3 Amishai-Maisels, 1993; Kampf, 1984; Roskies, 1984; Young, 2000.
4 Brutin, 2015: 9–10.
5 In 1986 Maor met Suzanna Birgit-Willeh, who came that year from Germany to Kibbutz Givat Haim (Meuhad) where Maor lived at the time as a volunteer and stayed there for eight months. Maor and Suzanna met while working across from each other in the Kibbutz's *Prigat* juice factory. They became friends and, through their conversations, they each determined their own identity. As part of the process that brought them closer, Suzanna could start talking of the existence of a Nazi past in her family, while Maor was confronting his parents' trauma on the one hand and his new experience of meeting a German woman on the other hand. The author's interview with Haim Maor, December 20, 2021, Meitar, Israel; Raz, 1988: 7; Shapira, 1994: 25.
6 The author's interviews with Pnina Liebermann, December 8, 2021; January 1, 2022.
7 Brutin, 2015: 203–208.
8 The author's interviews with Dvora Morag, December 15, 2021; January 19, 2022.
9 The author's correspondence and interview with Arnon Avni, October 31, 2021; January 18, 2022.
10 The author's correspondence and interview with *Nechama Golan*, January 24, 2008; January 18, 2022. Brutin, 2008: 12.
11 The author's correspondence and interview with *Nechama Golan*, January 24, 2008; January 18, 2022.
12 According to tradition Hillel HaZaken (Babylon c. 110 BCE – Jerusalem 10 CE) was a sage, scholar, and Jewish religious leader, associated with the development of the Mishnah and the Talmud.
13 The author's correspondence and interview with Arnon Avni, October 31, 2021; January 18, 2022.
14 The author's correspondence and interview with Michel Kichka, December 3, 2020; December 13, 2021.
15 Alma Rosé (1944–06) was a well-known Austrian Jewish violinist. When she was imprisoned in Auschwitz-Birkenau in April 1943, armed with a violin, a conductor's wand, and strong willpower, she managed to form a group of women prisoners and created an orchestra. Their participation in the orchestra was their only hope of survival. From August 1943 she was the capo of the music block, a special block for her and the orchestra members, which gave them improved conditions. Rosé conducted and managed the orchestra until April 4, 1944, when she died under mysterious circumstances. Brutin, 2022: 20–21.
16 The author's correspondence and interview with Haim Maor, December 30, 2021; January 19, 24, 2022.
17 The author's correspondence and interview with Ayana Friedman, January 8–9, 2021; January 21, 2022.

Bibliography

Amishai-Maisels, Ziva, 1993. *Depiction and Interpretation: The Influence of the Holocaust on the Visual Arts*, Oxford: Pergamon.

Brutin, Batya, 2008. *In the Shadow of the Holocaust, "Second Generation" Israeli Artists*, Budapest: Peter Wilhelm Art Projects (Catalog, Hungarian and English).

Brutin, Batya, 2015. *Hayerusha, Hashoah Beyetzirotehem Shel Omanim Israelim Bnei Hador Hasheni (The Inheritance, The Holocaust in the Artworks of Second Generation Israeli Artists)*, Jerusalem: Magnes and Yad Vashem (Hebrew).

Brutin, Batya, 2022. *Haim Maor: My Dear Herose*, Rishon Lezion: Beit Yad Lebanim (Catalog, Hebrew).

Diefenbach, Lorenz, 1873. *Arbeit Macht Frei – Erzählung*, Bremen: J. Kühtmann's Buchhandlung (German).

Gutman, Israel, and Berenbaum, Michael, 2003. *Anatomy of the Auschwitz Death Camp*, Jerusalem: Yad Vashem (Hebrew).

Kampf, Avram, 1984. *Jewish Experience in the Art of the Twentieth Century*, South Hadley: Bergin and Garvey.

Levi, Primo, 2013. *If This is a Man, the Truce*, London: Abacus.

Raz, Sari, 1988. "Netivei Ha-Zikaron" (Paths of Memory), *Maariv* 7 (Hebrew).

Roskies, David G., 1984. *Against the Apocalypse: Responses to Catastrophe in Modern Jewish Culture*, Cambridge, MA: Harvard University Press.

Shapira, Ruth, 1994. "Et Ha-Shoah Asu Anashim Tarbutiim" (The Holocaust Was Perpetrated by Civilized People), *Maariv*, Weekend Supplement: 25 (Hebrew).

Young, James E., 2000. *At Memory's Edge: After-Images of the Holocaust in Contemporary Art and Architecture*, New Haven: Yale University Press.

8

THE ROLE OF MUSIC IN SHAPING HOLOCAUST MEMORY

An Intergenerational Process of Preservation and Transmission

Rachel Kollender

Preface

Musical activity was part of everyday life during the Holocaust – in the ghettos and camps and among the partisan groups. The musical repertoire that survived the war is still meaningful for the survivors and plays an important role in the process of preserving the memory and transmitting it to the next generations. It is a direct and indirect means of transmitting facts about the past. On one hand it is a "live" testimony, as oral artifacts preserve the original voice of the past. On the other hand, it tells the story of similar events that other people (or victims) experienced. This duality enables the survivors to tell their stories and express repressed feelings as if they are "bystanders" without involving hidden emotions. My focus is on songs (mostly in Yiddish but also in other languages) that were performed during the Holocaust and immediately afterwards and the ways in which they function as vehicles of memory. Everyday life; struggles within the ghettos and camps; behavior of Jewish officials; emotions of fear, despair, and hope; and spiritual resistance[1] – all are hinted and described in the songs.

Many studies have been conducted over the past 60 years, dealing with memory influencing post-trauma behavior. Only few of them are based on the role of music.[2] The results have been inconsistent,[3] usually emphasizing the survivors and disregarding the children's experience. My research, presented here, focuses on both – survivors and next generations. It is based on music that was performed and is still remembered and performed and relies on a case study that is analyzed from three aspects:

1 My own experience as member of the Second Generation.
2 As teacher and lecturer of the Holocaust music to youngsters and students who are Third Generation, many of whom are not offspring of Holocaust survivors and do not have direct family ties to the Holocaust.
3 Field work – recording and interviewing survivors who are willing to preserve, for the next generations, the music that they had heard and that was sung during the Nazi era.

They willingly share recollections of their musical experiences. This exposure to both old and young generations (survivors, my parents, my children, students) seems to me fundamental in order

DOI: 10.4324/b23365-10

to understand the interpersonal process of passing on the memory of the Holocaust to the next generations.[4]

The Lyrical, Historical, Traditional, and Emotional Power of Music

Music is one of the most important media through which ideas and attitudes about the past are constructed and shared.[5] Thus music of the Holocaust offers an insight into the inner lives of Jewish communities before and during the Holocaust. The repertoire of this current research includes three categories:

1 Old prewar popular tunes and folk songs in Yiddish, Hebrew, Ladino, Russian, Polish, Italian, German, and Dutch that became popular during the Holocaust: the texts of these songs commemorate the community that was ruined. Some of these songs quote excerpts of Jewish liturgy; some of them came later to be viewed as prophetic. A famous example is the song "Our little village is in flame", created in 1938 by Mordekhai Gebirtig or "ghetto", the text written in 1932 by Abraham Reisen and music composed by Arie Ben Erez Abrahamson:

A gezunt zalber acht	Healthy eight persons
Und bettn nur zwei	And beds only two
Und kumt un di nacht	And the night draws near,
Wu schlufen zei . . .	Where shall they all sleep . . .[6]

2 Songs composed during the war, documenting the killing, struggle, dreadful and devastating conditions, despair, and fear of ghetto life: Every ghetto had its own local character and system of survival, which were reflected in its unique brand of cultural and musical activity. Therefore, every ghetto had its own pattern of musical activities.[7] Some of the songs include new texts adapted to familiar old melodies. On the one hand, this includes using popular Jewish tunes as part of the need to remember the past by preserving the musical Jewish heritage, while on the other hand it shows the desire to document the daily life in the ghettos and concentration camps. One of these songs is the famous *Oifn Prijpechik* – "On the stove":

Oifn Prijpetchik	On the stove
Brent a Faierl	A fire burns
Un in Schtub is hejss . . .	And the room is warm . . .[8]

This song, with same melody, was recast as *Zurick fun der Arbet* – "Back from work", documenting the gate and life in Kovno ghetto:

Baym geto toyerl	Near the ghetto gate
Brent a fayerl	A fire burns
Di kontrol is groys . . .	The control is fierce . . .[9]

Also new songs were composed in the ghettos, as for example the song "*Arois is gegangen a Jid*" (One morning a Jew went out into the street), of Warsaw ghetto – providing a revealing picture of the life in the ghetto – or the song about Haim Rumkovsky in Lodz ghetto, describing the system of governing the ghetto by the leader. Ghetto songs from the Soviet Union are based upon Soviet popular melodies, stressing march-like style.

Songs were created also in the labor and extermination camps, documenting the killing, hard labor, humiliation, and hunger. In addition to "forced" music, which was performed according to orders of the Nazis,[10] the songs were performed silently and intimately, far from the suppressors' ears. This was a declaration of Jewish identity, in many cases as substitute for holy rituals and spiritual exclamation. Survivors from Thessaloniki, for example, recall their singing in Ladino in Auschwitz. They chose old traditional folk tunes, changing the original texts into curses for the oppressors and expressions of longing for their homeland. An example of such lament is the song "Sweet Saloniki", composed by Yakov Levi, TheSalonoki and Auschwitz survivor. The tune is based on a popular Greek tune.[11]

But laments, as "fragments of the tragedy",[12] were not the only type of popular songs sung in the ghettos and death camps during that time. We can also find humoristic and satirical songs, full of hatred for the tormentors and contempt towards oppressors, side by side with songs of hope, optimism, calls for revenge, and proclamations of enduring faith, as means of fighting despair. These announcements of endurance and hope give the songs their vitality, thus presenting the past in colors that the young generations, many years after the war, can easier absorb. For example, the songs "*minuten fun* Bitokhen" (Moments of confidence) or "*Yidn Zol zayn freilekh*" (Jews rejoice), by Mordekhai Gebirtig:

Yidn zol zayn freylekh	Jews rejoice
Shoyn nit lang ikh hof . . .	The day is not far off . . .[13]

Singing became also part of the partisan activities, expressing homesickness, desire for revenge, and praise of the partisans' brave activities. These songs, partly composed by musicians, mainly based on Russian tunes with texts of poets who had managed to escape from the ghetto and join up with partisan bands, have short symmetrical phrases, skipping intervals, fast tempo, and dotted rhythmic values. For example, we can mention the well-known "Partisan Hymn" by Hirsch Glik and "*Shtey oyf tsum Kamf*" (Get up and fight) by Lea Svirsky, both based on Soviet folk tunes. It seems to me that the combination of bravery, resistance, and protest, in addition to the march-like tunes, gives the songs a special flavor, and therefore they are still very popular among the partisan survivors and catch easily the attention of young listeners.

3 Heterogeneous musical activities flourished in the Displaced Persons camps in Germany and elsewhere in Europe immediately after the war: Songs from the pre-war period, songs from the ghettos and concentration camps, as well as songs newly created were sung and performed on improvised stages.[14] The desire of "togetherness" was very strong among the survivors, and because of the variety of languages among them, songs were mainly in Yiddish, which was the common known language. In addition, Hebrew arranged songs became popular among the residents of these camps. Many new, easily absorbed melodies, which had been "transported" from the concentration camps to the DP camps, were set to liturgical and para-liturgical texts, declaring again the victory of the Jewish spirit.[15]

Most of these songs resulted from collaboration between anonymous poets and musicians, who probably were amateur artists. Only few of them were well-known professional artists. The texts and the music were created almost simultaneously. These songs spread orally. They were not written down, and they may therefore be considered part of an oral tradition. The musical style of the songs is based, as mentioned, on Western tonality, repeated rhythmic patterns, simple melodic motives, and a symmetrical melodic contour. Some of them are inspired by the spirit of Hassidic melodies. Most of the songs are syllabic.

Music is, therefore, a kind of testimony that combines many contradictory elements: it documents in detail concrete events, places, and people but also hints of hushed details;[16] it sorrowfully sheds light on the past and on the world that was destroyed[17] but also encourages and expresses optimism and hope; it is a combination of personal stories and memories as well as collective remembrance; it reflects the conflict of survivors between the wish to forget their stories and the need to tell them.

Psychological and historical reasons encouraged initiatives of collecting and preserving the songs that were sung during the Holocaust. This activity had started already during the Holocaust and in its immediate aftermath. The collectors, for example Shmerke Kaczerginski, David Boder, Zami Feder, and Ben Stonehill, wanted to preserve the music and stories while they were still fresh in the memory of the survivors.[18] Their aim was to save the songs not for those who were alive and singing but for those who would come after, so that they would know what had happened. The corpus of recordings and documents of this precious material, preserving the voices of the victims, is the basis for my research.[19]

My Personal Musical Story

The tragic past penetrated my childhood: I was raised by Holocaust survivor parents who were believing, religious, full of confidence, and had the drive to fulfill their mission of rebuilding their family and community. The Holocaust was always hovering above, but the atmosphere at home was optimistic and vital. Stories of their past were not silenced, and I was aware of their history and felt myself to be a "memorial candle",[20] mainly because I was told that my aunt, who had been murdered in the ghetto, was an amateur pianist (as well as a student of mathematics). The piano was my beloved instrument; I studied piano and music theory from a very young age and was proud to carry the burden, replacing my murdered aunt. I felt that my duty was to preserve her memory by playing the conventional repertoire that she had probably played, which included mainly European art music (what we used to call "classic"). But the repertoire of my grandmother (the surviving mother of my aunt) was different. She knew many pre-war songs but preferred to hum, quietly, songs that she had learned in the concentration camps. These songs were fascinating and encouraged me to learn more about her story and the story of my parents, their spiritual heroism and the function of music as a memorial vehicle. I realized that these "Holocaust songs" were in danger of disappearing forever, therefore I directed my efforts to record and document this music and teach it to the next generations, thus expanding my individual-personal process of memory into collective-communal memory. By transmitting this music, which I receive from surviving witnesses, I can proudly call myself "witness of witnesses". I am sure that the experiences of my family, as well as the role of music in commemorating the Holocaust, shaped my personal identity.

Documenting Music of Survivors

The echoes of the Holocaust can easily be identified among the survivors who have music reminiscent from the Nazi era. The ability of music to stimulate memory, evoking and helping in the process of reminding details and transmitting them across generations, was ascertained while interviewing the survivors, who come from various socio-cultural environments; their background and life experiences are as diverse as their geographical origins.[21] I was aware of the survivors' difficulty in opening up in front of a stranger. I understood that they could not tell me everything, but I wanted to achieve intimacy with them. Therefore, a combined approach of singing and dialogue, encouraging the survivors to present their testimony freely, was used. I discovered that, while expressing emotions, it is easier to sing them than to testify verbally. When songs evoked strong emotions, the survivors were more likely to describe their autobiographical memory. During the interviews they explained how music was a means through which they had acted and how music helped them to respond to what was happening.[22] Each survivor painted, by singing, a personal picture of what had happened, trying to express his (or her) own story. These musical pieces associated with specific periods and events helped them remember details, thus creating an individual-personal expression.[23] As we know, each song mentioned by the survivors is an individual testimony, therefore multiple versions of the same song, sung by different survivors, show that every survivor remembered things differently. This means that we cannot point at one "correct" version. For some of them, songs served as a tombstone, recalling the past as they knew it before the war, as well as commemorating the life and death of the murdered victims.[24] For others, singing was a means to tell what cannot be expressed otherwise. All of the survivors who were interviewed declared that they tried to leave a concrete reminder for coming generations, perpetuating their stories by songs.[25] Thus the songs of the Holocaust can be considered as "small stories"[26] that may lead to greater experiences of empathy on the side of the listeners.

While recording and interviewing, I also used memoirs as sources of information about the musical activity of the surviving writers. I discovered that as a result of the fact that the repertoire was transmitted, spread, and preserved orally, some songs had more than one version. Nobody could point at the authentic text and melodic line, therefore each version serves as an authentic document and should be preserved.

Difficulties concerning the language arose several times during interviews with the survivors, while making an effort to explain the songs sung in foreign languages. The survivors usually sang only one stanza of the songs and preferred to explain the content of the full text.

During the process of documenting music, I discovered that memory founded on family talks[27] and familial communication is fundamental in the process of transmitting the memory to the next generations. Survivors with close family ties, who spoke openly about their Holocaust experience, have easily transmitted their Holocaust legacy to their children and grandchildren. Their musical repertoire has been absorbed and corresponded fluently, giving voice also to unspoken stories and feelings. This encouraged them to transmit the memory also to the general public.[28]

Holocaust-related Musical Activity of the Second and Third Generations

Memory of the Holocaust among members of the Second and Third Generations poses a challenge to scholars who focus mainly on history and social subjects. The young generations are busy with daily life and pay less attention to commemorating the past. But since the 1980s, a new voice about the Holocaust is being heard – the voice of the survivors' offspring, those who were not "there".[29] Among the causes that stimulated this process were the production of films on the subject of the Holocaust; Eastern Europe opening the gates for visitors; survivors visiting the places they had known before and during the Nazi era; high school students' visits, as organized groups, under the supervision of ministry of education; and new patterns that have been shaped for the activities and events of the Holocaust Memorial Day. It is also important to mention that the ageing of the survivors has focused public attention on the need to preserve their testimony, including their musical repertoire.[30] As the private and collective memory undergoes a process of change, thus the unwillingness of the young generations to bear the weight of the Holocaust memory also has changed. They express a desire to "melt" the past into the present. In some cases, their connection to the Holocaust has started and developed as a result of listening to music of the survivors, which has become a mediator between the past and the present life of the survivors.

The results of my personal study, based on lengthy conversations and meetings with Holocaust survivor offspring, show that they are eager to hear the musical testimony of the survivors but feel ashamed that they cannot really experience the pain. They experience a dichotomy in relation to the subject of Holocaust: on the one hand Holocaust music functions as a window into a world that they want desperately to blot out, while on the other hand they desire to express what has not been experienced directly by them. In these cases, music is a means that helps them express their feelings.

My study has identified two categories of musical activity among Second and Third Generations, based on the musical and textual repertoires of the Holocaust. These categories reflect different perspectives of preservation and transmission of the memory:

1 Students who participate in courses[31] and lectures that deal with the music of the Holocaust – they consider the repertoire of the Holocaust as a historical testimony. They are stimulated by the music and analyze the historical background of the songs. They try to understand the musical elements that are "Western" oriented and remind them of popular European music,[32] and in some cases they refer to their grandparents and ask about additional information.[33] For them, Holocaust memory is shaped by creating knowledge. They consider the songs as providing historical and social information, regarding the authentic music of the past as testimony.

2 Artists,[34] students, and youngsters who create original music and infuse Holocaust themes into their musical composition They abandon the traditional Western style – which is typical of the songs that survived – and prefer to compose in rock, pop, or acoustic folk styles. In some cases, they use lyrics and poems from the Holocaust era,[35] but in most cases they create new texts on which the music is based. This is the solution of the dichotomy presented earlier: they recognize the importance of the Holocaust memory but prefer not to quote the music of previous generations. Modern music is created, based on what the composers heard from the survivors. The new musical repertoire matches the current popular musical style and reaches a much greater audience. In this way memory is spread to a larger population and becomes a synthesis of past and present,[36] symbolizing the ongoing process of memory. It is clear that the representation of the Holocaust in modern Israeli music is created by Second, Third, and Fourth Generations. It includes performances of music composed during the Holocaust as well as new compositions on Holocaust themes. This authentic modern approach combines old and new and is part of the model that summarizes the process of transmission. It seems to me that these recent works fulfill the will of the previous generations to preserve the old world but also built a new one.

Conclusion

"My ancestors are chanting psalms
Their voices blossom like tiny cotton-flowers,
And I join them with
"here I am, poor and needy".[37]

In my case study I tried to shed light on the diverse ways in which music functions as stimulating the memory of the Holocaust. Driven by my private musical story, I realized the urgency of collecting the music of the survivors before it is irrevocably lost. My project started with documenting and recording and expanded into an intergenerational study of memory and music. I discovered that the memory of the Holocaust, transmitted from survivors to the next generations is multi-faceted, and various modes of interpersonal patterns of communication can be identified.

For the survivors, music serves the purpose of nostalgia, memory, and commemoration. By singing the old songs they come back to where they, their family, and their community had been, thus creating a "monument" for those who perished.

Being confronted with this musical repertoire of the survivors creates a sense of mutual understanding, therefore it is a meaningful factor in transmitting the memory of the Holocaust. The Second, Third, and Fourth Generations who undertake the mission of preserving the memory study the music and create new styles, composed on Holocaust themes. This authentic modern style combines old and new and is part of the model that summarizes the process of memory transmission:

Song → Stimulating memory → Survivor → Transmission to next generations
Private story Collective memory

No doubt that, thanks to the music that is preserved and rearranged, the sounds of the victims will reverberate forever. They did not survive the war, but their sounds continue to resonate.

Notes

1 Gilbert, 2008: 118; Gilbert, 2010: 302.
2 For example, Fisher, 2019; Wiseman and Barber, 2008.
3 Friedman, 2017: 155–157. Also the way in which the Holocaust memory has shaped Israeli identity has not necessarily been uniform. Gampel, 1988.
4 This bond between the past and future generations is a central factor in understanding the power of music. See Baumel, 1995: 151, in relation to literature.
5 Gilbert, 2008: 109.
6 The song was written in Yiddish. Full text and translation, including reference – see Kollender, 2010: 94.
7 Kollender, 2010: 96.
8 Janda and Sprecher, 1962: 140–143.
9 Vinkovetzky and others, 1987: 133–135.
10 The repertoire of this sort of music included mainly well-known Western compositions.
11 Hoch, 2002: 223.
12 Gilbert, 2008: 118.
13 Vinkovetzky and others, 1987: 157–159.
14 Gilbert, 2010: 289.
15 It is interesting to note that this attitude of demonstrating the Jewish identity and spiritual endurance is a very meaningful issue transmitted by the survivors.
16 Ofer, 2009: 13; Belfi, 2016: 979.
17 Sometimes there is an idealization of pre-war communal life.
18 There is also a detailed inventory of musical performances that is the project of the Hamburg University, see Werb, 2010: 75.
19 Gilbert, 2010: 301. As mentioned later, I go on with this project, collecting and documenting the songs of the victims.
20 Wardi, 1992: 214–258.
21 During the last 15 years I have recorded and documented the musical repertoires and personal stories of around 25 survivors, creating a corpus of around 250 songs. I met each of the witnesses several times. At the end of the sessions, I provided them with recordings of the interviews, which included spoken and sung testimony. Almost all of the witnesses told me that they gave the recordings to their offspring.
22 Gilbert, 2008: 117.
23 It is interesting to note that the same song, performed by two different survivors, evoked different memories.
24 Rosen, 2010: 107; Gilbert, 2008: 108; Gilbert, 2010: 295.
25 Baumel, 1995: 146.
26 Breznitz, 2006: 43.

27 Ofer, 2009: 6.
28 Ofer, 2009: 12.
29 Ofer, 2009: 10; Sicher, 1998: 170.
30 Meyers and Zandberg, 2002: 392.
31 I give such a course in the music department at Bar Ilan University. During 12 meetings they become aware of the rich repertoire that was created and performed during the Nazi era and afterwards. They learn about historical facts, social organizations, values, and morals. They have a chance to express their emotions and attitudes towards dilemmas that are hinted at in the songs. I encourage them to "find" survivors and record their testimony, including the music they still remember.
32 Most of the songs – like "Partisan song", "sleep my child", "Therezin Hymn", etc. are completely based on Western musical elements such as harmonic intervals, symmetry, and tonality. This familiar musical structure enables them to focus on the textual material of the songs and pay attention to events, persons, places, dilemmas, and values that are represented in the songs.
33 This is, in my opinion, the way the offspring help the survivors to cope with the difficulties of trauma and memory.
34 Mainly musicians, for example Yehuda Poliker, Hava Alberstein, and others, who compose, arrange, and perform.
35 As for example the original music of Uri Meiselman, set to text by Abramek Kopelowitz, a boy of Lodz who was murdered in the ghetto.
36 Friedman, 2017: 165.
37 Psalm chapter 102, verse 1. Poem by Tania Hadar. See Hadar-Klein, 2014: 63.

Bibliography

Baumel, Judith, 1995. "In Everlasting Memory: Individual and Communal Holocaust Commemoration in Israel", in: Robert Wistrich and David Ohana (eds.), *The Shaping of Israeli Identity: Myth, Memory and Trauma*, London: Frank Cass: 146–170.

Belfi, Ami M. et al., 2016. "Music Evokes Vivid Autobiographical Memories", *Memory* 24 (7): 979–989.

Breznitz, Shlomo, 2006. "The Advantage of Delay", in: Steven T. Katz and Alan Rosen (eds.), *Obliged by Memory: Literature, Religion, Ethics*, Syracuse: Syracuse University Press: 43–51.

Fisher, Atarah, 2019. "The Role of Music on Holocaust Survivor Offspring and How It Influenced Their Relationship with Their Parents", *Psychology of Music* 49 (3): 311–332.

Friedman, Jonathan C., 2017. "Performing Grief: The Music of Three Children of Holocaust Survivors – Geddy Lee, Yehuda Poliker and Mike Brant", *Journal of Modern Jewish Studies* 16 (1): 153–167.

Gampel, Jolanda, 1988. "Identification, Identity and Transgenerational Transmission", in: Yitzhak Kashti et al. (eds.), *A Quest for Identity – Post War Jewish Biographies*, Tel Aviv: School of Education, Tel Aviv University: 157–186.

Gilbert, Shirli, 2008. "Buried Monuments: Yiddish Songs and Holocaust Memory", *History Workshop Journal* 66: 108–128.

Gilbert, Shilri, 2010. "We Long for a Home: Songs and Survival Among Jewish Displaced Persons", in: Avinoam J. Patt and Michael Berkowitz (eds.), *We Are Here: New Approaches to Jewish Displaced Persons in Postwar Germany*, Detroit: Wayne State University Press: 289–307.

Hadar-Klein, Rebeka-Tania, 2014. *Insinged Psalms*, Tel-Aviv: Hakibutz Hameuchad.

Hoch, Moshe, 2002. *Kolot Mitoch Hachoshech*, Jerusalem: Yad Vashem (In Hebrew).

Janda, Elsbeth, and Sprecher, Max M., 1962. *Lieder aus dem Ghetto*, Munchen: Ehrenwirth.

Kollender, Rachel, 2010. "Jewish Music in the Holocaust: An Assertion of Plural Identities", in: Kevin C. Karnes and Lewi Sheptovitsky (eds.), *Across Centuries and Countries*, Frankfurt am Mein: Peter Lang: 93–108.

Meyers, Oren, and Zandberg, Eyal, 2002. "The Sound Track of Memory: Ashes and Dust and the Commemoration of the Holocaust in Israeli Popular Culture", *Media, Culture and Society* 24: 389–408.

Ofer, Dalia, 2009. "The Past That Does Not Pass: Israelis and Holocaust Memory", *Israel Studies* 14 (1): 1–35.

Rosen, Alan, 2010. *The Wonder of their Voices*, Oxford: Oxford University Press.

Sicher, Efraim, 1998. "In the Shadow of History: Second Generation Witness and Artists and the Shaping of Holocaust Memory in Israel and America", *Judaism* 47 (2): 169–185.

Vinkovetzky, Aharon, et al., 1987. *Anthology of Yiddish Folksongs*, vol. IV, Jerusalem: Mount Scopus Publications.
Wardi, Dina, 1992. *Memorial Candles: Children of the Holocaust*, London: Routhledge.
Werb, Bret, 2010. "*Vu ahin zol ich geyn*? Music of Displaced Persons", in: Kevin C. Karnes and Lewi Sheptovitsky (eds.), *Across Centuries and Countries*, Frankfurt am Mein: Peter Lang: 75–91.
Wiseman, Hadas, and Barber, Jack P., 2008. "Growing Up to the Music of Knowing – Not Knowing: Reflections and Clinical Implications", in: Hadas Wiseman and Jacques P. Barber (eds.), *Echoes of the Trauma: Rational Themes and Emotions in Children of Holocaust Survivors*, New York: Cambridge University Press: 230–248.

9

HOLOCAUST REMEMBRANCE

Music as a Therapeutic Tool That Mediates Between Holocaust Survivors and Their Offspring

Atarah Fisher

Background

Music is known for its means to affect us emotionally and physically, making it a unique therapeutic tool capable of offering a broad range of health and wellness benefits, both psychological and physiological. It is known that it can bring a change in behavior, can penetrate the subconscious, and can develop awareness of the environment, regardless of the individual's mental or physical state or level of intelligence or education.[1] Music therapy researchers argue that the benefits of musical activities include mood improvement, self-expression, catharsis, facilitating grieving, relaxation, reflection, socialization, community building, stress reduction, and more.

Music Therapy for Trauma Victims

Music can also play a role in helping individuals and communities to cope with trauma, whether it be through the intervention of music therapists, community music making programs, or individual music listening.

The fact that music can be used to enhance coping with distress and with traumatic and post-traumatic situations is well documented in music therapy literature. For example, children who experienced war and other mass trauma, refugees both adolescent and adults, and post-war soldiers.[2]

Music therapists, working with victims of trauma, use their musical skills to create an interpersonal relationship such that they can relate to their client's different emotions, to help raise different memories relating to their loses, to come to terms with their identity, and to reach deeper understandings leading to a state of relaxation.[3] Different techniques are used to ameliorate post-traumatic symptoms. For example, guided imagery, improvising with musical instruments, singing with a client, and song writing.

Guided Imagery

During the 1970s Helen Bonny, a music therapist, developed a technique where she plays a music extract, suited to the client's specific needs, and using verbal processing she can help recognize the traumatic fears from the past. It is a form of self-hypnosis. Thus, it enables the client to be able to come to terms with fears that previously weren't able to be resolved.

 DOI: 10.4324/b23365-11

Improvisation

Another technique is using improvisation, giving the trauma a voice, and bringing harmony to the soul. As described by Amir:[4]

> Throughout the process, the client's playing serves as a mirror to her inner being. Playing only classical compositions at the beginning of the process fulfilled the client's need to feel secure and showed her strong need for control. As the process continued and more trust was gained, the client was able to improvise. These improvisations started the journey into her inner world and served as a vehicle to expose the trauma and to evoke emotions, images, memories, and events that were connected to it. Through the improvisations the trauma was processed and dealt with. By telling the story of the trauma, grieving the pain, and working through it, both musically and verbally, the traumatic memory slowly transformed into a healthier memory.

Singing With a Client

Diane Austin[5] developed a technique in music therapy based on singing. She explains that there are three reasons that explain how singing aids traumatized victims. First, singing requires control of our breathing, specifically involving breathing deeply. This control has an effect that causes slowing down of the heart-rate, calming the nervous system, leading to the person being more relaxed. Second, by taking a deep breath we can control our feelings. "The way we breathe influences how we feel, and what we feel has a direct effect on how we breathe". Third, the muscular patterns when singing not only reflect our emotions but can provide an outlet for intense internal feelings.

Song Writing

The power of songs is best described by Bruscia:[6]

> Songs are ways that human beings explore emotions. They express who we are and how we feel, they bring us closer together, they keep us company when we are alone. They articulate our beliefs and values. As the years pass, songs bear witness to our lives. They allow us to relive the past, to examine the present, and to voice our dreams for the future. Songs weave tales of our joys and sorrows, they reveal our innermost secrets, and they express our hopes and disappointments, our fears and triumphs. They are our musical diaries. They are the sounds of our personal development.

For trauma victims, actually writing songs enables them to process their emotions and to reach some form of individual relaxation. Song writing with groups in music therapy reported that the process of writing about their trauma allows them to regain their agency to tell their own stories.[7]

Second Generation

In his book *One Generation After*, Elie Wiesel,[8] a Holocaust survivor, wrote: "One can die in Auschwitz after Auschwitz". Although members of the Second Generation were not in the Holocaust, their lives are lived in the shadow of their parents' trauma. Numerous studies have discussed the intergenerational transmission of trauma from survivors to their children, the second generation relationship, and communication with their parents. Such studies focused on aspects such as fear of separation, obsession with food, preoccupation with death, and impending disaster. Symptoms such as outbursts of anger, tension, depression, and sadness were found to be prevalent.[9] Other issues concerning parent-child relationships that became apparent in the literature focused on the lack of emotional connections, leading to a number of common behaviors. For example, anger that their parents weren't there for them and feelings of shame about their parents' past.[10] In contrast, some members of the Second Generation experienced over-protection to the extreme of inhibiting their freedom and independence. Evidence further suggests that there may be specific factors linking parental PTSD with secondary traumatization, depressive symptoms, and parentification of the child's role,[11] due to guilt feelings that evolved into empathic distress for their parent's suffering.[12]

The form of communication between the parent and the child stemmed from the trauma. When there was no communication relating to the Holocaust between the two generations, it is referred to by Bar-On as a "wall of silence", whereas Danieli called this a "conspiracy of silence".[13] On the other end of the spectrum there are cases where too much information about the traumatic experience was revealed. Another issue that arises in relation to the Second Generation is the challenge to find its members' self-identity. Wardi[14] referred to the way surviving parents transmitted their trauma, memories, and hopes to their children, turning them into a "memorial candle", leading to the need of these children to seek professional aid in establishing a new identity and self-esteem. The Second Generation had an additional role: to remember not only the family that perished but also the community and traditions. Sometimes parents saw their children as a substitute for an entire nation that became extinct in the Holocaust and not just for family members who perished.

Music Therapy with Second Generation

There are not many case studies referring to music therapy both with Holocaust survivors and with the Second Generation. Timmerman,[15] a German music therapist, describes how he worked with Ludmilla, a 43-year-old musician who had emigrated with her parents from Russia to Germany. Her Jewish mother escaped from the Nazis, but her family perished in the Holocaust. During the treatment, Ludmila revealed fears and phobias she had about the dead and the funerals. The highlight of the therapy was her improvisation with seven different percussion instruments in memory of her relatives who had perished in the Holocaust while she read their names. Until then, Ludmila had refrained from mentioning the family members who perished in the Holocaust. This experience enabled her to grieve for family members she had never met, highlighting the intergenerational transference discussed earlier and the power of music to soften the conspiracy of silence. Schulberg[16] described her experiences as Second Generation to a Holocaust survivor. With the help of guided imagery and music (GIM), she managed to process Holocaust themes that were an inseparable part of her life and enabled her to independently control her life.

No doubt the conventional form of music therapy helps aids victims of trauma – but what happens when there is no real framework? This research investigates the way musicians, who are Second Generation to the Holocaust trauma, chose and use their music in their daily lives and explores the effect it had on their traumatic childhood.

Case Studies with Second-generation Musicians

Representatives of the Second Generation, aged 55–67, all of whom engage in music, were interviewed. The interview was conducted based on a semi-structured questionnaire, in which the interviewee was asked to talk about their musical experiences, focusing on the meaning of music regarding their relationship with their parents. In addition, prior to the interview, each participant was asked to prepare three musical extracts: one extract which, according to the interviewee, represents their father; another that represents their mother; and a third musical extract that the interviewee considers to best represent themselves. These musical extracts were played during the interview in order to enrich the interview and gain a deeper understanding of the musical world of the participant.

A wide range of themes emerged from the data analysis, some of which fall outside the focus of this article. In order to understand the therapeutic role of music in terms of the relationship between Holocaust survivors and their children, I wish to discuss three of the interviewees whom I call Ella, Naphtali, and Yocheved.[17]

Ella: "This Is My Mission, to Tell the World My Parents' Story, Through Music"

Background

Ella described her childhood as difficult and sad. She remembered the many times she ran away from home to friends. Her friends, on the other hand, did not come to her house because of their fear of her father, "from the hard look in his eyes". Although her parents did not talk about the Holocaust, the Holocaust was present from morning to evening. "It was to eat it for breakfast, lunch and dinner".

"The motive of silence was strongly emphasized in our home. On the one hand, I knew that they had a very dark past in the Holocaust and suffered terribly, but on the other hand, we were not told any details". Ella spoke about her feelings as a child, emphasizing the feeling of sadness and loneliness. She testified that she inherited her "sadness" from her parents and found a place to express her sadness through music. "I naturally invested all my sadness and all my soul in music. . . . My pain, my sadness I can express through music". In addition, her mother constantly made her feel anxious about her father; if something happened to him, Ella and her sister would be blamed, so they should not upset him.

A turning point happened at the age of 13; Ella accidentally found her father's diary. In this diary he wrote about his life during the war. For the first time, Ella learned that her father was married before the war and that he had a three-year-old son. The Nazis murdered her father's family, his wife and son. In 1983 her father decided that he wanted to write a book based on the diary he wrote during the war and asked Ella and her sister to proofread the book. Years later Ella was offered to compose music. She immediately knew what the theme would be: "I said to myself I have to write an opera based on my father's diary.[18] This is the right thing to do. It is my mission".

Ella described her relationship with her father as a complex one. In fact, her real relationship with him started only after his death, "I now have a dialogue with my father. A positive dialogue". Ella relates to her father's life story through music, she came to understand him and through her music formed a means of communication.

Ella chose to represent her father with the musical opera that she composed *Can Heaven be Void*, which is based on her father's diary, the one he wrote during the war. The highlight of the opera, the actual extract that Ella chose to represent her father, is her father's ten commandments[19] on which she was brought up. In this extract the narrator reads aloud in a voice that gradually becomes louder together with the orchestra, crescendoing, leading the listener to feel the tension and horror, up to the final commandment that is shouted aloud: "Do not believe – the heavens are void", then a few seconds of silence. The audience is left breathless.

Ella described her relationship with her mother as a harsh one. A mother that didn't believe in her musical talent. Only years later after she heard Ella's composition *Can Heaven be Void*, did she understand and appreciate her daughter's talent. Her mother suffered from manic depression. On one exceptional moment, when her mother was in a "high", her mother related to her a traumatic experience that she suffered towards the end of the war.

Ella chose to represent her mother with the eighth scene from the chamber opera "Baruchs Schweigen" (Baruch's Silence) that she transcribed and composed in 2010.[20] The opera is based on the true story of her family; the plot of the eighth scene describes what happened to her mother, a young lady right after the war. Her mother and grandmother were refugees and, on their way, they met a Russian officer who seemed to want to help them, but all he really wanted was the young beautiful girl. At night he raped Ella's mother. From the rape, her mother became pregnant and had an abortion without anesthesia.

The music that accompanies this scene with the Soviet soldiers is accompanied by a pleasant love song "Rina, I love the sky". "My mother used to sing this song to me as a child, in Russian". This song, as used by Ella, expresses two contrasting emotions. On the one hand, it is a love song; the words express a man's great love for a woman, and on the other hand, in the context of the opera, it is a song that accompanies the rape. This combination conveys a message of horror and trauma, a message that cannot always be conveyed in words but can perhaps be conveyed symbolically through music. Ella leads the listener to a harsh, mysterious, and frightening atmosphere. The music has a minor scale and dynamics that often change, where the orchestra plays dissonant tones. The same musical technique is repeated with the opera *Can Heaven be Void*, representing her father.

Ella chose to represent herself with the second movement from a piano concerto that she composed. Ella described this concerto as a prayer. The musical style in this chapter clearly reflects certain periods in her life. Ella described the whole concerto as an autobiographical work that, in fact, embraces her life from her childhood to the present day. She explained that the concerto contains various emotions since it was written when her mother, the last immediate member of her family, was critically ill. Ella used a major mode, the tempo is slow, the timbre is soft, and the atmosphere is a romantic, longing, nostalgic, typical of tenderness.

Naftali: "Music Is My Main Communication with My Mother, We Speak via Music"

Background

Naftali defines not only his mother as a Holocaust survivor but also himself, even though he was born many years after the Holocaust.[21] Naftali grew up in a musical environment; his mother was a music teacher, and his father a cantor. Even though he had no real musical education, today he is a musical composer.

Naftali had mixed feelings regarding his mother. On the one hand he was sent to a boarding school but would talk with his mother regularly and recounts that he missed home. But on the other hand, he remembers feeling a lack of warmth and physical love from his mother. As he grew up, he recounts how his mother had periods of depression, where she could spend days in bed. As a result, Naftali found himself spending even less time at home.

There was a special moment when Naftali felt that he was emotionally close to his mother. Every Friday evening when she lit the Shabbat candles, she would sing the song "The sun at the top of the trees"[22] written by Bialik, and sang it according to a composition by Naftali's grandfather.[23] Naftali chose to represent his mother with this song. His mother didn't expose Naftali to her Holocaust experience, and, as a child, Naftali avoided Holocaust ceremonies. He would skip school on Holocaust memorial days.

After returning from a family roots journey to Europe, where his mother opened up, breaking the silence, Naftali rearranged the tune as composed by his grandfather. Until now, the Holocaust had been taboo, but rearranging this tune marked a new relationship to the Holocaust for Naftali. He now writes songs for Holocaust ceremonies and retells his mother's Holocaust story. No longer does he avoid Holocaust ceremonies; he is now on the stage.

Naftali starts the song accompanied by a piano, side flute, electronic music, and xylophone. His voice inspires purity, calmness, serenity, and warmth. The melody reflects tenderness, purity, calmness, and warmth. He used a slow tempo, consonance melody, and soft timbre to create this atmosphere.

Naftali chose to represent himself with the song "I had a Child", a song that he composed to the words written by a mother who lost her son in a plane crash. This song reminds him of his son, who died at the age of three after a serious illness. Naftali seldomly hears the song, since it helps him to relax.

Yocheved: "My Role Was to Make My Father Laugh, and to Keep Him Happy"

Background

Yocheved described the climate of her house as very difficult. Both her parents were Holocaust survivors. Her father didn't talk about the Holocaust, and she only learned about her father's Holocaust experience on his deathbed. However, Yocheved pressured her mother to open up. To try to persuade her mother, she claimed that all her friends were aware of their parents' experiences. But the truth was that her friends' parents also remained silent. They were all afraid to expose their children to their traumatic past. After many requests, her mother would sometimes share very shocking incidents from the Holocaust.

There was constant tension in Yocheved's home. It was necessary to remain silent, due to her father being a very stressed person. The emotional atmosphere was of deprivation of warmth and love. Yocheved described a house without hugs and kisses, except after lighting Shabbat candles on Friday night. The feeling that was engraved in Yocheved was sadness. Yocheved testified that she was a very sad girl and that she grew up with parents who did not provide for her emotional needs. Yocheved described a dissonance between her emotional needs and her parents' attitude towards her. "I needed to be awakened in the morning calmly, not in thunderous voices, like my mother used to shout". The communication was through commands: "come", "go", "bring". Yocheved spent much of her time away from home.

Her relationship with her father can be divided into two; the everyday connection, a connection in which she described how she was afraid of him, and a musical connection, a connection of warmth and love. When Yocheved's father was in a good mood her family would sing traditional tunes around the table. Specifically, during the Saturday traditional meal, they would sing tunes that her father remembered from his childhood. Yocheved was particularly proud since these tunes are not commonly known, since they are local tunes from her father's hometown. Yocheved chose a song representing her father, based on an extract from the Babylonian Talmud: "Extinguishing the candle".[24] Analyzing the music shows that there is a long recitative opening section. The tune is very challenging regarding the harmonies. The scale changes from a minor scale to a major scale. The rhythm changes from slow to a cheerful and bouncy style and then again returns to the first style.

Yocheved's relationship with her mother was different. Her mother instructed her as a young girl to become a music teacher. Yocheved listened to her mother, however she appreciated her mother for encouraging her to develop her musical talent. She described how her mother insisted that she and her sisters should all learn to play instruments. Her mother would accompany them to the Conservatory, spending all her savings on her daughters' music lessons, even at the expense of buying food and clothing. She chose to represent her mother with a musical extract called "*Les yeux noirs*", a musical extract she played on the accordion, in her first concert. It seems to be a kind of tribute to her mother. Yocheved progressed, making a profession from her music, unsurprisingly becoming a music teacher.

Yocheved could not think of a musical piece that represented herself.

Discussion

Through my analysis of the case studies, I saw how Ella, Naftali, and Yocheved unconsciously used musical therapeutic techniques in order to cope with their childhood trauma and how they overcame characteristics that typify the Second Generation: transmission of trauma, identity issues, and specifically their connection with their parents.

All the interviewees described growing up in homes with a harsh environment. Tension and sadness were part of their daily lives.

Analyzing the Means They Used to Overcome Second Generation Phenomena

Naftali, for example, who understood how much the song "The sun at the top of the trees" was significant for his mother, surprised her by reviving the song and creating a new musical arrangement. Singing this new arrangement became a ritual in the house every Friday evening, changing the atmosphere to being far calmer and more emotional. Yocheved would sing to her father, out of an understanding that she was raising his morale and changing the atmosphere that was in the house. Yocheved became protective of her parents, known as parentification of the child. Instead of returning anger with anger, she turned to her music, singing songs together with her parents, often songs that she taught them, thus, creating an atmosphere of normality and pleasantness.

During their childhood, Naftali and Yocheved managed to please and calm their parents by music, as opposed to Ella who used her music just to calm herself. Ella's parents didn't appreciate her music. Only at a later age when Ella became a famous musician did her mother recognize her talents and ability. Her father did not live to see her musical success.

Music also had a significant role in breaking the conspiracy of silence. Naftali, as described earlier, grew up in an environment where the Holocaust was taboo. A family roots trip with his mother broke the silence. The trigger that changed everything happened while standing in a forest in Europe when his mother asked all to hold hands together and then to sing "The sun at the top of the trees". Naftali asked whether they sang like this in the Holocaust; she answered: "Of course not" and then opened up.

Ella grew up in a home that did not talk about the Holocaust, even though the Holocaust was present at all hours of the day. The silence ended when her father, reaching old age, demanded that she and her sister take the diary that he wrote and turn it into a book. Ella described that the process of writing her father's story as very difficult and often quite shocking. While writing, she often cried without being able to stop her tears. After publishing the book, Ella took his request one step further. She composed two operas that were based on her parents' past. The operas were translated in a number of languages and performed in Israel, Europe, and the United States.

As a child, Ella spoke about dealing with complicated identity issues. She was ashamed of her parents' culture and language and refused to speak Polish. She wanted to feel Israeli. Her music brought her to an understanding that her identity is a combination of being Israeli, with European roots. She learned to live peacefully with her identity.

As a result of breaking the silence, the interviewees now revive their parents' story and culture. Taking upon themselves the role to remember the perished, they revive the forgotten past. Yocheved felt responsible for preserving tunes from her father's community, a community that almost totally perished in the Holocaust, teaching them to her children and grandchildren on every possible occasion. She was content that I, as a musician, didn't know the melody that she chose to represent her father.

Naftali, who as a child ran away from every Holocaust symbol, now composes songs related to the Holocaust, sings them, and tells his mother's story at Holocaust memorial ceremonies and in front of large audiences.

Self-music Therapy

All the interviewees were qualified musicians; none of them had music therapy backgrounds, yet they all unconsciously used therapeutic musical techniques to overcome their inherited trauma. They used their musical skills to tell their own story.

In this study I saw a clear type of "self-music therapy" that was evident from the way the interviewees presented their music. This type of self-music therapy is also called in the literature "health musicking".[25] The interviewees who used music and especially their own music making (musicking) were oblivious to the health-promoting functions of music. The context of music therapy is not restricted to a clinical one.

After composing the opera based on her father's life, Ella understood him in a different perspective, as if she could now have a positive dialogue with him, even thought he was no longer alive. This feeling was a kind of therapy for her. As a child she was ashamed of her parents speaking Polish, and Yiddish, yet now she used that same language to retell her parents' and her family's Holocaust stories. She was no longer embarrassed. On the contrary, she is now proud of her heritage and identity and sees it as her mission in life to perform her operas on the Holocaust, specifically in Europe, in countries that had been occupied by the Nazis. This became a kind of closure of her childhood.

Ella's father in his diary wrote how he sought revenge after his immediate family were killed. The revenge and victory came years later through Ella's music. Her music is played all over Europe also by German actors.

> My father who so sought for revenge after the murder of his family members, did not get to see the revenge, that a German orchestra should sit there, a German actor should read his text, and a German audience should hear it, this is the revenge, that my father so wanted and could not fulfill in his life.

Through her music, the victory that her father so much needed for his mental calmness she has now achieved. The mental calmness is now hers.

Yocheved's music that she played that she sang and the songs that she taught her family had a calming and joyful effect, not only on herself but also for the rest of the family. "Music has a role in our home, to bring happiness". Yocheved sought and longed for those magical moments where the trauma was set aside and happiness would be present, thus promoting a healthier atmosphere, a family therapy.

After composing the song "The sun at the top of the trees", the relationship between Naftali and his mother changed. Singing together created the means for a social media where they could communicate without any obstacles, one of the goals in music therapy.

Epilogue

I will end on a personal note. The interviewees taught me that you need not immerse yourself within trauma. With the aid of music, it is possible to see life in a more positive way, finding tranquility instead of despair. As a music therapist, this research has strengthened my understanding that music has the power to heal mental pain and to strengthen parental communication wherever it is impaired by trauma.

Notes

1 Alvin and Warwick, 1997.
2 Gerber, 2014; Loewy and Stewart, 2004; Wiess and Bensimon, 2020; Sunderland et al., 2019; Bensimon, 2020.
3 Orth, 2005.
4 Amir, 2004: 103.
5 Austin, 2002.
6 Bruscia, 1998: 9.
7 Garrido et al., 2015.
8 Wiesel, 1970: 168–169.
9 Hogman, 1998; Kellerman, 2001; Lev-Wiesel, 2007.
10 Epstein, 1979.
11 Hoffman and Shrira, 2019.
12 Krell et al., 2004; Winik, 1988.
13 Bar-On, 1992; Danieli, 1984, 1998.
14 Wardi, 1992.
15 Timmerman, 2011.
16 Schulberg, 1999.
17 Except for Ella, who has allowed me to use her name, all the other names are pseudonyms.
18 The diary was originally written during the Holocaust but got lost. Her father rewrote the diary from memory years after the Holocaust. Later on, two months after her father passed away, the family received a phone call relating to the original version that was found in Poland. The reconstructed version did not miss any detail from the original version. Quoting from the introduction to the diary:

> "He remembered everything, he wasn't able to forget".

19 And these are my commandments:

> One: You shall not have other g-ds before yourself.
> Two: Only do what benefits you, and do not sacrifice yourself for others.
> Three: Live life to the fullest and enjoy every moment.
> Four: Love yourself above all.
> Five: Do not do for your fellow man that which you favor the most.
> Six: Do not exert your mind.
> Seven: Harden your heart. Do not listen to him.
> Eight: Do not get too close to people and do not bring them close to you.
> Nine: Do not count on anyone.
> Ten: Do not believe – the heavens are empty

20 Composed eight years after *The Heavens Are Void.*

21 His father was born and lived in Israel.
22 The sun has set beyond the treetops

> Come join us to welcome the Sabbath, our Queen
> Behold her descending, the holy, the blessed
> And together with her angels – cohorts of peace and rest
> Come come, Queen Sabbath
> Come come, Queen Sabbath.

23 His Grandfather was also a composer who died of typhus in Bergen-Belsen.
24 "If one extinguishes a lamp (on the sabbath) because he is afraid of the officers of the government, or of robbers, or of an evil spirit, or in order that a sick person may be able to sleep, he is exempt".

> One must say three things in his house on Friday, when it is getting dark.--viz. 'Have you set aside the tithes (from the fruit, which is to be eaten on the Sabbath)?' 'Have you put up the Erubh?' and 'Light ye the lamp.'

25 Health musicking can be understood as the common core of any use of music experiences to regulate emotional or relational states or to promote wellbeing, be it therapeutic or not, professionally assisted or self-made. Bonde, 2011; Ruud, 2010, 2013; Stige, 2002.

Bibliography

Alvin, Juliette, and Warwick, Auriel, 1997. *Music Therapy for the Autistic Child*, New York: Oxford University Press.

Amir, Dorit, 2004. "Giving Trauma a Voice: The Role of Improvisational Music Therapy in Exposing, Dealing with and Healing a Traumatic Experience of Sexual Abuse", *Music Therapy Perspectives* 22 (2): 96–103.

Austin, Diane, 2002. "Voice of Trauma: A Wounded Healer's Perspective", in: Julie Sutton (ed.), *Music, Music Therapy and Trauma: International Perspectives*, London: Jessica Kingsley Publishers: 231–259.

Bar-On, Dan, 1992. "Israeli and German Students Encounter the Holocaust Through a Group Process: 'Working Through' and 'Partial Relevance'", *International Journal of Group Tensions* 22 (2): 81–118.

Bensimon, Moshe, 2020. "Relational Needs in Music Therapy with Trauma Victims: The Perspective of Music Therapists", *Nordic Journal of Music Therapy* 29 (3): 240–254.

Bonde, Lars Ole, 2011. "Health Musicing – Music Therapy or Music and Health? A Model, Empirical Examples and Personal Reflections", *Music and Arts in Action* 3 (2): 120–139.

Bruscia, Kenneth, 1998. "An Introduction to Music Psychotherapy", in: Kenneth Bruscia (ed.), *The Dynamics of Music Psychotherapy*, Barcelona: Gilsum N H.

Danieli, Yael, 1984. "Psychotherapists' Participation in the Conspiracy of Silence About the Holocaust", *Psychoanalytic Psychology* 1 (1): 23–42.

Danieli, Yael, 1998. *International Handbook of Multigenerational Legacies of Trauma*, New York: Plenum.

Eliram, Talila, 2006. *'Come, Thou Hebrew Song' the Songs of the Land of Israel – Musical and Social Aspects*, Jerusalem: Keter Press.

Epstein, Helen, 1979. *Children of the Holocaust: Conversations with Sons and Daughters of Survivors*, New York: Penguin.

Garrido, Sandra, Baker, Felicity, Davidson, Jane, Moore, Grace, and Wasserman, Steve, 2015. "Music and Trauma: The Relationship Between Music, Personality, and Coping Style", *Frontiers in Psychology* 6: 1–3.

Gerber, Monica, Hogan, Lindsey, and Maxwell, Kendall, 2014. "Children After War: A Novel Approach to Promoting Resilience Through Music", *Traumatology: An International Journal* 20 (2): 112–118.

Hoffman, Yaakov, and Shrira, Amit, 2019. "Variables Connecting Parental PTSD to Offspring Successful Aging: Parent–Child Role Reversal, Secondary Traumatization, and Depressive Symptoms", *Frontiers in Psychiatry* 10 (718).

Hogman, Flora, 1998. "Trauma and Identity Through Two Generations of the Holocaust", *Psychoanalytic Review* 85 (4): 551–578.

Kellerman, Nathan, 2001. "The Long-Term Psychological Effects and Treatment of Holocaust Trauma", *Journal of Loss and Trauma* 6: 197–218.

Krell, Robert, Suedfeld, and Soriano, Erin, 2004. "Child Holocaust Survivors as Parents: A Transgenerational Perspective", *American Journal of Orthopsychiatry* 74 (4): 502–508.

Lev-Wiesel, Rachel, 2007. "Intergenerational Transmission of Trauma across Three Generations: A Preliminary Study", *Qualitative Social Work* 6 (1): 75–94.

Loewy, Joanne V., and Stewart, Kristen, 2004. "Music Therapy to Help Traumatized Children and Caregivers", in: Nancy Boyd Webb (ed.), *Mass Trauma and Violence: Helping Families and Children Cope*, New York: Guilford Press: 191–215.

Orth, Jaap, 2005. "Music Therapy with Traumatized Refugees in a Clinical Setting", *Voices: A World Forum for Music Therapy* 5 (2). https://doi.org/10.15845/voices.v5i2.227.

Ruud, Even, 2010. *Music Therapy: A Perspective from the Humanities*, New Hampshire: Barcelona Publishers.

Ruud, Even, 2013. "Can Music Serve as a 'Cultural Immunogen'? An Explorative Study", *International Journal of Qualitative Studies on Health and Well-being* 8: 17–28.

Schulberg, Cecilia H., 1999. "Out of the Ashes: Transforming Despair into Hope with Music and Imagery", in: Julie Hiben (ed.), *Inside Music Therapy: Client Experiences*, New Hampshire: Barcelona Publishers: 7–11.

Stige, Brynjulf, 2002. *Culture-Centered Music Therapy*, Gilsum: Barcelona Publishers.

Sunderland, Naomi, Harrison, Klisala, and Jacobsen, Kristina, 2019. "New Skies Above: Sense-bound and Place-based Songwriting as a Trauma Response for Asylum Seekers and Refugees", *Journal of Applied Arts & Health* 10 (2): 147–167.

Timmermann, Tonius, 2011. "Transgenerational Interactions in Music Therapy", *British Journal of Music Therapy*, June 1: 32–47. https://doi.org/10.1177/135945751102500104.

Wardi, Dina, 1992. *Memorial Candles: Children of the Holocaust*, London: Routledge.

Wiesel, Elie, 1970. *One Generation After*, New York: Random House.

Wiess, Chava, and Bensimon, Moshe, 2020. "Group Music Therapy with Uprooted Teenagers: The Importance of Structure", *Nordic Journal of Music Therapy* 29 (2): 174–189.

Winik, Marta, 1988. "Generation to Generation – A Discussion with Children of Jewish Holocaust Survivors", *Family Therapy* 15 (3): 271–284.

PART II

The Social Sciences and Health-related Sciences

10

EFFECTS OF THE HOLOCAUST ON THE SECOND GENERATION

A Preliminary Analysis of an Ongoing Survey

Samuel Juni

Introduction

Beginning with Danieli's[1] research highlighting differences in Holocaust survivors' familial adaptational styles as crucial determinants of the health vs. pathology of 2gs, many studies have elaborated on and detailed the importance of familial functioning modes in shaping individual and attachment/relational styles of children of trauma survivors.[2]

In the last two decades, the intergenerational transmission of trauma-related psychological difficulties and resiliencies has been the focus of considerable research. An approach that has gained particular traction among scholars is Relational Competence Theory (RCT)[3] as formulated by L'Abate and his colleagues, positing that individual personality is shaped – and relational styles are transmitted – through close family relationships – which comprise the primary medium of cross-generational transmission. The premise of RCT is that intimate relationships promote the close vs. distant feeling through the process of modeling. The construct essentially harkens back to observational learning during child development when children typically imitate parental behavioral and interactional styles and is central to the studies of Holocaust repercussions on 2gs and 3gs.[4] Our adaptation of RCT represents a specific framework in which dynamics affect intimacy levels within survivor families. These effects, which escalate and profoundly influence 2gs, are posited to constitute the transmission mechanism of anomalies in personality, relational styles, and personal attitudes/beliefs.

There is a sizable Holocaust literature focusing on survivors.[5] A comprehensive literature review of data-based 2g studies published between 2000 and 2018[6] confirmed that mental health problems, problematic parenting styles, and poor attachment quality negatively affected the mental wellbeing and stress vulnerability of children of survivors. Another comprehensive review of research findings[7] stresses that maladaptive parenting styles of survivors (including overinvolvement and overprotectiveness) that interfered with developmental separation and autonomy are inherent in the many loveless "marriages of despair"[8] in which survivors lacked the resources to enhance emotional nurturance and capacity for intimacy in 2gs.[9] Alas, there is a dearth of non-anecdotal empirical quantitative data that examine directly (rather than inferentially or statistically) the mediation (or transmission) of Holocaust effects on 2gs.[10]

Characteristics of 2gs common in the literature are often found under the headings of self-perception and intergenerational functioning (i.e., the level of adaption that typifies a familial unit across generations)[11] and feature occasional diagnostic overlaps with personality disorders.[12]

DOI: 10.4324/b23365-13

Self-perception is a key qualifier here, based on the phenomenological postmodern orientation that asserts that the "facts" are not as salient in terms of trauma effects as are the reconstruction of these facts in the human mind.[13] In other words, it is what people make of the "facts" that is of consequence to their lives. The key aspects of self-perception here relate especially to self-identity and overidentification with survivor role, where the latter is defined as viewing oneself first and foremost as a 2g survivor. Trauma-related difficulties, self-perception, danger vigilance, affective stance, and relationship style/capacity are typically seen as prone to intergenerational transmission. Some researchers argue that these features are particularly linked to the overprotectiveness of survivors with their children.[14] Deficits in separation-individuation from parents often result,[15] which engender a diminished capacity for intimacy in 2gs.[16] A particular facet of this over-protectiveness is expressed in the symbiotic relationship between the children and their survivor parents.[17]

Reading many of the studies in detail, one notices that the samples are typically limited to small numbers and to very specific geographic locations – with some notable exceptions.[18] The classic studies that defined the field for decades focused primarily on psychiatric syndromes, while others focused on anxiety and depression as well. Data-based studies typically focus on personality, and interactional patterns are based on comparisons of scale scores and interview measures between 2gs and non-2gs. Although results of the latter are moderately objective, comparative control groups often apparently differ from the 2gs in a number of demographics and background variables, besides the fact that 2gs were raised by survivor parents. Methodologically, the ideal comparison group should differ from the study group in only a single facet, so that differences between the two groups can then be definitively attributed to that facet. A case in point: a study that examined the beliefs of 2gs related to G-d and to notions of the divine (utilizing a design that matched 2gs with other immigrant families and nonimmigrants)[19] found that the beliefs of the 2gs were unrelated to parental survivor status. Instead, the beliefs were actually determined by another demographic shared by children of survivors (i.e., their immigration status and relocation experiences) so that they shared similar theological notions with immigrants from non-survivor families. As for the effect of the Holocaust per se on the religiosity of 2gs, there is little in the empirical literature.

The author was raised in a community of Holocaust survivors and their families and noticed early on specific behaviors and orientations clearly attributable to the Holocaust among his peers. Based on multiple discussions with his childhood friends and survivors and his clinical experience in psychiatric diagnostics with many Holocaust survivor families – in conjunction with detailed comparisons of his impressions with those of his colleagues and former students specializing in treating survivor families – the author formulated personality and coping profiles of survivors and 2gs. These profiles focused primarily on family constellations, intra-familial relationship qualities, parents' personality, religiosity, and Holocaust experiences. The development of these profiles and their theoretical conceptualizations – including patterns gleaned from psychoanalytic explorations – have been presented in a series of studies referenced at the end of this chapter.[20]

Key factors of these profiles were culled and included in a self-report survey for 2gs examining various aspects of their demographics, background, behaviors, attitudes, and relationships – as well those of their parents (as the 2gs perceived them). Major sections of the survey contain detailed background questions about the 2gs and their parents. The survey included, in addition, a number of exploratory items that are not key factors in the coping profiles of survivors and 2gs but appeared inconsistently in the profiles.

Theoretical Orientation

Our conceptual approach to the understanding of 2gs is based on the premise that some of their personal and relational attributes are derived from modeling parental styles. Our theoretical stance entails an adaptation of communication theory constructs to the analysis of interpersonal relationships.

Watzlawick et al.[21] revolutionized the understanding of interpersonal communication by positing that it is not monolithic, pointing to symmetric vs. complementary dyadic communication constellations. Essentially, there is one communication style from partner *a* to partner *b* and another for the converse. These two styles may be symmetric (i.e., similar) or complementary (i.e., different or even opposite), as each communicative style or role capitalizes on the strengths of the other and somehow makes up in aspects where they fall short (e.g., *a* may be the initiator of ideas but superficial with details or implications, while *b* may be the critic who responds, evaluates, and questions whether and how to follow up with practical applications).

Watzlawick with his Palo Alto Group elaborated an important caveat in applying this differential to family therapy – that complementary communication styles often *escalate*. Escalation entails the augmentation (and entrenchment) of each partner's diametrically oriented communicative role that occurs as the dyadic relationship solidifies. Recently, the concepts of symmetry, complementarity, and escalation were adapted from communication patterns to the conceptualization of dyadic conflict.[22]

In our clinical and research work with dyads, we expanded the application of interactional symmetry vs. complementary from communication to the closeness/distance aspect of dyadic relationships. In addition, paralleling Watzlawick's differentiation between dyadic communication roles, we found that dyadic relationships, too, essentially consist of two different valences: one defines the relationship of *a* to *b*, while another defines the relationship of *b* to *a*. It is argued that a unitary depiction of a relationship *between* two individuals is basically a misnomer. When dyads are asked how close they felt to the other and also how close they believed the other felt towards them, the respective feelings of closeness are asymmetric, especially in comparisons of perceived closeness between parents and children.[23] Arguably, a unitary qualifier of a dyadic relationship is misleading since any "relationship" entails a combination of two bidirectional "relationships". This survey therefore refers separately – for example – to the perceived closeness or distance of the respondent *to* his or her parent, as distinct from the converse closeness or distance of the parent *to* the respondent. Never is the deceptive preposition of "between" used to describe any aspect of dyadic relationships throughout this study.

Our conceptualization of relationships subsumes two dimensional constructs: Closeness and Relatedness. Closeness – measuring the closeness vs. distance of *a* to *b* – is based on the truism that becoming more distant from someone or closer to him/her is diametrically opposite to reactions along a dimension of positivity vs. negativity in relationships. However, from the psychoanalytic perspective of Object Relations, it may be appropriate to consider Relatedness, per se, as a salient construct, which focuses on the intensity of the relationship regardless of the direction of its positivity or negativity. The dimension of Relatedness ranges from a total lack of relationship on one end of the continuum – to the "common denominator" between feeling bothered/disturbed/upset *and* feeling close/positive in a relationship. In fact, this commonality is a basic tenet in psychoanalysis[24] that is conceptualized as a function of the Reaction Formation defense mechanism.[25] The salience of Relatedness is best captioned by Elie Wiesel's[26] iconic aphorism relating to the Holocaust: "The opposite of love is not hate, it's indifference".

Method

To study the effects of a monumental event on people, there are two ideal designs. The first entails comparing measurements of the people before and after the event. This is clearly impossible with individuals (such as 2gs) who were born after the event. The second design is to compare findings of the individuals being studied with a comparably matched control group who are very similar to these individuals in all key demographic, social background, and experiential variables – with the exception that they were not subjected to the event. In studying 2gs, it is difficult, if not impossible, to find a control population that matches the confounded and unique background of 2gs – particularly with large-scale online studies.

It is posited that the most appropriate option, albeit not ideal in terms of design, is to ask 2gs to share their subjective judgments about specific effects the Holocaust may have had on them. In a sense, limiting the scope of the research to perceived effects by 2gs, rather than attempting to discover the "actual" objective effects (which is practically impossible to achieve), renders the self-report design most suitable to study such effects.

From a psychodynamic perspective, arguably, subjective self-perceptions are indeed far more relevant to understanding personality and emotional life than objective events might be. More pointedly, psychoanalytic theory is emphatic that subjective perception is the singular determinant of motivation and the primary component of relationship styles, life satisfaction, and adjustment. Objective reality hardly matters when it comes to an individuals' understanding of their cognitions, emotions, or relationships.

A self-report survey of 2gs was posted online using Google Forms. Directions specified that only respondents who had either one or two Holocaust survivor parents complete and submit their forms. Respondents were solicited by announcements on social media. In addition, respondents passed on the link to friends and acquaintances (the snowball effect).

The initial survey format featured open-ended questions. Feedback from a number of respondents indicated that answering the items was too laborious and time consuming. This resulted in some individuals responding tersely (and incompletely) to items asking for longer answers and others to skip some items, while a significant number abandoned the survey altogether midway. Moreover, a coding trial with eight of the protocols to convert phrases and free-style sentences into categorical and numeric data protocols showed potential reliability complications for unclear or complex responses, requiring multiple raters to minimize judgement errors. It was therefore decided to extract key response categories from the open-ended responses of the first 176 forms received and to design a new forced-choice format to replace the open-ended version. This study reports preliminary results of the first 305 forced-choice forms.

There was also one item omitted midway through the data collection. Noticing that there was a lack of response from respondents who self-identified as Very Orthodox, we initiated discussions with some members of the cohort to discover why this was happening. It turned out that these individuals took serious exception to items concerning religiosity. Moreover, they were totally aghast at the item asking respondents to categorize their sexual preference. In fact, some of the respondents revealed that they abandoned the survey upon encountering the sexual preference item. Although none of the religiosity items were changed, the item concerning sexual preference was omitted as a result of this feedback.

Completed forms were received from a number of countries. 114 men and 191 women submitted responses. The modal age was 70 (s.d. = 5.3). The modal level of secular education was 18 years (s.d. = 4.1). 280 respondents were Jewish; a sizable majority of the remainder did not indicate their religion, and very few indicated religions other than Jewish. 219 of the respondents were married, 37 divorced, 19 widowed, 19 were single, and 18 were living with partners. Belief in G-d was rated by 51 respondents as totally absent, 65 as somewhat, 47 as moderate, and 140 as very much. 63 respondents rated their degree of Religious Observance as totally absent, 86 as somewhat, 70 as moderate, and 86 as very much.

Results[27]

All of the variables in this study and their respective response breakdowns are presented as follows:

Table 10.1 The Variables in This Study and Their Response Breakdowns.

Personal Reactions to the Holocaust	
How much does the Holocaust negatively affect your personality?	
Not at all	66 (22%)
Somewhat	125 (41%)
Moderately	58 (19%)
Very much	56 (18%)
How much does the Holocaust negatively affect your quality of life?	
Not at all	115 (38%)
Somewhat	116 (38%)
Moderately	42 (14%)
Very much	32 (10%)
Religiosity Reactions to the Holocaust	
How does the Holocaust affect your belief in G-d?	
Has no effect	155 (50%)
Strengthens it	66 (21%)
Weakens it	86 (28%)
How does the Holocaust affect your religious observance?	
Has no effect	158 (52%)
Strengthens it	87 (29%)
Weakens it	56 (19%)
Effect of Holocaust on 2g Relationships to Others	
How does the Holocaust affect your relationship to your father?	
It does not affect it	107 (37%)
I am more distant	59 (20%)
I am closer	123 (43%)
How does the Holocaust affect your relationship to your mother?	
It does not affect it	108 (38%)
I am more distant	55 (19%)
I am closer	124 (43%)
How does the Holocaust affect your relationship to your children?	
It does not affect it	111 (42%)
I am more distant	18 (7%)
I am closer	133 (51%)
How does the Holocaust affect your relationship to your siblings?	
It does not affect it	123 (47%)
I am more distant	41 (16%)
I am closer	98 (37%)
How does the Holocaust affect your relationship to your friends?	
It does not affect it	153 (53%)
I am more distant	67 (23%)
I am closer	66 (23%)

(*Continued*)

Table 10.1 (Continued)

How does the Holocaust affect your relationship to your professional/business associates?	
It does not affect it	188 (70%)
I am more distant	60 (22%)
I am closer	21 (8%)
Effect of Holocaust on Parental Relationships to 2gs	
How was your father's relationship to you affected by the Holocaust?	
It was unaffected	31 (16 %)
It made him more distant from me	72 (38 %)
It made him closer to me	87 (46 %)
Don't know	(excluded from statistical analyses)
How was your mother's relationship to you affected by the Holocaust?	
It was unaffected	67 (28%)
It made her more distant from me	55 (23 %)
It made her closer to me	117 (49 %)
Don't know	(excluded from statistical analyses)

Analyses of Findings

The analyses are based exclusively on the data just presented in the Results section. However, the tables that follow juxtapose different variables and also features new combined response options.

Personal Reactions to the Holocaust

Table 10.1 shows that personality and the quality of life of were both affected negatively to some extent for most 2gs in this sample. However, the distribution patterns are different. To get a clearer sense of this difference, the responses were split at the center, adding *Not at All* + *Somewhat* vs. *Moderately* + *Very Much*. As can be seen on Table 10.2, personality was negatively affected much less than quality of life.

Table 10.2 Negative Holocaust Effects on 2gs' Personality and Quality of Life.

	Personality	*Quality of Life*
Not at all + Somewhat	191	231
Moderately + Very Much	114	74
	χ^2 $(1, N = 610) = 12.30, p = .0004$.[28]	

Slightly more than half of the respondents reported that their religious belief and religious observance were unaffected by the Holocaust (as evident in Table 10.1).[29] For the 2gs whose religiosity was affected, there is a remarkable effect differential between two aspects of religiosity, as evident on Table 10.3:

Table 10.3 Effects of the Holocaust on the Religiosity of 2gs.

	Belief in G-d	*Religious Observance*
Strengthens it	66	87
Weakens it	86	56
	χ^2 (1, N = 295) = 8.95, p = .03	

Religiosity Reactions to the Holocaust

It is clear that the notion of considering religiosity as a unitary construct is inapplicable to 2gs. Disregarding those whose religiosity was unaffected, belief in G-d was weakened for most 2gs in this sample, while religious observance was strengthened. How can this be understood?

There is evidence in the literature that the religiosity of many survivors decreased significantly due to their Holocaust experiences; many abandoned religion altogether.[30] There are also reports of some survivors becoming more religious.[31] However, the divergence evidenced in this study, where the same population shows strengthening of observance and weakening of belief, seems dissonant.

Interviews and discussions with Holocaust survivors who abandoned religion – excluding those who did so for pragmatic considerations – revealed a fairly consistent rationale exemplified by the following typical explanation: *If G-d existed, He never would have allowed such atrocities. I don't believe in G-d.* This stance seemed arguably logical and intuitively understandable.

By contrast, the explanations presented by survivors whose religiosity increased were inconsistent with each other. It was remarkable that the explanations of a good number were often difficult to understand to the point that some seemed illogical. Of the responses that were coherent, commonly verbalized rationales seemed to fall into several categories, typified by the following respectively:

- *If I stopped being religious, then Hitler would have won; No way am I allowing that.*[32]
- *Scripture and our Rabbis predicted that the Jewish people would be punished for their sins. . . . We got what was coming to us. . . . I got the message and changed my ways; I experienced quite a few incredible strokes of good fortune – maybe even miracles – that saved my life. . . . I knew G-d was watching over me all the time.*
- *What happened to us could not have been random. . . . It could only have happened by a major concerted effort by G-d. . . . If I had any doubts before about G-d managing the world, this was the ultimate proof.*

Evidently, these rationales refer to one of two aspects of religiosity: belief in G-d vs. religious observance. Many survivors claiming to having become more religious were referring exclusively to an increase in observance of rituals. It is suggested that the reason why some explanations proved difficult to understand was because increased adherence to religious practices was often powered by unconscious (perhaps neurotic) fears that the survivors themselves were unaware of consciously – and certainly could not convey clearly to the interviewers.[33]

Once the explanations of those whose religiosity increased were categorized according to this behavior vs. cognitive divide, it appeared that the majority of the cohort who became more religious actually enhanced their involvement with religious ritual practices rather than enhancing their belief in G-d – let alone enhancing their relationship with Him. Applying our understanding of the dynamics of the changes in religiosity of survivors to the responses of 2gs in the present study, we propose a rationale explaining the divergence – in opposite directions – between the diminution of belief in G-d vs. the increase in religious observance. Arguably, most 2gs in this sample (i.e., those who report No Effect + those who report that it had a negative effect) do not buy the arguments construing the Holocaust as a validation of the existence of G-d. If anything, they see it precisely in the other direction; hence the weakened belief in G-d. On the other hand, their behavioral reaction to the Holocaust and their identification with their parent-survivors leads most of those who report having been affected to increase their affiliative activities which identify them more strongly with the religious culture of their survivor parents.

It is also arguable, however, that the increase in religious observance of 2gs may well not entail rituals that are congruent with traditional religious practice. This might in fact be likely, given findings that children of survivors often tend to reject the traditions of pre-Holocaust Judaism, creating instead new forms of religious culture and imagery that are in part a response to the failure of a patriarchal god in the face of Nazi destruction.[34]

Juxtaposing the inconsistent Holocaust effects on religiosity vs. religious behavior on 2gs, it is argued that what we have here is a manifestation of maladaptive escalation that prompts alienation by inducing a host of personal and psychological differences.[21] The dynamic here is that these differences are secondary repercussions of intergenerational alienation that fosters oppositional identification for its own sake.

Holocaust Effects on 2g Relationships

Examining the percentages in Table 10.4,[35] we note a steadily decreasing effect for *Closer*, beginning at 51% for 2gs' relationship to their children and dropping down through the closeness level to parents, then siblings, then non-family relationships.[36]

Table 10.4 Effects of the Holocaust on Different Relationships of 2gs to Others.

	Children	*Father*	*Mother*	*Siblings*	*Friends*	*Professional/Business Associates*
No Effect	42%	37%	38%	47%	53%	70%
Distant	7%	20%	19%	16%	23%	22%
Closer	51%	43%	43%	37%	23%	8%
Distant + Closer	58%	63%	62%	53%	46%	30%

For *Distant*, similarly, the progression begins at 7% for children rising gradually towards the low 20s as the kinship valences approach non-family relationships, albeit with a displacement of the parental percentages that are somewhat higher than that for siblings. For *No Effect*, however, the upward percent progression (in gradations of kinship) deviates significantly in that the value for parents moves to the starting point (lowest percentage) of the progression after which the percentages rise for children, siblings, and then for non-family relationship to a high of 70.

Table 10.4 shows that the Holocaust affected relationships with family members for the majority of respondents in this sample. It is noted that the effects of the Holocaust in shaping 2gs' relationships to their parents is practically identical in the relationships to their fathers and mothers, respectively, as reflected in Table 10.5:

Table 10.5 A Comparison of Holocaust Effects on 2g's Relationships to Their Fathers and Mothers.

	Unaffected	*More Distant*	*Closer*
2g's relationships to their fathers	107 (37%)	59 (20%)	123 (43%)
2g's relationships to their mothers	108 (38%)	55 (19%)	124 (43%)
	No χ^2 test is called for here since the patterns are practically identical for fathers and mothers.		

Table 10.6 examines the converse effects of Table 10.5 – i.e., 2gs' perceived Holocaust effects on parents' relationships to them.[37]

Juxtaposing Tables 10.5 and 10.6, it is clear that 2gs perceive that the Holocaust made their fathers more distant to them (38%) than it made their fathers closer to them (20%).[37]

Analyzing the Holocaust effects on survivors' perceived relationships to their children (2gs), there is a significant difference between the stance of fathers and that of mothers, as seen in Table 10.6. Evidently 2gs perceive that their fathers became more distant to them than their mothers did, due to the Holocaust.

There are two evident nexi of the discrepancy: a) the likelihood of mothers' relationships to be unaffected by the Holocaust is much greater than the likelihood of the fathers' relationships to be unaffected; b) mothers are more than twice as likely to be closer to their children than to be distant, while fathers are only somewhat more likely to be closer to their children than to be distant. And yet, there is a fairly uniform raised level of the *unaffected* category relationship of the 2gs to their parents – both father and mother alike (as seen in Table 10.5) – despite the significant difference in the *unaffected* category in the relationships of the parents to their children (which is evident in Table 10.6).

To further explore the data, it is useful to separate the two dimensions of relationships – *closeness* and *relatedness* – to our study of Holocaust *effects on relationships*. Considering the options of *unaffected*, *more distant*, and *closer*, the *closeness* dimension is best seen by contrasting *distant* from *closer*; the *unaffected* option is irrelevant to this dimension. (Arguably, it might be considered a neutral point between the two salient options on either end.) However, for the relatedness dimension – measuring *whether* the Holocaust affected relationship valences – we clearly would be contrasting *unaffected* (on one end) from the options of *distant* and *closer* (on the other end).

Table 10.7 presents the bidirectional Holocaust effects on the *Closeness* of 2gs and their parents.

These results indicate that while the Holocaust enhanced the *closeness* of 2gs to their fathers more than closeness of fathers to 2gs (as noted earlier in the juxtaposition of Tables 10.5 and 10.6), it also had the reverse effect in the converse direction – as it made fathers more distant to 2gs than it made

Table 10.6 A Comparison of Holocaust Effects on Parents' Relationships to 2gs.

	Unaffected	*More Distant*	*Closer*
Fathers' relationships to 2gs	31 (16%)	72 (38%)	87 (46%)
Mothers' relationships to 2gs	67 (28%)	55 (23%)	117 (49%)
	χ^2 (2, *N* = 429) = 14.50, *p* = .0007. (Note that χ^2 is computed based on *ns*.)		

Table 10.7 A Comparison of Closer/Distant Holocaust Effects on 2gs' Relationships to Their Parents vs. Those of Parents to 2g.

	Distant	*Closer*		*Distant*	*Closer*
2gs to fathers	59 (32%)	123 (68%)	2gs to Mothers	59 (32%)	124 (68%)
Fathers to 2gs	72 (42%)	87 (55%)	Mothers to 2gs	55 (32%)	117 (68%)
	χ^2 (1, N = 341) = 5.94, p = .014		χ^2 is not statistically significant.		

2gs to their fathers.[38] However, the effect is not supported for the 2g-mother dyad.[39] The father-mother valence differences might be related to gender differences in parental overprotectiveness.[40]

Table 10.8 compares the Holocaust effects on 2gs' *relatedness* to their parents vs. those of parents to 2gs. These results show the following:

- The Holocaust enhanced the *relatedness* of 2gs to parents and of parents to 2gs, for both fathers and mothers.
- The *relatedness* enhancement of parents to 2gs was much stronger than the converse.
- The *relatedness* enhancement of 2gs to parents was moderate and similar for both parents (63%).
- The *relatedness* enhancement of fathers to 2gs was marked (over five-fold), while that of mothers was only half as pronounced (2½ times as much).

RCT posits that the essentials of individual interactive communication style are rooted within the family and social context, with modeling as its primary dynamic. Researchers in organizational dynamics adapted the constructs of relational symmetry, complementarity, and escalation from communication patterns to the conceptualization of dyadic conflict.[21] Our theoretical framework expands modeling dynamics further to the realm of relational maladaptation. Applying this perspective to the relationship development of the parent-child dyad, we conceptualize the escalation tendency of some individuals within dyadic interactions – epitomized in youngsters who identify with parental (or hero) figures by adopting more exaggerated versions of their behavioral and interactional styles – as a manifestation of identity formation. We posit a reciprocal-recursive dynamic as a key transmission mechanism of problematic relational styles from Holocaust survivors to 2gs.

The essence of what is transmitted in such cases is often a profound sense of alienation that engenders maladaptive reactive stances and personality anomalies. When trauma results in characterological alienation of survivors, it can be expected that their children – based on modeling – will adopt an alienated style as well based on modeling. Understandably, this style will also engender an alienated style of 2gs towards their parents. These dynamics become even more complex in the survivor-2g dyad as it will likely lead to reactive escalation, where the child reacts to the alienation experienced from the parent by becoming even more alienated from the parent. More than simply weakening the parent-child bond, this alienation may arguably further transform the stance of the 2g towards the parent into general contrariness and prompt a reactive disengagement from the parent's

Table 10.8 A Comparison of Unaffected/Affected Holocaust Effects on 2gs' Relationships to Their Parents vs. Those of Parents to 2gs.

	Unaffected	*Distant + Closer*		*Unaffected*	*Distant + Closer*
2gs to their fathers	107 (37%)	182 (63%)	2gs to their mothers	108 (37%)	183 (63%)
Fathers to 2gs	31 (16%	159 (84%)	Mothers to 2gs	67 (28%)	172 (72%)
χ^2 (1, N = 479) = 23.97, p < .00001.			χ^2 (1, N = 526) = 5.41, p = .02		

beliefs and values. Arguably, the dynamic may shed some light on the inconsistent position of the parental relationships (i.e., the far stronger relatedness of the survivor to the 2g than the converse, and the marked difference between maternal closeness to the 2g as compared to paternal closeness) and for the disparity between the *no effect* and *becoming closer* categories across relationship continuum ranging from the strongest valence to the weakest (children, parents, siblings, friends, professional/ business associates) evidenced on Table 10.4.[41]

Study Limitations

There are various limitations in the structure of the survey and in the generalizability of the findings of this study. A number of the limitations will be corrected in the more detailed data analyses that will be conducted following the final phase of data collection when the larger *n* will allow more differentiated statistical analytics (including demographic permutations).

Self-report data is always susceptible to distortion because of response sets. These are usually mind-sets that increase the likelihood that respondents will not respond truthfully. Sometimes this is intentional due to social or personal considerations. Often it is unwitting. In this study, this may particularly distort responses about religiosity and interpersonal relationships.[42] Anonymity reduced – but did not obviate – this limitation.

Moreover, in the absence of a matched control group of respondents from non-survivor families for comparison, the only evidence that the 2gs were affected in any domain is their subjective assessment of the effect – which cannot be said to be inherently reliable. In fact, the 2g's "knowledge" of such effects can be said to derive either from – a) their own comparisons with non-2g peers, followed by an attribution of differences to the fact that their parents were survivors or b) their introspection about their associations or thoughts that precede (or accompany) the behaviors, attitudes, or emotions in question. In the first case, their conclusions are subject to the same critiques that are relevant to scientific multi-respondent studies using allegedly matched comparison groups, only more so since most respondents are not trained researchers. In the second case, the validity of the data is predicated on the assumption that respondents have accurate (and unbiased) readings of their associations and thoughts despite the fact that most are not trained psychologists with experience in psychoanalysis or related methodologies.

Although the data for fathers and mothers were analyzed separately, there was no differentiation in the statistical tables between male and female 2gs. It is likely, however, that there were some differences in responses for male and female respondents. Furthermore, the gender-pairings of the respondent and parent (i.e., male 2g and mother, male 2g and father, female 2g and mother, female 2g and father) may have introduced variance in the patterns as well.

There is no accommodation in the presented breakdowns (Table 10.1) whether a parent in consideration was even a Holocaust survivor at all, which is important since a number of 2gs who participated in the survey had one parent who was not a survivor. While this still leaves the cross-generational interactional and relational findings as proper indices of the behavior and attitudes of 2g towards their parents, it does not necessarily have specific relevance about how they relate to parent survivors as such. In addition, it is feasible that data patterns would differ depending on whether both or only one of the parents are survivors, even in the 2g-survivor dyadic relationship. Indeed, studies have shown that having two survivor parents resulted in higher mental health problems in 2gs than did having one survivor parent.[6]

Our statistical analyses in this study did not differentiate between respondents based on the details of their parents' Holocaust experience or the degree of hardships suffered by the survivors during the Holocaust. However, the implications of various studies have shown that it is incorrect to view

Holocaust victimization in a binary fashion. As specific examples: empirical research has shown that anomalies in self-perception, as linked to an ambivalent attachment style, varied as a function of the severity of trauma suffered by survivors during the Holocaust,[43] while a correlational study showed an association between the mother's age during the Holocaust and anxiety/depression of 2gs.[44]

The data collection was managed by a computerized system. Though relatively insulated from human error, technological and program glitches cannot absolutely be ruled out. Moreover, the forced-choice format may well have led some 2gs to distort their intended responses to items when no options matched closely those offered.

As noted earlier, we decided mid-study to omit the item concerning sexual preference to avoid the likelihood that religiously orthodox individuals would decline to participate in the survey. This cost us demographic information that may have proven salient.

Our sampling is not truly random and thus subject to sampling bias. The study is dependent on respondents who happen to be connected to specific sites where the survey link was posted or were connected to others who knew about the survey. Some potential respondents may have doubted the assurances of anonymity, suspecting that their responses could be traced back to them. Also, based on our clinical and research interactions with ultra-orthodox populations, many in such cohorts did not participate since they manifest a disdain for – and even an abhorrence of –social science questionnaires, all the more so of anything internet-related, which they view as threatening. Moreover, as noted earlier, some of these individuals may have decided to not participate in the survey altogether, rather than simply leaving (potentially offensive) religion-relating items blank. In addition, there are respondents who have a reactive aversion to multiple-choice items and summarily refuse to answer them. Finally, some notes in the comment section (at the end of the survey) featured complaints that the questionnaire was too long, which suggests that this may have resulted in carelessness in reading the items and in non-responses to others – even on the forced-choice version.

The items that ask 2gs to rate whether their religiosity increased, decreased, or was unaffected have inherent response skew. The changes in question are clearly predicated on basic levels of religiosity. Based on the "regression towards the mean" phenomenon, those who have very high levels of religiosity (regardless of the Holocaust) could only be affected towards the negative direction, while those who are totally irreligious (regardless of the Holocaust) could only be affected towards more religiosity. Moreover, the dynamics of 2gs whose religiosity increased from moderate to high levels are qualitatively distinct from one who went from being totally irreligious to adopting religion; the two should ideally be analyzed separately. These limitations could have been accommodated for statistically, by including the initial levels (or family levels) of religiosity in the analyses.

Summary

Preliminary findings from an online survey completed by 305 2gs yielded evidence of significant Holocaust effects on their personality, quality of life, religiosity, and familial/interpersonal relationships. Personality and quality of life of were affected negatively to some extent for most 2gs in this sample. Within the area of religiosity – for those in this sample whose religiosity was affected by the Holocaust – belief in G-d was weakened for most 2gs, while religious observance was strengthened. The dynamics of cognitive-based attitudes are distinguished from behavioral and relational reactions.

Our analytic approach to the data is that the parent-child relationship is best conceptualized as consisting of two distinct components – the relationship of the parent to the child vs. the relationship of the child to the parent. These are analyzed in terms of dyadic closeness and relatedness.

Results showed different patterns for facets of the personal variables and divergent effects of religious belief vs. observance. Different patterns were revealed in 2g-to-parent and in parent-to-2g relationships based on the parents' gender. Inconsistent and asymmetric patterns are delineated, and anomalies are partially attributed to maladaptive relational and parenting styles by survivors.

The transmission of alienation and maladaptive relationship styles from survivors to 2gs is construed from the perspective of interactional reciprocal learning in addition to the percepts of RCT. Limitations in the survey design are annotated, as are a number of omissions in the analysis that will be reckoned with in the final data analyses upon the completion of the data collection.

Notes

1 Danieli, 1981.
2 As detailed in a number of meta-study reviews; e.g., Fossion et al., 2015; Lambert et al., 2014; Leen-Feldner et al., 2013.
3 L'Abate et al., 2010. The theory was developed in a series of L'Abate's publications.
4 E.g., Fonagy, 1999; Kellerman, 2001; Yehuda et al., 2008; Shmotkin et al., 2011; Shrira et al., 2011; Roitman, 2017.
5 See, for example, the meta-analysis by Barel et al., 2010, of 71 studies of over 12,000 survivors focusing on wellbeing and psychopathology.
6 Dashorst et al., 2019.
7 Bar-On and Chaitin, 2001.
8 Danieli, 1988.
9 This is acutely depicted by Bar-On and Chaitin, 2001: 4, as follows:

> Preoccupied with the issue of life and death, these parents often suffered from feelings of self-hatred and worthlessness. When these feelings remained unchanged, they hindered the development of a positive self-image in their children – one of the hallmarks of nurturance.

10 Notably, two more recent studies do feature items that examine transmission directly. Namely, Letzter-Pouw et al., 2014, asked respondents how much the Holocaust is salient in their daily lives, while Greenblatt-Kimron et al., 2021, asked respondents about the centrality of the Holocaust to their identity.
11 Kellerman, 2001.
12 Kellerman, 1999.
13 Bar-On and Chaitin, 2001.
14 E.g., Gangi et al., 2009.
15 Brom et al., 2001.
16 Zilberfein, 1996.
17 Vardi, 1990.
18 Danieli et al., 2016.
19 Weiss et al., 1986.
20 Juni, 2015–2021.
21 Watzlawick et al., 1967.
22 Valitova and Besson, 2021.
23 Aquilino, 1999.
24 Stekel, 1921.
25 Juni, 1999.
26 Wiesel, 1986: 68.
27 The following analyses are limited to survey items that ask respondents to rate how the Holocaust affects specific aspects of their personality, quality of life, religiosity, and interpersonal relationships.
28 Because of the exploratory nature of the results of this ongoing data collection, all of the chi-squared statistical tests in this paper are computed as Independent-Sample t-tests rather than paired t-tests. Despite not being as concise, as well as the inflation of the number of observations above the number of respondents, this mode allows a more inclusive analysis, since some respondents did not answer all items.
29 This is particularly salient in view of one of Elie Wiesel's lesser-known formulation: "The opposite of faith is not heresy, it's indifference", (1986: 68). Apparently, half of the 2gs in our survey were indifferent to the Holocaust as far as religiosity is concerned.

30 Lassley, 2015.
31 Juni, 2016b.
32 This is consistent with the 614th Commandment by Fackenheim, 1968 – that Jews should not grant Hitler a posthumous victory.
33 It is noteworthy that it was rare to hear pragmatic justifications for maintaining (if not increasing) religious observance – e.g., family/community affiliation, valuing the lifestyle, protection against assimilation.
34 Jacobs, 2015.
35 Table 10.4 is intended to visualize a trend rather than a basis for statistical comparison testing; thus, it features percentages rather than raw numbers.
36 This basic progression in kinship reflects the assumption that the valence of the parent-to-child relationship is higher than the converse. This hierarchy is not featured in the empirical research literature. However, it is formulated by Ben-Zeév, 2012, based on his analysis of differential grief reactions within the family. (Prof. Aaron Ben-Ze'ev, of the University of Haifa, specializes in the philosophy of psychology and is considered a leading authority in the study of emotions.)
37 The previous rationale of treating comparisons of father vs. mother ratings as independent vs. dependent ratings vis a vis independent-sample t-tests rather than paired t-tests is even more salient for the χ^2 comparisons in Tables 10.6–10.8. The *ns* here are relatively limited since respondents who only had one parent who was a survivor often only completed the items relating to that parent while leaving items relating to the other parent blank.
38 Here, again, the contrast may be construed as inconsistent with Aquilino's (1999) findings that parents see themselves as closer to their children than the converse.
39 This differential may be seen as consistent with the converse findings by Stephens, 2009 that children feel closer to their mothers than to their fathers. However, although Stephens' findings are not supported in Table 10.5. The fact that Stephens' closeness measure does not differentiate between the survivor's closeness to the 2g vs. the 2g's closeness to the survivor – while these two facets are separated in Tables 10.5 and 10.6 respectively – may explain why Stephens' findings are only partially supported by our data.
40 Studies are inconsistent here. E.g., Stephens, 2009, reports fathers are generally more overprotective than mothers; Way and Gillman, 2000 note higher level of overprotection of daughters by their fathers, while Majdandžić et al., 2016, found that mothers are more overprotective than fathers on some measures but not on others.
41 It is reasonable to argue, alternatively, that the latter disparity may be due to the fact that 2gs associate the Holocaust with the parent/survivor more than with other family members. This would translate into stronger Holocaust-related effects on their relationships to their parents.
42 Consider, for example, the findings by Brenner, 2012 that survey respondents generally overestimate church attendance.
43 Scharf, 2007.
44 Aviad-Wilchek et al., 2013.

Bibliography

Aquilino, W.S., 1999. "Two Views of One Relationship: Comparing Parents' and Young Adult Children's Reports of the Quality of Intergenerational Relations", *Journal of Marriage and the Family* 61 (4): 858–870.

Aviad-Wilchek, Y.A., Cohenca-Shiby, D., and Sasson, Y., 2013. "The Effects of the Survival Characteristics of Parent Holocaust Survivors on Offsprings' Anxiety and Depression Symptoms", *Israel Journal of Psychiatry and Related Sciences* 50 (3): 210–216.

Barel, E., Van IJzendoorn, M.H., Sagi-Schwartz, A., and Bakermans-Kranenburg, M.J., 2010. "Surviving the Holocaust: A Meta-analysis of the Long-Term Sequelae of a Genocide", *Psychological Bulletin* 136 (5): 677–698.

Bar-On, D., and Chaitin, J., 2001. *Parenthood and the Holocaust*, Jerusalem: Yad Vashem.

Ben-Zeév, A., 2012. "Mommy, Do You Love Me as Much as You Love Your Mommy?", *Psychology Today Online*, posted January 1, www.psychologytoday.com/us/blog/in-the-name-love/201201/mommy-do-you-love-me-much-you-love-your-mommy?amp'

Brenner, P.S., 2012. "Investigating the Effect of Bias in Survey Measures of Church Attendance", *Sociology of Religion* 73: 361–383.

Brom, D., Kfir, R., and Dasberg, H., 2001. "A Controlled Double-Blind Study on Children of Holocaust Survivors", *Israel Journal of Psychiatry and Related Sciences* 38 (1): 47–57.

Danieli, Y., 1981. "Differing Adaptational Styles in Families of Survivors of the Nazi Holocaust", *Children Today* 10 (5): 6–10, 34–36.

Danieli, Y., 1988. "The Heterogeneity of Postwar Adaptation in Families of Holocaust Survivors", in: R.L. Braham (ed.), *The Psychological Perspectives of the Holocaust and of its Aftermath*, Boulder, CO: Social Science Monographs, Holocaust Study Series: 109–127.

Danieli, Y., Norris, F.H., and Engdahl, B., 2016. "Multigenerational Legacies of Trauma: Modeling the What and How of Transmission", *American Journal of Orthopsychiatry*, advance online publication, January 14.

Dashorst, P., Mooren, T.M., Kleber, R.J., de Jong, P.J., and Huntjens, R.J.C., 2019. "Intergenerational Consequences of the Holocaust on Offspring Mental Health: A Systematic Review of Associated Factors and Mechanisms", *European Journal of Psychotraumatology* 10 (1): Article 1654065.

Fackenheim, E.L., 1968. "Jewish Faith and the Holocaust", *Commentary* 46: 30–36.

Fonagy, P., 1999. "The Transgenerational Transmission of Holocaust Trauma", *Attachment & Human Development* 1: 92–114.

Fossion, P., Leys, C., Vandeleur, C., Kempenaers, C., Braun, S., Verbanck, P., and Linkowski, P., 2015. "Transgenerational Transmission of Trauma in Families of Holocaust Survivors: The Consequences of Extreme Family Functioning on Resilience, Sense of Coherence, Anxiety and Depression", *Journal of Affective Disorders* 171: 48–53.

Gangi, S., Talam, A., and Ferracuti, S., 2009. "The Long-Term Effects of Extreme War-Related Trauma on the Second Generation of Holocaust Survivors", *Violence and Victims* 24 (5): 687–700.

Greenblatt-Kimron, L., Shrira, A., Rubinstein, T., and Palgi, Y., 2021. "Event Centrality and Secondary Traumatization among Holocaust Survivors' Offspring and Grandchildren: A Three-Generation Study", *Journal of Anxiety Disorders* 81: 102401.

Jacobs, J., 2015. "*Traumatic* Inheritance *and the Demasculinization of God*: Reimagining the Divine among Descendants of the Holocaust", *Journal of Feminist Studies in Religion* 31 (2): 65–82.

Juni, S., 1999. "The Defense Mechanisms Inventory: Theoretical and Psychometric Implications", *Current Psychology* 17: 313–332.

Juni, S., 2015a. "The Failed Education of Jewish Second Generation Holocaust Survivors", *Journal of the Institute for Jewish Ideas and Ideals* 23: 227–246.

Juni, S., 2015b. "Negative Emotionality and Relationships with God among Religious Jewish Holocaust Survivors", *Mental Health, Religion & Culture* 18: 165–174.

Juni, S., 2016a. "Second-Generation Holocaust Survivors: Psychological, Theological and Moral Challenges", *Journal of Trauma Dissociation* 17 (1): 97–111.

Juni, S., 2016b. "Identity Disorders of Second Generation Holocaust Survivors", *Journal of Loss and Trauma: International Perspectives on Stress and Coping* 2 (3): 203–212.

Juni, S., 2016c. "Theistic Dissonance among Religious Jewish Holocaust Survivors: A Psychodynamic Perspective", *Journal of Aggression, Maltreatment, and Trauma* 24: 1–19.

Juni, S., 2016d. "Survivor Guilt: A Critical Review from the Lens of the Holocaust", *International Review of Victimology* 22: 1–17.

Juni, S., 2021. "Righting a Life Which Started on the Wrong Foot", in: J.T. Baumel-Schwartz and S. Refael (eds.), *Researchers Remember: Research as an Arena of Memory for Offspring of Holocaust Survivors: A Collected Volume of Academic Autobiographies*, New York: Peter Lang Publishers: 41–54.

Kellerman, N., 1999. "Diagnosis of Holocaust Survivors and Their Children", *Israel Journal of Psychiatry and Related Sciences* 36 (1): 56–65.

Kellerman, N., 2001. "Transmission of Holocaust Trauma – An Integrative View", *Psychiatry* 64: 256–267.

L'Abate, L., Cusinato, M., Maino, E., Colesso, W., and Scilletta, C., 2010. *Relational Competence Theory: Research and Mental Health Applications*, New York: Springer-Science.

Lambert, J.E., Holzer, J., and Hasbun, A., 2014. "Association between Parents' PTSD Severity and Children's Psychological Distress: A Meta-Analysis", *Journal of Traumatic Stress* 27 (1): 9–17.

Lassley, J., 2015. "A *Defective Covenant*: Abandonment of Faith Among Jewish Survivors of the Holocaust", *International Social Science Review* 90 (2): 1–17.

Leen-Feldner, E.W., Feldner, M.T., Knapp, A., Bunaciu, L., Blumenthal, H., and Amstadter, A.B., 2013. "Offspring Psychological and Biological Correlates of Parental Posttraumatic Stress: Review of the Literature and Research Agenda", *Clinical Psychology Review* 33: 1106–1133.

Letzter-Pouw, S.E., Shrira, A., Ben-Ezra, M., and Palgi, Y., 2014. "Trauma Transmission Through Perceived Parental Burden among Holocaust Survivors' Offspring and Grandchildren", *Psychological Trauma: Theory, Research, Practice, and Policy* 6 (4): 420–429.

Majdandžić, M., de Vente, W., and Bögels, S.M., 2016. "Challenging Parenting Behavior from Infancy to Toddlerhood: Etiology, Measurement, and Differences Between Fathers and Mothers", *Infancy* 21 (4): 1–30.

Roitman, Y., 2017. "Intergenerational Transmission of Violence: Shattered Subjectivity and Relational Freedom", *Psychoanalytic Social Work* 24: 144–162.

Scharf, M., 2007. "Long-Term Effects of Trauma: Psychosocial Functioning of the Second and Third Generation of Holocaust Survivors", *Developmental Psychopathology* 19 (2): 603–622.

Shmotkin, D., Shrira, A., Goldberg, S.C., and Palgi, Y., 2011. "Resilience and Vulnerability among Aging Holocaust Survivors and Their Families: An Intergenerational Overview", *Journal of Intergenerational Relationships* 9: 7–21.

Shrira, A., Palgi, Y., Ben-Ezra, M., and Shmotkin, D., 2011. "Transgenerational Effects of Trauma in Midlife: Evidence for Resilience and Vulnerability in Offspring of Holocaust Survivors", *Psychological Trauma: Theory, Research, Practice, and Policy* 3: 394–402.

Stekel, W., 1921. *The Beloved Ego: Foundations of The New Study of the Psyche* (R. Gabler, Trans.), London: Kegan Paul, Trench, Trubner & Co.

Stephens, M.A., 2009. *Gender Differences in Parenting Styles and Effects on the Parent-Child Relationship*, Unpublished thesis, Texas State University-San Marcos, San Marcos, TX, https://digital.library.txstate.edu/handle/10877/3300

Valitova, A., and Besson, D., 2021. "Interpersonal Communications at Core of Conflicts' Escalation in Organization: The Interplay of Interpersonal Communication Escalation, People's Habitus and Psycho-Sociological Processes are More Important than Contextual Factors", *Journal of Organizational Change Management* 34 (1): 3–27.

Vardi, D., 1990. *Bearers of the Seal: A Dialog with Second Generation Holocaust Survivors* (Hebrew), Jerusalem: Keter.

Watzlawick, P., Bavelas, J.B., and Jackson, D.D., 1967. *Pragmatics of Human Communication: A Study of Interactional Patterns, Pathologies, and Paradoxes*, New York: W.W. Norton & Company.

Way, N., and Gillman, D., 2000. "Adolescent Girls' Perceptions of their Relationships with Their Fathers", *Journal of Early Adolescence* 20: 309–331.

Weiss, E., O'Connell, A.N., and Siiter, R., 1986. "Comparisons of Second-Generation Holocaust Survivors, and Measures of Mental Health", *Journal of Personality and Social Psychology* 50 (4): 828–831.

Wiesel, E., 1986. "One Must Not Forget: Interview with Alvin P. Sanoff.", *U.S. News & World Report*, October 27: 68.

Yehuda, R., Bell, A., Bierer, L.M., and Schmeidler, J., 2008. "Maternal, Not Paternal, PTSD is Related to Increased Risk for PTSD in Offspring of Holocaust Survivors", *Journal of Psychiatric Research* 42: 1104–1111.

Zilberfein, F., 1996. "Children of Holocaust Survivors: Separation Obstacles, Attachments and Anxiety", *Social Work & Health Care* 23: 35–56.

11

INTERGENERATIONAL TRANSMISSION IN THE EXPERIENCES OF AGING CHILDREN OF HOLOCAUST SURVIVORS DURING THE COVID-19 PANDEMIC IN THE USA

Irit Felsen

Previous Research with OHS

Evidence from studies in multiple trauma-exposed populations across the globe demonstrates that intergenerational trauma constitutes a biopsychological risk factor that manifests itself throughout the life cycle of offspring of trauma survivors.[1] Findings from prior research with adult offspring of Holocaust survivors (OHS) have demonstrated a profile of strengths and resiliencies that coexist alongside specific vulnerabilities.[2] While there is a great variability among OHS,[3] studies found common characteristics including higher levels of anxiety, depressive experiences, mistrustfulness, hypervigilance, and feelings of alienation in comparison with peers. Reports from psychotherapy with OHS have documented particular psychological burdens,[4] and empirical studies demonstrated heightened preoccupation with threats to survival[5] and sensitivity to life-threatening challenges[6] and to potential threats of annihilation.[7] It was suggested that this heightened sensitivity manifests a "hostile world scenario"[8] and expectations for bad things to happen. The COVID-19 pandemic posed a life-threatening risk, which was particularly elevated for adults over the age of 60,[9] the age cohort most OHS now belong to. Social distancing measures interrupted normal activities, created isolation, and heightened the sense of danger especially for these age cohorts. For many OHS, they activated underlying intergenerational sensitivities but also highlighted their unique resiliencies and adaptive capacities.

The COVID-19 pandemic converged with multiple cataclysmic political and socio-cultural events in the USA. The "syndemic", as these synergistic crises have been referred to, contributed to the sense of a changed and unstable world, more so in the United States in comparison with other high-income countries.[10] The generally heightened sense of vigilance and threat during this time in the USA presented particular triggers for the vulnerabilities of OHS.

As these words are being written, on top of the prolonged strain of the pandemic and the events of 2020–21, a new geopolitical threat has emerged with the Russian invasion of Ukraine. Recent findings from February and March 2022[11] demonstrate that 80% of adults indicated concerns about

DOI: 10.4324/b23365-14

potentially unbearable economic consequences and threats of nuclear war. This is a higher reported level of stress in comparison with any other issue in any of the Stress in America surveys conducted by the American Psychological Association since they began in 2007. These new threats undoubtedly impact OHS negatively. In recent weeks, OHS have expressed, individually and in virtual meetings, acute distress in response to images of women and children refugees fleeing, trying to cross the borders to safety. There are also complicated emotions, due to the role of Ukrainians in the Holocaust and the well-documented active participation of Ukrainian Militia, Ukrainian police, and individuals from the general population in the murder of the Jewish population in these parts.[12] L., the daughter of two concentration camp survivors, shared: "I'm having a hard time with the Ukrainian crisis. The war is on my mind constantly. I remember my father saying how cruel the Ukrainians were. That they were worse than the Germans". L's statement echoed what I remember hearing from my own father, who survived the Janowska concentration camp. She added: "However, we're 80 years later and Zelensky is Jewish. It's so hard seeing all the horrific images and not feeling awful".

Nightmarish images of war and displacement, evoking our families' Holocaust history, are playing on the screens in front of us, a live enactment of the "transposition"[13] of the past onto the present. There is a familiarity and visual similarity between these refugees and our own families. They look like us, they are dressed like us, and they are fleeing across the same landscape of our own haunted legacy. M. told me that she saw on TV refugees walking past the house that belonged to her family, in Hungary, which is located near the border crossing from the Ukraine. Like her, I find myself emotionally discombobulated by media coverage of refugees at the border crossing in Przemysl, the Polish town where my parents' families lived, where they were forced into the ghetto, and from where they were sent to their deaths.[14]

The high levels of stress that are currently experienced by many in the USA necessitate identifying vulnerable populations and tailoring appropriate interventions to alleviate the mental health burden of the pandemic. To that end, it is important to explore how different segments of the population have been impacted to varying degrees by different aspects of the syndemic. Some risk factors are related to more tangible variables, such as loss of a loved one to COVID, suffering persistent post-COVID related symptoms, concerns about increases in cost of living, job loss, or the effects of the pandemic on the development of young children.[15] Others might be related to less tangible variables, such as the psychological sensitivities of survivors of prior trauma and the intergenerational transmission of such vulnerabilities to descendants of trauma survivors.

The vulnerabilities of OHS might not interfere with daily functioning, but they can surface under particular conditions.[16] The syndemic presented such conditions. In particular, there were multiple potential triggers for the activation and confirmation of expectations of an unsafe, dangerous, "hostile world".

Soon after the "Stay at Home" decree in mid-March 2020, I was invited to lead virtual meetings for adult children of survivors, which included psycho-educational and social-interactive elements.[17] As the daughter of two Holocaust survivors, I have dedicated much of my professional life to clinical work, research, and psychoeducation related to the effects of the Holocaust on survivors and on their descendants. The requests for such gatherings emerged as a spontaneous response to a need that was noticed by organizations that cater to OHS in the USA, Canada, Europe, and Israel. Some of these organizations included: Now Initiative for Holocaust Survivors, MorseLife Health System; Amcha, Tel-Aviv; Hamakom, Tel-Aviv; SlidingDors, Hungary; Montreal Canadian Jewish Holocaust Survivors and Descendants, Liberation 75, World Federation of Jewish Child Survivors of the Holocaust and Descendants, Toronto Daughters of Holocaust survivors, and multiple Jewish agencies catering to Holocaust survivors and their families. The sheer numbers of participants who have attended these virtual forums during the past 2 years, over 3,500 so far, reflect the level of interest and need among OHS to come together, express, and process their experiences with others who share the same intergenerational background. Many of the gatherings were recorded,[18] and observations were later discussed with the leaders of the inviting organizations, most of whom are mental health professionals, who attended these meetings and listened again to the recordings. A series of 20 of these virtual meetings was invited and sponsored by a Florida-based organization that offers a wide range of social services to survivors and their families. Dr. Jenni Frumer, PhD, LCSW, MSEd, Director, NOW for Holocaust Initiative, MorseLife Health System attended all meetings and held post-meeting discussions with me following each webinar. The following sections describe and discuss the experiences shared by OHS during the COVID-19 pandemic in the USA.

Empirical Observations During 2020–21

An empirical study[19] conducted between the months of June and August 2020 utilized a North American convenience sample drawn from participants in the 2G webinars that I facilitated who responded to a request that I put out to the mailing list of those who had registered to the online meetings, as well as on social media including my own blog and Facebook pages of 2G groups. The participants responded to questionnaires online and rated posttraumatic stress disorder (PTSD) symptoms for their parents and for themselves using the International Trauma Questionnaire.[20] They further rated their psychological distress using the Patient Health Questionnaire for Depression and Anxiety, which includes four symptoms of anxiety and depression,[21] COVID-19-related worries (e.g., "That you will develop a serious case of coronavirus and your life will be at risk") were examined with five items,[22] loneliness was assessed with the three-item version of the UCLA Loneliness Scale,[23] and social support was assessed with eight items adapted from the twelve-item Multidimensional Scale of Perceived Social Support.[24] Respondents were divided into four groups: OHS with two parents with probable PTSD, with one such parent, with no such parent, and comparisons to those whose parents did not undergo the Holocaust. The results demonstrated that OHS with two parents with PTSD reported the highest levels of PTSD symptoms. Controlling for respondents' own PTSD, OHS with two parents with PTSD reported higher psychological distress relative to comparisons. Moreover, while acknowledging having good social support, those who perceive one or both parents as having (probable) PTSD nevertheless reported higher loneliness relative to OHS without parental PTSD or comparisons. In the absence of observed differences among the groups in perceived social support, this subjective loneliness during difficult times might represent an invisible vulnerability in OHS and might be related to experiences of intergenerational failed intersubjectivity recounted in the childhood recollections of family relationships by adult OHS.[25] Parental PTSD appears to be a risk factor associated with increased vulnerability of OHS to psychological distress and subjective loneliness in our study, consistent with other findings about the critical role of parental PTSD in intergenerational transmission.[26] Our findings support the perspective that prior exposure to traumatic or stressful events, in this case exposure to intergenerational transmission of historical trauma,[27] sensitizes individuals to novel threats.[28]

Surprisingly, the groups in our study did not differ in COVID-19-related worries. This finding might reflect the fact that the participants were mostly retired and had relatively high socioeconomic status, which protected them from direct risk of exposure or the impacts of lost income. The findings suggested that the distress experienced by OHS with parental PTSD, which was reflected in higher levels of anxiety and depressive symptoms, is more general, possibly related to the multiple converging crises that occurred since the pandemic began rather than to the health risk or other concerns directly associated with COVID-19. However, the differences observed might have predated the current situation, which could not be established by our study.

Qualitative Observations During 2020–21

Further insight into the empirical findings was gained from the virtual meetings, in which participants articulated their experiences in their own words. Experiences shared in these group forums evidenced the influence of intergenerational transmission of trauma among aging OHS. Associations to parental Holocaust trauma reverberated in the reactions of OHS to the current challenges they were experiencing and sensitized them, in particular to threats of antisemitism and violence.

Stressors and Reactions to the Pandemic and Events During This Time

The participants shared a torrent of Holocaust associations, which varied as the pandemic lingered and circumstances changed. Worries about safety and concerns about shortages and scarcity were triggered during the early weeks. Some OHS went out shopping and stocked their homes with as many provisions as possible. Others, in contrast, resisted such behavior and expressed being averse to memories of their parents' tendencies to be always preparing for a disaster, to hoard food. E., a mental health professional herself, said:

> I avoided allowing myself to get overly anxious. Perhaps to a fault, numbing myself to what was going on around me, perhaps somewhat dissociating . . . I did not go to the shops, and I refused to hoard food or toilet paper. But then . . . when there was shortage . . . I was gripped by fear . . . and I started having thoughts about what might happen, what people might do if there is not enough food in the stores.

Fears about scarcity and its potential to set off violence were very close to the surface from very early on. Many OHS discussed being deeply troubled by the fact that guns and ammunition sales sharply spiked during the early months of the pandemic and have continued to increase in the USA, including many first-time buyers, a fifth of Americans who purchased guns.[29] Some OHS, many of whom had never before considered owning guns, were among these first-time buyers. The rising feeling of unsafety, of the potential for violence, was expressed by many and reflected in statements such as: "we know how neighbors can become murderers". Many expressed deep concerns about the rise of antisemitism and antisemitic attacks in the USA, which have rendered 2020 the third year with the highest number of violent incidents since the Anti-Defamation League began tracking this data.[30] The rise of violent attacks against Jews and Jewish institutions, including the deadly attack in a Kosher grocery store in Jersey City at the end of 2019 and the recent attack on a synagogue in Colleyville, Texas, has become a new part of life in America.

Concerns about violence intensified after the violent death of George Floyd, on May 25, 2020, while he was in police custody. The video of this horrifying event, showing him handcuffed and pinned to the ground under the knee of a white policeman for over nine minutes, sparked nationwide protests. Black Lives Matter, established in 2013, had grown into a national movement following the deaths of Michael Brown in Missouri and Eric Garner in New York, but in the aftermath of George Floyd's death, BLM spread around the globe. Many OHS were profoundly appalled by the inhuman behavior and brutality of the policemen who caused Floyd's death. In New York, the abandoned streets, eerily empty during the first months, took on an even more apocalyptic appearance, as department stores boarded up their storefront windows to protect against potential vandalism. Fears about potential mob violence were expressed by many OHS, as mass demonstrations took place in the cities. Some disorderly behavior led to images of shattered glass in the streets, which for many OHS was a visceral, frightening reminder of "Kristallnacht" (November 9, 1938), known as the

"Night of Broken Glass" on which Nazis in Germany and Austria torched synagogues; vandalized Jewish homes, schools, and businesses; and killed nearly one hundred Jews.[31] Many OHS expressed the sense of waking up to a reality that is profoundly disturbing and different from their previous perceptions about America. As one participant put it, echoing many others:

> We were lucky, for our entire life, yes, there was the missile crisis with Cuba, but . . . the world seemed to be getting more . . . sane, the country seemed to be getting ahead, women's lib, the Civil Rights movement, the end of the cold war.

L. said tearfully:

> So was my mother right?! Growing up, in the arguments with my mother . . . I said, it's ancient history [the Holocaust]. It's different now. She said, people are the same, no matter where they live or what generation. . . . Sometimes there is an increased sense of threat, sometimes I could dismiss it more. Now, I cannot dismiss it. When your children are hiding their Mezuzas and star of David, you know the world is dangerous. It's like Pandora's Box was closed after the Holocaust, and now it's reopened, and it's been multiplying in there!

The year 2020 was also a presidential election year in the USA and a watershed event with regard to political discourse and political culture, exposing profound ruptures in the social fabric of the country. Many of the events were triggers for fears and potential confirmations of a view of people, from government officials to one's next-door neighbors, as untrustworthy, hostile, dangerous, and violent. A presidency characterized from its inception by inflammatory language and disregard of verifiable evidence culminated in an armed insurrection on Capitol Hill on January 6, 2021. Many of the demonstrators donned Nazi and antisemitic symbols, and at least seven people lost their lives as a result of the insurrection.[32] The images on TV and the media were terrifying, a frenzied rampage in the nation's most revered seat of government. This unprecedented event, incited by the former president, Donald Trump,[33] was especially frightening to OHS. It called forth the memory of the Reichstag fire, the catastrophic demise of democracy, and the intoxicating effect of inciting hatred and mob violence. The protracted and baseless contesting of the results of the elections was another continued stressor and 'proof' that the very basis of democracy is threatened and that the world can no longer be trusted to operate according to predictable and decent rules.

As the pandemic persisted, participants expressed a sense of mounting anxiety about antisemitism that they have never experienced before in their lifetime. Direct and offensive associations to the Holocaust were voiced publicly by celebrities, including, for example, the anti-vaccine activist Robert F. Kennedy, Jr., who stated in a public rally that things are worse for people living under COVID restrictions and mandates than they were for Anne Frank, the teenager who died in a Nazi concentration camp after hiding for two years in an annex in an Amsterdam house.[34] Such incidents repeatedly shocked OHS, some of whom stated, "Are we not seeing the writing on the wall?!" and "Now I understand how hard it was to leave Europe before it was too late!" Others expressed being flooded with panic when Israel closed its borders to non-citizens due to COVID-19 restrictions. Some OHS reported feeling like there was no safe place for them to go, similar to their parents' situation just before WWII. A constant stream of additional reminders of the Holocaust seemed to occur. In January 2021, a school board in Tennessee voted unanimously to ban the illustrated Pulitzer Prize-winning novel *Maus*[35] from being taught in the classroom.[36] In several places across the USA, there were incidents of book burnings,[37] and OHS expressed the dread evoked by these images, reminiscent of the book burnings in Nazi Germany and indicative of similar dangerous attitudes and sentiments about differences and diversity. These direct references and reminders of the Holocaust and indications of rising antisemitism have been a growing stressor for the Jewish community in the USA and for OHS in particular.[38]

Alongside the overarching sense of hypervigilance and anxiety, many OHS acknowledged perceived hardiness and resilience, which they felt made it easier for them to cope with the current circumstances, in comparison with non-Holocaust related others. OHS expressed recognition of an inherent preparedness for disaster, conferred by the legacy of trauma: "The feeling of doom? I kind of feel this is the feeling I have been expecting my whole life . . . It is not at all a surprise". Many expressed an awareness of the adaptive benefits of hypersensitivity to signs of danger. One participant who left her job while others, including her boss, were still underestimating the risk of COVID-19 and avoiding protective measures, said: "I am like the canary in the mine. I sense things before other people do. I tried to warn them, but I was viewed as an alarmist". A sense of one's own fortitude was also frequently revealed:

> We [OHS] are interestingly appreciative [of the current situation we are in] while comparing with what our parents went through. This is setting me apart from others [not OHS] who are struggling more. I have the acceptance that things can change within seconds, and I know I have extreme resources to adapt to new situations.

Yet another shared a dream in which she relived her parents' survival story:

> I spent the night running from the Nazis . . . I was in a modern village running through alleyways. Jews were being herded through the alleys and pushed on school busses . . . some were wearing *tallits* . . . all heads were down. I couldn't believe that this was happening again. I knew I needed to escape to the woods on the outskirts of the city . . . I knew how to survive this . . . I needed to find guns to fight. The dream went on and on to where I hid, to peeing in the woods, to watching Jews silently walking to the buses . . . a real nightmare. But my resilience was ever present.

Some OHS commented sorrowfully about their chronic hypervigilance and scanning for danger, which interferes with their sense of wellbeing and with the atmosphere of family relations: "It's my experience and observation that many of us 2Gs are faring better emotionally than others [during the pandemic] – we are accustomed to extreme situations of threat and danger. The challenge is: how do we live in more 'normal' times?"

Subjective Loneliness: An Intergenerational Vulnerability

While isolation can cause loneliness, loneliness is a subjective experience that can be experienced also in the company of others. Loneliness is the discrepancy individuals experience between their desired and achieved level of social relationships[39] and reflects the psychological perception of one's social relationships as insufficient. Individuals may have a social network but still feel lonely when these relations are perceived as not rewarding enough or not meaningful and satisfying.[40] Multiple participants in the webinars shared that they felt they could not be understood by family and friends who are not children of survivors. Some feared their reactions would be judged as "too extreme" because of their hypersensitivity to perceived reminders of the Holocaust in response to current events. In contrast, some felt that others would be alienated or offended if they shared that being children of survivors "relativizes" their experience of the current hardships. They felt others could not understand that, as children of survivors, they experience the present as less difficult, because it is compared with what survivor parents endured during the Holocaust. This observation of an emotional and communicative gap, of not being able to share meaningful aspects of one's experience during a time of crisis, is particularly relevant to the finding from our empirical study, that OHS with parental PTSD demonstrated elevated loneliness in comparison with others, despite equally perceived social support.

The rapid emergence of COVID-19 and the measures taken to minimize its spread have severely disrupted normal life. Concerns about the negative mental health effects of the pandemic and of social distancing were unfortunately confirmed by reports of rising psychological distress from around the world.[41] In the USA, a study conducted as early as the third week of "shelter at home" showed that loneliness was significantly higher than normal during the COVID-19 pandemic and was associated with increased depression and suicidal ideation. The authors cautioned that loneliness was "a signature mental health concern in the era of COVID-19" and that public health efforts must address increased loneliness during the COVID-19 pandemic.[42] These findings came on top of what has already been referred to as "the epidemic of loneliness" by the former surgeon general of the USA, Dr. Vivek H. Murthy, who identified it as a major public health issue prior to COVID-19.[43] Loneliness and isolation have been associated with elevated risk for mental and physical health consequences.[44] The pandemic highlighted the need to identify vulnerable populations and to design protective measures for circumstances that might again place them at risk of isolation and loneliness. Prior trauma might constitute such a vulnerability, as it has been associated with elevated subjective loneliness. Individuals who endured trauma may feel that those who did not share their experiences are not capable of understanding them and that they are not able to communicate such experiences.[45] Elie Wiesel, Holocaust survivor and Nobel Prize laureate, was an internationally revered writer and professor of the humanities at Boston University who dedicated his life to telling the world about the evil he experienced as a prisoner in Auschwitz, to political activism, and to fighting against oppression across the globe.[46] Wiesel stated, "The survivor speaks in an alien tongue. You will never break its code". Subjective loneliness associated with the intergenerational transmission of trauma related to the Holocaust was one of the main findings in our empirical study and was articulated and shared by many participants in the virtual forums. A subjective difficulty in benefiting from social support, especially during times when one's social engagement is limited, might represent a vulnerability that increases feelings of loneliness and isolation and could place offspring of trauma survivors at higher risk regarding the mental health burden of the pandemic.

Transmission of Effects Related to Parental PTSD

Our empirical findings highlighted the role of intergenerational transmission of trauma, in particular parental PTSD, in the responses of aging children of survivors of genocide to the novel challenges they encountered during the pandemic. The intergenerational transmission of parental PTSD and its impact on the mental health of children in the family is a major issue globally and in the USA. The recent decades have witnessed the largest population migration due to political conflicts and natural disasters since the end of WWII.[47] In the USA, the trauma of historical and ongoing racism, recent military conflicts, and terrorism have left many parents and would-be parents with full or partial PTSD. Recent migrants, undocumented immigrants and the "dreamers" (undocumented immigrants who are minors, granted conditional residency under The Development, Relief and Education for Alien Minors Act) live in the USA with constant fear of deportation and separation from family members. The horrific conditions of asylum seekers, especially unaccompanied Mexican minors, have been an inconceivable travesty.[48] In addition, there are those whose lives have been recently directly impacted by loss of a loved one, one of the 964,831 COVID-deaths in the USA at the time this chapter was written.[49] Understanding the intergenerational transmission of effects related to parental trauma has never been more globally and nationally relevant.

Aging and Ageism

In the USA, the 65 and older population is rapidly growing as Baby Boomers age.[50] Globally, it is predicted that, by mid-century, 1 in 6 people will be aged 65 years or older.[51] The "graying" of the population[52] makes it urgent to understand the interaction of effects of intergenerational transmission of trauma with aging and with the endemic problems of ageism and loneliness. COVID-19 amplified stereotypes of all older people as frail and helpless. These views were spread by social media, the press, and public announcements by government officials throughout the world[53] and exacerbated perennial pre-pandemic ageism. Some of the indelible images from the pandemic in the USA will forever be the photographs of countless bodies awaiting burial, heaped on top of each other in nursing facilities, where death rates sky-rocketed.

Older adults, many of whom have been professionally and socially active and engaged until the "shelter at home" decree, were lumped together with frail older adults requiring long-term care. Such lumping together and undervaluing the contribution of older adults is a form of ageism.[54] Contrary to stereotypes, the process of aging shows great variability and is context- and cohort-dependent. Chronological age is not the most important measure of an individual's level of functioning.[55] A "lifespan perspective"[56] on aging posits that individual reactions to the many challenges of aging differ according to personal life histories. From this contextual perspective, it is particularly important to examine how previous massive trauma – and its reverberations in intergenerational transmission – impact the way older people experience novel challenges and traumatic events such as those that took place during the COVID-19 pandemic. A better understanding of such risk factors and the identification of strengths, resiliencies, and protective factors can help design interventions and prevention programs for potential future circumstances requiring social distancing for personal reasons (such as health and mobility issues) or collective reasons, such as a potential future pandemic.

Closing Thoughts: The Need for Novel Strategies

Given the magnitude of the pandemic, mental health needs will have to be addressed on a large scale. International organizations, including the WHO, advocate for integration of mental health and psychosocial support into the COVID-19 response, and a UN policy brief,[57] as well as an executive report from the World Economic Forum,[58] emphasize that investments now will reduce the burden of negative mental health effects later.[59]

This chapter described virtual psycho-social meetings that emerged as a spontaneous response to a need that was expressed by OHS and responded to by social networks of OHS around the globe. The new digital technologies offer novel, efficient, global tools for virtual group meetings that facilitate connection and engagement when circumstances hinder in-person contact. The meetings described were distinct from mental health interventions and specifically focused on facilitating shared experience and connection. Such forums offer collective spaces for individuals who share similar traumatic backgrounds to contain common vulnerabilities. Gathering with other children of survivors created a potential space for expressing and processing trauma-related experiences that participants feel cannot be shared or fully understood elsewhere. This experience proved to be uniquely suitable in addressing subjective feelings of loneliness, which might constitute a particular intergenerational vulnerability among aging offspring of trauma survivors, especially those with parental PTSD. Virtual forums can be tailored around the specific social identity of particular groups and can provide relevant, culturally sensitive psychosocial intervention and prevention strategies, offering also an opportunity to share, articulate, and amplify unique resiliencies associated with the experience of growing up with survivor parents and with the strengths and endurance of previous generations. Our observations are consistent with the Social Identity Approach to Health (SIAH, also referred to as "the social cure,"[60]), which posits that people feel a sense of belonging in groups where they are able to express shared identities and that social interaction involving people who share a social identity will usually be experienced as more positive and meaningful compared to an interaction with an outgroup member.

The widespread use of the technological platforms during COVID-19 has mobilized people who were not previously utilizing digital technology for social activities to become more open to them and more facile at using them. However, accessibility is not the only obstacle to overcome. There can be functional barriers amongst older adults, as even those who utilize digital communication to maintain existing relationships do not usually view it as a way to create new connections.[61] Furthermore, many popular digital tools have not been designed to address the needs of older adults during times of limited contact. Stuart et al.[62] offer groundbreaking, almost futuristic ideas for designing digital loneliness interventions. They argue for a multidisciplinary integration of the psychology of loneliness and social identity theory with Human-Computer Interaction research to build digital interventions that enable older people and their social networks to socially engage in ways that are meaningful to them, thus addressing loneliness created by social isolation.

Novel strategies are necessary to improve accessibility to electronic devices and increase basic computer literacy among older adults, especially among vulnerable populations. Cooperation among government and private sector stakeholders is necessary to redesign social policies, insurance regulations, and more, in view of the lessons from the COVID-19 pandemic. It will need to be determined who will pay for these much-needed new services that might help protect older adults from the accentuated negative effects of social distancing now and in the future. Previous public health campaigns have succeeded in changing behaviors, and various types of health-related devices and wellness services are provided and paid for by insurance companies. To combat the endemic problems of loneliness and the added risks of social distancing, efforts to increase the beneficial potential of digital technology must be introduced to policies regarding retirement and healthcare benefits and to the classes and trainings that are available through social services. The interconnectedness of the world made society vulnerable to the pandemic[63] but has also highlighted the critical role of developing novel ways to facilitate connections as protection against psychological distress. Psychologists, mental health professionals, and researchers have an important role in implementing lessons learned from the pandemic to social change. We have to communicate our observations and findings outside our own circles, interact with stakeholders and the media, and advocate for the necessary innovations and for progress and inclusion regarding the needs of older adults in particular.

Notes

1 Lambert et al., 2014; Leen-Feldner et al., 2013.
2 Felsen, 1998; Kellerman, 2001; Prince, 2015; Shmotkin et al., 2011.
3 Danieli et al., 2017; Dashorst et al., 2019; Letzter Pouw et al., 2014.
4 Auerhahn, 2013; Grünberg, 2007; Kogan, 1995; Peskin et al., 1997; Solomon and Chaitin, 2007.
5 Scharf and Mayseless, 2011.
6 Baider et al., 2006; Solomon et al., 1988; Waldfogel, 1991; Yehuda et al., 1998.
7 Shrira, 2015.

8 Shmotkin, 2005.
9 CDC, 2020.
10 Arpaci et al., 2022; Williams et al., 2020.
11 "Stress in America," 2022.
12 Gilbert, 1985.
13 Kestenberg, 1982.
14 *Los Angeles Times*, 2022.
15 "Stress in America," 2022.
16 Shrira and Felsen, 2021.
17 Felsen, 2021.
18 Felsen, 2021.
19 Shrira and Felsen, 2021.
20 Cloitre et al., 2018.
21 Kroenke et al., 2009.
22 Bergman et al., 2020.
23 Hughes et al., 2004.
24 Zimet et al., 1988.
25 Wiseman, 2008.
26 Lambert et al., 2014; Leen-Feldner et al., 2013.
27 SAMSHA, 2014.
28 Solomon, 1993.
29 Helmore, 2021.
30 "Antisemitism in the US," n.d.
31 Gilbert, 1985: 69–75, 471.
32 "Capitol Riot Investigations," n.d.
33 New York Times, 2022.
34 Frank, 1947/1993; Mueller, 1998.
35 Spiegelman, 1986.
36 Gross, 2022.
37 Levin, 2021.
38 Milbank, 2022.
39 Gierveld et al., 2018.
40 Hughes et al., 2004.
41 *Psychological Trauma: Theory, Research, Practice, Policy,* 2020, July, vol. 12, issue 5.
42 Killgore et al., 2020.
43 McGregor, 2017.
44 Holt-Lunstad et al., 2010.
45 Amery, 1995; LaMothe, 1999; Laub and Auerhahn, 1989; Stolorow, 2007.
46 Wiesel, 1978: 175.
47 United Nations, n.d.
48 Human Rights Watch, 2022.
49 CDC, 2020.
50 US Census Bureau, n.d.
51 United Nations, 2020.
52 United Nations Department of Economics and Social Affairs, Population Division, 2019.
53 Ayalon et al., 2021.
54 Staudinger, 2020.
55 Staudinger, 2020.
56 Wahl et al., 2017.
57 United Nations, 2020.
58 World Economic Forum, 2020.
59 Moreno et al., 2020.
60 Haslam et al., 2018; Jetten, 2020; Jetten et al., 2012.
61 Stuart et al., 2022.
62 Stuart et al., 2022.
63 Moreno et al., 2020.

Bibliography

Amery, Jean, 1995. "Torture", in: Lawrence L. Langer (ed.), *Art from the Ashes: A Holocaust Anthology*, New York: Oxford University Press: 121–137.

Anti-Defamation League, n.d. *Antisemitism in the US*, www.adl.org/what-we-do/anti-semitism/antisemitism-in-the-us retrieved on March 19, 2022.

Arpaci, Ibrahim, Karatas, Kasim, Baloglu, Mustafa, and Haktanir, Abdulkadir, 2022. "COVID-19 Phobia in the United States: Validation of the COVID-19 Phobia Scale (C19P-SE)", *Death Studies* 46 (3): 553–559.

Auerhahn, Nanette C., 2013. "Evolution of Traumatic Narratives: Impact of the Holocaust on Children of Survivors", *The Psychoanalytic Study of the Child* 67 (1): 215–246.

Ayalon, Liat, Chasteen, Alison, Diehl, Manfred, Levy, Becca R., Neupert, Shevaun D., Rothermund, Klaus, Tesch-Römer, Clemens, and Wahl, Hans-Werner, 2021. "Aging in Times of the COVID-19 Pandemic: Avoiding Ageism and Fostering Intergenerational Solidarity", *The Journal of Gerontology: Series B* 76 (2): e49–e52.

Baider, Lea, Goldzeig, Gil, Ever-Hadani, Pnina, and Peretz, Tamar, 2006. "Psychological Distress and Coping in Breast Cancer Patients and Healthy Women Whose Parents Survived the Holocaust", *Psycho-Oncology* 15 (7): 635–646.

Bergman, Yoav S., Cohen-Fridel, Sara, Shrira, Amit, Bodner, Ehud, and Palgi, Yuval, 2020. "COVID-19 Health Worries and Anxiety Symptoms Among Older Adults: The Moderating Role of Ageism", *International Psychogeriatrics* 32 (11): 1371–1375.

"Capitol Riot Investigations", n.d. *The New York Times*, www.nytimes.com/spotlight/us-capitol-riots-investigations retrieved on March 19, 2022.

Centers for Disease Control and Prevention (CDC), 2020. *Coronavirus Disease 2019 (COVID-19) Older Adults*. https://stacks.cdc.gov/view/cdc/85964

Cloitre, Marylene, Shevlin, Mark, Brewin, Christopher R., Bisson, Jonathan I., Roberts, Neil P., Maercker, Andreas, Karatzias, Thanos, and Hyland, Philip, 2018. "The International Trauma Questionnaire: Development of a Self-Report Measure of ICD-11 PTSD and Complex PTSD", *Acta Psychiatrica Scandinavica* 138 (6): 536–546.

Danieli, Yael, Norris, H. Fran, and Engdahl, Brian, 2017. "A Question of Who, Not If: Psychological Disorders in Holocaust Survivors' Children", *Psychological Trauma: Theory, Research, Practice, and Policy* 9 (S1): 98–106.

Dashorst, Patricia, Moorenb, Trudy M., Kleber, Rolf J., de Jong, Peter J., and Huntjensd, Rafaele J.C., 2019. "Intergenerational Consequences of the Holocaust on Offspring Mental Health: A Systematic Review of Associated Factors and Mechani", *European Journal of Psychotraumatology* 10 (1): 1654065.

Felsen, Irit, 1998. "Transgenerational Transmission of Effects of the Holocaust: The North American Research Perspective", in: Yael Danieli (ed.), *International Handbook of Multigenerational Legacies of Trauma*, New York, NY: Plenum: 43–68.

Felsen, Irit, 2021. "'Web-Based, Second-Best Togetherness': Psychosocial Group Intervention with Children of Holocaust Survivors During COVID-19", *American Journal of Orthopsychiatry* 91 (2): 171–180. https://www.youtube.com/playlist?list=PL98TejO6Vy3qoYCkt71NEKjfHw431dvet

Frank, Anne, 1947. *The Diary of a Young Girl*, London: Bantam Books (re-released in English in 1993).

Gierveld, J.D.J., Van Tilburg, T.G., and Dykstra, P.A., 2018. "New Ways of Theorizing and Conducting Research in the Field of Loneliness and Social Isolation", in: A. L. Vangelisti and D. Perlman (eds.), *The Cambridge Handbook of Personal Relationships,* Cambridge: Cambridge University Press: 391–404. https://doi.org/10.1017/9781316417867.031

Gilbert, Martin, 1985. *The Holocaust: A History of the Jews of Europe During the Second World War*, New York: Henry Holt and Company.

Gross, Jenny, 2022. "School Board in Tennessee Bans Teaching of Holocaust Novel 'Maus'", *The New York Times*. January 27, 2022.

Grünberg, Kurt, 2007. "Contaminated Generativity: Holocaust Survivors and Their Children in Germany", *American Journal of Psychoanalysis* 67 (1): 82–96.

Haslam, Alexander, McMahon, S. Charlotte, Cruwys, Tegan, Haslam, Catherine, Jetten, Jolanda J., and Steffens, Niklas K., 2018. "Social Cure, What Social Cure? The Propensity to Underestimate the Importance of Social Factors for Health", *Social Science & Medicine* 198: 14–21.

Helmore, Edward, 2021. "US Gun Sales Spiked During Pandemic and Continue to Rise", *The Guardian*. May 31.

Holt-Lunstad, Julianne, Smith, Timothy B., and Layton, J. Bradley, 2010. "Social Relationships and Mortality Risk: A Meta-Analytic Review", *PLoS Medicine* 7 (7): e1000316.

Hughes, Mary Elithabeth, Waite, Linda J., Hawkley, Lewis C., and Cacioppo, John T., 2004. "A Short Scale for Measuring Loneliness in Large Surveys: Results from Two Population-Based Studies", *Research on Aging* 26 (6): 655–672.

Jetten, Jolanda, 2020. *Together Apart: The Psychology of COVID-19*, Thousand Oaks, CA: SAGE Publications.

Jetten, Jolanda, Catherine Haslam, and Alexander S. Haslam (eds.), 2012. *The Social Cure: Identity, Health and Well-Being*, London: Psychology Press.

Kellerman, Nathan P., 2001. "Psychopathology in Children of Holocaust Survivors: A Review of the Research Literature", *Israeli Journal of Psychiatry and Related Sciences* 38 (1): 36–46.

Kestenberg, Judith S., 1982. *Survivor-Parents and Their Children*, New York, NY: Basic Books.

Killgore, William D.S., Cloonan, Sara A., Taylor, Emily C., and Dailey, Natalie S., 2020. "Loneliness: A Signature Mental Health Concern in the Era of COVID-19", *Psychiatry Research* 290: 113117.

Kogan, Illany, 1995. *The Cry of Muted Children A Psychoanalytic Perspective of the Second Generation of the Holocaust*, London: Free Association Books.

Kroenke, Kurt, Spitzer, Robert L., Williams, Janet B.W., and Löwe, Bernd, 2009. "An Ultra-Brief Screening Scale for Anxiety and Depression: The PHQ–4", *Psychosomatics* 50 (6): 613–621.

Lambert, Jessica E., Holzer, Jessica, and Hasbun, Amber, 2014. "Association Between Parents' PTSD Severity and Childrens' Psychological Distress: A Meta-Analysis", *Journal of Traumatic Stress* 27 (1): 9–17.

LaMothe, Ryan, 1999. "The Absence of Cure of Malignant Trauma and Symbolization", *Journal of Interpersonal Violence* 14 (11): 1193–1210.

Laub, D., and Auerhahn, N., 1989. "Failed Empathy – A Central Theme in the Survivor's Holocaust Experience", *Psychoanalytic Psychology* 6 (4): 377–400.

Leen-Feldner, Ellen W., Feldner, Matthew T., Knapp, Ashley, Bunaciu, Liviu, Blumenthal, Heidemarie, and Amstadter, A.B., 2013. "Offspring Psychological and Biological Correlates of Parental Posttraumatic Stress: Review of the Literature and Research Agenda", *Clinical Psychology Review* 33: 1106–1133.

Letzter Pouw, Sonia E., Shrira, Amit, Ben-Ezra, Menachem, and Palgi, Yuval, 2014. "Trauma Transmission Through Perceived Parental Burden Among Holocaust Survivors' Offspring and Grandchildren", *Psychological Trauma: Theory, Research, Practice, and Policy* 6 (4): 420–429.

Levin, B., 2021. "Conservatives Are Just Openly Endorsing Book Burning Now", *Vanity Fair*. November 11, 2021.

McGregor, Jena, 2017. "This Former Surgeon General Says There's a 'Loneliness Epidemic' and Work is Partly to Blame", *The Washington Post*. October 4, 2017.

Milbank, Dana, 2022. "American Jews Start to Think the Unthinkable", *The Washington Post*, October 28, www.washingtonpost.com/opinions/2022/10/28/american-jews-exile-fears/

Moreno, Carmen, Wykes, Til T., Galderisi, Silvana, Nordentoft, Merete, Crossley, Nicolas, Jones, Nev, Cannon, Mary, Correll, Christof U., Byrne, Louise, Carr, Sarah, Chen, Eric Y.H., Gorwood, Phillip, Johnson, Sonia, Kärkkäinen, Hillka, Krystal, John H., Lee, Jimmy, Lieberman, Jeffry, López-Jaramillo, Carlos, Männikkö, Miia, Phillips, Michael R., Uchida, Hiroyuki, Vieta, Eduard, Vita, Antonio, and Arango, Celso, 2020. "How Mental Health Care Should Change as a Consequence of the COVID-19 Pandemic", *The Lancet Psychiatry* 7 (9): 813–824.

Mueller, Melissa, 1998. *Anne Frank the Biography*, New York: Henry Holt and Company.

Peskin, Harvey, Auerhahn, Nanette C., and Laub, Dori, 1997, "The Second Holocaust: Therapeutic Rescue When Life Threatens", *Journal of Personal & Interpersonal Loss* 2 (1): 1–25.

Prince, Robert M., 2015. "The Holocaust after 70 Years: Holocaust Survivors in the United States", *American Journal of Psychoanalysis* 75 (3): 267–286.

SAMSHA, 2014. *Trauma-Informed Care in Behavioral Health Services, TIP 57*. Rockville, MD: U.S. Department of Health and Human Services.

Scharf, Miri, and Mayseless, Ofra, 2011. "Disorganizing Experiences in Second- and Third-Generation Holocaust Survivors", *Qualitative Health Research* 21 (11): 1539–1553.

Shmotkin, Dov, 2005. "Happiness in the Face of Adversity: Reformulating the Dynamic and Modular Bases of Subjective Well-Being", *Review of General Psychology* 9 (4): 291–325.

Shmotkin, Dov, Shrira, Amit, Goldberg, Shira C., and Palgi, Yuval, 2011. "Resilience and Vulnerability Among Aging Holocaust Survivors and Their Families: An Intergenerational Overview", *Journal of Intergenerational Relationships* 9 (1): 7–21.

Shrira, Amit, 2015. "Transmitting the Sum of All Fears: Iranian Nuclear Threat Salience Among Offspring of Holocaust Survivors", *Psychological Trauma: Theory, Research, Practice and Policy* 7 (4): 364–371.

Shrira, Amit, and Felsen, Irit, 2021. "Parental PTSD and Psychological Reactions During the COVID-19 Pandemic Among Offspring of Holocaust Survivors", *Psychological Trauma: Theory, Research, Practice* 13 (4): 438–445.

Solomon, Zahava, 1993. *Combat Stress Reaction: The Enduring Toll of War*, New York, NY: Plenum Press.

Solomon, Zahava, and Chaitin, Julia, 2007. *Childhood in the Shadow of the Holocaust: Child Survivors and Second Generation* (in Hebrew), Bnei Brak: Hakibbutz Hameuchad.

Solomon, Zahava, Kotler, Moshe, and Mikulincer, Mario, 1988. "Combat-Related Posttraumatic Stress Disorder Among Second-Generation Holocaust Survivors Preliminary Findings", *American Journal of Psychiatry* 145: 865–868.

Spiegelman, Art, 1986. *Maus: A Survivor's Tale, I: My Father Bleeds History*, New York, NY: Pantheon Books.

Staudinger, Ursula M., 2020. "The Positive Plasticity of Adult Development: Potential for the 21st Century", *The American Psychologist* 75 (4): 540–553.

Stolorow, Robert D., 2007. *Trauma and Human Existence: Autobiographical, Psychoanalytic, and Philosophical Reflections*, London: Routledge.

Stress in America: On Second COVID-19 Anniversary, Money, Inflation, War Pile on to Nation Stuck in Survival Mode, 2022, www.apa.org/news/press/releases/stress/2022/march-2022-survival-mode

Stuart, Avelie, Katz, Dmitri, Stevenson, Clifford, Gooch, Daniel, Harkin, Lydia, Bennasar, Mohamed, Sanderson, Lisa, Liddle, Jacki, Bennaceur, Amel, Levine, Mark, Mehta, Vikram, Wijesundara, Akshika, Talbot, Catherine, Bandara, Arosha, Price, Blaine, and Nuseibeh, Bashar, 2022. "Loneliness in Older People and COVID-19: Applying the Social Identity Approach to Digital Intervention Design", *Computers in Human Behavior Reports* 6: 100179. https://doi.org/10.1016/j.chbr.2022.100179

"Ukrainian Refugees at the Main Train Station in Przemysl, Poland", 2022. *Los Angeles Times*, March 6.

United Nations, 2020. *Policy Brief: Covid-19 and the Need for Action on Mental Health & World Population Aging 2020.* https://unsdg.un.org/resources/policy-brief-covid-19-and-need-action-mental-health

United Nations, n.d. *Refugees.* United Nations; United Nations, www.un.org/en/global-issues/refugees retrieved on March 19, 2022.

United Nations, Department of Economic and Social Affairs, Population Division, 2019. *World Population Ageing 2019: Highlights* (ST/ESA/SER.A/430), www.un.org/en/development/desa/population/publications/pdf/ageing/WorldPopulationAgeing2019-Highlights.pdf

"US Border Program's Huge Toll on Children", 2022. *Human Rights Watch*, February 4, www.hrw.org/news/2022/02/04/us-border-programs-huge-toll-children

US Census Bureau, n.d. *65 and Older Population Grows Rapidly as Baby Boomers Age.* Census.Gov, www.census.gov/newsroom/press-releases/2020/65-older-population-grows.html retrieved on March 17, 2022.

Wahl, Hans-Werner, Tesch-Römer, Clemens, and Hoff, Andreas (eds.), 2017. *New Dynamics in Old Age: Individual, Environmental and Societal Perspectives*, London: Routledge.

Waldfogel, Shimon, 1991. "Physical Illness in Children of Holocaust Survivors", *General Hospital Psychiatry* 13 (4): 267–269.

Wiesel, Eli, 1978. *A Jew Today*, New York, NY: Random House, Inc.

Williams, Reginald D., II, Shah, Arnav, Tikkanen, Roosa, Schneider, Eric C., and Doty, Michelle M., 2020. "Do Americans Face Greater Mental Health and Economic Consequences from COVID-19? Comparing the U.S. with Other High-Income Countries", *The Commomwealth Fund.* https://www.commonwealthfund.org/publications/issue-briefs/2020/aug/americans-mental-health-and-economic-consequences-COVID19 retrieved April 13, 2023.

Wiseman, Hadas, 2008. "On Failed Intersubjectivity: Recollections of Loneliness Experiences in Offspring of Holocaust Survivors", *American Journal of Orthopsychiatry* 78 (3): 350–358.

World Economic Forum, 2020. *COVID and Longer Lives: Combating Ageism and Creating Solutions.* https://www3.weforum.org/docs/WEF_Combating_ageism_and_creating_solutions_2020.pdf

Yehuda, Rachel, Schmeidler, James, Wainberg, Milton, Binder-Brynes, Karen, and Duvdevani, Tamar, 1998. "Vulnerability to Posttraumatic Stress Disorder in Adult Offspring of Holocaust Survivors", *American Journal of Psychiatry* 155: 1163–1171.

Zimet, Gregory D., Dahlem, Nancy W., Zimet, Sara G., and Farley, Gordon K., 1988. "The Multidimensional Scale of Perceived Social Support", *Journal of Personality Assessment* 52 (1): 30–41.

12

PAST, PRESENT, AND FUTURE PERSPECTIVES OF HOLOCAUST TRAUMA TRANSMISSION

Natan P.F. Kellermann

Can Parental Traumatization Be Transmitted to Their Offspring?

This question has repeatedly been asked ever since the Second World War in connection with the offspring of Holocaust survivors (OHS). This population has regularly been studied almost since they were born, from infancy, childhood, and adolescence, throughout their early adulthood and midlife,[1] to the present stage of mature adulthood and old age. For more than 70 years, qualitative and quantitative data have been collected, resulting in a sizeable cumulative database that provides a unique long-term perspective of a population at risk due to their parents' war-time experiences.

The knowledge gained from Holocaust trauma transmission (HTT) has substantial translational applications, since it is relevant also for the offspring of survivors from a wide variety of other traumatic events. This includes the offspring of survivors of other types of mass trauma,[2] victims of Apartheid-era human rights violations,[3] Native Americans,[4] natural disasters,[5] as well as the offspring of combat veterans,[6] ex-POWs,[7] survivors of terrorist attacks,[8] and victims of torture and domestic violence.[9] Indeed, anyone who has experienced an adverse event may wonder how the impact on themselves may also have affected (or will affect) their children.

The question is not only limited to the transmission of anxiety disorders and complex stress-related disorders such as post-traumatic stress disorder (PTSD), which are moderately hereditary.[10] It is also relevant to a wide range of mental disorders that can be passed on from parent to child. For example, the offspring of parents with severe mental illness are at increased risk for a range of psychiatric disorders.[11] However, despite substantial progress in other areas of psychiatric genetics, few risk factors have been identified,[12] and there are still many open questions regarding trauma transmission in general: *who* is more likely to transmit, *what* is transmitted, *who* is more susceptible, *where* and *when* is it more likely to happen, and *how* does such a transmission transpire?

Since no definitive answers have been found to these questions, the purpose of this chapter is to take a new look at the underlying assumptions of trauma transmission. By focusing on the past, present, and future perspectives, the review will critically evaluate the strengths and weaknesses in past research, highlight important issues that have been left unresolved, and suggest how future research can produce new information on the relevant variables in the study of trauma transmission. In conclusion, a more comprehensive and integrative conceptual model of transmission will be suggested from a developmental systems perspective that can guide future research in this field with a variety of populations.

DOI: 10.4324/b23365-15

Past Perspectives

During more than half a century, studies on OHS have advanced through the following simplified and roughly estimated six decades:

The 1960s: initial case studies were based on clinical observations and anecdotal reports of adolescent OHS who suffered from anxieties and who seemed to be different from their peers.[13]

The 1970s: based on similar observations of OHS who had now reached early adulthood, several psychoanalytic case studies were published. Preliminary empirical investigations were also carried out[14] but later criticized for methodological flaws.[15] When the book *Children of the Holocaust*[16] was published, it resonated well with OHS and gave them a distinct identity as the Second Generation.

The 1980s: various conceptualizations of HTT were suggested, and the professional literature increased in scope.[17] Concurrent with the increased application of PTSD in the treatment of Holocaust survivors, clinicians started to question if this disorder could be intrinsically transmittable to offspring. Individual and group psychotherapies for young adult OHS were therefore provided in many countries. At this time, many OHS became parents themselves and thus gained a deeper understanding of what it meant to be a parent.

The 1990s: the number of controlled studies increased and shifted to nonclinical samples.[18] Even though these studies did not find more psychopathology in adult OHS,[19] more wide-ranging study designs were used to investigate the interaction between parents and offspring in Holocaust survivor families.[20] Different outcomes in these studies led to an attempt to integrate earlier findings of vulnerability and resilience, and the entire field became more diversified and multi-faceted. Initial results from studies on possible biological correlates also began to appear.[21]

The 2000s: when OHS had reached mid-adulthood, a more integrative understanding of trauma transmission had evolved,[22] with an increasing focus on the aggravating and mitigating factors.[23] In comparative studies on representative samples, OHS were not found to differ in secondary traumatization[24] or in physical morbidity.[25] Similar results were reported in a later review of studies on the impact of genocide on children's psychopathology in general.[26] The clinical subgroup, however, continued to present emotional problems and utilize mental health services. Possible epigenetic pathways of transmission were suggested for this population.[27]

The 2010s: as OHS reached late adulthood, the number of OHS studies declined, with a focus on the aging process[28] and the biological basis for Holocaust trauma (HT).

The 2020s: the present COVID-19 pandemic era brought social isolation and a threat of infection that impacted the entire world as a collective trauma.[29] The past concerns of OHS became less important than the present ones.

In sum, studies from the early years investigated whether OHS were different from other populations and, if so, in what way. Were they more disturbed than others? Were they more vulnerable or more resilient? Were they more predisposed to PTSD when serving in the army?[30] Were they more prone to commit suicide? Did they smoke more, divorce more, and suffer more from being diagnosed with cancer? As these differences were highlighted, further differentiation was made between, for example, OHS and other children of immigrants, men and women, and OHS in different countries. Studies continued to be conducted in small, often self-selected samples. Descriptive studies were replaced by more controlled, empirical, large-scale studies with more sophisticated empirical research methodologies, but they did not bring about objective measures that provided valuable and generalizable data on OHS. There were few conclusive answers to many of the questions that remained. In fact, one may argue that they were less illuminating in terms of what they conveyed, in contrast to the early single case histories that were based on in-depth interviews, autographic memoirs, and the accounts of homogeneous OHS groups.[31] These early and sometimes psychoanalytic reports provided (and still provide) a colorful glimpse into the inner worlds, conflicts, associations, and actual feelings self-reported by the OHS.

Most previous studies were based on descriptive, epidemiological, and correlational data from retrospective cohort studies on small samples.[32] These studies did not fulfill the essential methodological criteria that transmission research should meet, such as prospective designs, large representative samples, valid and reliable measures, and different reporters for each generation.[33] These and other methodological problems have restricted many efforts that were invested in studying OHS. It seems therefore to be difficult, at this time, to give a final assessment of the trauma transmission hypothesis. Even though much progress has been made, past studies failed to produce a definitive answer to the question of whether Holocaust traumatization can indeed be transmitted to OHS.

To understand the changes in OHS over time,[34] a historical and life course approach may be useful. Simultaneously with the advance in research on OHS, the population also changed across time, through childhood, adolescence, young adulthood, adulthood, and old age. Each stage of development required a different coping strategy. Most importantly, their perception of the Holocaust and its impact on themselves gradually shifted. Findings from the 1970s, when OHS were young adults, were unlike those reported in 2015 when they were middle-aged or older. Younger OHS presented more identity problems than older OHS who had developed a more stable personality. Meta-analytic studies that did not consider such a time perspective may, therefore, have reached faulty conclusions on the population of OHS as a whole. Earlier studies should, thus, be understood from when the specific studies were conducted and the biographical ages of the participants when the studies examined them.

Changes in post-war readjustment were also reported in contemporary studies on Holocaust survivors, completed with regular intervals 10, 20, 30, 40, 50, 60, and 70 years after the war.[35] When surveyed together, these studies indicate that most survivors gradually reversed the harmful effects of trauma, instead of succumbing to the emotional effects of their past tragedies. The Holocaust survivor parents who transformed their lives by finding a new meaning to their legacy also helped OHS to find some closure to their multi-generational saga.

Present Perspectives

A small number of OHS who were born early after the war have already passed away. Most OHS are now approaching retirement age or have retired. Those who were born later have reached mature adulthood. A few of them are still caring for their older adult parents,[36] while the majority have lost them. As a result, their focus of attention has shifted to their own children and grandchildren. Numerous OHS built successful careers and seem to have transformed the legacy of the Holocaust into post-traumatic growth. For them, the impact of the Holocaust has become less important in their lives, and they seem no longer to be "lost in transmission".[37] The scientific debate about whether OHS suffer from more psychopathology than comparable populations is largely settled. It is now widely acknowledged that parental trauma does not have a universal detrimental effect on OHS in general. Only a few OHS meet the criteria for mental disorders and require mental health treatments from time to time. Many more are preoccupied with disorganizing experiences[38] and have occasional Holocaust associations from time to time. Some also struggle with stress-related problems and a lack of emotional resources when faced with adversity. This OHS minority continues to suffer from life-long generalized anxiety disorders. Despite years of therapy, psychopharmacological treatments, and various attempts to get on with their lives, they remain chronically depressed with significant functional impairment.

For many years, the paradoxical coexistence of both vulnerability and resilience in OHS was confusing to clinicians and researchers who were unable to understand how this population could function so well and achieve so much while struggling with emotional stress symptoms throughout their lives. The current shift from a psychosocial to a neurobiological focus offers an explanation for this observation. Epigenetic "vulnerability markers" can lie inactive and do no harm for years until suddenly being switched on in a threatening situation. Thus, it is suggested that OHS might have inherited a kind of chemical marking upon their chromosomes (similar to the numbers tattooed on their parents' forearms) that lead to their "inherited nightmares".[39] These marks would make it possible for the children to "remember" in their bodies what their parents repressed. Thus, it is now generally recognized that OHS who were earlier regarded as being either vulnerable or resilient are now viewed as being more or less biologically susceptible to a more-or-less accommodating environment.

Various theories have been suggested to explain how traumatization can be transmitted from parent to offspring, either from a psychosocial or from a biological perspective. The psychosocial perspective included psychoanalytic notions, behavioral conditioning models, and principles of cognitive appraisal, attention bias/information processing, interpersonal coping styles, parent-child interaction schemes (e.g., contagion, modeling), socialization models, and family systems perspectives.[40] These theories tacitly assumed that there was a "mediating agent" between the transmitting parent and the absorbing child, similar to the one observed in the transmission of a virus, in which a mosquito carries the virus from one person to another. Or, in today's vocabulary, how COVID-19 is spread in a population.

The psychoanalytic theory assumed that the unconscious in itself may be "infectious", especially if it is disavowed. If Holocaust survivor parents became aware of their loss and worked through their repressed emotions, they would be less likely to pass them on to their children. Family system theory assumed that unhealthy communication was the main mediating agent. If the Holocaust trauma was talked about in a balanced manner, it would be easier for the child to digest it. However, if it was talked about too much or too little, it would become malignant. Socialization theory assumed that parenting style was the primary mediating agent of trauma transmission. Inadequate parenting would lead to enmeshment and affect the general family atmosphere with a detrimental effect on the child's behavior. Biological theories were based on the assumption that there was a genetic predisposition to a person's illness and that parents passed on "acquired traits" to their offspring through physiological pathways.

Manifestation of HTT was thus understood, first as displaced unconscious fears in parents. The children internalized what the parents themselves could not handle. Second, it was explained as the result of social learning and parenting. The child responded to the anxieties indirectly expressed in unhealthy child-rearing behavior. Third, it was the result of family enmeshment and tacit communication. The child was trapped in a closed setting where it adopted a threatening worldview that regulated their thoughts, feelings, and behavior. Finally, it was the result of hereditary transmission of the parents' neural fear network, allostatic physiological stress-response system, and HPA-axis regulating system. As a result, OHS would become physiologically predisposed to vulnerability, even though they did not necessarily manifest psychopathology.

At first glance, these theories of the process of trauma transmission seem to make perfect sense. Upon further examination, however, they are too general to explain the specific process of how the impact of trauma can cross generations. First, psychoanalytic theories cannot fully explain how repressed traumatic experiences in parents can enter into the minds of offspring, even with concepts such as "projective identification", "transposition", "internalization", and "role induction".[41] Neither is the theory of a disruption of the dialogic self[42] sufficient to explain the actual process of HTT.

Second, while deficient parenting and flawed socialization had important effects on OHS, these factors cannot fully explain the process of HTT, since "good-enough" parenting was also found to transmit the emotional residues of the Holocaust to OHS. Third, family systems and communication models have produced a similar indefinite explanation of the transmission process. Emotional ties in Holocaust survivor families have consistently been reported as being strong, but there is also much ambivalence manifested in such families, and it is not clear how changes in family structures during their lives affected the impact of HTT, as both the parents and their offspring grew older.[43] Also, while too much talk about the Holocaust would lead to a burden being passed upon the children, many parents did not share their traumatic experiences, but the children still absorbed much of their past trauma. Finally, HTT has also been reported in harmonious families with plenty of opportunities for separation-individuation.

Fourth, while findings from animal studies have indicated that acquired traits from the past can be transmitted to offspring, there is insufficient evidence on the epigenetic transmission of such characteristics in humans,[44] and fundamental questions remain regarding the transgenerational transmission of epigenetic alterations to future generations.[45] Holocaust survivor parents suffered from malnutrition during the war and also experienced extreme death anxiety that may have caused their cortisol to be elevated for long periods. However, there is still insufficient evidence of the assumption that the stress responses of Holocaust survivor parents became permanently dysregulated and that OHS inherited stable constitutional tendencies or robust epigenetic alterations. It is, therefore, currently impossible to attribute transmission effects in humans to a single set of biological or other determinants.[46]

Epigenetics provides a plausible theory to explain how early life traumas can produce functional "scars" in parents[47] and also transmit them to offspring in the form of epigenetic methylation marks – the reversible chemical modification to DNA that typically blocks transcription of a gene without altering its sequence. During the last decade, exhaustive reviews have been published on transgenerational epigenetics and psychiatric disorders,[48] fear memory and biomarkers,[49] epigenetic risk factors in PTSD and depression,[50] epigenetic mechanisms in learned fear,[51] neural fear network and PTSD,[52] early life stress,[53] the inheritance of learned behaviors,[54] recent genetics and epigenetics approaches to PTSD[55] and most recently on the inter- and transgenerational inheritance of behavioral phenotypes.[56] Contrary to previous notions, ground-breaking research showed that DNA methylation could escape the "reset" mechanism or "reprogramming" in human germ cells.[57] Because of these emerging findings, there was a paradigmatic shift in the study of HTT. While HTT was earlier investigated mostly within psycho-social disciplines, an increasing number of transmission studies include a measurement of the neuroendocrine, neuroanatomic, and epigenetic systems.[58]

1. *Neuroendocrine*: amongst psychobiological correlates, altered HPA axis reactivity was the most investigated in OHS with parental PTSD.[59] OHS were found to have significantly lower cortisol – but better cortisol suppression in their blood – than offspring of survivors without PTSD.[60] There is no consensus, however, on how to interpret these findings. Cortisol responses show large intra- and inter-individual variability[61] and it is not clear if the contra-intuitive findings of low cortisol signified a preexisting vulnerability, a reaction to new exposure, or an attempt to regain an inner balance. There is also disagreement regarding baseline levels of cortisol observed in people with PTSD. The finding of low cortisol levels in trauma survivors and their offspring have, therefore, been the subject of much debate, and their current clinical application remains limited.[62] While reduced cortisol levels and enhanced GR sensitivity are still assumed to be risk factors for developing PTSD,[63] other pathways of traumatization are increasingly investigated.
2. *Neuroanatomic*: HTT suggests that traumatic stress can cause irreversible effects on the parent's brain and that irregular neural brain circuits can be inherited by OHS. If this is the case, the

child would be born with a preprogrammed salience network and thus respond with excessive anxiety when faced with stressful situations that resemble the war. To investigate this assumption, there is an ongoing search for the location in the brain where trauma memories are located.[64] If these locations are found, they can be correlated with similar findings in offspring to determine a possible hereditary path. For example, exposure to excessive stress hormones has been shown to influence brain structures involved in cognition and mental health.[65] Non-invasive brain imaging techniques, such as fMRI and PET, made it possible to identify such brain circuits affected by traumatization. Studies have detected changes in brain structure and function in patients with PTSD.[66] Such changes were observed, for example in the hippocampus and in the amygdala, as well as in cortical regions including the anterior cingulate, insula, and orbitofrontal region,[67] which are involved in the processing and regulation of emotion.[68] Episodic memories of fear were found to be located in the dentate gyrus in the hippocampus.[69] Abnormalities in processing involving the salience network within the amygdala, anterior cingulate cortex, and insula were also found. These would play an important role in a successful PTSD treatment response.[70]

3 *Epigenetic*: the first actual findings of epigenetic transmission in Holocaust survivor parents and their offspring were published by Yehuda and her colleagues.[71] They found that Holocaust exposure affected FKBP5 methylation in parents and also in their offspring, a correlation not found in the control group and their children.[72] These findings created a lively debate in the scientific community,[73] and the study became known as the "most over-interpreted epigenetics study of the week" in a blog.[74] In response to this, Yehuda and her colleagues[75] claimed that their findings had been over-interpreted in the popular media and that methodological difficulties remain to confirm the epigenetic transmission hypothesis. A great deal of controversy remains within the study of transgenerational epigenetics in humans[76] since biological data has come mostly from animal studies.

Research on epigenetic HTT comprises multiple stages. Proving the existence of a psychobiological predisposition involves showing not only that the body of the parent actually can "keep the score" of trauma[77] and that mental stress is physically manifested in biological correlates[78] but also that such manifestations can be inherited by the following generations. While several laboratories have made progress in finding the biochemical origins to stress responses,[79] as for now, no valid and clinically applicable biomarkers for PTSD have been found.[80] As a result, there is still insufficient evidence of the assumption that massive stress exposure in parents can influence the risk of stress-related mental problems in their children. Consequently, there is no tangible evidence for the epigenetic inheritance of phenotypes in the etiology of HTT, and no "Geiger-counter" for Holocaust traumatization[81] has been developed.

The interpretability of epigenetic findings of a psychological phenomenon such as HTT is a complex undertaking.[82] Obstacles are caused not only by methodological constraints but also because HT cannot merely be regarded as one specific and persistent disorder detached from the human mind. It is difficult to find biomarkers of HT since it a) cannot be easily measured in human beings; b) is not clearly identified; c) tends to vary between individuals and populations; d) is not constant over time; and e) is the result of a failure to regain physiological homeostasis rather than a simple physiological response to stress.[83] While these obstacles make future research on psychobiological HTT a challenging undertaking, some evidence has been found to show that chronic stress in the first generation has documented effects on the development of physiological, neural, and behavioral phenotypes in the Second Generation.[84] An epigenetic perspective[85] across the lifespan of OHS seems, therefore, currently to be the most promising avenue for future progress.[86]

Future Perspectives

Where do we continue from here? Which new perspective of HTT is best suited to answer the question of whether parental traumatization can be transmitted to their offspring? Assuming that trauma can indeed be transmitted, how can the aggravating and mitigating factors that increase or decrease the likelihood of offspring psychopathology be further investigated?

It is now recognized that the essential variables in future research on trauma transmission include *particular* parents who transmit *various* influences to *certain* individual children under *specific* circumstances and during *different* critical time periods.[87] This model of trauma transmission suggests that future research on HTT with a variety of populations will benefit from a psychosocial and neurobiological life-course developmental perspective.

It will be the task of future studies to specify the diverse parental, offspring, environmental, and time factors that increase or decrease the transmission of trauma from parents to their offspring. These variables together will explain more precisely how various kinds of transmission occur from both a psychosocial and biological point of view (see the "three-hit" concept).[88] Since transmission tends to be highly volatile, it will also have to take the adaptability of parents and children into account, as well as the shifting environments and critical periods when the transmission is more likely to occur. A systems biology perspective may be needed to measure the quantity and connectivity of all these variables.[89]

Future transmission studies will benefit from both neurobiological and psychosocial measures in conjunction with one another. Until recently, transmission was studied from either one of them; each with its own conceptualizations, methodology, and scientific frame of reference. One would investigate the influence of various parent-child interactions, while the other would search for biomarkers within biological psychiatry. These two assumed pathways of HTT should no longer be regarded as mutually exclusive since the pathways of HTT can occur at multiple levels, including epigenetic alterations of stress responses, changes in individuals' psychological wellbeing, family functioning, community integrity, and cultural identity.[90]

The possible applicability in future longitudinal studies of diverse traumatized populations could thus include a combination of psychosocial (e.g. subjective stress ratings) and biological (e.g. psychophysiological assessment of HPA-axis dysregulation) in several generations.

Various manifestations of trauma transmission can thus be explained as being determined by any or all of these factors or by an ecological combination of them.[91] Such a combination can be exemplified in the amalgamation of neurobiology and psychoanalysis within neuro-psychoanalysis. It also appears in studies on the biosocial context of parenting,[92] on the telomere length in PoW,[93] and on the limbic-hypothalamic-pituitary-adrenal (LHPA) axis reactivity on separation-individuation in subjects from three generations removed from the Holocaust.[94] Both approaches were emphasized when explaining the possible parental transmission of a variety of disorders, including chronic pain and immune deficiencies.[95] The usefulness of such a broad-based approach was evident in a review of over a hundred studies on offspring with parents who suffered from PTSD.[96] The multitude of biological and environmental factors that influence individual development can thus be considered, especially those factors that can be reliably transmitted.[97] The challenge will be to integrate findings from both fields of research and include all the systemic and central biological and psychosocial mechanisms underlying stress-related disorders.[98] This approach can pave the way for multi-disciplinary intervention strategies for offspring at risk.

Genetic disposition and socialization factors brought together within a single framework contradict the nature-nurture dichotomy.[99] It shows how our understanding of transmission and heredity has changed through the development of new concepts within Mendelian genetics and neo-Lamarckism. It also corresponds to the appreciation of transmission in evolutionary biology, as described by Jablonka and Lamb in their book *Evolution in Four Dimensions*.[100] From this theoretical background, transmission occurs not just through genes per se but through the heritable variations transmitted from generation to generation by whatever means. Such variations can occur a) at the physical level of genetics, b) at the epigenetic level, c) at the level of social learning, and d) at the level of culture. This complex environment-biology interface has shown promise as a possible route for the intergenerational transmission of the effects of trauma.[101] Within such an integrative bio-psycho-social explanatory model of traumatization, all the essential hereditary variations must be taken into account, rather than only a purely biological reductionist one.[102] When trying to understand the causal pathways through which individuals show resilience or vulnerability in the face of adversity,[103] this explanatory model becomes particularly useful.

Conclusion

Can parental traumatization be transmitted to offspring? The present overview of the literature suggests that traumatization in the first generation can indeed be a risk factor for adverse long-term outcomes in the second. Risk factors, however, are multi-determined and to specify and disentangle all the origins of transmission is a daunting task. A range of vulnerability and resilience factors, environmental pressures (and provisions), psychological outfit, and subjective appraisal of the traumatic event will all influence the process of trauma transmission.[104]

In the past, research of HTT sought to discover the general characteristics of OHS behaviors and suggested formulations of resilience in conjunction with specific vulnerabilities. A developmental psychopathology model is here suggested as an alternative. This model illuminates the numerous factors that yield different effects along various stages of transmission. It recognizes a "matrix of child-intrinsic factors, developmental maturation and experience, life events, and evolving family and social ecologies".[105] From this life-course developmental point of view, particular parents passed on various influences to individual children under specific circumstances and at different critical periods through a combination of biological and psychosocial mechanisms. A condensed summary of findings from earlier studies on HTT would thus imply that Holocaust survivor parents who experienced adverse experiences in childhood were more likely to transmit their accumulated emotional residues to sensitive offspring during adolescence if a supportive social network was absent.

This differential appraisal recognizes that *any* child will somehow be affected by their parents' war experiences. But rather than focusing on one or the other outcome of HT, it seems more relevant today to reflect on the journey of post-war adjustment as a whole. Even simple organisms learn fundamental survival skills and pass these on to their offspring, and it is not surprising that life-changing experiences in Holocaust survivor parents, which result in knowledge useful for survival, would be passed on to OHS. If survival is the name of the game of evolution, the post-war generation of Holocaust survivors and their offspring became masters in it. It has become part of their very nature and, as such, it will probably be passed on also to future generations.

Notes

1 Shrira et al., 2011.
2 Bezo and Maggi, 2018.
3 Adonis, 2016; Felsen, 1998.
4 Brown-Rice, 2013.
5 Juth et al., 2015.
6 Dekel and Goldblatt, 2008; Creech and Misca, 2017.

7 Costa et al., 2018.
8 Weinstein et al., 2018.
9 Daud et al., 2005; DeGregorio, 2012; Timshel et al., 2017.
10 Banerjee et al., 2017; Duncan et al., 2017.
11 Rasic et al., 2014.
12 Smoller, 2016.
13 Rakoff et al., 1966.
14 Sigal, 1971.
15 Solkoff, 1981; Albeck, 1994.
16 Epstein, 1979.
17 Bergmann and Jacovy, 1982.
18 Felsen, 1998.
19 Major, 1996.
20 Bar-On et al., 1998.
21 Yehuda, 1999.
22 Kellermann, 2001.
23 Kellermann, 2008.
24 Van IJzendoorn et al., 2003; Barel et al., 2010.
25 Levav et al., 2007.
26 Lindert et al., 2017.
27 Yehuda and Bierer, 2009; Yehuda and Lehrner, 2018.
28 Shrira et al., 2017; Shrira, 2019.
29 Shrira and Felsen, 2021.
30 Solomon et al., 1988.
31 Wardi, 1992.
32 Lindert et al., 2017.
33 Thornberry et al., 2012.
34 Hareven, 1994; Hareven, 2000.
35 Kellermann, 2018.
36 Shrira et al., 2019.
37 Fromm, 2012.
38 Scharf and Mayseless, 2011.
39 Kellermann, 2013.
40 Kellermann, 2009.
41 Kahn, 2006.
42 Bradfield, 2013.
43 Shmotkin et al., 2011.
44 Daxinger and Whitelaw, 2010.
45 Grossniklaus et al., 2013.
46 Yehuda et al., 2018.
47 Skinner et al., 2012; Gröger et al., 2016; McEwen, 2017.
48 Franklin et al., 2010.
49 Maddox et al., 2013.
50 Raabe and Spengler, 2013.
51 Zovkic and Sweatt, 2013.
52 Vukojevic et al., 2014.
53 Provençal and Binder, 2014.
54 Dias et al., 2015.
55 Daskalakis et al., 2018.
56 Jawaid and Mansuy, 2019.
57 Bohacek and Mansuy, 2015.
58 Bowers and Yehuda, 2016; Klengel et al., 2016.
59 Yehuda and Bierer, 2007; Yehuda et al., 2007.
60 Yehuda, 2009.
61 Yehuda and Seckl, 2011.
62 Olff and van Zuiden, 2017.

63 Szeszko et al., 2018.
64 Sartory et al., 2013.
65 Lupien et al., 2009.
66 Rauch et al., 2006.
67 Wager et al., 2008.
68 Sherin and Nemeroff, 2011.
69 Besnard and Sahay, 2016.
70 Szeszko and Yehuda, 2019.
71 Yehuda et al., 2014.
72 Yehuda et al., 2016.
73 Yasmin, 2017.
74 Birney, 2015.
75 Yehuda et al., 2018.
76 Albert, 2010; Heard and Martienssen, 2014; Nagy and Turecki, 2015.
77 van der Kolk, 1994.
78 McEwen, 2018; Nasca et al., 2018.
79 Kandel, 2009; Skinner et al., 2012; McEwen, 2017.
80 Schmidt and Vermetten, 2017
81 Kellermann, 2019.
82 Jones et al., 2018.
83 Kellermann, 2018.
84 Crews et al., 2012; Hanson and Skinner, 2016; Gillette et al., 2018.
85 McEwen, 2019.
86 Petronis, 2010.
87 Kellermann, 2020.
88 Daskalakis et al., 2013.
89 Ma'ayan, 2017.
90 Sotero, 2006.
91 Kellermann, 2001.
92 Feldman, 2016.
93 Solomon et al., 2017.
94 Ullmann et al., 2018.
95 Segerstrom and Miller, 2004; Olff and van Zuiden, 2017; Jonker et al., 2017.
96 Leen-Feldner et al., 2013.
97 Blumberg, 2017.
98 Nasca et al., 2018.
99 Cavalli-Sforza and Feldman, 1973; Bouchard and McGue, 2003; Lewkowicz, 2011.
100 Jablonka and Lamb, 2005.
101 Lehrner and Yehuda, 2018.
102 Kendler, 2005; Omidi, 2013.
103 Bowes and Jaffee, 2013.
104 Qi et al., 2016.
105 Pynoos et al., 2000: 1542.

References

Adonis, Cyril K., 2016. "Exploring the Salience of Intergenerational Trauma Among Children and Grandchildren of Victims of Apartheid-Era Gross Human Rights Violations", *Indo-Pacific Journal of Phenomenology* 16 (1–2): 163–179.

Albeck, Joseph H., 1994. "Intergenerational Consequences of Trauma: Reframing Traps in Treatment Theory: A Second Generation Perspective", in: John F. Sommer and Marybeth Williams (eds.), *Handbook of Post-traumatic Therapy*, Westport, CT: Greenwood Press: 106–128.

Albert, Paul R., 2010. "Epigenetics in Mental Illness: Hope or Hype?", *Journal of Psychiatry & Neuroscience* 35: 366–368.

Banerjee, Sunayana B., Morris, Filomene G., and Ressler, Kerry J., 2017. "Genetic Approaches for the Study of PTSD: Advances and Challenges", *Neuroscience Letters* 649: 139–146.

Barel, Efrat, IJzendoorn, Marinus H. van, Sagi-Schwartz, Abraham, and Bakermans-Kranenburg, Marian J., 2010. "Surviving the Holocaust: A Meta-Analysis of the Long-Term Sequelae of a Genocide", *Psychological Bulletin* 136 (5): 677–698.

Bar-On, Dan, Eland, Jeanette, Kleber, Rolf J., Krell, Robert, Moore, Yael, Sagi, Abraham, Soriano, Erin, Suedfeld, Peter, Velden, Peter G. van der, and IJzendoorn, Marinus H. van, 1998. "Multigenerational Perspectives on Coping with the Holocaust Experience: An Attachment Perspective for Understanding the Developmental Sequelae of Trauma Across Generations", *International Journal of Behavioral Development* 22: 315–338.

Bergmann, Martin, and Jacovy, Milton E., 1982. *Generations of the Holocaust*, New York: Basic Books.

Besnard, Antoine, and Amar, Sahay, 2016. "Adult Hippocampal Neurogenesis, Fear Generalization, and Stress", *Neuropsychopharmacology* 41 (1): 24–44.

Bezo, Brent, and Maggi, Stefania, 2018. "Intergenerational Perceptions of Mass Trauma's Impact on Physical Health and Well-Being", *Psychological Trauma: Theory, Research, Practice, and Policy* 10 (1): 87–94.

Birney, Ewan, 2015. "Study of Holocaust Survivors Finds Trauma Passed on the Children's Genes", *The Guardian August* 21, www.theguardian.com/science/2015/aug/21/study-of-holocaust-survivors-finds-trauma-passed-on-to-childrens-genes?CMP=share_btn_tw

Blumberg, Mark S., 2017. "Development Evolving: The Origins and Meanings of Instinct", *Wiley Interdisciplinary Reviews. Cognitive Science* 8 (1–2).

Bohacek, Johannes, and Mansuy, Isabelle M., 2015. "Molecular Insights into Transgenerational Non-Genetic Inheritance of Acquired Behaviours", *Nature Reviews Genetics* 16 (11): 641–652.

Bouchard, Thomas J., and McGue, Matt, 2003. "Genetic and Environmental Influences on Human Psychological Differences", *Journal of Neurobiology* 54 (1): 4–45.

Bowers, Mallory E., and Yehuda, Rachel, 2016. "Intergenerational Transmission of Stress in Humans", *Neuropsychopharmacology* 41 (1): 232–244.

Bowes, Lucy, and Jaffee, Sara R., 2013. "Biology, Genes, and Resilience", *Trauma, Violence, & Abuse* 14 (3): 195–208.

Bradfield, Bruce C., 2013. "The Intergenerational Transmission of Trauma as a Disruption of the Dialogical Self", *Journal of Trauma and Dissociation* 14 (4): 390–403.

Brown-Rice, Kathleen, 2013. "Examining the Theory of Historical Trauma Among Native Americans", *The Professional Counselor* 3 (3): 117–130.

Cavalli-Sforza, Luigi L., and Feldman, Marcus W., 1973. "Cultural Versus Biological Inheritance: Phenotypic Transmission from Parents to Children", *American Journal of Human Genetics* 25 (6): 618–637.

Costa, Dora L., Yetter, Noelle, and DeSomer, Heather, 2018. "Intergenerational Transmission of Paternal Trauma Among US Civil War ex-POWs", *Proceedings of the National Academy of Sciences of the United States of America* 115 (44): 11215–11220.

Creech, Suzannah, K., and Misca, Gabriela, 2017. "Parenting with PTSD: A Review of Research on the Influence of PTSD on Parent-Child Functioning in Military and Veteran families", *Frontiers in Psychology* 8: 1101.

Crews, David, Gillette, Ross, Scarpino, Samuel V., Manikkam, Mohan, Savenkova, Marina I., and Skinner, Michael K., 2012. "Epigenetic Transgenerational Inheritance of Altered Stress Responses", *Proceedings of the National Academy of Sciences of the United States of America* 109 (23): 9143–9148.

Daskalakis, Nikolaos P., Bagot, Rosemary C., Parker, Karen J., Vinkers, Christiaan H., and Kloet, Edo de, 2013. "The Three-Hit Concept of Vulnerability and Resilience: Toward Understanding Adaptation to Early-Life Adversity Outcome", *Psychoneuroendocrinology* 38 (9): 1858–1873.

Daskalakis, Nikolaos P., Rijal, Chuda M., King, Christopher, Huckins, Laura M., and Ressler, Kerry J., 2018. "Recent Genetics and Epigenetics Approaches to PTSD", *Current Psychiatry Reports* 20: 30.

Daud, Atia, Erling, Skoglund, and Per-Anders, Rydelius, 2005. "Children in Families of Torture Victims: Transgenerational Transmission of Parents' Traumatic Experiences to their Children", *International Journal of Social Welfare* 14: 23–32.

Daxinger, Lucia, and Whitelaw, Emma, 2010. "Transgenerational Epigenetic Inheritance: More Questions Than Answers", *Genome Research* 20 (12): 1623–1628.

DeGregorio, Lisa J., 2012. "Intergenerational Transmission of Abuse: Implication for Parenting Interventions from a Neuropsychological Perspective", *Traumatology* 19 (2): 158–166.

Dekel, Rachel, and Goldblatt, Hadass, 2008. "Is There Intergenerational Transmission of Trauma? The Case of Combat Veterans' Children", *American Journal of Orthopsychiatry* 78 (3): 281–289.

Dias, Brian G., Maddox, Stephanie A., Klengel, Torsten, and Ressler, Kerry J., 2015. "Epigenetic Mechanisms Underlying Learning and the Inheritance of Learned Behaviors", *Trends in Neurosciences* 38 (2): 96–107.

Duncan, Laramie et al., 2017. "Largest GWAS of PTSD (N=20 070) Yields Genetic Overlap with Schizophrenia and Sex Differences in Heritability", *Molecular Psychiatry* 23 (3): 666–673.

Epstein, Hellen, 1979. *Children of the Holocaust: Conversations with Sons and Daughters of Survivors*, New York: Penguin Books.

Feldman, Ruth, 2016. "The Neurobiology of Mammalian Parenting and the Biosocial Context of Human Caregiving", *Hormones and Behavior* 77: 3–17.

Felsen, Irit, 1998. "Transgenerational Transmission of Effects of the Holocaust: The North American Research Perspective", in Yael Danieli (ed.), *International Handbook of Multigenerational Legacies of Trauma*, New York: Plenum: 43–68.

Franklin, Tamara B., Russig, Holder, Weiss, Isabelle C., Gräff, Johannes, Linder, Natacha, Michalon, Aubin, Visi, Sandor, and Mansuy, Isabelle M., 2010. "Epigenetic Transmission of the Impact of Early Stress Across Generations", *Biological Psychiatry* 68 (5): 408–415.

Fromm, Gerard M. (ed.), 2012. *Lost in Transmission: Studies of Trauma across Generations*, London: Karnac Books.

Gillette, Ross, Son, Min Ji, Ton, Lexi, Gore, Andrea C., and Crews, David, 2018. "Passing Experiences on to Future Generations: Endocrine Disruptors and Transgenerational Inheritance of Epimutations in Brain and Sperm", *Epigenetics* 13 (10–11): 1106–1126.

Gröger, Nicole, Matas, Emmanuel, Gos, Tomasz, Lesse, Alexandra, Poeggel, Gerd, Braun, Katharina Braun, and Bock, Jörg, 2016. "The Transgenerational Transmission of Childhood Adversity: Behavioral, Cellular, and Epigenetic Correlates", *Journal of Neural Transmission* 123 (9): 1037–1052.

Grossniklaus, Ueli, Kelley, William G., Ferguson-Smith, Anne C., Pembrey, Marcus, and Lindquist, Suzan, 2013, "Transgenerational Epigenetic Inheritance: How Important Is It?", *Nature Reviews. Genetics* 14 (3): 228–235.

Hanson, Mark A., and Skinner, Michael K., 2016. "Developmental Origins of Epigenetic Transgenerational Inheritance", *Environmental Epigenetics* 2 (1).

Hareven, Tamara K., 1994. "Aging and Generational Relations: A Historical and Life Course Perspective", *Annual Review of Sociology* 20 (1): 437–461.

Hareven, Tamara K., 2000. *Families, History and Social Change. Life-Course and Cross-Cultural Perspectives*, Boulder: Westview.

Heard, Edith, and Martienssen, Robert A., 2014. "Transgenerational Epigenetic Inheritance: Myths and Mechanisms", *Cell* 157 (1): 95–109.

Jablonka, Eva, and Lamb, Marion, 2005. *Evolution in Four Dimensions*. Cumberland: MIT.

Jawaid, Ali, and Mansuy, Isabelle M., 2019. "Inter- and Transgenerational Inheritance of Behavioral Phenotypes", *Current Opinion in Behavioral Sciences* 25: 96–101.

Jones, Meaghan J., Moore, Sarah R., and Kobor, Michael S., 2018. "Principles and Challenges of Applying Epigenetic Epidemiology to Psychology", *Annual Review of Psychology* 69 (1): 459–485.

Jonker, Iris, Rosmalen, Judith G.M., and Schoevers, Robert A., 2017. "Childhood Life Events, Immune Activation and the Development of Mood and Anxiety Disorders: The TRAILS Study", *Translational Psychiatry* 7 (5): e1112.

Juth, Vanessa, Silver, Roxan Cohen, Seyle, Conor D., Widyatmoko, Siswa C., and Tan, Edwin T., 2015. "Post-Disaster Mental Health Among Parent-Child Dyads After a Major Earthquake in Indonesia", *Journal of Abnormal Child Psychology* 43 (7): 1309–1318.

Kahn, Charlotte, 2006. "Some Determinants of the Multigenerational Transmission Process", *The Psychoanalytic Review* 93 (1): 71–92.

Kandel, Eric R., 2009. "The Biology of Memory: A Forty-Year Perspective", *Journal of Neuroscience* 29 (41): 12748–12756.

Kellermann, Natan P.F., 2001. "Transmission of Holocaust Trauma – An Integrative View", *Psychiatry: Interpersonal and Biological Processes* 64 (1): 256–267.

Kellermann, Natan P.F., 2008. "Transmitted Holocaust Trauma: Curse or Legacy? The Aggravating and Mitigating Factors of Holocaust Transmission", *Israel Journal of Psychiatry and Related Sciences* 45 (4): 263–271.

Kellermann, Natan P.F., 2009. *Holocaust Trauma: Psychological Effects and Treatment*, New York, NY: iUniverse.

Kellermann, Natan P.F., 2012. "What's in a Name? Eight Variations on a Theme", *Kavod: Honoring Aging Survivors* 2, http://kavod.claimscon.org/2012/02/whats-in-a-name/

Kellermann, Natan P.F., 2013. "Epigenetic Transmission of Holocaust Trauma: Can Nightmares be Inherited", *The Israel Journal of Psychiatry and Related Sciences* 50 (1): 33–39.

Kellermann, Natan P.F., 2018. "The Search for Biomarkers of Holocaust Trauma", *Journal of Traumatic Stress Disorders & Treatment* 7 (1): 1–13.

Kellermann, Natan P.F., 2019. "No Geiger-Counter for Holocaust Radioactivity: Possible or Impossible Biomarkers of Holocaust Traumatization?", *Israel Journal of Psychiatry* 55 (3): 41–44.

Kellermann, Natan P.F., 2020. "Major Variables of Holocaust Trauma Transmission", in: Ori Z. Soltes (ed.), *Immortality, Memory, Creativity and Survival: The Arts of Alice Lok Cahana, Ronnie Cahana and Kitra Cahana*, The Fritz Ascher Society for Persecuted, New York, NY: Ostracized and Banned Art: 85–136.

Kendler, Kenneth S., 2005. "Toward a Philosophical Structure for Psychiatry", *American Journal of Psychiatry* 162: 433–440.

Klengel, Torsten, Dias, Brian G., and Ressler, Kerry J., 2016. "Models of Intergenerational and Transgenerational Transmission of Risk for Psychopathology in Mice", *Neuropsychopharmacology* 41 (1): 219–231.

Leen-Feldner, Ellen W., Feldner, Matthew T., Knapp, Ashley, Bunaciu, Liviu, Blumenthal, Heudemarie, and Amstadter, Ananda B., 2013. "Offspring Psychological and Biological Correlates of Parental Posttraumatic Stress: Review of the Literature and Research Agenda", *Clinical Psychology Review* 33 (8): 1106–1133.

Lehrner, Amy, and Yehuda, Rachel, 2018. "Cultural Trauma and Epigenetic Inheritance", *Development and Psychopathology* 30 (5): 1763–1777.

Levav, Itzhak, Levinson, Daphna, Radomislensky, Irina, Shemesh, Annarosa A., and Kohn, Robert, 2007. "Psychopathology and Other Health Dimensions Among the Offspring of Holocaust Survivors: Results From the Israel National Health Survey", *Israel Journal of Psychiatry and Related Sciences* 44 (2): 144–151.

Lewkowicz, David J., 2011. "The Biological Implausibility of the Nature-Nurture Dichotomy and What It Means for the Study of Infancy", *Infancy* 16 (4): 331–367.

Lindert, Jutta, Knobler, Haim Y., Kawachi, Ichiro, Bain, Paul A., Abramowitz, Moshe Z., McKee, Charlotte, Reinharz, Shula, and McKee, Martin M., 2017. "Psychopathology of Children of Genocide Survivors: A Systematic Review of the Impact of Genocide on their Children`s Psychopathology from Five Countries", *International Journal of Epidemiology* 46 (1): 246–257.

Lupien, Sonia J., McEwen, Bruce S., Gunnar, Megan R., and Heim, Christine, 2009. "Effects of Stress Throughout the Lifespan on the Brain, Behavior, and Cognition", *Nature Reviews Neuroscience* 10 (6): 434–445.

Ma'ayan, Avi, 2017. "Complex Systems Biology", *Journal of the Royal Society Interface* 14 (134).

Maddox, Stephanie A., Schafe, Glenn E., and Ressler, Kerry J., 2013. "Exploring Epigenetic Regulation of Fear Memory and Biomarkers Associated with Post-Traumatic Stress Disorder", *Frontiers in Psychiatry* 4: 62.

Major, Ellinor F., 1996. "The Impact of the Holocaust on the Second Generation: Norwegian Jewish Holocaust Survivors and Their Children", *Journal of Traumatic Stress* 9 (3): 441–454.

McEwen, Bruce S., 2017. "Epigenetic Interactions and the Brain-Body Communication", *Psychotherapy and Psychosomatic* 8: 1–4.

McEwen, Bruce S., 2018. "Redefining Neuroendocrinology: Epigenetics of Brain-Body Communication Over the Life Course", *Frontiers in Neuroendocrinology* 49: 8–30.

McEwen, Bruce S., 2019. "Prenatal Programming of Neuropsychiatric Disorders: An Epigenetic Perspective Across the Lifespan", *Biological Psychiatry* 85 (2): 91–93.

Nagy, Carina, and Turecki, Gustavo, 2015. "Transgenerational Epigenetic Inheritance: An Open Discussion", *Epigenomics* 7 (5): 781–790.

Nasca, Carla, Rasgon, Natalie, and McEwen, Bruce, 2018. "An Emerging Epigenetic Framework of Systemic and Central Mechanisms Underlying Stress-Related Disorders", *Neuro-psychopharmacology* 44 (1): 235–236.

Olff, Miranda, and van Zuiden, Mirjam, 2017. "Neuroendocrine and Neuroimmune Markers in PTSD: Pre-, Peri- and Post-Trauma Glucocorticoid and Inflammatory Dysregulation", *Current Opinion in Psychology* 14: 132–137.

Omidi, Abdollah, 2013. "Towards an Integrative Approach to Trauma Study", *Archives of Trauma Research* 2 (1): 1–2.

Petronis, Arturas, 2010. "Epigenetics as a Unifying Principle in the Aetiology of Complex Traits and Diseases", *Nature* 465 (7299): 721–727.

Provençal, Nadine, and Binder, Elisabeth B., 2014. "The Effects of Early Life Stress on the Epigenome: From the Womb to Adulthood and Even Before", *Experimental Neurology* 268: 10–20.

Pynoos, Robert S., Steinberg, Alan M., and Piacenini, John C., 2000. "A Developmental Psychopathology Model of Childhood Traumatic Stress and Intersection with Anxiety Disorders", *Biological Psychiatry* 46 (11): 1542–1554.

Qi, Wei, Gevonden, Martin, and Shalev, Arieh, 2016. "Prevention of Post-Traumatic Stress Disorder After Trauma: Current Evidence and Future Directions", *Current Psychiatry Reports* 18 (2): 20.

Raabe, Florian J., and Spengler, Dietmar, 2013. "Epigenetic Risk Factors in PTSD and Depression", *Frontiers in Psychiatry* 4: 80.

Rakoff, Vivian M., Sigal, John J., and Epstein, Norman B., 1966. "Children and Families of Concentration Camp Survivors", *Canadian Mental Health* 14: 24–26.

Rasic, Daniel, Hajek, Tomas, Alda, Martin, and Uher, Rudolf, 2014. "Risk of Mental Illness in Offspring of Parents with Schizophrenia, Bipolar Disorder, and Major Depressive Disorder: A Meta-Analysis of Family High-Risk Studies", *Schizophrenia Bulletin* 40 (1): 28–38.

Rauch, Scott L., Shin, Lisa M., and Phelps, Elizabeth A., 2006. "Neurocircuitry Models of Posttraumatic Stress Disorder and Extinction: Human Neuroimaging Research – Past, Present, and Future", *Biological Psychiatry* 60 (4): 376–382.

Sartory, Gudrun, Cwik, Jan, Knuppertz, Helge, Schürholt, Benjamin, Lebens, Morena, Seitz, Rüdiger J., and Schulze, Ralf, 2013. "In Search of the Trauma Memory: A Meta-Analysis of Functional Neuroimaging Studies of Symptom Provocation in Posttraumatic Stress Disorder (PTSD)", *PLoS ONE* 8: e58150.

Scharf, Miri, and Mayseless, Ofra, 2011. "Disorganizing Experiences in Second- and Third-Generation Holocaust Survivors", *Qualitative Health Research* 21: 1539–1553.

Schmidt, Ulrike, and Vermetten, Eric, 2017. "Integrating NIMH Research Domain Criteria (RDoC) into PTSD Research", in Eric Vermetten, Dewleen G. Baker, and Victoria B. Risbrough (eds.), *Behavioral Neurobiology of PTSD. Current Topics in Behavioral Neurosciences*, Cham: Springer: 69–91.

Segerstrom, Suzanne C., and Miller, Gregory E., 2004. "Psychological Stress and the Human Immune System: A Meta-Analytic Study of 30 Years of Inquiry", *Psychological Bulletin* 130 (4): 601–630.

Sherin, Jonathan E., and Nemeroff, Charles B., 2011. "Post-Traumatic Stress Disorder: The Neurobiological Impact of Psychological Trauma", *Dialogues in Clinical Neuroscience* 13 (3): 263–278.

Shmotkin, Dov, Shrira, Amit, and Palgi, Yuval, 2011. "Does Trauma Linger into Old-Old Age? Using the Holocaust Experience as a Paradigm", in: Leonard W. Poon and Jiska Cohen-Mansfield (eds.), *Understanding Well-being in the Oldest Old*, Cambridge, MA: Cambridge University Press: 81–95.

Shrira, Amit, 2019. "Parental PTSD, Health Behaviors and Successful Aging Among Offspring of Holocaust Survivors", *Psychiatry Research* 271: 265–271.

Shrira, Amit, Ayalon, Liat, Bensimon, Moshe, Bodner, Ehud, Rosenbloom, Tova, and Yadid, Gal, 2017. "Parental Post-Traumatic Stress Disorder Symptoms Are Related to Successful Aging in Offspring of Holocaust Survivors", *Frontiers in Psychology* 8: 1099.

Shrira, Amit, and Felsen, Irit, 2021. "Parental PTSD and Psychological Reactions During the COVID-19 Pandemic Among Offspring of Holocaust Survivors", *Psychological Trauma: Theory, Research, Practice, and Policy* 13 (4): 438–445.

Shrira, Amit, Menashe, Ravit, and Bensimon, Moshe, 2019. "Filial Anxiety and Sense of Obligation Among Offspring of Holocaust Survivors", *Aging & Mental Health* 23 (6): 752–761.

Shrira, Amit, Palgi, Yuval, Ben-Ezra, Menachem, and Shmotkin, Dov, 2011. "Transgenerational Effects of Trauma in Midlife: Evidence for Resilience and Vulnerability in Offspring of Holocaust Survivors", *Psychological Trauma: Theory, Research, Practice, and Policy* 3 (4): 394–402.

Sigal, John J., 1971. "Second-Generation Effects of Massive Psychic Trauma", *International Psychiatry Clinics* 8 (1): 55–65.

Skinner, Michael K., Mohan, Mannikam, Haque, Md M., Zhang, Bin, and Savenkova, Marina, 2012. "Epigenetic Transgenerational Inheritance of Somatic Transcriptomes and Epigenetic Control Regions", *Genome Biology* 13 (10): R91.

Smoller, Jordan W., 2016. "The Genetics of Stress-Related Disorders: PTSD, Depression, and Anxiety Disorders", *Neuropsychopharmacology* 41 (1): 297–319.

Solkoff, Norman, 1981. "Children of Survivors of the Nazi Holocaust: A Critical Review of the Literature", *American Journal of Orthopsychiatry* 51 (3): 29–42.

Solomon, Zahava, Kotler, Moshe, and Mikulincer, Mario, 1988. "Combat-Related Posttraumatic Stress Disorder Among Second-Generation Holocaust Survivors: Preliminary Findings", *The American Journal of Psychiatry* 145 (7): 865–868.

Solomon, Zahava, Tsur, Noga, Levin, Yafit, Uziel, Orit, Lahav, Meir, and Ohry, Avi, 2017. "The Implications of War Captivity and Long-Term Psychopathology Trajectories for Telomere Length", *Psychoneuroendocrinology* 19: 855–856.

Sotero, Michelle, 2006. "A Conceptual Model of Historical Trauma: Implications for Public Health Practice and Research", *Journal of Health Disparities Research and Practice* 1 (1): 93–108.

Stone, Amanda L., and Wilson, Anna C., 2016. "Transmission of Risk from Parents with Chronic Pain to Offspring: An Integrative Conceptual Model", *Pain* 157 (12): 2628–2639.

Szeszko, Phlip R., Lehrner, Amy, and Yehuda, Rachel, 2018. "Glucocorticoids and Hippocampal Structure and Function in PTSD", *Harvard Review of Psychiatry* 26 (3): 142–157.

Szeszko, Philip R., and Yehuda, Rachel, 2019. "Magnetic Resonance Imaging Predictors of Psychotherapy Treatment Response in Post-Traumatic Stress Disorder: A Role for the Salience Network", *Psychiatry Research* 277: 52–57.

Thornberry, Terence P., Knight, Kelly E., and Lovegrove, Peter J., 2012. "Does Maltreatment Beget Maltreatment? A Systematic Review of the Intergenerational Literature", *Trauma, Violence & Abuse* 13 (3): 135–152.

Timshel, Isabelle, Montgomery, Edith, and Dalgaard, Nina T., 2017. "A Systematic Review of Risk and Protective Factors Associated with Family-Related Violence in Refugee Families", *Child Abuse & Neglect* 70: 315–330.

Ullmann, Enrico, Licinio, Julio, Perry, Steve W., White, L.O., Klein, A.M., Barthel, A., Petrowski, K., Stalder, T., Oratovski, B., von Klitzing, K., Bornstein, S.R., and Kirschbaum, C., 2018. "Inherited Anxiety-Related Parent-Infant Dyads Alter LHPA Activity", *Stress* 13: 1–9.

Van der Kolk, Bessel A., 1994. "The Body Keeps the Score: Memory and the Evolving Psychobiology of Posttraumatic Stress", *Harvard Review of Psychiatry* 1 (5): 253–265.

Van IJzendoorn, Marinus H., Bakermans-Kranenburg, Marian J., and Sagi-Schwartz, Abraham, 2003. "Are Children of Holocaust Survivors Less Well-Adapted? A Meta-Analytic Investigation of Secondary Traumatization", *Journal of Traumatic Stress* 16 (5): 459–469.

Vukojevic, Vanja, Kolassa, Iris-T., Fastenrath, Matthias, Gschwind, Leo, Spalek, Klara, Milnik, Annette, Heck, Angela, Vogler, Christian, Wilker, Sarah, Demougin, Philippe, Peter, Fabian, Atucha, Erika, Stetak, Attila, Roozendaal, Benno, Elbert, Thomas, Papassotiropoulos, Andreas, and Quervain, Dominique J-F de, 2014. "Epigenetic Modification of the Gucocorticoid Receptor Gene is Linked to Traumatic Memory and Post-Traumatic Stress Disorder Risk in Genocide Survivors", *The Journal of Neuroscience* 34 (31): 10274–10274.

Wager, Tor D., Davidson, Matthew L., Hughes, Brent L., Lindquist, Martin A., and Ochsner, Kevin N., 2008. "Prefrontal-Subcortical Pathways Mediating Success", *Neuron* 59 (6): 1037–1050.

Wardi, Dina, 1992. *Memorial Candles: Children of the Holocaust*, London: Routledge.

Weinstein, Yael, Levav, Itzhak, Gelkopf, Marc, Roe, David, Yoffe, Rinat, Pugachova, Inna, and Levine, Stephen Z., 2018. "Association of Maternal Exposure to Terror Attacks During Pregnancy and the Risk of Schizophrenia in the Offspring: A Population-Based Study", *Schizophrenia Research* 199: 163–167.

Yasmin, Seema, 2017. "Experts Debunk Study that Found Holocaust Trauma Inherited", *Chicago Tribune*, www.chicagotribune.com/lifestyles/health/ct-holocaust-trauma-not-inherited-20170609-story.html

Yehuda, Rachel, 1999. "Biological Factors Associated with Susceptibility to Posttraumatic Stress Disorder", *Canadian Journal of Psychiatry* 44 (1): 34–39.

Yehuda, Rachel, 2009. "Status of Glucocorticoid Alterations in Post-Traumatic Stress Disorder", *Annals of the New York Academy of Sciences* 1179: 56–69.

Yehuda, Rachel, and Bierer, Linda M., 2007. "Transgenerational Transmission of Cortisol and PTSD Risk", *Progress in Brain Research* 167: 121–135.

Yehuda, Rachel, and Bierer, Linda M., 2009. "The Relevance of Epigenetics to PTSD: Implications for the DSM-V", *Journal of Traumatic Stress* 22 (5): 427–434.

Yehuda, Rachel, Daskalakis, Nikolaos P., Bierer, Linda M., Bader, Heather N., Klengel, Torsten, Holsboer, Florian, and Binder, Elisabeth, 2016. "Holocaust Exposure Induced Intergenerational Effects on FKBP5 Methylation", *Biological Psychiatry* 80 (5): 372–380.

Yehuda, Rachel, Daskalakis, Nokolaos P., Lehrner, Amy, Desarnaud, Frank, Bader, Heather, Makotkine, Iouri, Flory, Janin D., Bierer, Linda M., and Meaney, Michael J., 2014. "Influences of Maternal and Paternal PTSD on Epigenetic Regulation of the Glucocorticoid Receptor Gene in Holocaust Survivor Offspring", *American Journal of Psychiatry* 171 (8): 872–880.

Yehuda, Rachel, and Lehrner, Amy, 2018. "Intergenerational Transmission of Trauma Effects: Putative Role of Epigenetic Mechanisms", *World Psychiatry: Official Journal of the World Psychiatric Association* 17 (3): 243–257.

Yehuda, Rachel, Lehrner, Amy, and Bierer, Linda M., 2018. "The Public Reception of Putative Epigenetic Mechanisms in the Transgenerational Effects of Trauma", *Environmental Epigenetics* 4 (2): dvy018.

Yehuda, Rachel, and Seckl, Jonathan, 2011. "Minireview: Stress-Related Psychiatric Disorders with Low Cortisol Levels: A Metabolic Hypothesis", *Endocrinology* 152: 4496–4503.

Yehuda, Rachel, Teicher, Martin H., Seckl, Jonathan, Grossman, Robert A., Morris, Adam, and Bierer, Linda M., 2007. "Parental Posttraumatic Stress Disorder as a Vulnerability Factor for Low Cortisol Trait in Offspring of Holocaust Survivors", *Archives of General Psychiatry* 64 (9): 1040–1048.

Zovkic, Iva B., and Sweatt, David J., 2013. "Epigenetic Mechanisms in Learned Fear: Implications for PTSD", *Neuropsychopharmacology* 38 (1): 77–93.

13

ETHNOGRAPHIC ACCOUNTS OF ISRAELI HOLOCAUST DESCENDANT RESILIENT-VULNERABILITY

Moral-Political Worldviews and the Emergence of Empowering Distress

Carol A. Kidron, Dan M. Kotliar, and Laurence J. Kirmayer

Scholarship on cultural idioms of distress sheds light on illness experience as complementing symptom-based nosological systems.[1] At the same time, the recent salutogenic turn in health research has called for greater attention to processes of mental and physical wellbeing, including transcultural work on resilience and protective factors.[2] A number of questions remain. Does our understanding of particular conceptions of wellbeing and distress require a re-evaluation of culturally mediated experiences of vulnerability and resilience and the interpretive processes that link and mutually qualify them? This case study presents self-perceptions of resilience and vulnerability of Jewish-Israeli trauma descendants of Holocaust survivors. We explore the ways that cultural worldviews mediate wellbeing and emotional distress. We argue that descendant valorization of the transmitted emotional scars of the parental-survivor past constitutes a context-specific form of "resilient vulnerability", differing from the constructs of trauma descendant distress and/or resilience.

Transmitted Trauma and Resilience

Post-traumatic Stress Disorder (PTSD) has been found to impair survivor parenting, potentially transmitting the effects of trauma exposure to the children of survivors.[3] According to the construct of Intergenerational Transmission of the Effects of Trauma (TET or ITT),[4] descendants of genocide, mass violence, terrorism, and natural disasters may be at risk of pathology decades or even centuries after the traumatizing event. Researchers and clinicians have critiqued the theory of intergenerational trauma, warning that resilient survivors and descendants may be needlessly pathologized.[5]

Resilience theory seeks to recognize trauma victims' hardiness and capacity for emotional regulation.[6] Agaibi and Wilson have defined trauma resilience as "efficacious adaptation regardless of significant traumatic threats to personal and physical integrity".[7] Adaptation to multiple forms of adversity in diverse populations has been examined, including Holocaust survivors,[8] war veterans,[9] genocide survivors,[10] victims of terror,[11] historical trauma descendants,[12] and survivors of natural

 DOI: 10.4324/b23365-16

disasters.[13] Recent work has highlighted processes that underlie resilience,[14] conceptualizing pathways through which individuals and collectives may flourish in the face of adversity.[15] Scholars have identified protective factors that enable trauma victims to cope with adversity.[16] Clusters of psychological and communal factors are thought to contribute to "post-traumatic resilience".[17]

From a more critical perspective, the language of resilience may signify that pathology is the usual consequence of trauma exposure and that only the special traits of some individuals spare them these consequences.[18] Yet, epidemiological studies find that the majority of individuals exposed to traumatic events do not develop PTSD or other forms of chronic emotional distress, reflecting the fact that humans have evolved to adapt to environmental stressors, including traumatic events, as part of the human condition.[19] Others have called for more "ecological" and culturally informed models of resilience.[20] Transcultural perspectives on the diversity of self-concepts imply that research must examine the self as embedded in relations with others in the family, community, wider collectivities, and the environment.[21] Finally, scholars have yet to fully explore how resilience is defined normatively across cultures.[22] Insufficient attention has been paid to how particular protective factors interact to create local configurations of meaning and experience that mitigate or exacerbate psycho-social risk and vulnerability.[23]

In response to this critique, critical psychiatrists, mental health practitioners, and psychological and medical anthropologists have explored the ways that local meanings and practices mediate culturally particular modes of suffering.[24] Cultural psychiatrists have examined the beneficial effects of Buddhist worldviews and healing practices among Cambodian genocide survivors.[25] Foxen examined resilience in post-war Guatemala, where the Mayan connection to the land mitigated the impact of trauma.[26] Somasundaram identified Tamil coping strategies, including religious ceremonies, as sources of strength, support, and meaning.[27]

Scholars have also examined the ambiguous role of cultural values, both promoting and obstructing resilience. Exploring narratives of poverty-stricken adults and children in Afghanistan, Eggerman and Panter-Brick found that faith, family unity, and the value of honor and service foster hope and resilience, even though these same values may also entrap the poor in debilitating contexts of structural violence.[28] Argenti-Pillen highlighted the role of cosmological conceptions of memory and the silencing of expressions of the traumatic past as markers of distress and culture-specific coping mechanisms.[29] In a comparative study of Cambodian and Israeli trauma descendants, Kidron found that Cambodian Buddhist conceptions of Karma and acceptance of suffering validate and even promote the choice to forget past suffering. Framed as such, the choice to avoid thinking or speaking about the evil past was perceived by Cambodian interlocutors as a source of resilience.[30]

These studies reveal the ways in which complex networks of survivor personal and collective meaning may give rise to both resilience and vulnerability. Given the cultural basis of these networks, Pedersen and colleagues call for additional "naturalistic studies" of lived experience that might identify interactions among protective factors, risk of chronic distress, and resilience.[31] In this chapter we respond to this call, presenting a phenomenological study of Holocaust trauma descendant perceptions of Holocaust-related vulnerability and resilience.

Holocaust Descendant Legacies of Vulnerability and Resilience

Early theories of transmitted trauma (TT) postulated direct transmission of the effects of trauma. These theories suggested that vicarious trauma in Holocaust descendants involved the transposition of parental defensive structures and repressed or dissociated trauma memories.[32] However, as Kellermann notes, this initial wave of research may have been biased, over-generalizing from a small number of clinical case studies of maladapted families.[33] According to Sagi-Schwartz, subsequent meta-analyses of larger studies of non-clinical samples have failed to find evidence of psychopathology or psychosocial differences between descendant samples and control groups.[34] In a more recent meta-analysis, Payne and Berle found increased levels of PTSD symptoms for children of survivors as compared to control.[35] Transgenerational effects are now conceptualized as the potential transmitted effects of trauma (TET; rather than direct transmission), recognizing that transgenerational transmission of trauma effects involve different mechanisms than those involved in direct trauma.[36]

Although recent studies on TET adopt a salutogenic perspective, they also focus on markers of latent vulnerability and the risk of dysfunction. For example, Shrira and colleagues propose a "mixed functional profile" of descendant wellbeing and vulnerability.[37] While exhibiting "a high sense of wellbeing", descendants are considered at risk for mid-life health problems, due to the physical toll of repressive coping.[38] Van IJzendoorn and colleagues assert that vulnerability may emerge in later life with the onset of health issues and retirement.[39] Scharf found that, compared to control groups, descendants reported less-positive representations of their childhood experiences of parenting, perceiving parents as less autonomy-granting and less accepting.[40] Giladi and Bell found poorer levels of family communication as a risk factor for TET.[41]

In contrast to the extensive research on survivor resilience and protective factors, there have been few attempts to examine how cultural meaning mediates the subjective experience of Holocaust descendant vulnerability or resilience. This study examined Israeli Holocaust trauma descendants' accounts of identity and illness experience and the way descendants depict their legacy as conferring resilience and/or vulnerability. Our results problematize both the universalization of the construct of TET and the construct of transmitted trauma resilience, as they fail to encompass the ways culturally mediated vulnerability and resilience interact to constitute what we term "resilient vulnerability".

Methods

This qualitative ethnographic study of second generation Holocaust survivors used a snowball method to recruit participants. Sampling did not include clinical participants, and we did not sample from Holocaust-related organizations. A total of 55 in-depth interviews were conducted with second generation Holocaust survivors in Israel in 2001–04 and another 20 interviews in 2010–11. Second generation participants ranged in age from 35 to 55 with equal gender representation. The great majority (92%) were born in Israel to one (23%) or two (77%) survivor parents who had emigrated there from Europe in the late 1940s and early 1950s after surviving Nazi extermination camps, forced labor camps, ghetto incarceration, or extended periods of hiding.[42] The minority born in Europe were extremely young when immigrating to Israel. After an initial period of economic hardship, the majority achieved middle- to upper-middle-class status and had some form of higher education.

Semi-structured ethnographic interviews took place in respondents' homes or in cafés and lasted two to four hours.[43] Interviews used a phenomenological approach, which allows in-depth exploration of subjective experience, while ensuring that all respondents are exposed to the same questions, enabling systematic comparison of responses.[44] The topic guide covered: self-perceived wellness/distress; parental wellness/distress; the meanings of perceived silence and/or lack of communication around parental Holocaust experience; and the social contexts, norms, and values framing these perceptions and experiences. With respondents' consent, interviews were recorded and transcribed. All interviews were conducted in Hebrew, with English translation validated by the second author, a native-born Hebrew speaker.

We followed Giorgi's procedure for analysis of mid-sized qualitative ethnographic studies.[45] Two research assistants and the first two authors read each transcript. During these readings, we explored the text as a narrative whole, as well as identified recurring themes within each interview. We then identified and discussed recurring themes shared across interviews. As a next step we reread transcripts, tagging the appropriate text under the identified themes. Thematic files were created containing interview segments from the various participants. Prior to 2005/11, when the data for this study were collected, universities in Israel did not require IRB approval for ethnographic studies. However, the study was conducted in conformity with current research ethics guidelines. All participants gave written informed consent. All names and other identifying factors have been changed to preserve confidentiality.

Results

The results present two dominant themes emergent in descendant accounts relating to the overarching topic of vulnerability and resilience. All respondent accounts presented herein are emblematic of the wider data set. In keeping with the presentation of ethnographic interview data in qualitative sociology and anthropology, the results section includes interpretation of data excerpts.

Srutim ("Scratched"): Normalizing Descendant Vulnerability

When asked about parental mental health, 68% (52/75) of the descendant sample stated that their parents suffered from symptoms of post-trauma; however, the majority (80%) insisted that their parents did not require therapy. The great majority of descendants asserted that they were not suffering from transmitted effects of parental PTSD. The entire sample showed familiarity with popular literature on transmitted PTSD and about 25% (19/75) had participated in short- or long-term psychotherapy or support groups.

A closer reading of descendant accounts, however, reveals that many descendants acknowledged that they were in fact marked by their parents' trauma experience, referring to themselves as *srutim* (30/75 of descendant sample). The terms *srita* (Hebrew for "scratch"), *sarut* (adjective of *srita* signifying being *sarut* or "scratched") or *srutim* (plural of *sarut*) are colloquial descriptors signifying the emotional and behavioral consequences of adverse situations. In colloquial accounts, the *sarut* self is non-normative, at times abnormal, or even "crazy". When describing themselves as *srutim* in popular culture, Israelis refer to the harmful and irreparable effects of difficult events. The fact that the term *srita*, signifying a minor wound, is used to refer to the outcomes of major adversities, allows for a prosaic, often humorous, depiction of the blow, without understating the gravity of the experience and its impact: traumatic scars or wounds are rendered mere scratches. The usage of the term *srita* calls attention to hardships, while downplaying and normalizing them. By highlighting both the superficiality *and* the permanence of events, the term *srita* refers to the way one successfully copes with, without erasing the impact of, emotional blows.

Descendants claimed that their *srita* was not a sign of pathology but rather a relatively benign emotive marker of difference. Bella explained:

> In my childhood I never thought I was different, even now – I would say I'm definitely not traumatized by my parents! I mean, sure we are *srutim* [laughing]. I did therapy for three years. Blamed everything on the Holocaust. But there's a point where you say obsessing about yourself is self-indulgent. We are different, how could we not be different and see the world differently – as a place full of evil, for gosh sake we were almost not born!

Beyond her critique of therapeutic "self-indulgence", Bella presents descendants as *srutim*. Instead of highlighting traumatization or other maladaptive psychosocial conditions, Bella emphasized descendants' particular emotive worldviews regarding the past and the world as an evil place. David recounted the commemorative function of the scratch:

> How could you grow up with parents crying in their sleep, empathizing with their pain before you even knew what it was and not have *sritot?* No matter what we do they are permanent, part of who we are. I tried to understand why I am like I am for many years. But I have come to terms with who I am, and I think there is a meaningful part to all this, we are like monuments to the past. It's not just about us – we have to make sure people don't forget. There is comfort and strength in that, I think.

David clearly traces intergenerational transmission of an emotional legacy of empathy and identification. The descendant depicts what has become iconic founding events of his identity – such as parents crying at night. The inevitability of a wounded legacy is brought home in his question: "how could children of survivors not have *sritot*?" Like Bella, David depicts the permanence of *sritot* – while he too has "come to terms" with wounds that are "part of who I am". However, his almost taken for granted acceptance of his legacy went beyond the intrapsychic management of years of attempted self-analysis ("I tried to understand why I am like I am") as David claims the *srita* also provided meaning and a moral mission of ethnic/national collective memory. The descendant illustrates the way Jewish-Israeli worldviews mediate the self-construal of the descendant's suffering self as empowered carrier of memory, who finds "comfort and strength" in this emotionally demanding legacy. If cultural meanings differentially frame the moral order[46] by assigning value to genocide memory, then descendants' emotional experience of trauma-related memories may be differentially experienced, interpreted, tolerated – even valorized. In descendant accounts, wounds are experienced as particular normative emotional modes of being ("see[ing] the world differently"), rather than as evidence of disorder. If such emotional experience signifies a morally valuable Holocaust presence and not a personally maladaptive form of suffering, then psychotherapeutic treatment to achieve better coping or adaptation is not simply undesirable but untenable (a kind of "self indulgence"). The assertion of collective meaning appears to perpetuate individual scars ("they are permanent") as socially valorized markers of collective trauma carrier status.[47]

How does this cultural mediation of the legacy of woundedness impact descendant subjective experience of vulnerability and resilience? Are these constructs applicable to those who normalize their wounds as "scratches"? If one defines the word *vulnerability* based on its Latin origin as the capability of being physically or emotionally wounded,[48] then Holocaust descendants are depicting themselves as vulnerable to the long-term effects of the Holocaust. Yet if the Israeli Holocaust descendant legacy is experienced as a valorized collective identity and not as an individual psychological disorder, is it nevertheless a marker of 'latent vulnerability', leaving individuals at risk for future maladaptive behavior?[49]

Although descendants experience what they recognize as emotional 'effects' of parental trauma, they describe this as a desirable burden of memory and not as a maladaptive psychological disorder. Descendants therefore cannot be characterized simply as vulnerable or resilient because they remain both vulnerable and empowered by the scars of past and present 'difference'. If resilience is defined as coping with or adapting to a legacy of adversity,[50] then the Jewish burden of collective memory protectively buffers the self and fosters resilient 'coping'. Could Jewish-Israeli paradigms of memory and the politics of Israeli memory be both a risk factor and a protective buffer?

Jewish Paradigms of Memory: Risk or Protective Factor?

The commemorative role of the descendant wound must be contextualized within Jewish paradigms of memory and Israeli-Jewish politics of memory. The remembrance and re-enactment of the past are key Jewish ethno-cultural tropes.[51] The individual, perceived as the eternal witness who embodies memory, and the community of which they are a part, which erects monuments and organizes commemorative ceremonies, loop back to make the past present by embedding memories of individual and collective events in current depictions of history. Filial responsibility to the memory of one's parents and ancestors is of great importance, embedded in Jewish cosmology and praxis. Children are burdened with the "sins of their forefathers", completing the destinies of ancestral namesakes, and they are obligated to yearly commemorative prayers sustaining the presence of familial dead among the living. The individual must transmit the collective past to future generations. These paradigms of memory are ever present in the Israeli state as government-sponsored commemoration valorizes Holocaust survivors and fallen war heroes, collectively enlists survivors and bereaved families, and engineers pedagogic pilgrimages to Holocaust death camps.[52] Holocaust-related commemorative pedagogy is widely disseminated in everyday Israeli life, including in non-Jewish Arab-Israeli classrooms. Within the context of the Arab-Israeli conflict, carriers of Holocaust memory act as an essential commemorative role in the politics of memory and victimhood,[53] serving to legitimate the nation state in the face of competing historical narratives. These forms of memory work weave the past into the everyday lives of the nation and constitute the moral mission of those citizens prepared to carry the burden of collective and personal memory.

In keeping with these Jewish cultural and national tropes of memory, descendants in our study all expressed concern with the future of commemoration. Beyond the embodied emotive commemoration of the transmitted *srita* of the Holocaust past, the majority described private practices of lighting candles in memory of the Holocaust dead. The more religiously observant participated in synagogue-based communal prayers commemorating family killed in the Holocaust and communities lost to the genocide. However, when asked about the transmission of the Holocaust past to their children or participation in public forms of commemoration, the majority of descendants preferred to remain silent – despite national rhetoric concerning the dwindling survivor-witness generation – and relied on survivor grandparents and the educational system to transmit personal and collective legacies. After recounting their own exposure to survivors' wounds and memories, descendants noted that their children (the Third Generation) would also have to "learn to know and to feel" the wounds of the past "for all those who had died" – again fusing emotional vulnerability with a collective moral mission. Regarding descendant avoidance of public commemoration, respondents described the silent presence in the home as commemorative, obviating the need for objectification in the public domain and constituting descendants as walking testament to the past. At the same time, descendants did undertake "roots trips" to death camps and became members of local grassroots descendant organizations.[54] For example, Rafi, a 50-year-old descendant, depicted his experience visiting Auschwitz as an Israeli soldier in uniform:

> We descendants, we are like an elite unit in the army, we have an important duty to fulfill, we have to make sure no one forgets, like when I stood in Auschwitz in uniform and reminded everyone of what happened to our families, to our people and that they can't do it to us again. But we have scars to show for it, service does not come without its costs. We're *srutim*. I'm more sensitive than the next guy, maybe even more paranoid . . . I drive my kids crazy like my father did worrying about them . . . but I'm tougher than the others and I'll survive. I know that from the battlefield. . . . You get it from looking into your father's eyes holding his shaking hand during the memorial service in synagogue for the dead [his hand clenches and his voice breaks]. This is what we do best, we survive and when it's engraved in your heart and soul [touches his chest and long pause], from those moments, no one can take that away.

Rafi depicts the emotional toll of valorized participation in the "elite unit" of carriers of collective memory. Although describing his emotional scars as *sritot,* Rafi normalizes the early experiences of intergenerational transmission, presenting them as taken-for-granted empathic parent-child relations and embodied memories of the silent presence of the past. Rafi traces a causal connection between his early memories of silent identification ("you get it from looking in your father's eyes") and his superior skills of survival. Rafi "gets" his survival skills from survivor-parent-child emotive interaction in moments that are depicted in the literature as potentially transmitting the effects of trauma. In keeping with the work of Sagi-Schwarz and colleagues and Barel and colleagues,[55] the transmitted trauma legacy may result in adaptive coping skills. Rafi's account thus describes the constitutive process of latent vulnerability and resilience.

We would claim, however, that Rafi's account illustrates a more complex configuration of vulnerability and resilience. In the Jewish-Israeli context, the legacy "engraved" in Rafi's heart and soul, is a marker of the elite status of the authentic carrier of collective memory. Resonant with other descendant accounts in our sample (53/75); beyond adaptive skills of survival, his scars enable and require collective testimony that, in turn, acts as a normative protective factor – providing empowering cultural capital, status and meaning. Rafi asserts that "when it's engraved in one's heart and soul from those moments no one can take them [strength and survival skills] away" – implying that markers of emotional vulnerability and strength and the resultant carrier status may not only be permanent, but as normative protective factors (contributing capital, self-esteem and resilience) they sustain vulnerability. Thus, the data suggest that resilience and vulnerability may be mutually constitutive and reinforcing. Rafi is empowered by the act of classification as "wounded" because this recognizes him as a publicly valorized carrier of collective memory. In this way, the interface between personal and collective memory in the Jewish-Israeli political context further sustains the mutually constitutive relationship of vulnerability and resilience of survivor and descendant identities in the service of the nation.[56] In the Israeli context, resilience in everyday life is informed by particular notions of value[57] and human worth where the moral message of the valorized resilient-vulnerable descendant may be put to work to articulate a sense of national belonging.

Rebecca gave the following account of her wounds and resilient public sacrifice:

> When my husband had a heart attack, I became very calm. I called the paramedics. They put him in the ambulance. As they were leaving, I went to leave food for the dog. They yelled at me 'what are you doing.' I ran and caught up with them and I said to myself, 'this is what I have been waiting for all my life'. Second Generation are always prepared for disaster and death. We are ready and will always be strong. My daughter was with me. I could see my calm scared her. We are not the same as everyone else. We suffer from an awareness of all that can go wrong in life. We have scenarios running in our head. We are *srutim*, no way to change, but we don't break. Not like the soldiers after the war – this is not trauma. . . . Our parents suffered real life situations, and these are the lessons we learned from them. Can you tell me some of those situations will never happen again? My daughter does not understand this yet, but she too is strong, maybe some of this terrible history affects the next generation too. She was very close to her grandmother. Who knows . . . she tasted the shadow. . . . She is a social worker, she works with broken families. You know a lot of descendants are caregivers. . . . We use our pain to help others. There is a sad honor [*kavod atzuv*] to this life we have, no? We like to talk about ourselves like we have a badge of honor [*ot kavod*]. We grew up with iconic survivors . . . we contribute to others, but this badge also has hidden thorns.

Despite depicting herself as emotionally wounded, Rebecca depathologizes descendants asserting that their *srita* are not marks of trauma but rather a transmitted mode of being, characterized by heightened preparedness for survival in a dangerous world. Recalling Shrira's findings pertaining to Second Generation depictions of scenarios of a "hostile world", Rebecca's preparedness (as she "waits all her life" for the inevitable crisis), aided by the "scenarios in her head" give her strength.[58] Describing her vulnerability or "scratch" as a permanent wound that entails anxious anticipation of potential disasters, she insists that, despite their *srita*, descendants do not "break" as the lessons of the past also confer resilience.

Rebecca depicts her daughter as inheriting an emotive legacy of intergenerational transmission, positioning her daughter as sacrificially serving the collective. Recalling Rafi's "elite unit", Rebecca ends with reference to descendant "sad honor" symbolized as a badge of honor, while hidden thorns signify the trade-off of transmitted emotional vulnerability. The Hebrew idiom "badge of honor" (in Hebrew: *ot kavod,* literally translated as "a sign or badge of honor") is a symbol of ascribed and displayed status. Social valorization for ones' collective commemorative sacrifice resonates with collective and individual self-esteem. However, as evident in many of the accounts of the scarring of the commemorative *srita*, descendant honor is forever pained or "saddened" by the emotional weight or "thorns" of their honorable sacrifice. The tropes of "sad honor" and "badge of honor with thorns" point to the interaction of vulnerability and resilience, as each qualifies the other in the configuration of Israeli descendant wellbeing and distress.

Discussion

This study has explored Jewish-Israeli trauma descendants' sense of resilience and vulnerability. Consistent with earlier findings on Holocaust descendant perceptions of familial wellness and distress,[59] respondents describe trauma descendant wellbeing, challenging the commonly accepted profile in the literature of pathology and vulnerability. However, descendants also acknowledge they have an emotional *srita* – a scar, which one study participant described as a "badge of honor with thorns". This normalization and valorization of woundedness is embedded within particular cultural practices of collective commemoration and sociomoral modes of being that mediate a distinctive configuration of emotional vulnerability and resilience that we have termed "resilient vulnerability". At first glance, our data appear to support Shrira and colleagues' "mixed functional profile" of trauma descendants.[60] Yet, a closer look at the dialectic of Israeli descendant resilient-vulnerability points to the need for a culturally and socio-politically grounded approach to resilience, in which the Jewish filial obligation to emotively embody sacrificial markers of the Holocaust past transforms what might otherwise be maladaptive effects of transmitted trauma into a valued testament to familial and collective survival and a source of resilience. The proposed concept *resilient vulnerability* aims to capture the way the two processes reinforce each other, while underscoring the experience of an enduring vulnerability that is qualified by its contribution to resilience. Moreover, the concept also reflects the culturally esteemed norm of "sustaining" survivor and descendant vulnerability central to Holocaust commemoration.

Depathologizing Transmitted Trauma

Descendant accounts in our study are incongruent in a number of respects with the pathologizing constructs of transmitted and intergenerational trauma. The descendant *srita* is presented as a Holocaust-related idiom of distress that signifies emotional difference, transmitted by the matrix of silent Holocaust survivor presence and empathic parent-child relations. The Holocaust descendant's emotive scar is seen by respondents as a culturally valorized form of commemorative remembering and worn as an empowering badge of honor. Although describing themselves as wounded, descendants' emotional legacy is not experienced as univocally distressing. Unlike psychological readings of silence as a potential mechanism of intergenerational transmission and risk factor for vulnerability,[61] descendant accounts of parent-child relations and the familial "wall of silence" depicted silence as an alternative channel for intimate parent-child interaction and the culturally esteemed presence of the genocide past. Such intergenerational transmission was perceived as constituting unique embodied emotional relationships, not parental emotional detachment, pathogenic identification, vicarious trauma, or longing for the voided past.[62] Accounts presented herein also illustrate the potential diversity of culturally mediated familial emotion work and corresponding adaptive and valued emotional modes of being.[63] Understanding descendant psychosocial legacies requires moving beyond a narrow therapeutic gaze to consider culture-specific modes of parenting, intergenerational relational hierarchies, and emotion management.

In keeping with previous critiques of the transmitted trauma construct,[64] because descendants have not experienced the foundational traumatizing event and psychological studies have failed to show evidence of descendants' first-hand traumatic adversity during childhood, descendants' legacy of trauma consists primarily of culturally transmitted moral modes of being rather than adversity. This suggests that the construct of transmitted trauma resilience may be better understood through a phenomenological analysis of the culturally situated lived experience of familial relations – and by deconstruction of the discursive and institutional mediation of wellbeing and distress – than through its impact on the construct of "survivor PTSD".[65]

Ethno-religious Modes of Being and Paradigms of Memory as Protective Buffers

When recounting their experience, descendants appealed to culturally specific moral modes of being to account for familial wellbeing and/or distress. Paradigms of memory and forgetting embedded in Jewish-Israeli worldviews mediated differential self-perceived senses of emotional vulnerability and resilience. In keeping with the work of Argenti-Pillen,[66] we could not decipher psychosocial responses to parental traumatizing events without examining the mediation of Jewish paradigms of filial obligation to familial and collective commemoration. Holocaust memory work valorizes emotive wounds as markers of personal and familial genocide memory, countering the logic of healing in which the disappearance of superficial and temporary scars would culminate in forgetting. Jewish-Israeli political ideology also esteems, empowers, and sustains descendant emotional experience as a living testament to the past, commemoratively re-presenting historical collective suffering and thereby legitimating contemporary national agendas.[67] Recalling the studies by Kaplan and colleagues and Plotkin-Amrami on the ways that Jewish-Israeli religious-Zionist beliefs acted as protective buffers in the case of potentially traumatized terror victims and those who lost their homes in the 2005 disengagement from Gaza (the dismantling of Israeli settlements from the Gaza strip),[68] we might conclude that Jewish-Israeli worldviews buffer the wounded self, permitting what resilience theory would term "adaptive coping" with the psychosocial legacies of the Holocaust. Beyond the beneficial effects of collective meaning making, however, religious and political worldviews not only make distress culturally meaningful but potentially transform vulnerability into an honorable identity and desirable mode of being.

Conclusion: The Interaction of Vulnerability and Resilience as a Culturally Mediated Process of Meaning Making

In keeping with Panter-Brick's distinction between the functional/outcome-centered dimension of resilience research and normative dimensions of resilience research,[69] this study problematizes models and composite measures of vulnerability and resilience that gauge resilience in terms of a dichotomous tally of vulnerability and protective factors.[70] These models fail to represent the complex interaction between protective factors and risk factors that emerge in specific cultural and socio-political contexts.[71] In the absence of qualitative ethnographic accounts, depictions of mixed profiles of wellbeing in the face of vulnerability may appear surprising and remain unexplained.[72]

Descendant accounts reveal the ways in which culturally mediated perceptions of the self as resilient and vulnerable co-exist and interact, qualifying and mutually reinforcing one another to generate particular local conceptions of wellbeing and distress. Although Jewish paradigms of memory buffer the self confronted with traumatic memory, they sustain vulnerability by insisting on the value of the carrier of traumatic memory. The Holocaust descendant experiences a trade-off between wellness and recovery and the valorized burden of memory. In this context, silence acts simultaneously as a potential stressor and buffer transmitting an alternative form of parent-child interaction. Expanding on Eggerman and Panter-Brick's conceptualization of the way Afghani values may both exacerbate and mitigate distress[73] and Kirmayer and colleagues' analyses of psychosocial political trade-offs related to historical trauma among Indigenous peoples,[74] our findings illustrate how the lived experience of Holocaust descendants does not frame resilience and vulnerability as distinct, contradictory experiences of increased and decreased distress or wellbeing. Building upon Kidron et al.'s findings pertaining to descendant accounts of vulnerability and resilience, this chapter highlights the way culturally mediated sociomoral and political values uniquely shape descendant experiences of distress and wellbeing as mutually reinforcing.[75]

Notes

1 Argenti-Pillen, 2000; Foxen, 2010; Lewis-Fernández et al., 2017.
2 Eggerman and Panter-Brick, 2010; Panter-Brick, 2014.
3 Scharf, 2007.
4 Kellerman, 2001; Scharf, 2007.
5 Summerfield, 1998; Sagi-Schwartz et al., 2003.
6 Bonanno, 2004; Luthar, 2003; Masten, 2001.
7 Agaibi and Wilson, 2005: 199.
8 Shmotkin, 2003.
9 King et al., 1998.
10 Rousseau et al., 1998.
11 Kaitz et al., 2008.
12 Brave Heart, 2000.
13 Goodman and West-Olatunji, 2008.
14 Ungar, 2012; Masten, 2014.
15 Theron and Theron, 2013; Kirmayer et al., 2012.
16 Steinhardt and Dolbier, 2007.
17 Agaibi and Wilson, 2005: 203.
18 Kidron and Kirmayer, 2019; Kidron et al., 2019.
19 Summerfield, 2002: 1107; Konner, 2007.
20 Harvey, 1996.
21 Kirmayer et al., 2011; Argenti-Pillen, 2000.
22 Panter-Brick, 2014.
23 Foxen, 2010; Kirmayer et al., 2009; Eggerman and Panter-Brick, 2010.
24 Hinton and Kirmayer, 2013.
25 Nickerson and Hinton, 2011.
26 Foxen, 2010.
27 Somasundaram, 2014.
28 Eggerman and Panter-Brick, 2010.
29 Argenti-Pillen, 2003.
30 Kidron, 2012.

31 Pedersen et al., 2015: 20.
32 Kellerman, 2001.
33 Kellerman, 2001: 39.
34 Sagi-Schwartz et al., 2003; Barel et al., 2010. See also Solkoff's (1992) critique on mechanisms of intergenerational transmission.
35 Payne and Berle, 2021.
36 Kaitz, 2008; Shrira et al., 2011.
37 Shrira et al., 2011.
38 Shrira et al., 2011: 400.
39 Van IJzendoorn et al., 2003.
40 Scharf, 2007: 617–619.
41 Giladi and Bell, 2013: 1.
42 The definition of Holocaust survivor utilized herein was based on the Israeli Census Bureau of Statistics, 2000. Although this definition was subsequently broadened to include those suffering from Nazi occupation, descendants interviewed during the initial pilot study expressed strong support for the narrow definition.
43 Ethnographic interviewing is informal and dialogic permitting open-ended questions and emergent conversation pertaining to interlocutor lived experience. See Rinaldo and Guhin, 2019.
44 Charmaz, 2014.
45 Giorgi, 1975.
46 Eggerman and Panter-Brick, 2010.
47 Kidron, 2012.
48 Collins English Dictionary, 2009.
49 Scharf, 2007.
50 Kirmayer et al., 2009.
51 Yerushalmi, 1982.
52 Feldman, 2008.
53 Kotliar, 2016.
54 Kidron, 2013.
55 Sagi Schwartz et al., 2003; Barel et al., 2010.
56 Feldman, 2008.
57 Shweder, 2000.
58 Shrira, 2015.
59 Kidron, 2009.
60 Shrira et al., 2011.
61 Danieli, 1998.
62 Kidron, 2009.
63 Butler et al., 2007.
64 Barel et al., 2010; Sagi Schwartz et al., 2003.
65 Barton, 2005.
66 Argenti-Pillen, 2000.
67 Feldman, 2008.
68 Kaplan et al., 2005; Plotkin Amrami, 2013.
69 Panter-Brick, 2014: 440.
70 Shrira et al., 2011.
71 Gone and Kirmayer, 2010; Foxen, 2010.
72 Barel et al., 2010; Barton, 2005; Sagi-Schwartz et al., 2003.
73 Eggerman and Panter-Brick, 2010.
74 Kirmayer et al., 2011.
75 Kidron et al., 2019.

References

Agaibi, Christin E., and Wilson, John P., 2005. "Trauma, PTSD, and Resilience: A Review of the Literature", *Trauma, Violence, & Abuse* 6 (3): 195–216.

Argenti-Pillen, Alex, 2000. "The Discourse on Trauma in Non-Western Cultural Contexts: Contribution of an Ethnographic Method", in: Arieh Y. Shalev, Rachel Yehuda, and Alexander C. McFarlane (eds.), *International Handbook of Human Response to Trauma*, New York: Plenum Publishers: 87–102.

Argenti-Pillen, Alex, 2003. *Masking Terror: How Women Contain Violence in Southern Sri Lanka*, Philadelphia, PA: University of Pennsylvania Press.

Barel, Efrat D., Van IJzendoorn, Marinus H., Sagi-Schwartz, Abraham, and Bakermans-Kranenburg, Marian J., 2010. "Surviving the Holocaust: A Meta-Analysis of the Long-Term Sequelae of a Genocide", *Psychological Bulletin* 136 (5): 677–98.

Barton, William H., 2005. "Methodological Challenges in the Study of Resilience", in: Michal Ungar (ed.), *Handbook for Working with Children and Youth: Pathways to Resilience across Cultures and Contexts*, Thousand Oaks, CA: Sage: 135–148.

Bonanno, George A., 2004. "Loss, Trauma and Human Resilience: Have we Underestimated the Human Capacity to Thrive after Extremely Aversive Events?", *American Psychologist* 59: 20–28.

Brave Heart, Maria Y., 2000. "Wakiksuyapi: Carrying the Historical/trauma of the Lakota", *Tulane Studies Social Welfare* 21 (22): 245–266.

Butler, Emily A., Lee, Tiane L., and Gross, James J., 2007. "Emotion Regulation and Culture: Are the Social Consequences of Emotion Suppression Culture-Specific?", *Emotion* 7 (1): 30–48.

Charmaz, Kathy, 2014. *Constructing Grounded Theory*, London: Sage.

Collins English Dictionary, 2009. *Vulnerability*, Glasgow: Harper Collins Publishers.

Danieli, Yael, 1998. "Introduction: History and Conceptual Foundations", in: Yael Danieli (ed.), *International Handbook of Multigenerational Legacies of Trauma*, New York: Plenum Press: 1–17.

Eggerman, Mark B., and Panter-Brick, Catherine, 2010. "Suffering, Hope, and Entrapment: Resilience and Cultural Values in Afghanistan", *Social Science & Medicine* 71 (1): 71–83.

Feldman, Jackie, 2008. *Above the Death Pits, Beneath the Flag: Youth Voyages to Holocaust Poland and Israeli National Identity*, New York: Berghahn Books.

Foxen, Patricia, 2010. "Local Narratives of Distress and Resilience: Lessons in Psychosocial Well-being among the 'Kiche' Maya in postwar Guatemala", *Journal Latin American Caribbean Anthropology* 15 (1): 66–89.

Giladi, Lotem, and Bell, Terece S., 2013. "Protective Factors for Intergenerational Transmission of Trauma among Second and Third Generation Holocaust Survivors", *Psychological Trauma, Theory, Research, Practice, and Policy* 5 (4): 384–391.

Giorgi, Amedeo, 1975. "An Application of Phenomenological Method in Psychology", in: Amadeo Giorgi, Constance T. Fisher, and Edward L. Murray (eds.), *Duquesne Studies in Phenomenological Psychology*, Pittsburgh, PA: Duquesne University Press: 82–103.

Gone, Joseph P., and Kirmayer, Laurence J., 2010. "On the Wisdom of Considering Culture and Context in Psychopathology", in: Theodore Millon, Robert F. Krueger, and Erik Simonsen (eds.), *Contemporary Directions in Psychopathology: Scientific Foundations of the DSM-V and ICD-11*, New York: The Guilford Press: 72–96.

Goodman, Rachael D., and West-Olatunji, Cirecie E., 2008. "Transgenerational Trauma and Resilience: Improving Mental Health Counseling for Survivors of Hurricane Katrina", *Journal Mental Health Counseling* 30 (2): 121–136.

Harvey, Mary R., 1996. "An Ecological View of Psychological Trauma and Trauma Recovery", *Journal of Trauma Stress* 9 (1): 3–23.

Hinton, Devon E., and Kirmayer, Laurence J., 2013. "Local Responses to Trauma: Symptom, Affect, and Healing", *Transcultural Psychiatry* 50 (5): 607–621.

Kaitz, Marsha, 2008. "The Transgenerational Effects of Trauma from Terror: A Developmental Model", in: R.A. Larch (ed.), *Global Terrorism Issues and Developments*, New York: Nova Science Publishers: 187–212.

Kaplan, Zeev, Matar, Michael A., Kamin, Ram, Sadan, Tamar, and Cohen, Hagar, 2005. "Stress-related Responses after 3 years of Exposure to Terror in Israel: Are Ideological-Religious Factors Associated with Resilience?", *Journal of Clinical Psychiatry* 66 (9): 1146–1154.

Kellerman, Natan P.F., 2001. "Psychopathology in Children of Holocaust Survivors: A Review of the Research Literature", *Israel Journal of Psychiatry and Related Sciences* 38 (1): 36–46.

Kidron, Carol A., 2009. "Toward an Ethnography of Silence: The Lived Presence of the Past in the Everyday Life of Holocaust Trauma Survivors and their Descendants in Israel", *Current Anthropology* 50 (1): 5–27.

Kidron, Carol A., 2012. "Alterity and the Particular Limits of Universalism: Comparing Jewish-Israeli Holocaust and Canadian-Cambodian Genocide Legacies", *Current Anthropology* 53 (6): 723–754.

Kidron, Carol A., 2013. "Being there Together: Dark Family Tourism and the Emotive Experience of Co-presence in the Holocaust Past", *Annals of Tourism Research* 41: 175–194.

Kidron, Carol A., and Kirmayer, Laurence J., 2019. "Global Mental Health and Idioms of Distress: The Paradox of Culture Sensitive Pathologization of Distress in Cambodia", *Culture Medicine and Psychiatry* 43: 211–235.

Kidron, Carol A., Kotliar, Dan, and Kirmayer, Laurence J., 2019. "Trauma as Badge of Honor: Phenomenological Experiences of Holocaust Descendant Resilient Vulnerability", *Social Science & Medicine* 239: 112524.

King, Lynda A., King, Daniel W., Fairbank, John A., Keane, Terence M., and Adams, Gary A., 1998. "Resilience–Recovery Factors in Post-Traumatic Stress Disorder among Female and Male Vietnam Veterans: Hardiness, Postwar Social Support, and Additional Stressful Life Events", *Journal of Personality and Social Psychology* 74 (2): 420–434.

Kirmayer, Laurence J., Dandeneau, Stéphane, Marshall, Elizabeth, Phillips, Morgan K., and Williamson, Karla J., 2011. "Rethinking Resilience from Indigenous Perspectives", *The Canadian Journal of Psychiatry* 56 (2): 84–91.

Kirmayer, Laurence J., Dandeneau, Stéphane, Marshall, Elizabeth, Phillips, Morgan K., and Williamson, Karla J., 2012. "Toward an Ecology of Stories: Indigenous Perspectives on Resilience", in: Michael Ungar (ed.), *The Social Ecology of Resilience*, New York: Springer: 399–414.

Kirmayer, Laurence J., Gone, Joseph P., and Moses, Joshua, 2014. "Rethinking Historical Trauma", *Transcultural Psychiatry* 51 (3): 299–319.

Kirmayer, Laurence J., Sehdev, Megha, Whitley, Robert, Dandeneau, Stéphane F., and Isaac, Colette, 2009. "Community Resilience: Models, Metaphors and Measures", *International Journal of Indigenous Health* 5 (1): 62.

Konner, Melvin, 2007. "Trauma, Adaptation, and Resilience: A Cross-cultural and Evolutionary Perspective", in: Laurence J. Kirmayer, Robert Lemelson, and M. Barad (eds.), *Understanding Trauma: Biological, Psychological and Cultural Perspectivesc*, New York: Cambridge University Press: 300–338.

Kotliar, Dan M., 2016. "Emotional Oppositions: The Political Struggle Over Citizens' Emotions", *Qualitative Sociology* 39: 267–286.

Lewis-Fernández, Roberto, and Aggarwal, Neal K., 2015. "Psychiatric Classification Beyond the DSM", in: Laurence J. Kirmayer, Robert Lemelson, and Constance A. Cummings (eds.), *Revisioning Psychiatry: Cultural Phenomenology, Critical Neuroscience, and Global Mental Health*, Cambridge: Cambridge University Press: 434.

Lewis-Fernández, Roberto, Kirmayer, Laurence J., Guarnaccia, Peter J., and Ruiz, Pedro, 2017. "Cultural Concepts of Distress", in: Benjamin J. Sadock, Pedro Ruiz, and Virginia A. Sadock (eds.), *Comprehensive Textbook of Psychiatry*, New York: Lippincott, Williams & Wilkins.

Luthar, Suniya S., 2003. *Resilience and Vulnerability*, New York: Cambridge University Press.

Masten, Ann S., 2001. "Ordinary Magic: Resilience Processes in Development", *American Psychologist* 56 (3): 227–238.

Masten, Ann S., 2014. "Global Perspectives on Resilience in Children and Youth", *Child Development* 85 (1): 6–20.

Nickerson, Angela, and Hinton, Devon E., 2011. "Anger Regulation in Traumatized Cambodian Refugees: The Perspectives of Buddhist Monks", *Culture Medicine and Psychiatry* 35 (3): 396–416.

Panter-Brick, Catherine, 2014.' Health, Risk and Resilience: Interdisciplinary Concepts and Applications", *Annual Review of Anthropology* 43: 431–448.

Payne, Emma A., and Berle, David, 2021. "Posttraumatic Stress Disorder Symptoms among Offspring of Holocaust Survivors: A Systematic Review and Meta-analysis", *Traumatology* 27 (3): 254–264.

Pedersen, Duncan, Kienzler, Hanna, and Guzder, Jaswant, 2015. "Searching for Best Practices: A Systematic Inquiry into the Nature of Psychosocial Interventions Aimed at Reducing the Mental Health Burden in Conflict and Post-Conflict Settings", *Sage Open* 5 (4).

Plotkin Amrami, Galia, 2013. "Between National Ideology and Western Therapy: On the Emergence of a New Culture of Trauma", *Transcultural Psychiatry* 50 (1): 47–67.

Rinaldo, Rachel, and Guhin, Jeffrey, 2019. "How and Why Interviews Work: Ethnographic Interviews and Meso-Level Public Culture", *Sociological Methods and Research*: 1–34.

Rousseau, Cécile, Said, Taher M., Gagné, Marie-Josée, and Bibeau, Gilles, 1998. "Resilience in Unaccompanied Minors from the North of Somalia", *The Psychoanalytic Review* 85 (4): 615–638.

Sagi-Schwartz, Abraham, Van IJzendoorn, Marinus H., Grossmann, Klaus E., Grossmann, Karin, Scharf, M., and Koren-Karie, Nina, 2003. "Attachment and Traumatic Stress in Female Holocaust Child Survivors and Their Daughters", *American Journal of Psychiatry* 160 (6): 1086–1092.

Scharf, Miri, 2007. "Long-Term Effects of Trauma: Psychosocial Functioning of the Second and Third Generation of Holocaust Survivors", *Development and Psychopathology* 19 (2): 603–622.

Schwartz, Sharon, Dohrenwend, Bruce P., and Levav, Itzhak, 1994. "Nongenetic Familial Transmission of Psychiatric Disorders? Evidence from Children of Holocaust Survivors", *Journal of Health and Social Behavior* 35 (4): 385–402.

Shmotkin, Dov, 2003. "Vulnerability and Resilience Intertwined: A Review of Research on Holocaust Survivors", in: Rebecca Jacoby and Giora Keinan (eds.), *Between Stress and Hope: From a Disease-Centered to a Health-Centered Perspective*, Westport, CT: Praeger: 213–233.

Shrira, Amit, 2015. "Transmitting the Sum of All Fears: Iranian Nuclear Threat Salience among Offspring of Holocaust Survivors", *Psychological Trauma: Theory, Research, Practice, and Policy* 7 (4): 364–371.

Shrira, Amit, Palgi, Yuval, Ben-Ezra, Menachem, and Shmotkin, Dov, 2011. "Transgenerational Effects of Trauma in Midlife: Evidence for Resilience and Vulnerability in Offspring of Holocaust Survivors", *Psychological Trauma: Theory, Research, Practice, and Policy* 3 (4): 394–402.

Shweder, Richard A., 2000. "Moral Maps, 'First World' Conceits and the New Evangelists", in: L.E. Harrison and P. Samuel (eds.), *Culture Matters: How Values Shape Human Progress*, New York: Basic Books: 158–176.

Solkoff, Norman, 1992. "Children of Survivors of the Nazi Holocaust: A Critical Review of the Literature", *American Journal of Orthopsychiatry* 62: 342–358.

Somasundaram, Daya, 2014. "Addressing Collective Trauma: Conceptualizations and Interventions", *Intervention* 12 (1): 43–60.

Steinhardt, Mary, and Dolbier, Christyn, 2007. "Evaluation of a Resilience Intervention to Enhance Coping Strategies and Protective Factors and Decrease Symptomatology", *Journal of American College Health* 56 (4): 445–453.

Summerfield, Derek, 1998. "The Social Experience of War and Some Issues for the Humanitarian Field", in: Patrick J. Bracken and Celia Petty (eds.), *Rethinking the Trauma of War*, London: Free Association Books: 9–37.

Summerfield, Derek, 2002. "Effects of War: Moral Knowledge, Revenge, Reconciliation, and Medicalised Concepts of 'Recovery'", *British Medical Journal* 325: 1105–1107.

Theron, Linda, C., and Theron, Adam, 2013. "Positive Adjustment to Poverty: How Family Communities Encourage Resilience in Traditional African Contexts", *Cultural and Psychology* 19 (3): 391–413.

Ungar, Michael (ed.), 2012. *The Social Ecology of Resilience: A Handbook of Theory and Practice*, Berlin: Springer Science & Business Media.

Van IJzendoorn, Marinus H., Bakermans-Kranenburg, Marian J., and Sagi-Schwartz, Abraham, 2003. "Are Children of Holocaust Survivors Less Well-adapted? No Meta-analytic Evidence for Secondary Traumatization", *Journal of Traumatic Stress* 16: 459–469.

Yerushalmi, Yosef H., 1982. *Zakhor – Jewish History and Jewish Memory*, Seattle: University of Washington Press.

14

A DIGITAL SAFE HAVEN

Six Functions of Social Media for Second Generation Holocaust Survivors

Motti Neiger and Miriam Neiger-Fleischmann

> You become our parents. But now we are closer than ever before because we have spoken and because you have spoken to one another.
>
> *Elie Wiesel, "To Our Children", 1984*[1]

Introduction

The private and social role and the cultural function of a shared venue wherein the daughters and sons of Holocaust survivors can speak to one another lies at the center of this chapter. This chapter explores a fascinating digital space: a Facebook group titled "Yes, I'm a Second Generation Holocaust survivor" (in Hebrew: "*Ken, Ani Dor Sheni LaShoah*"), which numbers 9,750 members. Decades after Wiesel's address "To Our Children", the digital age offers unique opportunities to communicate, remember, and share collective and personal experiences within closed online groups dedicated to the descendants of Holocaust survivors. This article seeks to understand if and how such forums serve as a haven for the Second Generation to build a sense of community constructed around shared collective experiences on the one hand and the private elaboration of the trauma on the other. The manifestations are diverse in form (e.g., original posts, shared materials, comments to others, or even mere emojis) and content (e.g., private reflections, discussions on mutual memories, or invitations to commemorative events). Still, these are all focused on and around the experiences that have and continue to shape the lives of Holocaust survivors' descendants.

The chapter will gauge the various functions used by second generation Holocaust survivors within the forum. However, before this analysis, we will provide three brief introductions that construct the foundations for the analysis: a) the forum's genesis story; b) the forum's members' screening policies; c) the forum's content guidelines.

The Founding of the Forum

On November 23, 2014, the Facebook group "Yes, I'm a Second Generation Holocaust survivor" opened. As Orit Lustig, the founder wrote:

> Welcome, this group was created for members who are proud Second Generation Holocaust survivors. This intermediate generation, caught between the first generation and the next. . . .

DOI: 10.4324/b23365-17

> This is a place for sharing, supporting, receiving support, asking, contributing, volunteering, and especially daring to share. Here, you can post any thought, poem, opinion, or experience, and together we will design our performance. Because outsiders will never understand. Important! Now is the time to gather our strength and give back to ourselves and future generations, because the first generation is slowly dying out.

The group was constructed around the shared experiences of second generation Holocaust survivors, which outsiders – as Lustig said, and as seen in other testimonies in this study – cannot truly understand.

In her interview,[2] Lustig spoke of a formative past experience that eventually led her to deal with the experiences of the Second Generation. At age 40, she went to a reunion where they began talking about childhood experiences. She mentioned a store she used to shop in, and her friend stated that she would never go into the moth-ball-scented, Holocaust-survivor-run store. "These new immigrants, you can recognize them immediately, especially the smell". Lustig then told her friend that she, too, is the daughter of Holocaust survivors, but her friend dismissed her, pointing out that her grandparents and parents, Hava and Yosef Lustig, were renowned educators in their city. Lustig's second post in the forum addressed this experience and her reaction:

> I kept quiet, a sort of defeating silence, the car we were in grew quiet, and on the Radio – Poliker was singing Holocaust Memorial Day songs. I'm sorry to tell you this, my dear childhood friend – in case you didn't notice or maybe forgot – I am the proud daughter of these new immigrants. Those who came here with no family or clothes or a toothbrush, those who were thrown in the Kibbutzim, sprayed with DDT and taken to the sheds; yes, those who could still smell the Holocaust and the smoke rising from the crematoriums . . . my dear, the desert bloomed thanks to those moth-ball-smelling new immigrants. And don't you forget that 'yes, I am a Second Generation survivor.' True story.

Lustig's story can explain the seemingly defiant name given to the forum. Nevertheless, it contains two significant components that come up repeatedly: the desire not to hide, expressed in the "Yes" that precedes the declaration "I am a Second Generation Holocaust survivor", alongside a demand to recognize this unique identity. In many ways, the forum was established as a continuation of the enterprise started by Orit Lustig's parents, the Memorial Museum of Hungarian Speaking Jewry in Safed, which deals with the various aspects of community life in pre-Holocaust Hungarian-speaking countries and preserves exhibits, documents, and testimonies of life in these communities during the Holocaust.

Screening Members: Second Generation Only

The founding of an online forum surrounding a shared topic is not, of course, a uniquely Holocaust-related phenomenon. Since the inception of the internet, online discussion boards that included user comments have been widespread. This phenomenon spread during the days of Web 2.0, also known as the "participatory" or "social" web stage in the development of the internet since the early 2000s, based on the creation of broadband and high-speed internet that enabled sharing of user-generated content (UGC). This new realm formed the basis for the establishment of massively large groups that could not have formed prior to the age of the internet.

However, as is common in these kinds of forums,[3] only a small number of members actually publish and comment. Yet nearly 10,000 people have shown an interest in the forum content. Regarding gatekeeping, the group admins have set a clear-cut rule. The group is a closed one, and those seeking entrance must declare that they are indeed the children of Holocaust survivors and disclose how they came upon the group. In online community terms, this group is categorized as private, visible, and general. That is, any member of the general public can find it and learn of its existence. However, to get through the door, a private group must accept your request to join, a decision that lies in the hands of group admins. In case the group is infiltrated by a person who does not meet its prerequisites or disrespects – according to the admins – its rules, the offender will either leave or be removed from the group.

For example, in February 2022, one group member posted the following: "Lucky for me, I am not a Second Generation Holocaust survivor. Because the atmosphere in those houses is reminiscent of the Holocaust. With constant talk of the suffering, they endured during the Holocaust". When this sentence appeared in white letters against a yellow-flowery backdrop, the group was enraged, and dozens of people reacted to it and its comments. Some suggested that the poster leave the group if this is how she feels. The poster, on her part, defended herself, saying her husband was a Holocaust survivor. The main sentiment that arose from the many comments – which we will tackle later in this article – was a sense of pride in the title "Yes, I am a Second Generation Holocaust survivor". The admin summarized the discussion with: "It is customary to provide true information when requesting to join the group. You should educate yourself about Second Generation Holocaust-survivors. The love and pride we feel for our parents". Thus, the writer of the post found herself removed from the forum. Forum walls protect those within it and provide them with a safe space among members of their peer group without infiltrators who would injure both the sanctity of the Holocaust and its memory – embodied in the parental generation.

Content Guidelines: A Description of the Group and Its Functions

The group's mission statement maintains that

> The forum is a stage for Second Generation Holocaust-survivors, in which we all tell, listen, ask, rely on, complain, search for our roots, and especially containing every member. In the spirit of 'outsiders will never understand,' and our pride in our parents. We are family.

Forum admins delineated the group's goals using six verbs that cover a wide range of uses and gratifications. Some of these verbs are more active, such as "tell" and "complain". At the same time, some are more passive, such as "listen" and "contain". According to the forum's founding principle, the connection among all these actions is its perception as a family whose members are responsible for one another and as a website that protects its members so that they feel safe enough to share and rely on each other. Under these terms, the forum quickly became popular. As one of the forum's Admin, Leviah Shalev, says in her interview:[4]

> Orit opened a door, and in no time – about a month – we already had 3,000 members without any PR. Word of it spread like wildfire; people needed this space where they could feel comfortable with like-minded people who they could trust and talk with. Later, we held non-virtual gatherings. Even before, Orit initiated "sharing meetings" in the house of one of the members, with each meeting comprising about 10–15 people. Orit led the discussion, and people spoke openly even though they did not know each other because they all came from similar homes. This space enabled revelations. We would cry there as if we had known each other for years.

Shalev mentions how quickly the forum grew and its clear advantage over the at-home meetings. While the latter are of a more personal nature, the number of participants is highly limited, as well as the duration and space. When people share online, they are exposed to thousands of participants simultaneously and remain visible for a long time. Therefore, many people can see their posts long after they were posted. By maintaining a strict adherence to both participant identity and the nature of the posts, the forum had gained the trust of its members.

Several months after the forum's inception, its admin wrote the following:

> We are getting bigger; this promotes and enhances our work. I thank each and every one of you for all the trust, support, encouraging emails, and most of all, for sharing. You have no idea – or maybe you do – how much it warms the heart and gets more projects and ideas underway. It is not easy and requires many hours. Still, just like I believed we would succeed in November 2014 when we went online, here we are, preserving the atmosphere, growing closer and creating . . . this Facebook group is closed and dedicated only to Second Generation survivors and not!!! [*sic*] to organizations, institutions, caregivers, institutes, associations, or any other governmental body. To maintain the personal framework and ambiance, we endeavor to preserve the uploaded commercial content and posts. We must all respect and follow these rules.

This strictness is the reason that, according to a survey we conducted among the forum's participants, 82% of them find content in the group that they consider as highly important for them (marked 4 or 5 on a scale of 1–5), with 79% claiming to find topics about which they feel very strongly.

Another notable content rule is the one that forbids political discussions in the group. In her interview, the group's founder stressed: "We do not talk about politics. Politics gets kicked out right away. This space is for conversations about emotional experiences". We should emphasize that "no politics" means no mentions of partisan power relations (Right vs Left). However, occasionally, current events do come up in relation to the memory of the Holocaust (e.g., following the war in Ukraine, we can see questions about the country's role in the annihilation of the Jews), upon which we will elaborate in the following sections.

Research Question and Methodology

The research questions at the heart of this study will examine the functions fulfilled by this closed Facebook group for second generation Holocaust survivors and how these functions make the forum unique.

This chapter will combine several research methods. We conducted a survey among forum participants, in which 71 of them answered a questionnaire, which mapped out their manner of using the forum and the uses and gratifications they find there. Most survey participants were women (72%), and the average age was 68.5. In addition, we analyzed all 351 posts published to the forum in January and February 2022, as random months of the group activity as a mature forum. We should note that, due to COVID-19 and unlike previous years, these months did not include offline member meetings. Moreover, we would like to point out two current events-related focal points: a) International Holocaust Remembrance Day was held at the end of January, around which an interesting discussion formed; b) during these months the tension grew between Russia and Ukraine, which led to a military campaign – an event that was debated in the forum. Apart from the survey and analysis of the posts, we also held – as presented earlier – interviews with forum admins, who are also active group members, and we heard from them about their motives as managers and about their guiding principles. The combination of all three research methods – interview, post analysis, and survey – covers the three points of the communication triangle: content creators–text–audience.

Many articles have already tackled the role of digital forums upon their various forms and the question of the meaning that users attribute to their forums. In an attempt to offer an original contribution towards understanding the role of digital platforms as community-building forums overall and in trying to figure out what it is that singles out the Second Generation's online group, we wish to revisit a veteran milestone theory from literary studies, Jakobson's model of linguistic functions, which maps out the various communicative functions of texts, and we wish to adopt it to our purpose to indicate the myriad uses and gratifications among the group members. Roman Jakobson's article,[5] "Linguistics and Poetics", suggests that at the center of verbal communication lies the utterance, the message itself. The initiator of a communicative act is the addresser, and the receiver of the utterance is the addressee.

Apart from these three basic elements, there are three others: the utterance operates within the context to which it is attributed. The context is the background for the interpretation of the message by the addressee and can be intertextual or hypertextual. Another element is the code: to avoid communication mishaps. The code must be shared and agreed upon by both addresser and addressee. The final element is contact, the technological and mental channel between addresser and addressee, which allows both to perform the act of communication. Jakobson outlines the following scheme:

Context
Addresser-----Utterance-----Addressee
Contact
Code

Jakobson's discussion raises six components of communication, each associated with a communication function. Indeed, communicative message may involve several functions, each attributed to one of the factors of communication, but only one function, according to Jakobson, is dominant, while others are secondary: utterances that focus on the context operate the referential function; those which focus on the addressers and their sentiments are associated with the emotive function; utterances centered on motivating the addressee to act (such as advertisements) are first and foremost associated with the conative function; utterances focusing on the arrangement and esthetics of the utterance are stressing the poetic functions; utterances that examine the existence of a communication channel are centered on contact and pertain to the phatic function (e.g., "Testing, one, two, three"); while utterances that explore the meaning of language activate the metalingual function.

Referential function (context)
Emotive func. (addresser)---Poetic func. (utterance)---Conative func. (addressee)
Phatic function (contact)
Metalingual function (code)

Jakobson was interested in the formalistic distinction between literary and non-literary texts. Therefore, while the poetic function can appear in different utterances (such as rhyming advertisements), this function – focusing on the utterance itself and its ascetics – is the essence and dominant element only in literature. We seek to use Jacobson's deconstruction with the required adjustments to understand better the various functions that arise from the group and the different roles the forum fulfills for Second Generation Holocaust-survivors.

a) The Referential-Educational Function – The Group's Role as a Classroom for the Realm of Memory

This category includes posts of stories about historical events or figures, narratives of the culture that flourished before the Holocaust, and reports of recent events within these contexts. Therefore, the temporal spectrum ranges from the far past, a time before the Holocaust, to the near present of recent days.

Thus, for example, one group member[6] writes to remind everyone: "On International Holocaust Remembrance Day we should also remember Wilfrid Israel, who deserved the honorific Righteous Among the Nations, having saved thousands of Jews, but was never awarded the title because he himself was a Jew". Some of the posts in this category were shared from other online sources, such as stories about children in the Holocaust regularly posted by one active group member.

One of the main functions of the forum is to learn about the Holocaust and the communities ravaged during that period. Almost 80% of survey participants stated this as their forum use. Only one participant completely denied using the forum to learn more about the Holocaust. Similarly, about 79% use the forum to find out what became of survivors after the war, their tales of immigration to Israel, and revival. However, less than 50% percent of participants agreed with the saying that the forum teaches them about pre-Holocaust communities and their cultures. While the forum does fulfill this function, it is not its focal point.

The introduction states that political information and opinions are not allowed in the forum. However, in rare contexts, current affairs do arise, such as the use or disrespectful misuse of the Holocaust and its memory by politicians, celebrities, or the media. Many survey participants agreed with the saying: "Reading posts and participating in the group alongside [other] Second Generation Holocaust survivors in Israel reminds me of [our] triumph over the Nazis" (47% highly agreed; 31% agreed).

During the sampling period, a prominent and currently relevant context involved the treatment of Ukraine after its attack by the Russians in February 2022. On the one hand, some voices expressed compassion – out of sympathy as second generation survivors – towards fleeing refugees. On the other hand, others had also mentioned what the Ukrainians did during the Holocaust as one member wrote: "Ukraine, Ukraine, Ukraine. I care for them as much as they cared for my uncle Yehoshua, whom they beat to death in the streets after he survived that terrible war". Therefore, while the group is prohibited from dealing with politics in its narrowest terms, despite this ban on politics and so-called separation between current affairs and forum ongoings, a mere fifth of survey participants agreed that reading group posts disconnect them from the political reality and day-to-day life. That is, even without discussions on partisan politics, participants felt that addressing the topic of the Holocaust is itself a political statement.

b) The Conative-motivational Function – The Group's Role in Motivating Participants to Join Holocaust Remembrance-related Activity

The survey revealed a comprehensive concurrence with the saying: "I think that at our age, members of the Second Generation should take place left by Holocaust survivors and tell their story" (over 80% highly agreed; 15% agreed). In the forum, many people convey the narratives of previous generations, and some also encourage participants to join activities associated with Holocaust remembrance. For example, one participant invited group members to the exhibition *Days Beyond Time – Artists Meet Testimony*. According to the post

> the exhibition introduces young Israeli artists to the testimonies of Holocaust survivors, giving the stage to testimonies that must be memorialized. The exhibition is open to the

> public, and entrance is free until 24 February . . . maybe you can still make it. [There,] you will experience a fascinating meeting between survivor and artist. These are our – the Second Generation's – parents. These are our children's grandparents.

Many members also aim to motivate their readers to join activities that are connected to their work. For example, one participant invited members to her book launch event:

> This Wednesday, I will be launching my fourth book, a historical novel depicting the story of Polish Jewry, exiled to Russia at the start of the war. You are invited to join or watch on Facebook Live from the Hebrew Writers Association in Israel homepage.

Interestingly, the height of motivational content surrounded the International Holocaust Remembrance Day, with invitations to various events associated with this day, which became commonplace in many cities.

Regarding motivation towards memorial activity outside of the online group, as well as activity in other forums in both formal and informal frameworks that memorialize the Holocaust, survey answers seem to vary greatly. Half of the survey participants are active in such frameworks, while the other half is inactive outside the Second Generation forum. Indeed, we must factor in the age of some forum members, who average 68.5, meaning that many of them are past the age of 70. Perhaps we should not marvel at the fact that over 90% believe in the necessity of passing the memory on throughout the generations, with the forum as a way of doing just that. The high percentage indicates that the Second Generation's inner circle knows that some of the sentiments and emotional turmoil they share there will vanish unless they are transferred to the next generation. The ten missing percent can be attributed to the general public. The doubt lies in whether the internal forum is indeed the correct way of preserving the memory, and there you will find the missing ten percent.

c) The Emotive Function – The Role of Sharing the Experiences and Emotions of Second Generation Survivors

Our survey shows that a meaningful function, which garnered the approval of 82% of participants, is that reading group posts evoke thoughts about the fate of one's family and the fate of the Jewish people. That is a different way of coping with forced repression caused by life circumstances, a release born of the ability to talk about the things that no one else wanted to hear with likeminded people who can echo your sentiments with a reliable empathy, rather than from a distant therapeutic stance (such as that of a psychologist), as well as a sense of belonging and social identity that defines one's emotions and eases stress and emotional loneliness. While this constitutes an escape, it is not to realms of entertainment but to the realm of memory and its lessons. A similar number of participants, 82%, agreed with the saying that the group is a place where they can raise topics that are important to them and other second generation members. One prominent way of doing this is by sharing personal experiences. Unlike the previous functions, this one focuses on the writer and their feelings.

For example, as one group participant wrote:

> Every time I face a difficulty, no matter how insignificant, like an itch, or when I'm cold, sad, etcetera, I just image I am in a camp or a ghetto, and think about how hard it was for them there, really feel the hardship, and think about how they managed to endure. And then I return to reality. Why am I even complaining? . . . Does this happen to any of you?

This question ignited a discussion and additional posts, and it seems that this side – the emotional side – is the core of the forum and that many of the more emotional posts are those that garner the most replies. Emotion is a force that connects generations – the "then" and "there" of the Holocaust in the far past with the lives of group members as children growing in the shadow of this trauma, to the experiences that they process and talk about in the present.

From another complementary perspective, many participants view the forum as an opportunity to get to know themselves: two thirds (67%) of survey participants reported that by reading group posts, they learn more about themselves (on a scale of 1–5, a third chose four and another third chose 5). Only 12% of participants did not find this function was applicable to them (choosing 1 or 2 on a scale of 1–5).

d) The Poetic Function – The Group as a Safe Space for Sharing and Reacting to Artwork

A surprising finding revealed that, although the forum does not include an escapist function in the sense of retreating to the entertainment world and although (and perhaps because) the topics discussed in the forum are serious and often traumatic, over 60% of responders agreed with the saying that reading and participation in the forum make them happy and that people who publish in the forum are given a platform and a safe space in which to upload the plastic and literary artwork they created on remembrance-related topics, where they will be heard and reacted to despite the difficult nature of the art, as some posters are not always professionals and fear getting criticism and attention in public spaces.

At the same time, some seek identification and empathy through artistic means. For example, as one poster wrote: "Yesterday, in honor of International Holocaust Day, I made this drawing in memory of my family members who died in the Holocaust. Always remember, never forget!" Another writes:

> I dedicate this poem to mother and father. Like many of my Second Generation siblings, only when I became an adult when I became a father myself, did I understand the mental strength they needed to give us a happy life

and another publishes what was written about her as an artist

> who operates across several mediums. She carries the family legacy and horrors of the Holocaust with her, which left a heavy emotional toll. In her work, she corresponds with the calamity that befell her parents and exposes the complexity of her relationship with her mother. She expresses her pain as a Second Generation survivor with precision, through a repetitive representation of her image as a girl, an only child, part doll, part woman.

Yet another poster writes of a sculpture he made alongside a picture:

> Six pieces of one branch cut and later unified. The star of David Ben Yishai [son of Jesse] guarded them even when the yellow star and barbed-wire fences were a part of their lives. A piece I created for the Holocaust Remembrance Day ceremony that I organized and ran in Netanya.

When survey participants were asked how many of them agree with the saying that reading group posts informs them of the work and creations of other Second Generation group members, the expectation was that all group members would agree that this is one of the group's central functions.

However, on a scale of 1–5, just one-third of responders chose the highest number, while most others chose 3 and 4. That is, for a rather large group of people, this function is secondary. Perhaps because for non-creators – which are most group members – other functions are far more meaningful.

e) The Metalingual-deliberative Function – The Group as a Space to Discuss Definitions and Identity

Most survey participants – nearly three-quarters – agreed and highly agreed with the more general saying that reading group posts brings them closer to people they feel a kinship. Of the responders, 82% highly agreed (64%) and agreed (18%) with the powerful saying that they feel solidarity between themselves and other group members. Over three-quarters of participants said they highly agree (54%) and agree (22%) with the saying that some group members can understand them better than the non-second generation people around them.

These result in occasional posts that present questions regarding key issues and meta-topics. That is, posts that deal with seemingly trivial questions seek to understand what lies beneath definitions and labels – especially the meaning of "second generation survivors". An example of one such discussion within the research sampling period is one that developed following a post by one participant, who addressed the forum in February 2022, asking: "Were you also raised not to throw away food, and to horde bags and other things, so that you don't run out?" This question garnered 49 replies. Many people agreed with the narrative that arose from the question, replying: "You bet. My mother would follow me around with the plate until I finished everything, and I am still quite traumatized. The motto of the family I built is 'in our home, no one will force you to eat'". Another replied:

> When it comes to food, yes, I was raised not to throw food away, [that] there are plenty of starving people with nothing to eat . . . and how my parents and family went hungry during the Holocaust and how they would dream about food . . . and that I must always be grateful that I lack for nothing, including clothes, toys, shoes, and so I learned to take good care of those.

Another member supported the statement: "Yes, yes, yes! Exactly that. I even look at the plates to see if they finished and ate well". One reply addresses the intergenerational transference of this behavior:

> I constantly tell my grandchildren not to leave leftovers. My children are already familiar with this quirk. My kids are quite sick of it and say that the Holocaust is in the past and the Austerity period is over.

Indeed, many people also share their attempts to avoid and, in fact, resist the experiences that shaped the first generation and filtered through to them – which manifested, among other things, in a spartan upbringing, food hoarding, anxiety regarding hunger, and frugality – to overcome this fate and everything that comes with being a "second generation Holocaust survivor".

f) The Phatic-performance Function: The Group's Role in Opening a Channel of Communication and Developing a Sense of Belonging

Almost all survey participants, about 96%, agreed that it is important to continue giving a voice to the Second Generation, with the group considered one of the spaces that makes this possible.

One reason this voice is considered significant is that "As descendants of Holocaust survivors, we have unique experiences, and the group is a place to share them", a statement with which 93% of participants agreed. Regarding participation practices, the variance was high, with about a third of respondents agreeing that, on occasion, they gladly raise a topic and post something themselves. About a third disagreed, and the rest fell somewhere in between. Most survey participants agreed with the opposite, saying: "On occasion, I gladly respond to the topics raised by other members, but do not post anything myself". This indicates that group members usually prefer to read others' posts rather than post anything themselves, although about 20–30% sometimes feel comfortable enough to raise a topic for debate.

One interesting and unique way in which the group raises subjects corresponds with a seemingly trivial function: opening a channel of communication. For example, at different moments, different people upload posts that merely echo the name of the group: "I am also a Second Generation Holocaust survivor". A possible equivalent for this practice is a technician going "testing, one, two, three" during a soundcheck or someone saying, "hello? Can you hear me?" during call disruptions.

On another occasion, the name also shows up in the comments, as one participant writes: "Yes . . . I am a Second Generation Holocaust survivor. And at home, no one spoke about the Holocaust . . ." or "I am a Second Generation Holocaust survivor on both my parents' sides, may they rest in peace. On my father's side, some of my uncles were lost, as well as grandma and grandpa". Such statements are especially fascinating in this forum because their communicative value is supposedly low. Seeing as all forum participants are the offspring of Holocaust survivors, those who write there are obviously Second Generation survivors. Therefore, such posts do not add any new information – or when they do, they add very little. Such posts testify to a need to be present, to say: "I am here". This may indicate that, for posters as well as reactors, this may be their most prominent membership group in the multifaceted and divided Israeli society, which may also explain the importance of it being homogeneously Second Generation, rather than ethnicity-dependent, with some of its members having raised mixed-ethnicity families.

Additionally, as mentioned in the introduction, this is a "pride group" that indicates its rise from a place of weakness and its remarkable victory. This message comes up again and again in the forum, and, as we suggested in the beginning, one of its main functions is to ensure that a proper communication channel is opened to provide a constant sense of belonging. However, it is just as important to note that, due to the fact that such posts receive both "likes" and "loves" reactions, as well as replies from other participants, this act, which only seems to be of low communicative value, becomes highly significant for the crystallization collective identity of both posters and other group members as Second Generation survivors. Comments on such posts can include succinct identification, such as users who write "me too", while others elaborate on their private histories, such as: "I am also a Second Generation Holocaust survivor of Auschwitz, Majdanek and Birkenau with almost no one left from my father and mother's large families, all perished and incinerated in the camps".

Discussion and Conclusions

In the quest to understand how society preserves the ties among its members in the modern age, Halbwachs[7] indicated that shared recollection could be perceived as a device serving to establish society's coherence and to cultivate integrity among its members. Although different collective memory scholars have offered various perspectives towards understanding the concept, they share a basic claim: a crucial component of any social community is strengthening its identity by constructing its story of the past. By these narratives, the group can forge the community since its members are those who accept these mutual interpretational boundaries of past events and processes.

The role of the media in understanding the term "collective memory" becomes clearer when we examine its oxymoronic nature at face value: a person can process and store memory, but societies do not have a brain. Thus, the physical and mental capacity of "memory" and "remembering" is foreign on the collective level. Indeed, memory per se is a faculty of an individual's mind.[8] Thus, the concept "collective memory" metaphorically refers to a communally agreed version of the past: the ways by which society inflects consent narratives regarding the past on the community members so that the personal and social interpretations of events coincide.

The topic at hand is a unique case involving the creation and preservation of the collective memory of a group that possesses similar sociological and age characteristics and shares the common denominator "forced" upon its members: having been born to Holocaust survivors. This shared fate then created a sense of community and need to preserve and even protect the collective memory, as well as resignation and acceptance alongside the construction of a narrative of overcoming hardship and converting trauma-based energy into a positive, Israeli productiveness. In his book, James Carey[9] indicates a connection between communication, common interest, and the creation of communities, which means that the **commun**ity is founded on **common**ality-based **commun**ication. This connection is not merely etymological-semantic but also inherent. Online forums in all their forms (message boards, dedicated forums, or social network groups) are complete expressions of the connection between communication – a common theme – and the creation of a community.

Many articles have addressed the role that forums play in the lives of their users. For example, studies noted how forums aid and support users in what is called "cyber-support".[10] Such forums are popular among people dealing with physical[11] and mental[12] problems and even aid suicide prevention.[13] Other studies were conducted on groups of professionals seeking to exchange opinions[14] or groups with a shared sociological-demographic denominator or ideological connection, such as members of the Ultra-Orthodox community.[15] The case of second generation Holocaust survivors is unique because its members come from different backgrounds, and their interests and political opinions vary. This diversity was explored by journalist Helen Epstein in the first study solely focused on the stories of children of survivors, published as an article in 1977 in the *New York Times*, titled "The Heirs of the Holocaust" and later in the book *Children of the Holocaust*:[16]

> Some say their parents' experience has affected them only slightly while others say it has determined their choice of profession, friends and despite this diversity, all described feelings of affinity to other children of survivors. "There's a tacit understanding between us," says one. "A completeness without conversation," said another. There's "the incredible experience of hearing from other people's mouths the thoughts I had lived alone with for years.

The human diversity in these forums is so broad that it is no surprise, therefore, that we can find such a wide range of content, uses, and gratifications there, all of which surprisingly meet the needs of most community members – a fact that indicates a most profound level of bonding. In this article, we tried to point out this diversity by identifying the various functions the group fulfills: the group as a classroom for the realm of memory; the group's role in motivating its members to join activities related to the realm of Holocaust remembrance and how they cope in the present; the group as a space for sharing the experiences and emotions of second generation Holocaust survivors; the group as a place for sharing artwork and commenting on it; the group as a place for discussions on definitions of identity; the group as a site for stating one's presence, opening a channel of communication and developing a sense of belonging.

All these roles are essential and are utilized because the group members feel safe and surrounded by like-minded people. We especially wish to emphasize the final function: the group as a site for stating one's presence as an individual and as part of the second generation community.

The famous song, the *Partizaner Lid* [Partisan Song], is a Yiddish song considered to be an anthem of Holocaust survivors, which one can hear in Holocaust memorial services across the globe. The last phrase of this song of faith is: "Our marching steps ring out: 'We are here!" (Yiddish transcription: *S'vet a poyk ton undzer trot: mir zaynen do*!). A careful reading of this online group comprised of the sons and daughters of Holocaust survivors echoes the same message: Yes! We are the Second Generation. We are here!

Notes

1 Wiesel, 2014: XV–XVII.
2 The authors interviewed Orit Lustig via Zoom on August 18, 2021.
3 Ahern et al., 2016.
4 The authors interviewed Leviah Shalev via Zoom on August 29, 2021.
5 Jakobson, 1960.
6 Posts will remain anonymous to protect the privacy of the writers.
7 Halbwachs, 1992 [1952].
8 Hoskins, 2009.
9 Carey, 1989.
10 Bauer et al., 2013.
11 Smailhodzic et al., 2016.
12 Gavin et al., 2008; Driolis Phillips et al., 2021.
13 Eichenberg, 2008.
14 Ahern et al., 2016.
15 Baumel-Schwartz, 2009; Barzilai-Nahon and Barzilai, 2005; Lev-On and Neriya-Ben Shahar, 2009.
16 Epstein, 1977, 1979.

Bibliography

Ahern, Liz, Feller, Joseph, and Nagle, Tadhg, 2016. "Social Media as a Support for Learning in Universities: An Empirical Study of Facebook Groups", *Journal of Decision Systems* 25 (Sup1): 35–49.

Barzilai-Nahon, Karin, and Barzilai, Gad, 2005. "Cultured Technology: The Internet and Religious Fundamentalism", *The Information Society* 21 (1): 25–40.

Bauer, Rita, Bauer, Michael, Spiessl, Hermann, and Kagerbauer, Tanja, 2013. "Cyber-Support: An Analysis of Online Self-help Forums (Online Self-help Forums in Bipolar Disorder)", *Nordic Journal of Psychiatry* 67 (3): 185–190.

Baumel-Schwartz, Judith Tydor, 2009. "Frum Surfing: Orthodox Jewish Women's Internet Forums as a Historical and Cultural Phenomenon", *Journal of Jewish Identities* 2 (1): 1–30.

Carey, James W., 1989. *Communications as Culture: Essays on Media and Society*, Winchester, MA: Unwin Hyman.

Drioli-Phillips, Phoebe G., Couteur, Amanda Le, Oxlad, Melissa, Feo, Rebecca, and Scholz, Brett, 2021. "'I Know You Shouldn't Compare to Other People, But I Can't do Anything Most People Can': Age, Family, and Occupation Categorisations in Men's Reasoning about Their Anxiety in an Online Discussion Forum", *Sociology of Health & Illness* 43 (3): 678–696.

Eichenberg, Christiane, 2008. "Internet Message Boards for Suicidal People: A Typology of Users", *CyberPsychology & Behavior* 11 (1): 107–113.

Epstein, Helen, 1977. "The Heirs of the Holocaust", *The New York Times*, June 19, p. 175.

Epstein, Helen, 1979, 1988. *Children of the Holocaust: Conversations with Sons and Daughters of Survivors*, New York: Penguin Books.

Gavin, Jeff, Rodham, Karen, and Poyer, Helen, 2008. "The Presentation of 'Pro-Anorexia' in Online Group Interactions", *Qualitative Health Research* 18 (3): 325–333.

Halbwachs, Maurice, 1992 [1952]. *On Collective Memory*, Chicago: University of Chicago Press.

Hoskins, Andrew, 2009. "The Mediatisation of Memory", in: *Save as . . . Digital Memories*, London: Palgrave Macmillan: 27–43.

Jakobson, Roman, 1960. "Linguistics and Poetics/Roman Jakobson", in: T. Sebeok (ed.), *Style in Language*, Cambridge, MA: Harvard University: 350–377.

Lev-On, A., and Neriya-Ben Shahar, R., 2009. "Forum of Their Own: Studying Discussion Forums of Ultra-Orthodox Women Online", *Media Frame* 4: 67–106 [in Hebrew].

Smailhodzic, Edin, Hooijsma, Wyanda, Boonstra, Albert, and Langley, David J., 2016. "Social Media Use in Healthcare: A Systematic Review of Effects on Patients and on Their Relationship with Healthcare Professionals", *BMC Health Services Research* 16 (1): 1–14.

Wiesel, Elie, 1984, May. "To Our Children", *In Keynote Address, Plenary Session of the First International Conference of Children of Holocaust Survivors*, New York.

Wiesel, Elie, 2014. "Prologue – To Our Children", in: Menachem Z. Rosensaft (ed.), *God, Faith and Identity from the Ashes, Reflections of Children and Grandchildren of Holocaust-survivors*, Woodstock, VT: Jewish Lights Publishing: XV–XVIII.

15

LATE-LIFE MANIFESTATIONS OF ANCESTRAL TRAUMA

The Case of Older Adult Offspring of Holocaust Survivors

Amit Shrira

Does the Holocaust Affect the Aging Process of Subsequent Generations?

The effects of massive trauma may linger into late adulthood and old age, leading to increased physical morbidity among those who were traumatized.[1] Evidence shows that that even early childhood trauma can linger and persist into older adulthood. These individuals demonstrate intensified psychological reactions to various late-life events due to depleted resources.[2] Accordingly, recent evidence from large-scale epidemiological studies points to higher prevalence of chronic medical conditions, such as cancer,[3] cardiovascular disease,[4] and dementia[5] among Holocaust survivors. Moreover, Holocaust survivors may manifest greater psychological distress when coping with medical conditions,[6] as such conditions may reverberate pain, frailty, and dependency experienced during the war. Surprisingly, survivors' life expectancy seems to be similar or even longer compared to other older adults,[7] rendering them a unique group where suffering and distress may co-reside with heightened desire to survive and continue living.[8]

While most Holocaust survivors are in the twilight of their lives, many of their descendants, the so-called Second Generation (2g), are now facing the challenges of later adulthood. Second Generations who were born following the end of WWII are now in their sixties and seventies. In view of the distinctive characteristics presented by their parents in late life, we need to better understand how 2g experience old age. The bulk of research focused on 2g in adolescents and young adults and showed that they are generally well functioning and resilient[9] yet may manifest lower stress tolerance in adverse situations, such as when coping with medical conditions.[10] Therefore, many questions arise as to how 2g experience old age and cope with its demands. For example, one can ask whether, similar to their parents, they too demonstrate an increased risk of developing physical conditions or how they perceive and cope with age-related changes, including the need to serve as caregivers for their parents or to grieve for their loss.

Physical health issues among 2g were underexplored. However, there is evidence for higher physical morbidity among offspring of mothers exposed to hunger during WWII, especially during the siege of Leningrad or during the Dutch famine.[11] Maternal exposure to hunger during pregnancy was related to various medical conditions among offspring decades later, including hypertension and hyperglycemia.[12] The few works conducted on 2g found mixed results. Two studies failed to find any group differences when comparing 2g to non-2g.[13] In these studies, it should be noted

DOI: 10.4324/b23365-18

that one sample included relatively young adults with a low prevalence of physical morbidity,[14] while another study was restricted to a female sample and had a unique group composition; whereas the 2g group included respondents with a survivor mother, the so-called comparison group included respondents with a survivor father as well as with parents who were not survivors.[15] A third study[16] found more signs of the metabolic syndrome among 2g. Yet, it also had its methodological limitations, as respondents were sampled from Holocaust-related organizations and did not represent a random sample.

The first published data on physical conditions among 2g using a national random sample of middle-aged Israelis was the Survey of Health, Ageing and Retirement-Israel (SHARE-Israel).[17] This survey included a wide variety of health-related measures including medical conditions, disability, somatic symptoms, medication use, visits to doctors, hospitalizations, and more. Although 2g had similar socio-demographic characteristics to non-2g, the former had a higher prevalence of hypertension, dyslipidemia, and sleep problems. Second Generations also reported more somatic symptoms and medication use.

In addition to initial evidence for higher physical morbidity, 2g may also find age-related events more strenuous. When faced with the diagnosis of breast cancer, for example, 2g women felt more helpless and hopeless and reported higher psychological distress than non-2g cancer patients.[18] Another related study[19] showed that 2g cancer patients demonstrated the highest distress levels compared to non-2g patients, healthy 2g, and healthy non-2g. Other works found that when serving as caregivers to their parents, 2g tended to provide more medical care and pragmatic help to their parents[20] and felt a stronger sense of duty, obligation, and responsibility compared with non-2g.[21] They also showed more worries and concerns about the anticipated decline and death of their aging parents and in regard to their ability to meet current or future caregiving needs.[22]

Despite the previously mentioned findings, the widespread proposition is that intergenerational effects of parental trauma are not omnipresent in Holocaust survivor families. In view of the varied responses seen among Holocaust survivors, it is plausible that intergenerational effects are shaped in different forms dependent on the characteristics of the particular parent, the specific offspring, the mechanisms underlying the transmission between them, and the specific circumstances they are in.[23] Therefore, it is premature to conclude that ancestral trauma affects the aging process of all 2gs. Rather, it is incumbent upon us to understand who is affected, how are they affected, and when, i.e., under which circumstances are they affected.

An Interdisciplinary, Integrative Model of Who Is Affected, How, and When

In an attempt to understand the complexity of the phenomenon, several factors were proposed as potential regulators of intergenerational effects of the Holocaust.

The effects may be dependent upon whether one parent or both parents experienced the Holocaust, their specific war-related experiences, or parental posttrauamtic reactions. It was suggested[24] that 2g absorbed much more parental distress when both parents were survivors who underwent extreme experiences, which remained unresolved in the shape of posttrauamtic stress disorder (PTSD) or other symptoms.

Effects may also be contingent on 2g characteristics, such as 2g gender. Some scholars propose that effects might be stronger among daughters compared to sons (especially when transmission occurs between mother and daughter).[25] Others refer to 2g time of birth or the number of children in the family, suggesting that effects may be more salient when 2g were born shortly after the war ended or in one-child families.[26]

This is by no means an exhustive list of parental and offspring characterestics, but even the factors listed here, as well as elsewhere,[27] were not systematically examined with regard to middle-aged or older 2g. It is possible, though, that 2g characteristics such as time of birth are connected to late-life physical morbidity, similar to the effects of maternal stress and famine exposure during pregnancy on impaired uterine blood flow, preterm birth, and low birthweight – all factors related to later morbidity.[28] With regard to parental characteristics, we do know, however, that physical morbidity and somatic symptoms were especially common among middle-aged or older 2g with two survivor parents[29] or those who had parents suffering from PTSD.[30] Second Generations who had parents suffering from PTSD also found it more difficult to cope with age-related challenges – such as serving as caregivers to their parents –[31] and tended to percieve old age as a period of losses.[32] Why is it so that 2gs with parental PTSD were most vulnerable?

Parental PTSD or other types of parental distress may catalyze psychological, behavioral, and biological mechanisms underlying later life morbidity among 2g. With regard to psychological mechanisms, it is possible that 2g exposed to parental distress are at a higher risk of developing secondary trauamtization symptoms. These symptoms reflect intensive, inmeshed parent-child dynamics[33] and intrusive, fragmented intrafamilial communication regarding parental trauma.[34] Secondary trauamtization symptoms parallel those experienced by trauma survivors, yet they evolve when one is in a close emotional relationship with the trauma survivor[35] – the parent in our case. These symptoms include intrusive thoughts and nightmares about the Holocaust, as well as a general sense of restlessness and hypervigilance. It is possible that these symptoms, when being repeatedly activated, bring about an allostatic load or the wear and tear on body systems leading to hypertension, hyperlipidemia, and atherosclerosis.[36] In a study conducted in 2017, 35% of Holocaust survivor families showed PTSD and subsequent increased secondary trauamtization.[31] Therefore, it is important to emphsize that many 2g manifested low distress levels and aging features similar to non-2Gg.[37]

On the behavioral level, it has been shown that PTSD is related to unhealthy behaviors[38] including lack of physical activity, smoking, over-consumption of alcohol, low adherence to medical treatment, and unbalanced diet. Traumatized individuals try to manage their distress through substance abuse and high-fat diet. It is possible that their accompanying depression reduces the motivation for self-care. Some of these behaviors were observed in Holocaust survivors with PTSD but also among 2g whose parents suffered from PTSD.[39] Second Generations might have modelled parental unhealthy behaviors. Moreover, it is possible that 2g turned to these behaviors in order to cope with a conflict-saturated and agitated familial environment produced by parental PTSD and hypervigilence or to cope with their own secondary traumatization.

Restlessness and hypersensitivity to threats also hamper interpersonal trust and support. Interpersonal conflicts, hostility, and loneliness are hazardous to physical health as they accentuate inflammation and other bodily dsyregulations.[40] In addition, the issue of social support and loneliness among 2g is underexplored.[41] In any case, these behavioral tendencies may have detrimental effects on 2g physical health, which become more visible as they age.

With regard to putative biological mechanisms, evidence accumulated so far suggests that late-life health problems among 2g may be traced back to endocrine dysregulation mediated by epigenetic processes.[42] Epigenetic mechanisms involve, among others, the modification of DNA methylation: the transfer of methyl groups to specific sites on the DNA string. When methylation takes place, it regulates the gene's ability to express itself, i.e., to synthesize proteins.[43] Various environmental changes, including exposure to extreme stress, bring about epigenetic processes. It has been suggested that these epigenetic changes may be long-lasting and may even be transmitted to offspring via the gametes, via the uterine environment during pregnancy, or during early postnatal care of newborns.[44] PTSD-related epigenetic modification may be evident especially in genes related to endocrine signalling, mostly including a lower cortisol level and a premature termination of the cortisol response.[45] These endocrine dysfunctions result in a failure to contain the nervous system response. Indeed, preliminary evidence suggests that there are unique methylation patterns in specific genes related to cortisol (e.g., FKBP5, NR3C1) among offspring of traumatized parents, as well as among 2g.[46] According to these findings, the effect of parental trauma and distress on offspring health may be explained by epigenetic modification in many other sites, namely in genes related to somatic complaints, as well as nervous system development and function.[47] This is an important avenue for future research.

Following the attempt to delineate who is affected by parental trauma and how, there is still a need to delineate *when* such effects are to be expected. There seem to be good reasons to assume that intergenerational effects of the Holocaust remain latent in low-stress circumstances and that they will manifest themselves when 2g experience new stress or trauma in their own lives. Indeed, in addition to the breast cancer study mentioned earlier,[48] 2g present distinctive reactions, mainly lower stress tolerance, in other adverse situations, including following combat[49] or when faced with threats of war.[50] These observartions align with evidence for neuroendocrine dysregulation in the hypothalamic–pituitary–adrenal axis in 2g,[51] as these biological processes mediate the effects of stressors by modulating numerous physiological processes. Therefore, although the focal parental trauma, the Holocaust, becomes more distant, as both survivors and 2g age, in view of the previous proposition and evidence, it is expected that intergenerational effects should be noticeable as aging 2g confront various late-life events. These include financial difficulties, interpersonal loss, physical and cognitive decline, hospitalization, and/or institutionalization.

Summarizing the evidence in an interdisciplinary, integrative model of intergenerational transmission of the Holocaust, we suggest the following four key propositions. a) Parental exposure to the Holocaust may be related to health and wellbeing of middle-aged and older 2g; b) intergenerational effects of the Holocaust may be contingent on parental and 2g characteristics, mainly parental PTSD and other parental manifestations of unresolved loss; c) parental exposure to the Holocaust and subsequent parental PTSD can relate to late-life health and wellbeing of 2g via psychological, behavioral, and biological mechanisms; d) The intergenerational effects of the Holocaust become most pronounced when 2g confront adverse circumstances, as common in old age.

Further supporting such a model, the next section presents some recent findings regarding 2g coping with age-related challenges during the COVID-19 pandemic.

Offspring of Holocaust Survivors Face the COVID-19 Pandemic

The global COVID-19 pandemic posed a severe risk of serious complications and fatality to older adults necessitating stringent social distance and shelter at home. Already at the onset of the pandemic, it was suggested that Holocaust survivors would show increased psychological distress during the COVID-19 crisis.[52] It was proposed that survivors' distress may be augmented due to Holocaust-related associations and imagery triggered by facets of the pandemic,[53] including the all-pervasive threat to life, confinement to one's home, shortages in medical and household supplies, massive job losses, and social chaos. Indeed, Holocaust survivors manifested amplified distress and loneliness during the pandemic, especially those whose WWII ordeals (e.g., suffering from infectious disease) were echoed by current threats[54] or those who suffered from PTSD.[55]

Similar to their parents, 2g could also present idiosyncratic reactions to the COVID-19 pandemic. Indeed, while some 2g negated associations between the Holocaust and the pandemic, others noted that their parents' trauma made them extra vigilant and anxious, and yet others indicated that their family background contributed to a sense of preparedness and competence. Given the diversity we already know exists among 2g, these mixed responses, as documented in online supportive webinars offered to 2g,[56] were not surprising.

A clinical case presented by Kogan[57] described how some 2g may intermingled their perception of the pandemic with their mental representation of the Holocaust. In this case, a 2g patient was feeling that the state is being taken over by a totalitarian regime, due to the restrictions imposed upon the population. She also had associations revolving around concentration camps, as she was watching reports of numbers of COVID-19 cases and deaths, as well as watching media reports of bodies piled up in hospitals around the world. The therapeutic process helped the patient to differentiate present reality from her fantasies about the Holocaust.

Quantitative research on 2g reactions during the pandemic is currently scarce. The few works published thus far indicate that, while most 2g managed to demonstrate resilience, some experienced severe anxiety and marked vulnerability during the pandemic. In what was probably the first published survey of 2g during COVID-19,[58] it was evident that parental PTSD played a critical role in explaining 2g reactions during the pandemic. Relative to non-2g or 2g whose parents did not have PTSD, psychological distress and loneliness were the most prevalent among 2g who reported that both of their parents had PTSD. Interestingly, perceived social support was similar across groups regardless of parental Holocaust background or PTSD, suggesting that, despite such support, some 2g still felt anxious, isolated, and lonely.

Another relevant aspect evident during the COVID-19 pandemic was the 2g's role as a caregiver for their parents.[59] In that study, my colleagues and I found that caregiver burden was much more prevalent among 2g who reported that their parents suffered from PTSD. A vast majority of them reported high levels of caregiver burden, and 60% reported that they felt their burden worsened during the pandemic. In contrast, among 2g without parental PTSD, 40% reported worsening in caregiving burden. Only 10% reported worsened burden among non-2g. Again, we see that there is a specific subgroup of 2g that requires special attention. They are at high risk for experiencing mental exhaustion due to their caregiver role, possibly because they feel a stronger obligation to help their parent. It is also possible that this finding reflects the higher support needs of survivor parents with PTSD when coping with the pandemic repercussions.

To recapitulate thus far, 2g's reactions to the COVID-19 pandemic further corroborate the proposition that intergenerational effects are notable as aging 2g confront late-life events, possibly especially when these events resonate with their ancestral trauma. Nevertheless, these reactions also testify to the strengths and coping abilities characteristic of most Holocaust survivors and their offspring.

Conclusions

The evidence amassed in recent years allows several conclusions regarding the potential effects of ancestral trauma on the aging process of 2g. While the majority of 2g demonstrate general resilience in middle and old age, some of them, mostly those whose parents suffered from PTSD and other indications of unresolved trauma, manifest higher prevalence of physical morbidity,[60] perceive old age and their own aging process more negatively,[61] and find it more difficult to cope with age-related challenges.[62] Parental PTSD is related to 2g aging via several mechanisms, including psychological (i.e., secondary traumatization and depression),[63] behavioral (i.e., unhealthy behaviors and avoiding healthy behaviors),[64] and biological processes (i.e., neuroendocrinological and epigenetic modification).[65]

The current chapter highlights the need for further research to understand the aging process of 2g. Current findings should be replicated using longitudinal multigenerational designs with objective as well as subjective indices of health. As the phenomenon of intergenerational effects of the Holocaust is determined by a range of psychological, behavioral, biological, and sociological[66] mechanisms, future works would advance our knowledge by taking a multidisciplinary approach. These works will provide the necessary evidence needed to guide recommendations for interventions designed to promote successful aging among 2g.

While there is a rich theoretical and empirical literature on the intergenerational effects of the Holocaust, much less is known about potential interventions with 2g. Because some 2g tend to be self-reliant, suspicious towards others outside the family circle, and are used to a caregiver role to their parents, 2g may show hesitance before reaching out for professional help either for themselves[67] or for their parents.[68] When they do, their needs are often pressing. Health practitioners need to overcome 2g's resistance to seeking help mostly by establishing a safe and trusting relationship – by making them feel understood and accepted.

In psychotherapy, 2g can be encouraged to freely express feeling, thoughts, and associations, increasing their awareness of processes that perpetuate secondary traumatization and depression and working through the roots of their problems.[69] Since many problems are focused on interpersonal relationships, the major task is to help separate them from enmeshed familial systems, find their own identities, and cultivate and maintain satisfying interpersonal relationships.[70] This is most important as social support is a fundamental resource required when confronting age-related challenges. Moreover, for those who serve as caregivers, practitioners may help 2g resolve conflictual relationships with care recipients, facilitating comprehension and empathy towards care recipients' incongruent behaviors. In other cases, they need to encourage 2g caregivers to express their needs and suggest the utilization of formal services.[71]

Additional interventions could include behavioral components aimed at encouraging preventive activities (e.g., performing common screening tests) and fostering a healthier lifestyle.[72] Interventions may address the manner by which 2g perceive their aging process in light of findings showing that favorable views of aging have a beneficial impact on future health.[73] Moreover, as certain substances have been found to be associated with reversal of harmful methylation patterns in animal models as well as in humans,[74] there is a potential for the development of pharmacological interventions aimed at attenuating biological effects on 2g health across the lifespan.

Notes

1 Shrira et al., 2021.
2 Palgi et al., 2015.
3 Keinan-Boker, 2018.
4 Zamstein et al., 2018; Kagansky et al., 2019.
5 Kodesh et al., 2019.
6 Baider et al., 1992; Hantman and Solomon, 2007.
7 Shrira et al., 2011a; Fund et al., 2019.
8 Shmotkin et al., 2011.
9 Van IJzendoorn et al., 2003; Lindert et al., 2017.
10 Dashorst et al., 2019; Payne and Berle, 2021.
11 Keinan-Boker, 2014.
12 Hazani and Shasha, 2008.
13 Levav et al., 2007; Fridman et al., 2011.
14 Hazani and Shasha, 2008.
15 Levav et al., 2007.
16 Flory et al., 2011.
17 Shrira et al., 2011b.
18 Baider et al., 2006.

19 Baider et al., 2008.
20 Alkalay et al., 2020.
21 Shrira et al., 2019.
22 Baider et al., 2006.
23 Kellermann, 2009; Danieli et al., 2017.
24 Kellermann, 2009.
25 Sagi-Schwartz, 2015.
26 Shrira et al., 2019.
27 Kellermann, 2020.
28 Barker, 2004.
29 Flory et al., 2011.
30 Shrira et al., 2017.
31 Alkalay et al., 2020.
32 Shrira, 2020.
33 Hoffman and Shrira, 2019.
34 Shrira, 2016.
35 Figley, 1995.
36 McEwen, 1998.
37 Kellermann, 2009.
38 Schnurr, 2017.
39 Shrira, 2019.
40 Miller et al., 2011.
41 Wiseman, 2008.
42 Kellermann, 2013.
43 Szyf, 2015.
44 Yehuda and Lehrner, 2018.
45 Yehuda et al., 2015.
46 Yehuda et al., 2014; Bierer et al., 2020.
47 Cao-Lei et al., 2014.
48 Shrira et al., 2011b.
49 Solomon et al., 1988.
50 Shrira, 2015.
51 Yehuda et al., 2000.
52 Cohn-Schwartz et al., 2020.
53 Steir-Livny, 2021.
54 Shrira et al., 2020; Sarfati et al., 2022.
55 Maytles et al., 2021a.
56 Felsen, 2021.
57 Kogan, 2021.
58 Shrira and Felsen, 2021.
59 Maytles et al., 2021b.
60 Flory et al., 2011.
61 Shrira et al., 2017.
62 Shrira et al., 2011b; Alkalay et al., 2020.
63 Shrira, 2020.
64 Schnurr, 2017.
65 Szyf, 2015.
66 Kidron et al., 2019.
67 Samson et al., 2013.
68 Anderson and Fields, 2013.
69 Kellermann, 2001.
70 Shrira et al., 2019.
71 Shrira and Felsen, 2021.
72 Payne and Berle, 2021.
73 Palgi et al., 2021.
74 Lax et al., 2018.

References

Alkalay, Sarit, Sagi-Schwartz, Abraham, and Wiseman, Hadas, 2020. "Increased Empathy and Helping Behavior Toward the Mother in Daughters of Holocaust Survivors", *Traumatology* 26 (1): 84–95.

Anderson, Keith A., Fields, Noelle L., and Dobb, Lynn A., 2013. "Caregiving and Early Life Trauma: Exploring the Experiences of Family Caregivers to Aging Holocaust Survivors", *Family Relations* 62 (2): 366–377.

Baider, Lea, Goldzweig, Gil, Ever-Hadani, Pnina, and Peretz, Tamar, 2006. "Psychological Distress and Coping in Breast Cancer Patients and Healthy Women Whose Parents Survived the Holocaust", *Psycho-Oncology: Journal of the Psychological, Social and Behavioral Dimensions of Cancer* 15 (7): 635–646.

Baider, Lea, Goldzweig, Gil, Ever-Hadani, Pnina, and Peretz, Tamar, 2008. "Breast Cancer and Psychological Distress: Mothers' and Daughters' Traumatic Experiences", *Supportive Care in Cancer* 16 (4): 407–414.

Baider, Lea, Peretz, Tamar, and Kaplan De-Nour, Atara, 1992. "Effect of the Holocaust on Coping with Cancer", *Social Science & Medicine* 34 (1): 11–15.

Barker, David Purslove James, 2004. "The Developmental Origins of Adult Disease", *Journal of the American College of Nutrition* 23 (sup6): 588S–595S.

Bierer, Linda M., Bader, Heather N., Daskalakis, Nikolaos P., Lehrner, Amy, Provençal, Nadine, Wiechmann, Tobias, Klengel, Torsten, Makotkine, Iouri, Binder, Elisabeth B., and Yehuda, Rachel, 2020. "Intergenerational Effects of Maternal Holocaust Exposure on FKBP5 Methylation", *American Journal of Psychiatry* 177 (8): 744–753.

Cao-Lei, Lei, Massart, Renaud, Suderman, Matthew J., Machnes, Ziv, Elgbeili, Guillaume, Laplante, David P., Szyf, Moshe, and King, Suzanne, 2014. "DNA Methylation Signatures Triggered by Prenatal Maternal Stress Exposure to a Natural Disaster: Project Ice Storm", *PLoS ONE* 9: e107653.

Cohn-Schwartz, Ella, Sagi, Doron, O'Rourke, Norm, and Bachner, Yaacov G., 2020. "The Coronavirus Pandemic and Holocaust Survivors in Israel", *Psychological Trauma: Theory, Research, Practice, and Policy* 12 (5): 502–504.

Danieli, Yael, Norris, Fran H., and Engdahl, Brian, 2017. "A Question of Who, Not If: Psychological Disorders in Holocaust Survivors' Children", *Psychological Trauma: Theory, Research, Practice, and Policy* 9 (S1): 98–106.

Dashorst, Patricia, Mooren, Trudy M., Kleber, Rolf J., Jong, Peter J. de, and Huntjens, Rafaele J.C., 2019. "Intergenerational Consequences of the Holocaust on Offspring Mental Health: A Systematic Review of Associated Factors and Mechanisms", *European Journal of Psychotraumatology* 10 (1): 1654065.

Felsen, Irit V., 2021. "'Web-Based, Second-Best Togetherness': Psychosocial Group Intervention with Children of Holocaust Survivors During COVID-19", *American Journal of Orthopsychiatry* 91 (2): 171–180.

Figley, Charles R., 1995. "Compassion Fatigue: Toward A New Understanding of the Costs of Caring", in Hudnall Stamm (ed.), *Secondary Traumatic Stress: Self-Care Issues for Clinicians, Researchers, and Educators*, Lutherville, MD: The Sidran Press: 3–28.

Flory, Janine D., Bierer, Linda M., and Yehuda, Rachel, 2011. "Maternal Exposure to the Holocaust and Health Complaints in Offspring", *Disease Markers* 30 (2): 133–139.

Fridman, Ayala, Bakermans-Kranenburg, Marian J., Sagi-Schwartz, Abraham, and Van IJzendoorn, Marinus H., 2011. "Coping in Old Age with Extreme Childhood Trauma: Aging Holocaust Survivors and Their Offspring Facing New Challenges", *Aging & Mental Health* 15 (2): 232–242.

Fund, Naama, Ash, Nachman, Porath, Avi, Shalev, Varda, and Koren, Gideon, 2019. "Comparison of Mortality and Comorbidity Rates Between Holocaust Survivors and Individuals in the General Population in Israel", *JAMA Network Open* 2 (1): e186643.

Hantman, Shira, and Solomon, Zahava, 2007. "Recurrent Trauma: Holocaust Survivors Cope with Aging and Cancer", *Social Psychiatry and Psychiatric Epidemiology* 42 (5): 396–402.

Hazani, Elizur, and Shasha, Shaul M., 2008. "Effects of the Holocaust on the Physical Health of the Offspring of Survivors", *The Israel Medical Association Journal* 10: 251–255.

Hoffman, Yaakov, and Shrira, Amit, 2019. "Variables Connecting Parental PTSD to Offspring Successful Aging: Parent–Child Role Reversal, Secondary Traumatization, and Depressive Symptoms", *Frontiers in Psychiatry* 10: 718.

Kagansky, Nadya, Knobler, Hilla, Stein-Babich, Marina, Voet, Hillary, Shalit, Adi, Lindert, Jutta, and Knobler, Haim Y., 2019. "Holocaust Survival and the Long-term Risk of Cardiovascular Disease in the Elderly", *The Israel Medical Association Journal: IMAJ* 21 (4): 241–245.

Keinan-Boker, Lital, 2014. "'The Mothers Have Eaten Unripe Grapes and the Children's Teeth Are Set on Edge': The Potential Inter-Generational Effects of the Holocaust on Chronic Morbidity in Holocaust Survivors' Offspring", *Israel Journal of Health Policy Research* 3 (1): 11.

Keinan-Boker, Lital, 2018. "Increased Cancer Incidence in Holocaust Survivors and the Implications for Survivors of Other Extreme Events", *Expert Review of Anticancer Therapy* 18 (11): 1059–1062.

Kellermann, Natan P.F., 2001. "The Long-Term Psychological Effects and Treatment of Holocaust Trauma", *Journal of Loss &Trauma* 6 (3): 197–218.

Kellermann, Natan P.F., 2009. *Holocaust Trauma: Psychological Effects and Treatment*, New York, NY: iUniverse.

Kellermann, Natan P.F., 2013. "Epigenetic Transmission of Holocaust Trauma: Can Nightmares be Inherited", *The Israel Journal of Psychiatry and Related Sciences* 50 (1): 33–39.

Kellermann, Natan P.F., 2020. "Major Variables of Holocaust Trauma Transmission", in: O.Z. Soltes (ed.), *Immortality, Memory, Creativity and Survival: The Arts of Alice Lok Cahana, Ronnie Cahana and Kitra Cahana*, New York, NY: The Fritz Ascher Society for Persecuted, Ostracized and Banned Art: 85–136.

Kidron, Carol A., Kotliar, Dan M., and Kirmayer, Laurence J., 2019. "Transmitted Trauma as Badge of Honor: Phenomenological Accounts of Holocaust Descendant Resilient Vulnerability", *Social Science & Medicine* 239: 112524.

Kodesh, Arad, Levav, Itzhak, and Levine, Stephen Z., 2019. "Exposure to Genocide and the Risk of Dementia", *Journal of Traumatic Stress* 32 (4): 536–545.

Kogan, Ilany, 2021. "Working with a Holocaust Survivor's Daughter During the Coronavirus Pandemic", *The Psychoanalytic Quarterly* 90 (4): 599–624.

Lax, Elad, Warhaftig, Gal, Ohana, David, Maayan, Rachel, Delayahu, Yael, Roska, Paola, Ponizovsky, Alexander M., Weizman, Abraham, Yadid, Gal, and Szyf, Moshe, 2018. "A DNA Methylation Signature of Addiction in T Cells and Its Reversal with DHEA Intervention", *Frontiers in Molecular Neuroscience* 11: 322.

Levav, Itzhak, Levinson, Daphna, Radomislensky, Irina, Shemesh, Annarosa A., and Kohn, Robert, 2007. "Psychopathology and Other Health Dimensions Among the Offspring of Holocaust Survivors: Results from the Israel National Health Survey", *Israel Journal of Psychiatry and Related Sciences* 44 (2): 144–151.

Lindert, Jutta, Knobler, Haim Y., Kawachi, Ichiro, Bain, Paul A., Abramowitz, Moshe Z., McKee, Charlotte, Reinharz, Shula, and McKee, Martin, 2017. "Psychopathology of Children of Genocide Survivors: A Systematic Review on the Impact of Genocide on Their Children's Psychopathology from Five Countries", *International Journal of Epidemiology* 46 (1): 246–257.

Maytles, Ruth, Frenkel-Yosef, Maya, and Shrira, Amit, 2021a. "Psychological Reactions of Holocaust Survivors with Low and High PTSD Symptom Levels During the COVID-19 Pandemic", *Journal of Affective Disorders* 282: 697–699.

Maytles, Ruth, Frenkel-Yosef, Maya, and Shrira, Amit, 2021b. "Caregiver Burden Among Adults Caring for Their Holocaust-Survivor Parents During the COVID-19 Pandemic", *International Psychogeriatrics* 33 (12): 1327–1332.

McEwen, Bruce S., 1998. "Protective and Damaging Effects of Stress Mediators", *New England Journal of Medicine* 338 (3): 171–179.

Miller, Gregory E., Chen, Edith, and Parker, Karen J., 2011. "Psychological Stress in Childhood and Susceptibility to the Chronic Diseases of Aging: Moving Toward a Model of Behavioral and Biological Mechanisms", *Psychological Bulletin* 137 (6): 959–997.

Palgi, Yuval, Shrira, Amit, and Neupert, Shevaun D., 2021. "Views on Aging and Health: A Multidimensional and Multitemporal Perspective", *The Journals of Gerontology: Series B* 76 (5): 821–824.

Palgi, Yuval, Shrira, Amit, and Shmotkin, Dov, 2015. "Aging with Trauma Across the Lifetime and Experiencing Trauma in Old Age: Vulnerability and Resilience Intertwined", in: Katie E. Cherry (ed.), *Traumatic Stress and Long-Term Recovery*, Cham: Springer: 293–308.

Payne, Emma A., and Berle, David, 2021. "Posttraumatic Stress Disorder Symptoms Among Offspring of Holocaust Survivors: A Systematic Review and Meta-Analysis", *Traumatology* 27 (3): 254–264.

Sagi-Schwartz, Abraham, 2015. "Does Extreme Trauma Transfer? The Case of Three Generations of the Holocaust", in: Katie E. Cherry (ed.), *Traumatic Stress and Long-Term Recovery*, Cham: Springer: 133–148.

Samson, Tali, Shvartzman, Pesach, and Biderman, Aya, 2013. "Palliative Care Among Second-Generation Holocaust Survivors: Communication Barriers", *Journal of Pain and Symptom Management* 45 (4): 798–802.

Sarfati, Samuel, Katz, Andrée, Cohen, Marc, Bantman, Patrick, Mimoun, Aviva, Sitruk, Patricia, Amson, Fabienne et al., 2022. "Psychological Impact of the Outbreak of COVID-19 on Holocaust Survivors in France", *European Journal of Trauma & Dissociation* 6 (2): 100242.

Schnurr, Paula P., 2017. "Physical Health and Health Services Utilization", in: Steven N. Gold (ed.), *APA Handbook of Trauma Psychology: Foundations in Knowledge*, Washington, DC: American Psychological Association: 349–370.

Shmotkin, Dov, Shrira, Amit, Goldberg, Shira C., and Palgi, Yuval, 2011. "Resilience and Vulnerability Among Aging Holocaust Survivors and Their Families: An Intergenerational Overview", *Journal of Intergenerational Relationships* 9 (1): 7–21.

Shrira, Amit, 2015. "Transmitting the Sum of All Fears: Iranian Nuclear Threat Salience Among Offspring of Holocaust Survivors", *Psychological Trauma: Theory, Research, Practice, and Policy* 7 (4): 364–371.

Shrira, Amit, 2016. "Perceptions of Aging Among Middle-Aged Offspring of Traumatized Parents: The Effects of Parental Holocaust-Related Communication and Secondary Traumatization", *Aging & Mental Health* 20 (1): 65–73.

Shrira, Amit, 2019. "Parental PTSD, Health Behaviors and Successful Aging Among Offspring of Holocaust Survivors", *Psychiatry Research* 271: 265–271.

Shrira, Amit, 2020. "Parental Holocaust Exposure, Related PTSD Symptoms and Subjective Aging Across the Generations", *The Journals of Gerontology: Series B* 75 (1): 30–41.

Shrira, Amit, Ayalon, Liat, Bensimon, Moshe, Bodner, Ehud, Rosenbloom, Tova, and Yadid, Gal, 2017. "Parental Post-Traumatic Stress Disorder Symptoms Are Related to Successful Aging in Offspring of Holocaust Survivors", *Frontiers in Psychology* 8: 1099.

Shrira, Amit, and Felsen, Irit, 2021. "Parental PTSD and Psychological Reactions During the COVID-19 Pandemic Among Offspring of Holocaust Survivors", *Psychological Trauma: Theory, Research, Practice, and Policy* 13 (4): 438–445.

Shrira, Amit, Maytles, Ruth, and Frenkel-Yosef, Maya, 2020. "Suffering From Infectious Diseases During the Holocaust Relates to Amplified Psychological Reactions During the COVID-19 Pandemic", *Journal of Psychiatric Research* 130: 421–423.

Shrira, Amit, Menashe, Ravit, and Bensimon, Moshe, 2019. "Filial Anxiety and Sense of Obligation Among Offspring of Holocaust Survivors", *Aging & Mental Health* 23 (6): 752–761.

Shrira, Amit, Palgi, Yuval, Ben-Ezra, Menachem, and Shmotkin, Dov, 2011a. "Functioning and Mortality of Holocaust Survivors: Physical Resilience and Psychosocial Vulnerabilities", *Journal of Loss and Trauma* 16 (1): 67–83.

Shrira, Amit, Palgi, Yuval, Ben-Ezra, Menachem, and Shmotkin, Dov, 2011b. "Transgenerational Effects of Trauma in Midlife: Evidence for Resilience and Vulnerability in Offspring of Holocaust Survivors", *Psychological Trauma: Theory, Research, Practice, and Policy* 3 (4): 394–402.

Shrira, Amit, Palgi, Yuval, and Lang, Frieder R., 2021. "Posttraumatic Manifestations among Older Adults", *GeroPsych: The Journal of Gerontopsychology and Geriatric Psychiatry* 34 (4): 167–168.

Solomon, Zahava, Kotler, Moshe, and Mikulincer, Mario, 1988. "Combat-Related Posttraumatic Stress Disorder Among Second-Generation Holocaust Survivors: Preliminary Findings", *The American Journal of Psychiatry* 145 (7): 865–868.

Steir-Livny, Liat, 2021. "Traumatic Past in The Present: COVID-19 and Holocaust Memory in Israeli Media, Digital Media, and Social Media", *Media, Culture & Society*, 01634437211036997.

Szyf, Moshe, 2015. "Nongenetic Inheritance and Transgenerational Epigenetics", *Trends in Molecular Medicine* 21 (2): 134–144.

Van IJzendoorn, Marinus H., Bakermans-Kranenburg, Marian J., and Sagi-Schwartz, Abraham, 2003. "Are Children of Holocaust Survivors Less Well-Adapted? A Meta-Analytic Investigation of Secondary Traumatization", *Journal of Traumatic Stress* 16 (5): 459–469.

Wiseman, Hadas, 2008. "On Failed Intersubjectivity: Recollections of Loneliness Experiences in Offspring of Holocaust Survivors", *American Journal of Orthopsychiatry* 78 (3): 350–358.

Yehuda, Rachel, Bierer, Linda M., Schmeidler, James, Aferiat, Daniel H., Breslau, Ilana, and Dolan, Susan, 2000. "Low Cortisol and Risk for PTSD in Adult Offspring of Holocaust Survivors", *American Journal of Psychiatry* 157 (8): 1252–1259.

Yehuda, Rachel, Daskalakis, Nikolaos P., Lehrner, Amy, Desarnaud, Frank, Bader, Heather N., Makotkine, Iouri, Flory, Janine D., Bierer, Linda M., and Meaney, Michael J., 2014. "Influences Of Maternal and Paternal PTSD on Epigenetic Regulation of the Glucocorticoid Receptor Gene in Holocaust Survivor Offspring", *American Journal of Psychiatry* 171 (8): 872–880.

Yehuda, Rachel, Hoge, Charles W., McFarlane, Alexander C., Vermetten, Eric, Lanius, Ruth A., Nievergelt, Caroline M., Hobfoll, Stevan E., Koenen, Karestan C., Neylan, Thomas C., and Hyman, Steven E., 2015. "Post-Traumatic Stress Disorder", *Nature Reviews Disease Primers* 1: 15057.

Yehuda, Rachel, and Lehrner, Amy, 2018. "Intergenerational Transmission of Trauma Effects: Putative Role of Epigenetic Mechanisms", *World Psychiatry* 17 (3): 243–257.

Zamstein, Omri, Biderman, Aya, Sherf, Michael, Ben David, Ran, and Dreiher, Jacob, 2018. "Cardiovascular Morbidity and Risk Factors in Holocaust Survivors in Israel", *Journal of the American Geriatrics Society* 66 (9): 1684–1691.

16

SPECIFIC ASPECTS IN THE LIFE AND CARE OF THE OFFSPRING OF SHOAH SURVIVORS IN GERMANY

Andrea Zielke-Nadkarni

Introduction

In 2021, Germany officially celebrated the jubilee of 1,700 years of Jewish presence in the realm of Germany today. In 321 CE, the Roman emperor Konstantin issued an edict by which he permitted the Jews in the city of Cologne to function as city councilors – thereby documenting the presence of Jews already there at that time. Numerous festivities in connection with the jubilee aim at making Jewish life visible and at setting a counterpoint against a rising right wing movement.[1]

The research taboo on the effects of the Shoah on the survivors and their offspring was lifted only in the late 1970s, then carried out in the USA, Canada, and Israel.[2] For Europe, such research remained an urgent desideratum even until the 1990s.[3] Now, about 80 years later, it can be shown that (grand)children still bear the burden of their (grand)parents' fate.

Background

In 1945, the majority of the about 15–20,000 Jewish citizens in post-Nazi Germany were Shoah survivors from Germany or Eastern Europe.[4] Owing to a special agreement between Germany and the CIS in 1991, about 200,000 Jews migrated to Germany.[5] With a new law in 2005, Jewish entry on that special agreement was terminated officially, which more or less ended Jewish immigration from the CIS. Most Jewish citizens in Germany today have an Eastern European background. Both the long history of persecution, starting in Russia with Tzar Ivan IV the Terrible (1533–84) and the concealment of their Jewish identity by many during the 75 years of communism in the Soviet Union,[6] resulted in atheistic Judaism for the majority. Some re-discovered their religiosity after entering Germany because of the support they received from the Jewish communities.[7]

The arrival of the Eastern European refugees led to the revival of Jewish culture. Berlin is the center of Orthodox Judaism in Germany today, including Orthodox institutions such as synagogues, kosher shops, museums, etc. Symbolic of this development is the School of Jewish Theology which houses, amongst other schools, the Zacharias Frankel College for the scientific training of Orthodox rabbis in Potsdam, just outside Berlin.

At the same time Judaism in Germany today consists of a variety of religious orientations including Progressive, Liberal, Conservative, and (Modern-)Orthodox believers, as well as people who feel

DOI: 10.4324/b23365-19

an ethnic affiliation to Judaism rather than a religiously founded one. In 2020, a total of 93,695 Jews were members of the Jewish communities in Germany[8] as not all of the immigrants from Eastern Europe became members. Many of the Jewish communities work at reconciling this somewhat contradictory plurality. In 2017 Koerber published an online survey comprising 267 men and women who either have a Jewish mother, are converted, or belong to the approximately 50% of immigrated Jews whose Jewish identity is based on the patrilineal Soviet nationality law. Koerber asked her interviewees how they understand Judaism: 51% described it as an ethnic affiliation, 23.9% described it as a cultural community, and only 13.1% defined Judaism as a religious identity. Some (40.8%) are members of a moderately Orthodox community (so called "Einheitsgemeinden" who strive at integrating all orientations), 13.5% belong to a neo-Orthodox community, 6.4% are members of a Liberal community, 2.2% chose a different religious community altogether, and 37.1% do not belong to any community at all.[9]

Another feature of both Jewish immigrants as well as German Jews is that many traditionally consider education, as well as high school and university degrees, as a very important goal of their children's socialization.[10] This view corresponds with some of Koerber's outcomes in that "Judaism is seen as an urban, cosmopolitan culture which is interpreted and practiced individually".[11] The diversity of 2g/3g Jewish persons in Germany based on the consequences of their family biographies and the sociopolitical views of this group has been researched, for example, by Haviv-Horiner and Heilbrunn[12] and will be confirmed to a smaller extent in the interview findings later.

Method

This chapter presents the results of a qualitative explorative study on the (health) biographies of the offspring of survivors of Nazi persecution in Germany today. It aims at eliciting their lived experience, their special trauma inheritance, resources and coping strategies, as well as the care needs of this clientele with a view to their dependence on professional carers when in need of nursing care.

The target group of this project was, therefore, members of the Jewish 2g/3g citizens of Germany with Holocaust surviving (grand)parents. Semi-structured interviews were conducted in November/December 2021 to investigate their socio-cultural background and its impact on their present life and health care needs. The method of grounded theory was employed to explore the ensuing categories presented in this chapter. The research aims at conceptualizing recommendations for a patient-oriented, culturally sensitive nursing care.

To avoid the fear of self-disclosure on the part of the interviewees a lengthy introductory telephone conversation was conducted, and the project's goals were explained in detail. Each participant was informed that s/he had the right to refuse to answer questions, interrupt at any point during the interview, or withdraw from the study altogether. With their permission, interviews were carried out online due to the COVID-19 pandemic using Zoom, then audiotaped, anonymized, transcribed verbatim, and checked by the interviewees before publication.

Sample: in general, it may be said that the more orthodox a person is, no matter what faith, the more rules regulate their lives and therefore apply when in need of nursing care. We were therefore looking ideally for Orthodox Jewesses, as women follow special rules of modesty and are usually responsible for nursing family members, both important in nursing care situations. However, it was extremely difficult to find participants, even with the much-appreciated help of members of the local Jewish community. Without them it might have been an impossible task, as the confrontation with trauma and its disclosure to an unknown non-Jewish German seemed too much to bear. In the end, the sample (Table 16.1) consisted of 3 Jewish participants, 1 man, 2 women, aged 23, 37,

Table 16.1 Sample

Sex/generation	*Female/3g*	*Female/2g*	*Male 3g*
Age	23	52	37
Religious orientation (self-portrayal)	Modern-Orthodox	Conservative	Modern-Orthodox
Survivor of camps and/or persecution	Grandparents	Father, grandmother	Grandfather, father-in-law
Profession	Administration employee	Teacher, runs a youth center of the city's Jewish community	Mathematician
Family status	Married	Married, 2 daughters	Married, 2 sons
National background	German (parents Ukrainian)	German	Russian
Year of immigration	Born in Germany	Born in Germany	2001

and 52. Their religious background is Orthodox in two cases and Conservative in one. They all are academics and the families of two them come from the CIS.

Findings and Discussion

To avoid repetitions, the presentation of the categories, which emerged from the interviews, is combined with the discussion.

Data analysis led to the core category (Figure 16.1) "Balancing Identity and Everyday Challenges", which is subdivided into the six categories:

- Living in Germany today as a Jew.
- Exercising one's religion according to individual needs and views.
- Being in the dark: biography of persecution.
- Living with the trauma.
- Strategies for coping with the trauma and the uncertainties of life in Germany.
- Requirements for the Health Care Service.

Living in Germany Today as a Jew

No matter how integrated a Jewish person lives her/his life in Germany there is always the feeling of being different. While Mrs. C, who has a German background relates that her Christian parents-in-law will always support her and her two daughters, thereby stressing that this is an issue, Mrs. B. feels well integrated into the Berlin Orthodox Jewish community and in the quasi-Jewish quarter where she lives. Born in Germany and with parents from Ukraine she says that her picture of Germany is not only associated with the Nazis but also that she knows well that Germany today is a different society. However, her life is mainly lived within the Jewish community and with Jewish friends. Mr. A., too, made a very conscious decision to live an Orthodox Jewish life – thus setting himself apart from

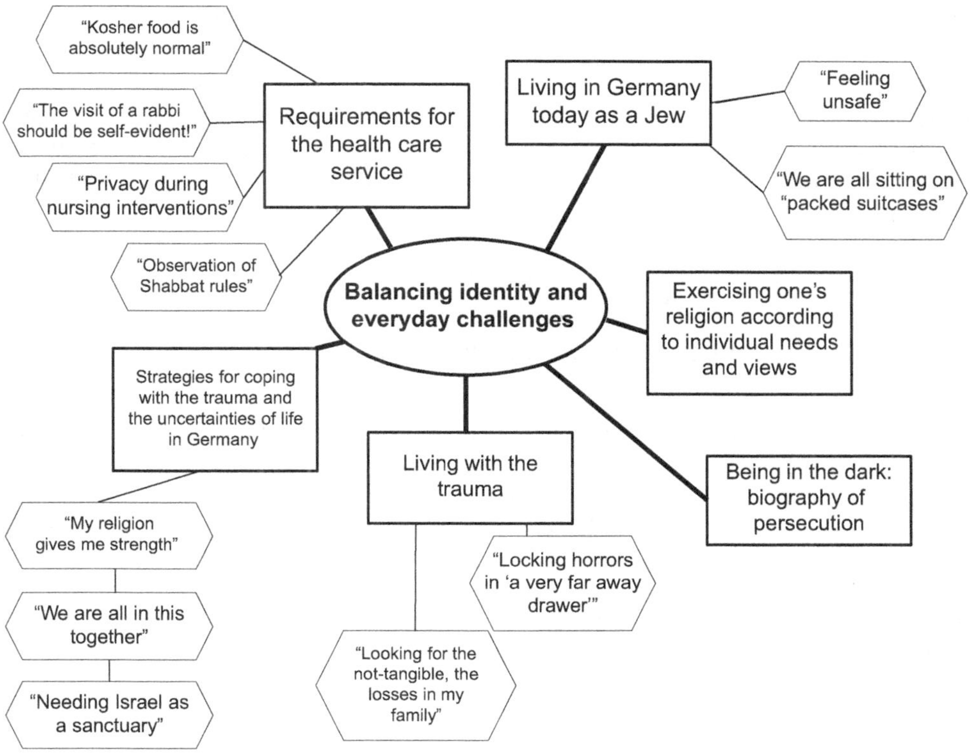

Figure 16.1 "Balancing identity and everyday challenges"

his Russian parents – at first at university, then in his wife's family and their community, thereafter in Berlin and lately in Vienna. For the sake of living in a very religious Jewish environment there, especially for their children, his wife gave up her well-paid job when they moved.

While their work life is the main area of contact with non-Jews for him and Mrs. B., Mrs. C. lives in two worlds with non-Jewish German friends and family on the one hand and the mainly Russian Jewish community on the other. This last aspect, unfortunately, makes her and her daughters feel like outsiders there as the main language spoken and the mentality are Russian. At the same time Mrs. C. takes great pride in her work as group leader for the young community members.

A subcategory of "Living in Germany today as a Jew" is:

"Feeling Unsafe"

All interviewees have been experiencing antisemitism themselves and know about incidences from others, starting with aggressive glances or verbal attacks up to physical violence. While women are rarely attacked as their outfit does not give their Jewish identity away easily, their negative experiences increase when they are accompanied by men wearing the kippah. The risks are larger if people live in big cities while in small towns, with a more homogenous population and few Jews, attacks are apparently very rare.

In addition to antisemitic aggression from strangers one of our interviewees also experienced a lack of support from her boss and colleagues who feared radical right-wing reactions. Her small daughter was attacked by classmates in the schoolyard several times, accumulating in a strangulation that was only ended by luck because the school bell chimed and a friend of hers intervened at that point in time. Here, like in all other incidences reported, for example a physical attack in a fitness studio, practically no one interfered. This was felt as the most hurtful aspect by all our interviewees.

In addition, there are shocking cyber-attacks whereby, for example, access to a university seminar was used to "step" right into the tale of a Shoah survivor with insinuating remarks and "Heil Hitler" shouts.

Official numbers of antisemitic incidences in Germany in 2020 totaled 1,909 of which 644 took place on the internet and physical violence amounted to 40 incidences.[13]

"We Are All Sitting on 'Packed Suitcases'"

The consequence for Mrs. B. and Mrs. C. is expressed in another subcategory: while there are no immediate plans for emigration, the interviewees report mentally "packed suitcases" for themselves and virtually all other Jews they know. Although he is still working in Germany, Mr. A. emigrated to Vienna – mainly for religious reasons: Vienna's infrastructure is more comprehensive than Berlin's, comprising not just more synagogues, kosher shops, and supermarkets but also Jewish kindergartens and schools. In Vienna's Jewish community, totaling about 7,000 Jews today, all his friends will serve his sons kosher food so he will not have to worry about a non-conformist diet. But he also feels that his sons can wear their kippah safely and he himself wears tzitzit in public and a kippah as well, with a baseball cap above it only as protection against the cold and not against possible attacks.

Exercising One's Religion According to Individual Needs and Views

The interviews revealed that Orthodoxy is not experienced as a clear-cut status within the larger Jewish community but to some extent due to individual definition. Mr. A. was regarded as ultra-Orthodox in Germany (only) because he sticks to the Shabbat laws. In Vienna, he is seen as just Orthodox as some Jews live much stricter according to Jewish laws. In Mrs. C.'s experience, Israeli Orthodoxy varies in several aspects from that of her German community where old and fragile women use the lift to reach the upper floor of the synagogue on Shabbat – unthinkable for her Israeli visitors. Mrs. C.'s Israeli family is Conservative; they keep their mobiles on during Shabbat, which is totally frowned upon in her German community. Her Conservative community celebrates Shabbat in dependence of the attendants: if there are more Orthodox Jews present, rules are stricter, the Torah is carried around the synagogue, and different prayers and songs are used than those at times when the majority of believers are Conservative.

Mrs. B. and Mr. A. term themselves "Modern Orthodox". Modern Orthodoxy includes for them having male and female friends, using the gadgets of today's world such as mobiles or laptops, as well as a Shabbat oven and Shabbat fridge, and adhering to many Orthodox laws concerning the religious holidays, Kashrut, or clothing.

Mr. A., who works as a mathematician at a German university, is convinced: "Germany today is no place for religious Jews!" For a genuinely Jewish environment for him, a kindergarten is needed where his sons do not have to celebrate "some St. Nicholas" and search for "strange eggs" at Easter. Mr. A. cherishes the freedom of living in an *Eruv* in Vienna, which facilitates observing the Shabbat rules for families. Similarly, Mrs. B. and her husband are thinking of moving to Israel to bring up their future children in a safe religious environment.

In St. Petersburg, where Mr. A. went to school, to him and his friends being Jewish used to mean being well educated and on a par with non-Jews. When he became a student in Berlin and a member of the Jewish student organization, his religious interest was awakened and later deepened due to a rabbi and his Orthodox wife and her family. Through them he experienced a proper Orthodox private life – different from his parents' – which now has become self-evident for him. In Mr. A.'s experience in the CIS, quite a number of people practice an Orthodox life without any deep knowledge of religious habits or items, while in Germany knowledge often exists, but on Shabbat they light candles while at the same time they watch the news on TV.

Mrs. B. also sees herself as a part of the modern world; she listens to modern music and does not cover her hair completely. She dresses modestly and wears a broad hair band, instead of a wig, thus meeting the minimum hairdressing propriety required of married women. She comes from a non-religious family who adhered only to the Jewish religious holidays, but she has a strong Jewish identity. Since the family had to keep their Jewish background a secret in the CIS, Mrs. B. became a believer only at the age of 14. She then spent a Jewish gap-year (between school and university) in Jewish communities in New York, London, and Israel. After she returned to Berlin, she attended Shabbat seminars, and since then her religiosity has become increasingly stricter. Her husband is "traditional". He does not keep the Shabbat, except for the Shabbat meal. But like his wife, he much appreciates the mutual support and friendship within the Jewish community.

Mrs. C. always felt Jewish, even if she does not visit the synagogue on Shabbat. She educated her children in the Jewish tradition and culture and celebrates the religious holidays. At the same time, she regards some of the Orthodox practices for dealing with religious laws as ridiculous, such as using an automatic time switch to heat up the Shabbat meal. For her, it is not the knowledge of the laws and the Torah, but finding one's faith within oneself that is the essential asset of a real believer as well as being a good person and passing on the faith.

She separates her crockery and kitchen equipment for meat and dairy products, but she has only one fridge. Her view is that all rules, which are enforced on people, are man-made. This includes many detailed kosher food rules. But she also seeks to avoid mistakes as the leader of a Jewish youth group. Mr. A.'s kitchen, on the other hand, is strictly divided into three compartments that separate meat and dairy products and allow for an area where neutral food can be cooked and thereafter mixed with either meat or dairy products. Mrs. B. eats kosher only. Her husband, however, although he will eat kosher food, has his own cooking kit for his non-kosher meals.

To all three interviewees their faith is very important. Jewish tradition passed down by the women in various ways and lived within the community means to be in good hands for them and forms the basis of a religious subculture in a secular society. An individualistic structure is closely connected to a life according to religious laws.[14]

Being in the Dark: Biography of Persecution

Mr. A.'s father was born in January 1941. When the Nazis invaded Russia on June 22 in that year, he was evacuated and, therefore, escaped, while Mr. A.'s grandfather died as a soldier in Leningrad. When his other grandfather, his mother's father, died, Mr. A. was three years old. He barely remembers him, and, therefore, heard most stories from his mother. This grandfather hated the Germans, and whenever he heard that language on the radio, he would switch to another station. His worst experience was the murder of all the Jewish children by the Nazis in a concentration camp, with the Russian army having to bury all these poor innocent children. Mr. A.'s parents never wanted to live in Germany. However, various factors reversed that view: the Chechen wars, the fact that there was no acceptable future for him as a mathematician, as well as Mr. A.'s knowledge of German, and, finally, that they were given a visa by the German embassy within just 11 months.

Mr. A.'s wife's father fought in the Russian army on the second Ukrainian front. He took part in the liberation of Bratislava and Vienna. So, living in Vienna gives Mr. A. a very good feeling.

Mrs. B. does not know anything about the history of her father's parents. Her mother's father fought in the Ukraine against Hitler's army. But for this he had to adopt a Russian name, which he even had tattooed on his wrist, to hide his Jewish identity. He was proud to have fought against the Nazis and May 9 was always a great personal holiday to him on which he was congratulated by the family. However, he was also traumatized: he lost his brother and many comrades: One night when they slept in tents in the woods, he left the camp to go to the toilet. When he returned, Nazi-soldiers had discovered the camp and killed everyone.

After the war, religiosity was prosecuted in the Soviet Union. So many Jews were secretive about their religion and identity.[15]

Mr. B.'s grandfather, therefore, attended the synagogue on Friday evenings secretly. In later years, many of the Jews in the Soviet Union considered themselves less a religious group than an ethnic group (they were given the nationality no. 5 by the state), and Jews who lived in the same quarter knew (about) each other.

Mrs. C.'s grandfather, a Christian, was pressured into divorcing his Jewish wife and while her father's brothers broke off all contact with him, her father and her grandmother, both Auschwitz survivors, forgave him because they realized how he would have been tortured had he not complied. After the liberation both Mrs. C.'s father and grandmother emigrated to pre-State Israel in 1946/47. While her father enjoyed life with his reunited family there, his mother felt permanently unwell because of the climate. She also found Hebrew very hard to learn and missed Germany a lot. She argued: "I survived those Hitler years. Why can't I have a good life in Germany again now!" After Auschwitz, her son had promised never to leave her again. So, after 10 years in Israel, Mrs. C.'s father returned to Germany with his mother where he fell head over heels in love with a Christian and stayed. Unfortunately, both families were against that marriage and the Jewish community also did not welcome his wife. But to their great surprise and happiness they had a daughter – Mrs. C. – and a son. In the concentration camp Mrs. C.'s father and his brothers were forcibly sterilized and therefore certain that they would not have any offspring. So, Mrs. C.'s father was overjoyed and especially proud to have fathered not only a daughter but also a son and heir.

One of the traumatic stories from the concentration camp he mentioned, which made her family proud at the same time, is about a Polish overseer who had blown the whistle on a friend. This friend was, therefore, beaten to death. In retaliation, Mrs. C.'s father and some friends ambushed this overseer one night, pulled a potato sack over him, beat him up, and took the potatoes he had taken for himself back to their barracks where they cooked them and shared them with everyone. To cross a line like that in the camps normally meant a death sentence. But the overseer did not dare give them away as this incident would have shown his weakness and inability to control them, which would have had bitter consequences.

A lot of studies confirm similar or worse horror stories,[16] as well as their effects on the next generations.[17]

Living with the Trauma

DSM-5 defines trauma as requiring "actual or threatened death, serious injury, or sexual violence" based on direct personal exposure, witnessing trauma, and indirect exposure through trauma experience of a close person[18] (secondary traumatization), which includes detainment and multiple trauma experience in concentration camps and the ensuing emotional distress symptoms years after exposure described here. Kellermann discusses the transmission terminology in detail and differentiates between "the *process* of transmission" and "the *content* of transmission" with a view to 2g and 3g.[19] The category "Living with the trauma" contains the two subcategories "Locking horrors in 'a very far away drawer'" and "Looking for the not-tangible, the losses in my family".

Locking Horrors in "A Very Far Away Drawer"

Asked whether and how the traumatic events experienced by his family affect him, Mr. A. replied that he always has to empty his plate completely. Food has to be totally eaten up; he cannot throw away any. The thought that his ancestors had to starve and ate shavings instead of bread makes him eat up even moldy bread after removing the fungus. Yet, he only realized the meaning of this habit as a post-reaction to the family trauma through talks he had with his wife and mother-in-law.

For Mrs. B. the traumas her family went through are so painful that she locked them in "a very far away drawer" and tries to continue her life without being too impaired by them. But films about this period on TV hit her very hard, especially when she imagines her parents in the circumstances shown.

This is a well-known phenomenon already described in many of the early studies: traumatic events are suppressed to avoid re-traumatization by the horrors, losses, and guilty feelings.[20]

"Looking for the Not-tangible, the Losses in My Family"

For Mrs. C., who was told very little about the Shoah, the effects of the trauma started during her childhood. Her performance in school was closely connected to her father's and grandmother's fate because their achieving survival made her feel that she had to achieve, too, i.e., to always have the best marks in school to suffice for her parents as well as for society.

Research shows that the children of Holocaust survivors try to reduce their guilty feelings and cope, for example, by a high commitment to perform well at school and in adult life. This "transgenerational trauma transmission" can go along with persisting identity problems and an overidentification with their parents' victimhood.[21]

Mrs. C.'s best possible performance was also the way to get love, as emotions were a difficult thing in her family. Her Christian mother, too, was traumatized: by the war, the famines, her flight as a child, and all the horrible pictures in her memory. She, therefore, had to suppress feelings and was unable to show her love to her daughter.

The early as well as recent literature reports apparent emotional restraints of traumatized parents towards their children who suffer from this lack of emotion. Life-threatening events that can cause a "freeze-reaction" and a de-realization to overcome deadly terror may lead to distorted attachments in personal relationships.[22]

Mrs. C.'s father grew up in a not very religious family. In the period before he was sent to the concentration camp as a child he was excluded from school because he was Jewish. All of a sudden everything was forbidden, and he lost all his friends. Except for secret meetings with one of them in the hallway of their house, he became a totally isolated boy.

As Freyberger et al.[23] amongst many others relate: traumatized children will have a heightened disposition for psychological impairments. This does not necessarily mean that they have to suffer them, although studies show a higher vulnerability to stress and PTSD.[24]

When the camp was liberated Mrs. C.'s father was a mentally and physically broken person suffering from nightmares and headaches. He had scars all over his body, the largest of which was on his head caused by an iron rod; his bottom had holes where chunks of flesh had been beaten out.

Many children internalize the victimhood of their (grand)parents and would love to compensate them – a frustrating and impossible task.[25]

Mrs. C. heard about all her father's sufferings at night when he was crying and in single jigsaw pieces, quasi on the side, related over the years. Based on these Mrs. C. created her own picture horror stories.

Safford[26] and later studies[27] found that uninformed children fantasize about the survival of their (grand)parents.

Mrs. C.'s worst memory is the terrible story of the ear-piercing scream of a mother whose baby is smashed against a train. Films such as *Schindler's List* were commented on by her father: "Nobody can imitate such an act!" And he told her how the Sinti did not suffer most from hunger and cold but from the forceful separation from their children and how they then committed suicide by running into the electric fence of the camp while the guards laughed: "Look, another one . . . and another one . . . and one more . . .!" Her father also suffered from (well-documented) survivor guilt[28] and the guilt of having taken a piece of bread from a dying inmate he knew well.

His nightmares increased in the 1990s when antisemitism was on the rise in Germany. At first, the ensuing protests encouraged him, but all in all it destroyed him. He always compared Nazism to a tumor and, in the end, he himself passed away from cancer.

Mrs. C. herself realizes her traumatization because she often wakes up at night and finds herself grinding her teeth. She is in trauma therapy, but it is not clear to her whether her problems at night stem from a car accident at 18 in which she nearly died or her family's history.

Another effect of the family trauma is that in the period around *Kristallnacht* (November 9/10 in 1938) every year Mrs. C. is pulled to the TV, spending hours and hours watching films of that period every night, unable to stop herself and go to bed, in an effort to find members of her family in the documentaries.

These are but few examples of how the manifold forms of transgenerational trauma transmission occur (see further examples in Kellermann).[29] All the more important are strategies developed by the offspring to cope with the past as well as the present, which often intermingle and shape their daily life, a phenomenon described as a "double biographic reality".[30]

Strategies for Coping with the Trauma and the Uncertainties of Life in Germany: "My Religion Gives Me Strength"

The basic strategy for coping with the trauma and the uncertainties of life in Germany seems to be leading a religious life. And although religion gives strength, a central question is how much Jewish citizens in Germany feel able to show their identity. Some of the time Mr. A. decides to wear a baseball cap over his kippah. Mrs. C. does not dare wear the Star of David, while Mrs. B. regards this as a self-evident right and a protective symbol, and she knows of many who also wear it. Mrs. B.'s friends are in part young Jewish activists who consciously demonstrate their Judaism while others do not directly talk about it in everyday encounters. All interviewees regard their faith and their Jewish community as the most important sources of support and inner calm. And if addressed they all will defend their faith and identity.

The literature, too, stresses the central function of the Jewish communities, which offer integration and strengthen Jewish identity, interrelated to the religious tradition and the connecting effect of rituals and symbols. Social integration, however, is described as correlating with the individual degree of education.[31]

"We Are All in This Together"

For the young Mrs. B. (3g) the community extends into the internet. Social media for her and her generation are a means of connecting, exchanging, interacting, planning actions, and receiving endorsement. "We are all in this together" sums up the feeling of unity and support she gains from Jews all over the country and the world, and: "we continue even when we are to be silenced!" The Berlin organization RIAS[32] offers contact persons victims can talk to after an attack. The mutual exchange, the shared celebration of memorial days such as the uproar in the Warsaw ghetto, or stories passed on by survivors strengthen the feelings of belonging and solidarity. Mrs. B.'s mother (2g), on the other hand, would rather hush things up than cause public attention.

Mrs. C.'s family is a (probably typical) example of the different generational reactions to the Nazi persecution. Her father, a survivor of the Shoah, was shocked when she called her daughter Sarah: "When we were hauled away by the Nazis all the girls were named Sarah, and all the boys Israel!" Mrs. C., however, gave her daughter this name "with pride and dignity!" She also built a house, which her father regarded as too risky: "A house can be taken away!" while she said: "isn't it time to build anew?!"

At the same time, she feels torn between the various positions. All through her childhood she heard from her father that "you have to be unobtrusive. Only those who are unobtrusive will survive!" She therefore learned to think ahead and calculate all eventualities – too much for any child! As an adult and a mother, she finds this continued demand for precaution and watchfulness on the one hand and the request to be a strong and proud Jewess on the other a difficult, contradictory, and even self-destructive task. As a personal consequence she opts for strict confrontation when verbally attacked as a Jewess: "Ours is a vengeful God, 'an eye for an eye, a tooth for a tooth' – not a forgiving God as in Christianity!" – "I want my faith to be tolerated, accepted, and respected!"

This may lead to more offensive reactions, but her experience is that usually her opponent gives up. She observed a similar inner conflict in her father: while he strongly advised "invisibility", he also refused to be "a sheep led to the slaughterhouse" again and therefore took an active part in many of the wars in Israel for which he returned from Germany. Forgiveness is another way her father chose in some incidences: for example, towards one of the very young guards the Nazis forced to work in the camps at the end. Her father recognized him after the war but did not reveal his Nazi past as he saw him as a victim: "a boy of 16, 17 or 18 who had to be a guard, but harmed no one – why give him away?"

As a result of the Shoah, survived by her father and grandmother, Mrs. C. (2g) is convinced that they both went through so much that she should bear up to almost any confrontation or verbal attack. A possible exception is a group of hostile people who might become very dangerous. Her daughters (3g) have very different personalities: while the older one is a strong character with clear views and a religious identity, the younger one has already been victimized a lot in her young life and will hopefully learn better defensive strategies rather than bear the antisemitic attacks she has already often been confronted with.

Needing Israel as a Sanctuary

"Those who survived the Shoah need Israel as a sanctuary to where they can withdraw and feel safe! – This is something many Germans do not understand!" (Mrs. C.). Reserving the right to emigrate is the last resort both for Mrs. B. and Mrs. C. – just as Mr. A. moved to Vienna, Mrs. B. may relocate to Israel once she has children to give them the chance to lead an Orthodox Jewish life more easily. Mrs. C. sees her base in Germany but can easily envisage moving to her family to the USA, Israel, or any other English-speaking country in an emergency situation.

To summarize, the coping strategies presented here include faith and the Jewish community within Germany but also the option to leave Germany for good. This is not just a theoretical game of thoughts but involves decisions that have to be taken – such as whether to buy a house or not – and pull the underlying question of whether and how living in Germany is possible into everyday life.

Requirements for the Health Care Service

At the center of the category "requirements from the Health Care Service" is the demand for respect for one's (orthodox) religious needs.

"Kosher Food Is Absolutely Normal"

This subcategory is the first request that sprang to mind for all three interviewees. Mr. A. related that, in Vienna hospitals, patients have the choice and will receive officially certified kosher food on demand. In Berlin, where this service is not offered, an organization for Jews who have to go into the hospital will bring kosher food to all patients who depend on this diet. The food is packed and can be warmed up without trespassing the Kashrut laws. The urge to support sick people goes far within the Jewish community in Berlin: even total strangers will bring the traditional chicken soup to the hospital if they hear about a sick Jewish person.

For Mrs. C., who sees herself as a Conservative Jewess, it would suffice that no pork is served and that dairy and meat are separated.

While most clinics in Germany adhere to basic Islamic nutrition rules, Jewish nutrition rules are ignored. This is certainly due to the extra cost and space needed to separate meat and dairy foods. However, this task could easily be outsourced.

"The Visit of a Rabbi Should Be Self-evident!"

While in Vienna a patient is self-evidently visited by a rabbi (as well as by other community members), this is unusual for Germany but an urgent matter for the interviewees. When in an intensive care unit after a heavy car accident and unable to speak, Mrs. C. was shocked that she was first visited by a Catholic priest who read to her from the Bible, then by a Protestant one and she "always had that fat cross dangling in front of her". She readily accepts a cross hanging in patients' rooms as justified for Protestant or Catholic hospitals, but demands that university clinics either do away with all religious symbols or offer those of the most important faiths.

A rabbi's visit should be offered to all Jewish patients, and a prayer room should be set aside for Shabbat prayer or any other personal prayer, ideally in combination with a Mikveh for spiritual cleansing.

"Privacy during Nursing Interventions"

Orthodox women need extensive privacy and a protection of their modest way of dressing during medical or nursing interventions. They prefer to be treated by women but accept male professionals if no women are available; however, before any intervention by a man, they would like to be asked if this is alright as a proof of respect. Equally, they want to be uncovered as minimally as possible and not stared at.

"Observation of Shabbat Rules"

The observing of Shabbat rules, for example no operation or examinations on that day, is also regarded as highly important. Both Mrs. B. and Mrs. C. regard this as even more important in Senior residences. For long-term inhabitants, besides Shabbat, the celebration of Jewish holidays is a matter of the heart. Being able to live Jewish culture is indispensable for the wellbeing of the elderly residents. This involves songs and music, mezuzahs on the doors, or a Hanukkiah available, as well as speaking their mother tongue, often Russian, sometimes Yiddish or Hebrew, especially when people become demented, rather than being exposed to the music and German folk songs they heard during the Nazi period.

In Germany there are quite a few Jewish Senior residences but also Jewish wards in general Senior residences. For many years already the literature reports that some older Jewish people decide to move into a Jewish Senior residence even though they are not (yet) in need of care. They want to live safely within a cultural environment that is Jewish, geared towards a religious structure of everyday life,[33] and – a necessity for many – with ideally Russian-speaking nursing and kitchen staff.[34]

Consequences for Nursing

In nursing situations, the role of religion and Jewish customs, rules, and expectations connected with them need to be assessed for each patient or inhabitant, as well as their traumatic family history and its consequences.[35] However, many Jewish persons cannot or will not be confronted again with the horrors of their family's past. Therefore, nurses need socio-historic knowledge as well as a distinctive sensitivity and empathy.

With view to hospitals and Senior residences, improved structures are needed to enable a religious Jewish life there. Therefore, nursing professionals have to develop an understanding of the practical meaning of spirituality and family trauma in the life of a person in their care.

We, the non-Jewish citizens of this country, too, carry the burden of our (grand)parents in the sense of a task: we must contribute to a more tolerant society, both in our private and professional lives.

Limitations of the Study

The most obvious limitation of this study is certainly the small number of only three participants. Another is that the author is not a psychologist or trauma expert, which would have elicited deeper and denser description. Therefore, its range is limited; however, supplemented by other research, key points for nursing are cautiously inferred.

Notes

1 1700 Jahre juedisches Leben in Deutschland e.V., 2021.
2 Honigman Cooper, 1979; Dasberg, 1987.
3 Bowling et al., 1992.
4 Sinn, 2020: 393 f.
5 Zentralrat der Juden in Deutschland, without date.
6 de Lange, 2000: 279 ff.
7 Zielke-Nadkarni, 2005.
8 Statista, 2021.
9 Koerber, 2014.
10 Bernstein, 2017.
11 Koerber, 2014, without page no.

12 Haviv-Horiner and Heilbrunn, 2013.
13 Bundesverband der Recherche- und Informationsstellen Antisemitismus e.V., 2021: 26.
14 Schrage, 2016: 148 f.
15 Zielke-Nadkarni, 2005.
16 Eitinger et al., 1985; Neurath et al., 2015.
17 Oren and Shavit, 2021; Payne and Berle, 2021.
18 American Psychiatric Association, 2013: 271.
19 Kellermann, 2009: 70 f.
20 Dor-Shav, 1978; Dasberg, 1987.
21 Freyberger et al., 2019: 112 ff.; Kellermann, 2009: 73.
22 Dasberg, 1987; Huber, 2004: 41 ff., Freyberger et al., 2019: 113 ff.
23 Freyberger et al., 2019: 119.
24 Kellermann, 2009: 73.
25 Freyberger et al., 2019: 112 ff.
26 Safford, 1995.
27 Freyberger et al., 2019: 118.
28 Fischer and Riedesser, 2009: 234 ff.
29 Kellermann, 2009: 74 ff.
30 Freyberger et al., 2019: 116.
31 Levinson, 2018: 127 ff.
32 Bundesverband der Recherche- und Informationsstellen Antisemitismus e.V.
33 Dasberg, 1987; Bloch and Weitzel-Polzer, 2001.
34 Zielke-Nadkarni, 2004.
35 See also Leonhard, 2003.

Bibliography

1700 Jahre juedisches Leben in Deutschland e.V. (ed.), 2021. https://2021jlid.de/ retrieved on February 11, 2022.

American Psychiatric Association, 2013. *Diagnostic and Statistical Manual of Mental Disorders*, 5th ed., Arlington, VA: American Psychiatric Association.

Bernstein, Julia, 2017. "Jüdische Perspektiven auf Antisemitismus", in: Kompetenzzentrum, Zentralwohlfahrtsstelle der Juden in Deutschland (ed.), Antisemitismus und Empowerment. Perspektiven, Ansätze, Projektionen, Berlin: Zentralwohlfahrtsstelle der Juden in Deutschland: 26–32.

Bloch, Benjamin, and Weitzel-Polzer, Esther, 2001. "Bewahrer der Tradition", *Juedische Altenhilfe* 11: 38–41.

Bowling, Ann, Farquhar, Morag, and Leaver, Jane, 1992. "Jewish People and Ageing: Their Emotional Wellbeing, Physical Health Status and Use of Services", *Nursing Practice* 5 (4): 5–16.

Bundesverband der Recherche- und Informationsstellen Antisemitismus e.V. (ed.), 2021. *Jahresbericht, Antisemitische Vorfaelle in Deutschland 2020*, Berlin, www.report-antisemitism.de/documents/Antisemitische_Vorfaelle_in_Deutschland_Jahresbericht_RIAS_Bund_2020.pdf retrieved on February 11, 2022.

Dasberg, Haim, 1987. "Psychological Distress of Holocaust Survivors and Offspring in Israel, Forty Years Later: A Review", *The Israel Journal of Psychiatry and Related Sciences* 24 (4): 243–256.

Dor-Shav, Netta K., 1978. "On the Long-Range Effects of Concentration Camp Internment on Nazi Victims: 25 Years Later", *Journal of Consulting and Clinical Psychology* 46 (1): 1–11.

Eitinger, Leo, Krell, Robert, and Rieck, Miriam, 1985. *The Psychological and Medical Effects of Concentration Camps and Related Persecutions on Survivors of the Holocaust: A Research Bibliography*, Vancouver: University of British Columbia Press.

Fischer, Gottfried, and Riedesser, Peter, 2009. *Lehrbuch der Psychotraumatologie*, 4th ed., Stuttgart: UTB.

Freyberger, Helmuth, Glaesmer, Heide, Kuwert, Philipp, and Freyberger, Harald J., 2019. "Transgenerationale Traumatransmission (am Beispiel der Ueberlebenden des Holocaust)", in: Guenter H. Seidler, Harald J. Freyberger, Heide Glaesmer, and Silke B. Gahleitner (eds.), *Handbuch der Psychotraumatologie*, 3rd ed., Stuttgart: Klett-Cotta: 111–126.

Haviv-Horiner, Anita, and Heilbrunn, Sibylle (eds.), 2013. *Heimat? – Vielleicht. Kinder von Holocaustüberlebenden zwischen Deutschland und Israel*, Bonn: Bundeszentrale für politische Bildung.

Honigman Cooper, R.H., 1979. "Concentration Camp Survivors: A Challenge for Geriatric Nursing", *Nursing Clinics of North America* 14: 621–629.

Huber, Michaela, 2004. *Multiple Persoenlichkeiten. Ueberlebende extremer Gewalt*, 9th ed., Frankfurt/Main: Fischer-Taschenbuch.

Kellermann, Natan P.F., 2009. *Holocaust Trauma. Psychological Effects and Treatment*, New York and Bloomington: iUniverse Inc.

Koerber, Karen, 2014. *Jung, Europaeisch, Saekular: Eine Studie ueber das Selbstverstaendnis der zweiten Zuwanderergeneration aus der Ex-Sowjetunion*, www.juedische-allgemeine.de/politik/die-aufsteiger-2/ retrieved on April 31, 2022.

Lange, de Nicolas (ed.), 2000. *Geschichte des Judentums*, Frankfurt and New York: Campus.

Leonhard, Birgit, 2003. "Pflege von Aelteren Holocaust-Ueberlebenden. Erfahrungen Israelischer Pflegepersonen vor dem Hintergrund Ihrer Eigenen Lebensgeschichte", *Pflege* 16: 31–39.

Levinson, David, 2018. *Jewish Germany: An Enduring Presence from the Fourth to the Twenty-First Century*, London and Portland, OR: Vallentine Mitchell.

Neurath, Paul, Stehr, Nico, and Fleck, Christian, 2015. *Society of Terror: Inside the Dachau and Buchenwald Concentration Camps*, London: Routledge.

Oren, Gila, and Shavit, Tal, 2021. "The Effect of the Subjective Holocaust Influence Level on Holocaust Survivors' Offspring", *Journal of Loss & Trauma* 26 (8): 767–781.

Payne, Emma A., and Berle, David, 2021. "Posttraumatic Stress Disorder Symptoms Among Offspring of Holocaust Survivors: A Systematic Review and Meta-Analysis", *Traumatology* 27 (3): 254–264.

Poser, Maerle, and Zielke-Nadkarni, Andrea, 2009. "Trauma", in: Zielke-Nadkarni Andrea, Hilgendorff Christina, Schlegel Sonja, and Poser Maerle (eds.), *Man Sieht Nur, Was Man Weiss. Fallgeschichten und Lehrmaterialien*, Frankfurt am Main: Mabuse: 163–170.

Safford, F., 1995. "Ageing Stressors for Holocaust Survivors and Their Families", *Journal of Gerontological and Social Work* 24 (1/2): 131–153.

Statista, 2021. *Anzahl der Mitglieder der juedischen Gemeinden in Deutschland von 2002 bis 2020*. https://de.statista.com/statistik/daten/studie/1232/umfrage/anzahl-der-juden-in-deutschland-seit-dem-jahr-2003/ retrieved on April 25, 2022.

Schrage, Eva-Maria, 2016. *Juedische Religion in Deutschland. Saekularitaet, Traditionsbewahrung und Erneuerung*, Wiesbaden: Springer VS.

Sinn, Andrea, 2020. "Returning to Stay? Jews in East and West Germany after the Holocaust", *Central European History* 53: 393–413.

Zentralrat der Juden in Deutschland, without date. *Fragen zur Jüdischen Gemeinschaft in Deutschland*. Berlin, www.zentralratderjuden.de/service/faq/ retrieved on April 25, 2022.

Zielke-Nadkarni, Andrea, 2004. "'Und das Leid Tragen Auch Noch Die Naechsten Generationen' – Eine Internationale Literaturstudie zur Pflege Juedischer PatientInnen", *Pflege* 17 (5): 319–328.

Zielke-Nadkarni, Andrea, 2005. *Juedische Fluechtlinge aus der GUS. Soziokulturelle Hintergruende, Versorgungsbedarf und Pflege*, Bern: Huber.

17

LONG-TERM PHYSICAL HEALTH OUTCOMES IN CHILD HOLOCAUST SURVIVORS AND IN OFFSPRING OF HOLOCAUST SURVIVORS

Lital Keinan Boker

Background

In the period between 1948 when the State of Israel was established and the end of 2020, over three million immigrants arrived in Israel.[1] Two thirds of them were of European origin, and many of those born before 1946 were Holocaust survivors (HS). By the end of 2015 only around 180,000 HS in Israel were still living,[2] most of whom were children during the Holocaust.

Early research on the consequences of exposure to the atrocities of World War II (WWII) and the Holocaust focused mostly on psychological and mental health outcomes.[3] Only since the 1990s, following the publication of several reports on the long-term physical effects of exposure to severe hunger during WWII and other extreme situations on non-Jewish populations,[4] was attention brought to these issues in Israeli HS. Indeed, it was found that long-term physical health outcomes in HS include higher risk of osteoporosis, particularly in women,[5] higher incidence of cancer,[6] and higher prevalence of chronic pain, fibromyalgia, and functional gastrointestinal complaints[7] as compared to population-based controls. In addition, based on the dataset of the largest healthcare fund in Israel ("Clalit"), it was shown that Holocaust survivors born before 1945 (mean age 83.8 ± 6.2) had significantly higher prevalence of cardiovascular risk factors compared to community-based controls (mean age 83.9 ± 7.3): hypertension (83% vs. 73%, $p < 0.001$), dyslipidemia (88% vs. 83%, $p < 0.001$), and diabetes mellitus (33% vs. 26%, $p < 0.001$), as well as significantly higher prevalence of ischemic heart disease (39% vs. 31%, $p < 0.001$), prior myocardial infarction (22% vs. 17%, $p < 0.001$), congestive heart failure (11% vs. 9%, $p < 0.001$), and prior stroke (16% vs. 13%, $p < 0.001$).[8]

Several mechanisms were suggested to explain the higher occurrence of chronic outcomes in HS. As suggested by the bio-psycho-social model,[9] chronic morbidity is the end-result of a complex interaction among genetic background, life adverse events, psychological and mental resources, or their lack of and social support. The exposure to extreme mental stress and severe malnutrition may have directly impacted certain metabolic pathways in ways that eventually increased the risk for future chronic morbidity.[10] The traumatic experiences were often associated with post-traumatic stress disorder (PTSD) and may have contributed to a lifestyle that promoted chronic morbidity, involving,

DOI: 10.4324/b23365-20

for instance, substance abuse (tobacco, alcohol) and sleep disturbances.[11] Exposure to horrific sanitary conditions, severe infections, as well as occupational hazards due to forced labor under the Nazi regime may have also played a role.[12]

Survivors that were children during the Holocaust (CHS) present a distinct group; they had not only been exposed to the aforementioned atrocities but often had concurrently become orphaned, abandoned, and forced to look after themselves, not always aware of their true identity or having memories of their prewar lives.[13] CHS are often defined as HS born in 1928 or 1930 and over, aged approximately 18y or 16y, respectively, at the end of WWII.[14] Previous reports on associations between adverse childhood experiences and high-risk behaviors (e.g., smoking, alcohol drinking, substance abuse), as well as adult morbidity (such as diabetes, coronary heart disease, stroke, depression, disability) and premature mortality suggest that a plausible explanatory mechanism may be biological embedding during sensitive periods in early life.[15] CHS may therefore be at a high risk for long-term health outcomes due to their Holocaust-related exposures.

The concept of Developmental Origin of Health and Disease (DOHaD) is based on the Barker theory, which suggested that the origin of some chronic adult conditions is rooted in fetal and other early exposures.[16] This conceptual framework is based on the plasticity of the human genome, which allows a given genotype to express different phenotypes; this process is mostly driven by DNA methylation and histone regulation in response to environmental and nutritional triggers at certain key developmental points.[17] The main motivation is apparently evolutional: to provide the best adaptation possible to challenging surroundings. However, these epigenetic changes are irreversible even if the environment later becomes more favorable. In light of the DOHaD theory and previous findings, concern was raised with respect to the potential transgenerational effects of exposure to the Holocaust and its impact on the Second Generation, i.e., offspring of HS (OHS).[18]

In this chapter the current literature on long-term **physical** morbidity in CHS is reviewed, since these subjects represent a unique subgroup with both direct (first generation) and parental (Second Generation) exposure to the Holocaust, as well as in OHS who were born after the end of WWII.

Methods

The scientific literature was reviewed for studies dealing with long-term **physical** health outcomes in CHS and in OHS, using the PUBMED, MEDLINE and Google Scholar databases. The terms "child Holocaust survivors", "offspring of Holocaust survivors", "Second Generation", "health", and "inter-/transgenerational" were used, including equivalent, related, and expanded terms. The search period was defined as 1965–2022, but there were no relevant papers before the mid-1970s and even early 1980s for some of the searches. The search was restricted to original papers, peer-reviewed journals, and English or Hebrew language only. The search process was redone using the comprehensive search engine of the library in the University of Haifa. The results retrieved from the different search engines and queries overlapped heavily. A quick screening of the titles, publishing journals, and abstracts assisted in identifying papers focusing on **physical** outcomes that represent original research. The references of relevant papers were screened to locate more publications. Out of **253** papers retrieved in the different searches (overlapping papers included), only **11** addressed the direct study questions, **5** referred to CHS and **6** referred to OHS. The supplementary figure presents PUBMED search results per each query.

The small number of relevant publications retrieved employed differing methodologies and studied different outcomes. Therefore, common risk estimators were not quantified.

Results

Most of the publications retrieved during the literature search referred to mental, psychological, traumatic, behavioral, societal, and other non-somatic health outcomes in HS, CHS, and OHS, particularly resilience, adaptation patterns, trauma coping, psychological disturbances, psychopathologies, and successful ageing. Only a very few focused on physical morbidity outcomes.

Child Holocaust Survivors (CHS)

Sperling et al.[19] reported on the relationship between PTSD and somatic manifestations. They compared 80 Jewish CHS (born in the period 1926–43 and residing in Israel or North and South America) who had been diagnosed with PTSD with 40 patients diagnosed with PTSD due to a single event unrelated to the Holocaust. All study participants applied for disability pensions from the German authorities. Expert assessments based on medical records, health reports, and self-declarations under oath served to ascertain the outcome. Notably, following adjustment for age and sex, the group of CHS showed significant increase in the prevalence of cardiovascular events between the first and the last expert assessment while the control group showed no significant changes. However, both groups showed significant increases in prevalence of gastrointestinal complaints, over time. The authors concluded that post-traumatic factors have an additive or interactive effect on somatic disease and that CHS may show an accelerated aging effect. This study had several problems, chief among them being that it was based on pension requests and thus may have been prone to biases resulting from secondary gain issues; the time gap between the first and second expert assessment differed between participants, and it had no control group of CHS without PTSD, thus limiting the generalizability of the results.

Three Israeli studies addressed a unique population of CHS, defined as subjects that were born during WWII (1940–45) in European countries that were under Nazi occupation or were Nazi-regime collaborators. It was assumed that the pregnancies of the mothers of these subjects were typified by harsh conditions of severe stress and nutritional deprivation, thus creating both pre- and postnatal exposure to these extreme circumstances.

In 2009, Keinan-Boker et al.[20] published on cancer risk in Holocaust survivors residing in Israel, linking the databases of the National Population Registry and the Israel National Cancer Registry (established in 1960). They found higher risk for cancer in HS as compared to the control group, with an inverse relationship with age at exposure. The subgroup of HS born in 1940–1945 presented the highest risk estimates: the risk ratio (RR) for all-site cancer in men was 3.50 (95% confidence interval, CI, 2.17–5.65) and in women, 2.33 (95% CI 1.69–3.21). The RR for female breast cancer was 2.44 (95% CI 1.46–4.06). Although based on high-validity national databases, the researchers could not directly ascertain the exposure status and relied on a proxy variable (year and place of birth and date of immigration to Israel) thus introducing some misclassifications that, while not expected to be differential, may have attenuated the results. In addition, they were unable to adjust for potential confounding factors such as smoking, obesity, and background morbidity.

Bercovich et al.[21] conducted a cross-sectional pilot study where they interviewed a convenience sample of CHS who were born in 1940–45 in European countries that were under Nazi occupation or were Nazi regime collaborators (exposed) and who self-reported on prevalent chronic morbidity. The researchers compared these prevalence rates to those of the general population (age-matched and of European origin) derived from a national health study. The prevalence of cardiovascular risk factors and morbidity was significantly higher in the exposed group compared to the general population: body mass index (BMI) (mean of 29.1 ± 3.2 kg/m^2 vs. 27.0 ± 4.4 kg/m^2, $p = 0.015$), hypertension (prevalence of 62.9% vs. 43.0%, $p = 0.003$), dyslipidemia (72.9% vs. 46.1%, $p < 0.001$), diabetes (32.9% vs. 17.4%, $p = 0.006$), angina pectoris (18.6% vs. 4.8%, $p = 0.001$), and congestive heart failure (8.6% vs. 1.7%, $p = 0.013$). The prevalence of cancer (30.0% vs. 8.7% $p < 0.001$), peptic ulcer disease (21.4% vs. 7.0%, $p = 0.001$), headaches/migraines (24.3% vs. 12.6%, $p < 0.001$) and anxiety/depression (50.0% vs. 8.3%, $p < 0.001$) was also significantly higher in the exposed group. As mentioned earlier, the study was based on a convenience sample, self-reported outcomes, and comparison with aggregated data; therefore, it may have been prone to both selection and information biases.

Consequently, another cross-sectional study using the same definition for CHS was carried out within the framework of the Northern District of Clalit Health Services, the largest healthcare fund in Israel.[22] In this study both the exposed subjects (CHS) and the non-exposed subjects (subjects of the same origin and age based on Clalit database, who were born in Israel) belonged to the same healthcare framework. The outcome data were derived from electronic medical records including computerized databases of medication procurement and medical procedures, thus considerably reducing the potential for selection or information biases. Interestingly, the results were very similar to those of the study by Bercovich et al.: CHS (exposed) were significantly more likely than non-exposed participants to present with dyslipidemia (81% vs. 72%, respectively), hypertension (67% vs. 53%), diabetes mellitus (41% vs. 28%), vascular disease (18% vs. 9%), and metabolic syndrome (17% vs. 9%). The exposed subjects also made less use of health services but used anti-depressive agents more often compared to the non-exposed subjects. In multivariable analyses, being born during WWII remained an independent and significant risk marker for hypertension (odds ratio, OR =1.52, 95% CI 1.17–1.99), diabetes mellitus (OR = 1.60, 95% CI 1.21–2.13) and vascular disease (OR = 1.99, 95% CI 1.33–2.99).

Furthermore, a study based on the total population of Maccabi Health Services, the second largest healthcare fund in Israel, which focused on HS born in Europe in 1911 through 1945 (some of whom represented CHS), replicated these findings.[23]

Table 17.1 summarizes the main findings with respect to chronic somatic morbidity in CHS.

Offspring of Holocaust Survivors (OHS) Who Were Born after the End of WWII

Levav et al.[24] explored the vulnerability of adult OHS in 2007. They compared 430 OHS to 417 offspring of Europe-born parents who did not reside in Nazi-occupied countries during WWII, using direct questions to ascertain exposure status. They found no differences between the groups regarding the prevalence of smoking, sleep problems, obesity, hypertension, cardiovascular disease, asthma, diabetes, or use of health services in the fortnight prior to the study. However, OHS were more likely than their counterparts to describe their general health as excellent or very good (OR [education-adjusted] = 1.3, 95% CI 1.0–1.7) and to report having chronic pain (OR [education-adjusted] = 1.3, 95% CI 1.0–1.7).

Zohar et al.[25] studied disordered eating in women belonging to the Second Generation (i.e., having one or two parents that are HS) and their daughters (the Third Generation). Interestingly, while no direct link was found between Holocaust exposure and disordered eating in the Second Generation, some inter-generational effect was suggested, with higher Holocaust exposure in the Second Generation associated with more disordered eating in the Third Generation. However, these findings, although statistically significant, are based on small numbers.

In 2011, Flory et al.[26] reported on the association between parental exposure to the Holocaust and offspring's self-reported health perception and disorders. They interviewed 137 subjects, 82 of whom had mothers who were HS. They found that maternal exposure to the Holocaust was

Table 17.1 Prevalence of Certain Chronic Somatic Conditions in Child Holocaust Survivors Compared to Controls

Condition	*Findings in CHS compared to controls*	*Reference*
Obesity	OR = 1.36 (95% CI 1.32–1.41)	Fund[a] et al., 2019
Dyslipidemia	OR = 3.1 (95% CI 1.7–5.7)	Bercovich[b] et al., 2014
	81% vs. 72%, p = 0.013	Keinan-Boker[c] et al., 2015
Hypertension	OR = 2.2 (95% CI 1.2–3.8)	Bercovich[b] et al., 2014
	OR = 1.52 (95% CI 1.17–1.99)	Keinan-Boker[c] et al., 2015
	OR = 1.61 (95% CI 1.54–1.67)	Fund[a] et al., 2019
Diabetes mellitus	OR = 2.2 (95% CI 1.2–4.2)	Bercovich[b] et al., 2014
	OR = 1.60 (95% CI 1.21–2.13)	Keinan-Boker[c] et al., 2015
Metabolic syndrome	17% vs. 9%, p < 0.001	Keinan-Boker[c] et al., 2015
Cardiovascular disease	Higher prevalence	Sperling[d] et al., 2012
	OR = 2.6 (95% CI 1.4–4.7) for any cardiovascular disease	Bercovich[b] et al., 2014
	OR = 1.99 (95% CI 1.33–2.99) for any vascular disease	Keinan-Boker[c] et al., 2015
	OR = 1.12 (95% CI 1.07–1.18) for ischemic heart disease	Fund[a] et al., 2019
	OR = 1.08 (95% CI 1.02–1.14) for myocardial infarction	
	OR = 1.06 (95% CI 1.01–1.11) for cerebrovascular disease	
Chronic respiratory disease	11% vs. 2%, p = 0.003	Bercovich[b] et al., 2014
	6% vs. 2%, p = 0.005	Keinan-Boker[c] et al., 2015
Chronic pain	34% vs. 5%, p < 0.001	Bercovich[b] et al., 2014
Osteoporosis	In women: OR = 1.11 (95% CI 1.06–1.16)	Fund[a] et al., 2019
Peptic ulcer disease	21% vs. 7%, p = 0.001	Bercovich[b] et al., 2014
Chronic kidney disease	OR = 1.17 (95% CI 1.13–1.22)	Fund[a] et al., 2019
Cancer	RR = 3.50 (95% CI 2.17–5.65) in men	Keinan-Boker[e] et al., 2009
	RR = 2.33 (95% CI 1.69–3.21) in women	
	OR = 4.3 (95% CI 2.1–8.7)	Bercovich[b] et al., 2014
	OR = 1.09 (95% CI 1.05–1.13)	Fund[a] et al., 2019

OR = Odds ratio; CI = Confidence interval; RR = Risk ratio

[a]Fund et al. (2019) study was based on Maccabi healthcare fund members, comparing HS born in Europe in 1911–45 (only part of them are CHS) with age- and origin-related non-HS members; [b]Bercovich et al. (2014) study was based on a convenience sample CHS born in Nazi-occupied or collaborating European countries in 1940–45 that was compared to aggregated data on the general Israeli age- and origin-related population, derived from a National Health Interview Survey; [c]Keinan-Boker et al. (2015) study was based on members of the Northern District of the Clalit Healthcare fund, comparing CHS born in Nazi-occupied or collaborating European countries in 1940–45 with age- and origin-related non-HS members; [d]Sperling et al. (2012) study was based on PTSD patients applying for disability pension from Germany, comparing 40 Jewish CHS born in 1926–43 to 80 non-Jewish applicants; [e]Keinan-Boker et al. (2009) study was based on the total Israel population and compared CHS born in Nazi-occupied or collaborating European countries in 1940–45 with age- and origin-related non-HS citizens

associated with poorer subjective emotional and physical health in offspring, significantly lower prevalence of current smoking (6.2% vs. 18.0%, $p = 0.03$), and greater use of medications (68.0% vs. 57.0%, $p = 0.03$), including psychotropic medications (23.0% vs. 5.7%, $p = 0.01$) and medications for the treatment of hypertension and lipid disorders. OHS (maternal exposure) were also more likely to have two or more components of metabolic syndrome than controls (15.0% vs. 2.0%, respectively, $p = 0.03$). These associations were not replicated in OHS with paternal exposure to the Holocaust. The authors hypothesized that while genetic, social, and behavioral factors may explain some of these findings, early developmental programming may also be involved, as suggested by the links with maternal but not paternal Holocaust exposure. However, in the very same year, Fridman et al.[27] conducted a study based on 32 elderly female HS and 47 daughters (OHS), who were compared to 33 elderly non-HS women and 32 daughters, regarding psychological adaptation and physical health. They reported no differences in the prevalence of physical health issues (general score on physical health and perceived physical health) between OHS daughters and matched controls. However, some daughters in the non-OHS comparison group were partially exposed, having an HS father.

Shrira et al.[28] studied age-related decline in 215 OHS and 149 controls at an average age of 55 years within the Israeli component of the Survey of Health, Ageing, and Retirement in Europe (SHARE-Israel). OHS reported significantly more major health problems and physical symptoms and reported higher consumption of medications and more contact with physicians. Specifically, OHS had higher prevalence of hypertension (36.3% vs. 23.5% in the controls, $p < 0.01$), hypercholesterolemia (34.9% vs. 23.5%, $p < 0.05$), and sleeping problems (22.3% vs. 11.4%, $p < 0.01$). There were no significant differences in health behaviors (i.e., smoking, obesity).

Another study by Shrira[29] examined three groups of parent-offspring dyads with respect to PTSD symptoms, health behaviors, and indices of successful aging: a) HS parents with probable PTSD ($n = 28$ dyads); b) HS parents without PTSD ($n = 86$ dyads); c) comparison parents without PTSD ($n = 73$ dyads). Health risk behaviors were assessed based on self-reports on smoking and lack of physical activity, summed to create a global score of risky behavior. Successful aging in offspring was determined by several indices including prevalence of certain chronic medical conditions (heart disease, hypertension, hypercholesterolemia, cerebral vascular disease, diabetes/high blood sugar, chronic lung disease, asthma, arthritis, osteoporosis, cancer, and Parkinson's disease), disability, somatic symptoms (based on the 18-item Brief Symptom Inventory (BSI-18) tool) and a global assessment of health (self-rated health). The results indicated significantly higher scores of risky health behavior in HS parents with probable PTSD compared to the other parent groups. Similarly, offspring of HS with probable PTSD showed higher scores of risky health behaviors compared to other offspring groups. Furthermore, offspring of HS with probable PTSD had lower successful aging score than each of the other two offspring groups. These findings suggest higher prevalence of risky health behaviors as well as certain chronic disease in offspring of HS who have probable PTSD.

Table 17.2 summarizes the main findings with respect to chronic somatic morbidity in OHS (the Second Generation).

Discussion

The aim of this chapter was to review the available scientific literature regarding chronic somatic morbidity in Israeli CHS and OHS, based on the assumption that extreme Holocaust-related experiences of CHS may have predisposed them to long-term physical outcomes and that OHS may have also be predisposed through transgenerational mechanisms. The findings, which unfortunately are based on a small number of publications, indicate that both populations may be at higher risk for

Table 17.2 Prevalence of Certain Chronic Somatic Conditions in OHS

Condition	*Finding in OHS compared to controls*	*Reference*
Smoking	OR = 1.1 (95% CI 0.8–1.6)	Levav[a] et al., 2007
	No differences	Shrira[b] et al., 2011
	6.2% vs. 18%, p = 0.03 (OHS – maternal exposure)	Flory[c] et al., 2011
Obesity	OR = 1.2 (95% CI 0.8–1.8)	Levav[a] et al., 2007
	No differences	Shrira[b] et al., 2011
Eating disorders	No differences	Zohar[d] et al., 2007
Risky health behavior score* ***Smoking and lack of physical activity**	Mean score: 2.67 ± 1.44 (OHS with probable parental PTSD) vs. 1.59 ± 1.24 (OHS/non-PTSD) and vs. 1.31 ± 1.19 (controls), p < 0.0001	Shrira[e], 2019
Dyslipidemia	Higher prevalence (OHS – maternal exposure)	Flory[c] et al., 2011
	34.9% vs. 23.5%, p < 0.05	Shrira[b] et al., 2011
Hypertension	OR = 0.9 (95% CI 0.7–1.2)	Levav[a] et al., 2007
	36.3% vs. 23.5%, p < 0.01	Shrira[b] et al., 2011
	Higher prevalence (OHS – maternal exposure)	Flory[c] et al., 2011
Asthma	OR = 1.0 (95% CI 0.6–1.8)	Levav[a] et al., 2007
Diabetes mellitus	OR = 0.8 (95% CI 0.5–1.2)	Levav[a] et al., 2007
Cardiovascular disease	OR = 0.9 (95% CI 0.7–1.2)	Levav[a] et al., 2007
Sleeping problems	OR = 1.1 (95% CI 0.8–1.6)	Levav[a] et al., 2007
	22.3% vs. 11.4%, p < 0.01	Shrira[b] et al., 2011
Chronic pain	OR = 1.3 (95% CI 1.0–1.7)	Levav[a] et al., 2007
Utilization of medical services/medications	OR = 1.0 (95% CI 0.8–1.4)	Levav[a] et al., 2007
	57% vs. 38%, p = 0.03 (OHS – maternal exposure)	Flory[c] et al., 2011
General physical health	Perceived as lower (OHS – maternal exposure)	Flory[c] et al., 2011
	No differences	Fridman[f] et al., 2011
Successful aging	Mean score: −0.41 ± 0.97 (OHS with probable parental PTSD) vs. −0.01 ± 0.73 (OHS/non-PTSD) and vs. 0.17 ± 0.60 (controls), p = 0.002	Shrira[e], 2019

OR = Odds ratio; CI = Confidence interval

[a]Levav et al. (2007) study compared OHS (n = 430) to offspring of Europe-born parents who did not reside in Nazi-occupied countries (n = 417) on psychopathological and physical health dimensions. Cardiovascular disease in this study referred to myocardial infarction, CVA, or hypertension while utilization of medical services/medications referred to the fortnight preceding the study; [b]Shrira et al. (2011) study was based on 50+y old subjects with European-born fathers and compared OHS (215) to non-OHS counterparts drawn from the Israeli component of the Survey of Health, Ageing, and Retirement in Europe (SHARE-Israel); [c]Flory et al. (2011) study was based on a sample of 137 adults aged 23 to 65 years, of them 82 were OHS and the rest (n = 55) served as a comparison group. In this study, data on hypertension was based on consumption of medications for this condition, and data on utilization of medications was based on non-psychotropic medication consumption; [d]Zohar et al. study was based on 108 dyads of mother (OHS) and daughter (Third Generation) who were Israeli college students 18–35 years of age. Information of the first generation (HS) was retrieved from the second- and third-generation participants; [e]Shrira (2019) study was based on a convenience sample including 114 dyads of HS and OHS and 73 dyads of non-HS parents and their offspring. All parents were Jews of European origin born before 1945, while all offspring were born after 1945; [f]Fridman et al. (2011) study was based on intergenerational comparison: 32 elderly female HS and 47 daughters (OHS) were compared to 33 elderly non-HS women and 32 non-OHS daughters. General physical health in this study referred to physical health score (objective) and perceived physical health (subjective).

chronic somatic conditions, particularly those associated with metabolic syndrome (hypertension, dyslipidemia, diabetes) as well as others.

These results are in accord with previous publications that referred to other exposed (mostly prenatally) populations, for example, the Dutch Famine Birth Cohort. In September 1944 the Nazi regime imposed an embargo on food delivery into occupied Dutch territories, leading to a period of severe hunger that lasted nine months, until the end of the war in May 1945. The Dutch Famine Birth Cohort included all babies born at the University of Amsterdam Teaching Hospital between August 1944 and April 1946, a period that preceded, encompassed, and followed the Hunger Winter. In this population, offspring of exposed mothers had lower birth weights and impaired glucose tolerance tests in adulthood.[30] Data from birth cohorts that were born before (1957–58), during (1959–61), and after (1962–63) the Great Chinese Famine, a result of the governmental policy of the "Great Leap Forward", showed that prenatal exposure to famine resulted in attenuated height, decreased adult BMI, and higher prevalence of hypertension,[31] although another study reported that the prevalence of hypertension was increased only in those exposed at infanthood, not prenatally.[32] It was also found that prenatal exposure to the famine was associated with higher levels of proteinuria[33] and higher risk for gastric cancer mortality (RR = 2.39, 95% CI 1.51–3.77 and RR = 1.64, 95% CI 1.02–2.62 for men and women, respectively).[34] In a study on survivors of the siege of Leningrad (1941–43), which included subjects born during the siege and subjects exposed at early childhood, significantly higher prevalence of hypertriglyceridemia was observed in those exposed prenatally (n = 13, 28.8%) compared to those exposed at early childhood (n = 33, 15.7%).[35]

Information on the transgenerational effects of famine in humans is still limited. A study from 2012 focused on adult offspring of Dutch subjects that had been prenatally exposed to the Dutch Hunger Winter. The results revealed significantly higher weight and higher BMI in offspring of exposed fathers compared to offspring of unexposed fathers. These findings were not replicated in offspring with maternal exposure,[36] but an earlier study on the same population indicated that maternal prenatal exposure to the Dutch famine was associated with decreased neonatal length and increased adiposity in the offspring, as well as with poorer health in later life.[37]

Prenatal exposure to the Great Chinese Famine was associated with hyperglycemia (OR = 1.93, 95% CI 1.51–2.48) and type 2 diabetes (OR = 1.75, 95% CI 1.20–2.54) in adult offspring, and these results were more pronounced when both parents were exposed.[38]

Basic science as well as animal studies provide evidence for several mechanisms that may explain these transgenerational effects: a) structural effects on tissues and organs; b) epigenetic programming of gene expression; c) glucocorticoid effects; and d) accelerated cellular ageing.[39] Indeed, a series of studies by Yehuda et al. showed a clear association between parental PTSD and cortisol levels in offspring, suggestive of glucocorticoid pathway programming.[40] The same research group also demonstrated that parental PTSD (including Holocaust-related PTSD) induced transgenerational effects on the methylation of certain genes including glucocorticoid receptor genes in OHS, with differential effects of maternal and paternal PTSD.[41] Furthermore, a set of glucocorticoid and immune-related genes have recently been found that show transgenerational changes associated with parental Holocaust exposure with differential effects based on parental exposure-related factors.[42]

In light of the paucity of data regarding long-term somatic outcomes in CHS and potential transgenerational effects in OHS, which may extend beyond the Second Generation, it is both a national priority and a matter of great scientific importance to establish an Israeli cohort of OHS, as previously suggested by Keinan-Boker.[43] Such a unique cohort may shed light on the potential transgenerational associations between extreme exposures and long-term outcomes in offspring of the exposed, information that may be useful with respect to many other global circumstances and that may enable tailoring of preventive measures and surveillance policies. On the national level, such a cohort may serve to fulfill a national obligation to Israeli HS and OHS.

Conclusions

CHS and OHS may be at a higher risk for certain chronic conditions, mostly metabolic diseases. Health caretakers' awareness should be focused on primary prevention and early detection in these populations. In addition, there is an urgent need to study long-term physical outcomes in OHS further, preferably using longitudinal study designs.

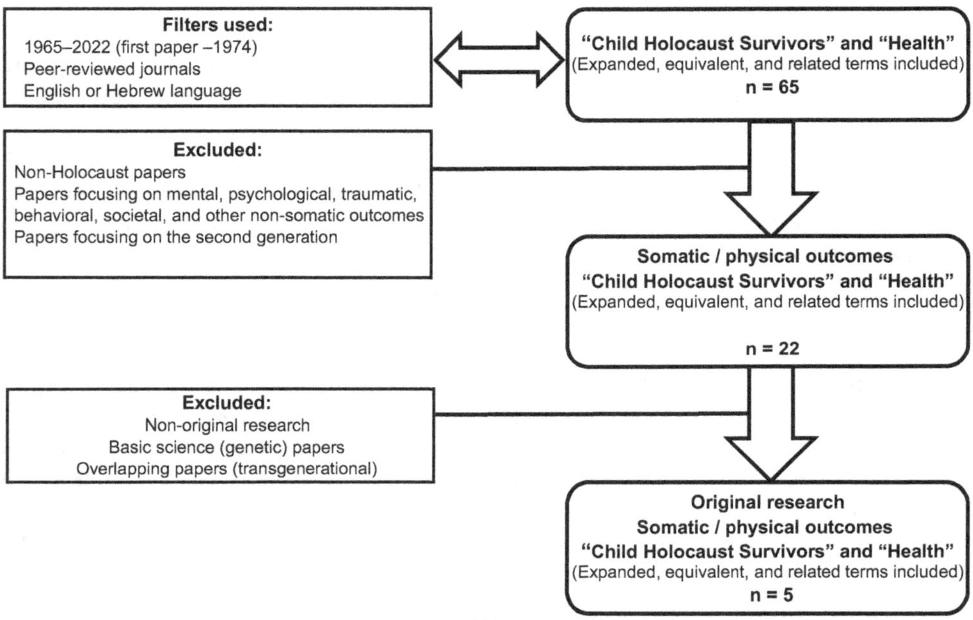

(A)

Figure 17.1

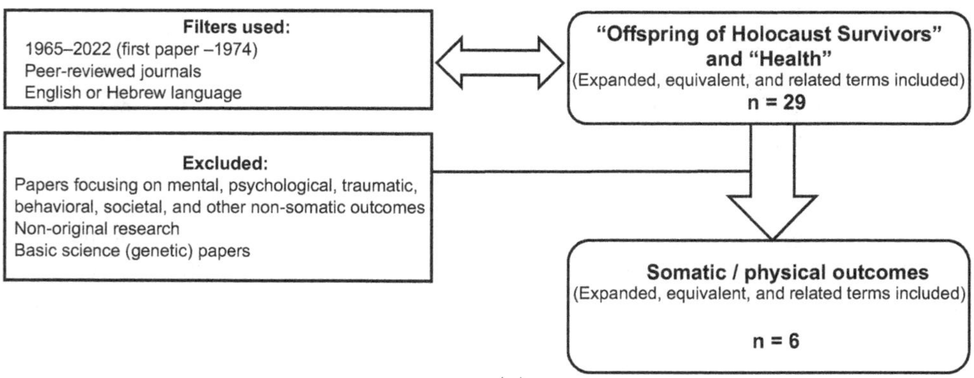

(B)

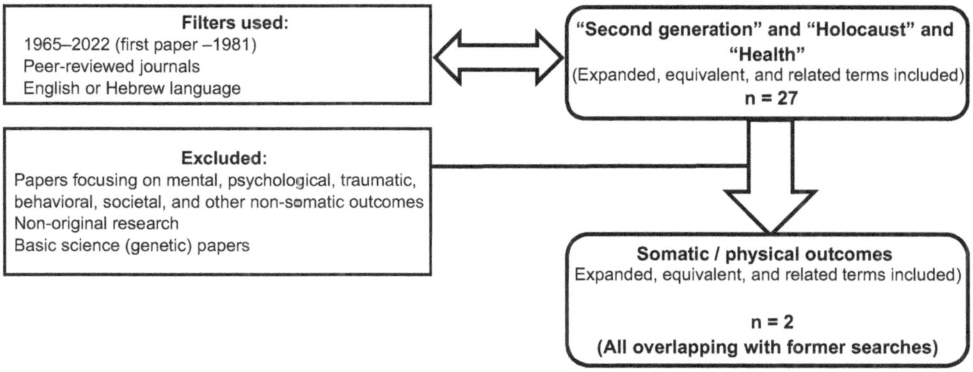

(C)

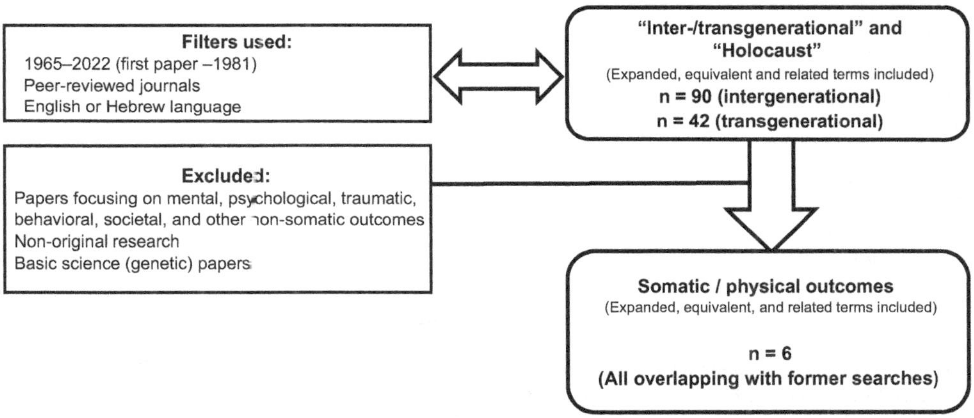

(D)

Notes

1 Central Bureau of Statistics, Annual Statistical Report, 2021.
2 Central Bureau of Statistics press release towards the National Holocaust Day 2021.
3 Barel et al., 2010.
4 Lumey and Van Poppel, 1994; Elias et al., 2004; Fentiman et al., 2007; Koupil et al., 2007; Head et al., 2008; Koupil et al., 2009; He et al., 2017.
5 Marcus and Menczel, 2007.
6 Keinan-Boker et al., 2009; Vin-Raviv et al., 2012; Keinan-Boker and Goldbourt, 2016; Sadetzki et al., 2017; Ben-David et al., 2018.
7 Yaari et al., 1999; Albin et al., 2010; Stermer et al., 1991.
8 Zamstein et al., 2018.
9 Engel, 1977.
10 Elias et al., 2004.
11 Landau et al., 2000.
12 Shasha et al., 2002.
13 Krell, 1985.
14 Krell, 1985; Claims Conference Israel website.
15 Campbell et al., 2016; Kelly-Irving et al., 2013.
16 Barker et al., 1992.

17 Dominguez-Salas et al., 2012; Lee, 2015.
18 Hazani and Shasha, 2008.
19 Sperling et al., 2012.
20 Keinan-Boker et al., 2009.
21 Bercovich et al., 2014.
22 Keinan-Boker et al., 2015.
23 Fund et al., 2019.
24 Levav et al., 2007.
25 Zohar et al., 2007.
26 Flory et al., 2011.
27 Fridman et al., 2011.
28 Shrira et al., 2011.
29 Shrira, 2019.
30 Stein et al., 1995; Lumey et al., 1997; De Rooij et al., 2006.
31 Huang et al., 2010; Wu et al., 2017.
32 Wang et al., 2016.
33 Huang et al., 2014.
34 Li et al., 2012.
35 Rotar et al., 2015.
36 Veenedaal et al., 2013.
37 Painter et al., 2008.
38 Li et al., 2017.
39 Aiken et al., 2016.
40 Yehuda et al., 2007; Bierer et al., 2014; Bader et al., 2014.
41 Yehuda et al., 2016; Yehuda et al., 2014.
42 Daskalakis et al., 2021.
43 Keinan-Boker, 2014.

Bibliography

Ablin, J.N., Cohen, H., Eisinger, M., and Buskila, D., 2010. "Holocaust Survivors: The Pain Behind the Agony. Increased Prevalence of Fibromyalgia among Holocaust Survivors", *Clinical and Experimental Rheumatology* 28 (6) (Suppl 63): S51–S56.

Aiken, C.E., Tarry-Adkins, J.L., and Ozanne, S.E., 2016. "Transgenerational Effects of Maternal Diet on Metabolic and Reproductive Ageing", *Mammalian Genome* 27: 430–439.

Bader, H.N., Bierer, L.M., Lehrner, A., Makotkine, I., Daskalakis, N.P., and Yehuda, R., 2014. "Maternal Age at Holocaust Exposure and Maternal PTSD Independently Influence Urinary Cortisol Levels in Adult Offspring", *Frontiers in Endocrinology* (Lausanne) 5: 103.

Barel, E., Van IJzendoorn, M.H., Sagi-Schwartz, A., and Bakermans-Kranenburg, M.J., 2010. "Surviving the Holocaust: A Meta-Analysis of the Long-Term Sequelae of a Genocide", *Psychological Bulletin* 136 (5): 677–698.

Barker, D.J.P., 1992. *Fetal and Infant Origin of Adult Disease*, London: BMJ Books. ISBN 0-7279-0743-3.

Ben-David, R., Biderman, A., Sherf, M., Zamstein, O., and Dreiher, J., 2018. "Elevated Cancer Risk in Holocaust Survivors Residing in Israel: A Retrospective Cohort Study", *European Journal of Cancer* 95: 85–92.

Bercovich, E., Keinan-Boker, L., and Shasha, S.M., 2014. "Long-Term Health Effects in Adults Born During the Holocaust", *Israel Medical Association Journal* 16 (4): 203–207.

Bierer, L.M., Bader, H.N., Daskalakis, N.P., Lehrner, A.L., Makotkine, I., Seckl, J.R., and Yehuda, R., 2014. "Elevation of 11β-hydroxysteroid Dehydrogenase Type 2 Activity in Holocaust Survivor Offspring: Evidence for an Intergenerational Effect of Maternal Trauma Exposure", *Psychoneuroendocrinology* 48: 1–10.

Campbell, J.A., Walker, R.J., and Egede, L.E., 2016. "Associations Between Adverse Childhood Experiences, High-Risk Behaviors, and Morbidity in Adulthood", *American Journal of Preventive Medicine* 50 (3): 344–352. http://doi.org/10.1016/j.amepre.2015.07.022.

Central Bureau of Statistics. Israel Annual Statistical Report, 2021, www.cbs.gov.il/he/publications/DocLib/2021/Shnaton72.pdf. retrieved on May 2022.

Central Bureau of Statistics. Press Release # 115/2021 Towards the National Holocaust Day, 2021, www.cbs.gov.il/he/mediarelease/pages/2021/%D7%A2%D7%A8%D7%91-%D7%99%D7%95%D7%9D-%D7%94%D7%96%D7%99%D7%9B%D7%A8%D7%95%D7%9F-%D7%9C%D7%A9%D7%95%D7%90%D7%94-%D7%95%D7%9C%D7%92%D7%91%D7%95%D7%A8%D7%94.aspx retrieved on May 2022.

Claims Conference Israel website, https://he.claimscon.org/child-survivor-fund-launched/ retrieved on May 2022.

Daskalakis, N.P., Xu, C., Bader, H.N., Chatzinakos, C., Weber, P., Makotkine, I., Lehrner, A., Bierer, L.M., Binder, E.B., and Yehuda, R., 2021. "Intergenerational Trauma is Associated with Expression Alterations in Glucocorticoid- and Immune-Related Genes", *Neuropsychopharmacology* 46 (4): 763–773.

de Rooij, S.R., Painter, R.C. Phillips, D.I., Osmond, C., Michels, R.P., Godsland, I.F, Bossuyt, P.M., Bleker, O.P., and Roseboom, T.J., 2006. "Impaired Insulin Secretion After Prenatal Exposure to the Dutch Famine", *Diabetes Care* 29 (8): 1897–1901.

Dominguez-Salas, P., Cox, S.E., Prentice, A.M., Hennig, B.J., and Moore, S.E., 2012. "Maternal Nutritional Status, C 1 Metabolism and Offspring DNA Methylation: A Review of Current Evidence in Human Subjects", *Proceedings of the Nutrition Society* 71: 154–165.

Elias, S.G., Keinan-Boker, L., Peeters, P.H., Van Gils, C.H., Kaaks, R., Grobbee, D.E., and Van Noord, P.A., 2004. "Long Term Consequences of the 1944–1945 Dutch Famine on the Insulin-like Growth Factor Axis", *International Journal of Cancer* 108 (4): 628–630.

Elias, S.G., Peeters, P.H., Grobbee, D.E., and van Noord, P.A., 2004. "Breast Cancer Risk after Caloric Restriction During the 1944–1945 Dutch Famine", *Journal of the National Cancer Institute* 96 (7): 539–546.

Engel, G.L., 1977. "The Need for A New Medical Model: A Challenge for Biomedicine", *Science* 196 (4286): 129–136.

Fentiman, I.S., Allen, D.S., and Ellison, G.T., 2007. "The Impact of the Occupation of Guernsey 1940–1945 on Breast Cancer Risk Factors and Incidence", *International Journal of Clinical Practice* 61 (6): 937–943.

Flory, J.D., Bierer, L.M., and Yehuda, R., 2011. "Maternal Exposure to the Holocaust and Health Complaints in Offspring", *Disease Markers* 30 (2–3): 133–139.

Fridman, A., Bakersman-Kranenburg, M.J., Sagi-Shwartz, A., and Van-Iizendoorn, M.H., 2011. "Coping in Old Age with Extreme Childhood Trauma: Aging Holocaust Survivors and Their Offspring Facing New Challenges", *Aging and Mental Health* 15 (2): 232–242.

Fund, N., Ash, N., Porath, A., Shalev, V., and Koren, G., 2019. "Comparison of Mortality and Comorbidity Rates between Holocaust Survivors and Individuals in the General Population in Israel", *JAMA Open* 2 (1): e186643.

Hazani, E., and Shasha, S.M., 2008. "Effects of the Holocaust on the Physical Health of the Offspring of Survivors", *Israel Medical Association Journal* 10: 251–255.

He, D., Fang, Y., Gunter, M.J., Xu, D., Zhao, Y., Zhou, J., Fang, H., and Xu, W.H., 2017. "Incidence of Breast Cancer in Chinese Women Exposed to the 1959–1961 Great Chinese Famine", *BMC Cancer* 17 (1): 824.

Head, R.F., Gilthorpe, M.S., Byrom, A., and Ellison, G.T., 2008. "Cardiovascular Disease in a Cohort Exposed to the 1940–45 Channel Islands Occupation", *BMC Public Health* 2: 303.

Huang, C., Guo, C., Nichols, C., Chen, S., and Martorell, R., 2014. "Elevated Levels of Protein in Urine in Adulthood after Exposure to the Chinese Famine of 1959–61 During Gestation and the Early Postnatal Period", *International Journal of Epidemiology* 43 (6): 1806–1814.

Huang, C., Li, Z., Wang, M., and Martorell, R., 2010. "Early Life Exposure to the 1959–1961 Chinese Famine Has Long-Term Health Consequences", *Journal of Nutrition* 140 (10): 1874–1878.

Keinan-Boker, L., 2014. "The Mothers Have Eaten Unripe Grapes and the Children's Teeth are Set on Edge: The Potential Inter-Generational Effects of the Holocaust on Chronic Morbidity in Holocaust Survivors' Offspring", *Israel Journal of Health Policy Research* 3 (1): 11.

Keinan-Boker, L., and Goldbourt, U., 2016. "Cancer Incidence in Holocaust Male Survivors-An Israeli Cohort Study", *International Journal of Cancer* 139 (11): 2426–2435.

Keinan-Boker, L., Shasha-Lavsky, H., Eilat-Zanani, S., Edri-Shur, A., and Shasha, S.M., 2015. "Chronic Health Conditions in Jewish Holocaust Survivors Born During World War II", *Israel Medical Association Journal* 17 (4): 206–212.

Keinan-Boker, L., Vin-Raviv, N., Liphshitz, I., Linn, S., and Barchana, M., 2009. "Cancer Incidence in Israeli Jewish Survivors of World War II", *Journal of the National Cancer Institute* 101 (21): 1489–1500.

Kelly-Irving, M., Lepage, B., Dedieu, D., Bartley, M., Blane, D., Grosclaude, P., Lang, T., and Delpierre, C., 2013. "Adverse Childhood Experiences and Premature All-Cause Mortality", *European Journal of Epidemiology* 28: 721–743.

Koupil, I., Plavinskaja, S., Parfenova, N., Shestov, D.B., Danziger, P.D., and Vågerö, D., 2009. "Cancer Mortality in Women and Men Who Survived the Siege of Leningrad (1941–1944)", *International Journal of Cancer* 124 (6): 1416–1421.

Koupil, I., Shestov, D.B., Sparén, P., Plavinskaja, S., Parfenova, N., and Vågerö, D., 2007. "Blood Pressure, Hypertension and Mortality from Circulatory Disease in Men and Women Who Survived the Siege of Leningrad", *European Journal of Epidemiology* 22 (4): 223–234.

Krell, R., 1985. "Child Survivors of the Holocaust – 40 Years Later", *Child Psychiatry* 24: 377–412.

Landau, R., and Litwin, H., 2000. "The Effects of Extreme Early Stress in Very Old Age", *Journal of Traumatic Stress* 13 (3): 473–487.

Lee, H.S., 2015. "Impact of Maternal Diet on the Epigenome During in Utero Life and the Developmental Programming of Diseases in Childhood and Adulthood", *Nutrients* 7 (11): 9492–9507.

Levav, I., Levinson, D., Radomislensky, I., Shemesh, A.A., and Kohn, R., 2007. "Psychopathology and Other Health Dimensions Among the Offspring of Holocaust Survivors: Results from the Israel National Health Survey", *Israel Journal of Psychiatry and Related Sciences* 44 (2): 144–151.

Li, J., Liu, S., Li, S., Feng, R., Na, L., Chu, X., Wu, X., Niu, Y., Sun, Z., Han, T., Deng, H., Meng, X., Xu, H., Zhang, Z., Qu, Q., Zhang, Q., Li, Y., and Sun, C., 2017. "Prenatal Exposure to Famine and the Development of Hyperglycemia and Type 2 Diabetes in Adulthood Across Consecutive Generations: A Population-Based Cohort Study of Families in Suihua, China", *American Journal of Clinical Nutrition* 105 (1): 221–227.

Li, Q.D., Li, H., Li, F.J., Wang, M.S., Li, Z.J., Han, J., Li, Q.H., Ma, X.J., and Wang, D.N., 2012. "Nutrition Deficiency Increases the Risk of Stomach Cancer Mortality", *BMC Cancer* 28: 315.

Lumey, L.H., and Stein, A.D., 1997. "Offspring Birth Weights After Maternal Intrauterine Undernutrition: A Comparison Within Sibships", *American Journal of Epidemiology* 146 (10): 810–819.

Lumey, L.H., and Van Poppel, F.W., 1994. "The Dutch Famine of 1944–45: Mortality and Morbidity in Past and Present Generations", *Social History of Medicine* 7 (2): 229–246.

Marcus, E.L., and Menczel, J., 2007. "Higher Prevalence of Osteoporosis Among Female Holocaust Survivors", *Osteoporosis International* 18: 1501–1506.

Painter, R.C., Osmond, C., Gluckman, P., Hanson, M., Phillips, D.I., and Roseboom, T.J., 2008. "Transgenerational Effects of Prenatal Exposure to the Dutch Famine on Neonatal Adiposity and Health in Later Life", *British Journal of Obstetrics and Gynecology* 115 (10): 1243–1249.

Rotar, O., Moguchaia, E., Boyarinova, M., Kolesova, E., Khromova, N., Freylikhman, O., Smolina, N., Solntsev, V., Kostareva, A., Konradi, A., and Shlyakhto, E., 2015. "Seventy Years After the Siege of Leningrad: Does Early Life Famine Still Affect Cardiovascular Risk and Aging?", *Journal of Hypertension* 33 (9): 1772–1779.

Sadetzki, S., Chetrit, A., Freedman, L.S., Hakak, N., Barchana, M., Catane, R., and Shani, M., 2017. "Cancer Risk Among Holocaust Survivors in Israel-A Nationwide Study", *Cancer* 123 (17): 3335–3345.

Shasha, S.M., 2002. "Morbidity in the Ghettos During the Holocaust", *Harefuah* 141 (4): 364–368, 408, 409 [Hebrew].

Shrira, A., 2019. "Parental PTSD, Health Behaviors and Successful Aging Among Offspring of Holocaust Survivors", *Psychiatric Research* 271: 265–271.

Shrira, A., Palgi, Y., Ben-Ezra, M., and Shmotkin, D., 2011. "Transgenerational Effects of Trauma in Midlife: Evidence for Resilience and Vulnerability in Offspring of Holocaust Survivors", *Psychological Trauma* 3 (4): 394–402.

Sperling, W., Kreil, S., and Biermann, T., 2012. "Somatic Diseases in Child Survivors of the Holocaust with Posttraumatic Stress Disorder: A Comparative Study", *The Journal of Nervous and Mental Disease* 200 (5): 423–428.

Stein, A.D., Ravelli, A.C., and Lumey, L.H., 1995. "Famine, Third-Trimester Pregnancy Weight Gain, and Intrauterine Growth: the Dutch Famine Birth Cohort Study", *Human Biology* 67 (1): 135–150.

Stermer, E., Bar, H., and Levy, N., 1991. "Chronic Functional Gastrointestinal Symptoms in Holocaust Survivors", *American Journal of Gastroenterology* 86 (4): 417–422.

Veenedaal, M.V.E., Painter, R.C., de Rooij, S.R., Bossuyt, P.M.M., van der Post, J.A.M., Gluckman, P.D., Hanson, M.A., and Roseboom, T.J., 2013. "Transgenerational Effects of Prenatal Exposure to the 1944–45 Dutch Famine", *British Journal of Obstetrics and Gynecology* 120 (5): 548–553.

Vin-Raviv, N., Barchana, M., Linn, S., and Keinan-Boker, L., 2012. "Severe Caloric Restriction in Young Women During World War II and Subsequent Breast Cancer Risk", *International Journal of Clinical Practice* 66 (10): 948–958.

Wang, Z., Li, C., Yang, Z., Zou, Z., and Ma, J., 2016. "Infant Exposure to Chinese Famine Increased the Risk of Hypertension in Adulthood: Results from the China Health and Retirement Longitudinal Study", *BMC Public Health* 16: 435.

Wu, L., Feng, X., He, A., Ding, Y., Zhou, X., and Xu, Z., 2017. "Prenatal Exposure to the Great Chinese Famine and Mid-Age Hypertension", *PLoS ONE* 12 (5): e0176413.

Yaari, A., Eisenberg, E., Adler, R., and Birkhan, J., 1999. "Chronic Pain in Holocaust Survivors", *Journal of Pain Symptom Management* 17 (3): 181–187.

Yehuda, R., Blair, W., Labinsky, E., and Bierer, L.M., 2007. "Effects of Parental PTSD on the Cortisol Response to Dexamethasone Administration in Their Adult Offspring", *American Journal of Psychiatry* 164 (1): 163–166.

Yehuda, R., Daskalakis, N.P., Bierer, L.M., Bader, H.N., Klengel, T., Holsboer, F., and Binder, E.B., 2016. "Holocaust Exposure Induced Intergenerational Effects on FKBP5 Methylation", *Biological Psychiatry* 80 (5): 372–380.

Yehuda, R., Daskalakis, N.P., Lehrner, A., Desarnaud, F., Bader, H.N., Makotkine, I., Flory, J.D., Bierer, L.M., and Meaney, M.J., 2014. "Influences of Maternal and Paternal PTSD on Epigenetic Regulation of the Glucocorticoid Receptor Gene in Holocaust Survivor Offspring", *American Journal of Psychiatry* 17 (18): 872–880.

Zamstein, O., Biderman, A., Sherf, M., Ben David, R., and Dreiher, J., 2018. "Cardiovascular Morbidity and Risk Factors in Holocaust Survivors in Israel", *Journal of the American Geriatric Society* 66: 1684–1691.

Zohar, A.H., Giladi, L., and Givati, T., 2007. "Holocaust Exposure and Disordered Eating: A Study of Multi-Generational Transmission", *European Eating Disorder Reviews* 15: 50–57.

INDEX

NAMES

PLACES

ORGANIZATIONS